In aid of The Railway Children charity

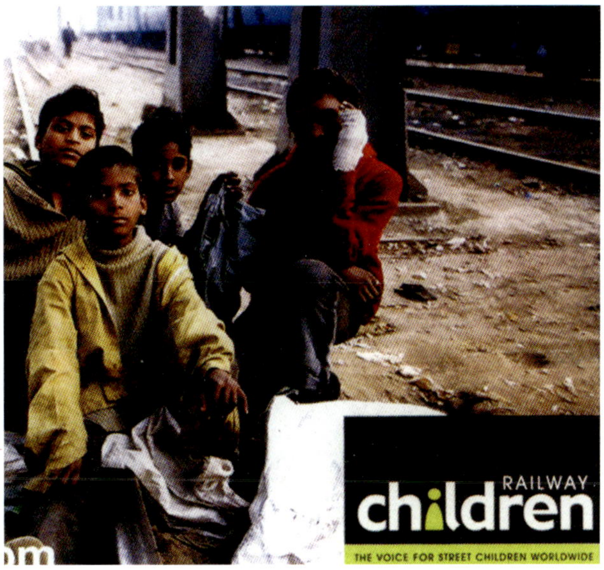

Railway Children helps children worldwide, who are alone, at risk, and living on the streets. Many of these children will suffer abuse verbally and physically; they will be sold, pimped, and beaten. Railway Children aims to make contact with the child before an abuser does. In the United Kingdom, one of the projects we support is in Glasgow and is run by The Aberlour Trust – the ROC shelter. It stands for "Running Other Choices". The shelter provides four beds as part of its outreach, preventative and follow-up work with young people who run away within Scotland. An incredible 100,000 children run away each year, yet this is one of only a handful of refuges available for them. There is a desperate need for more.

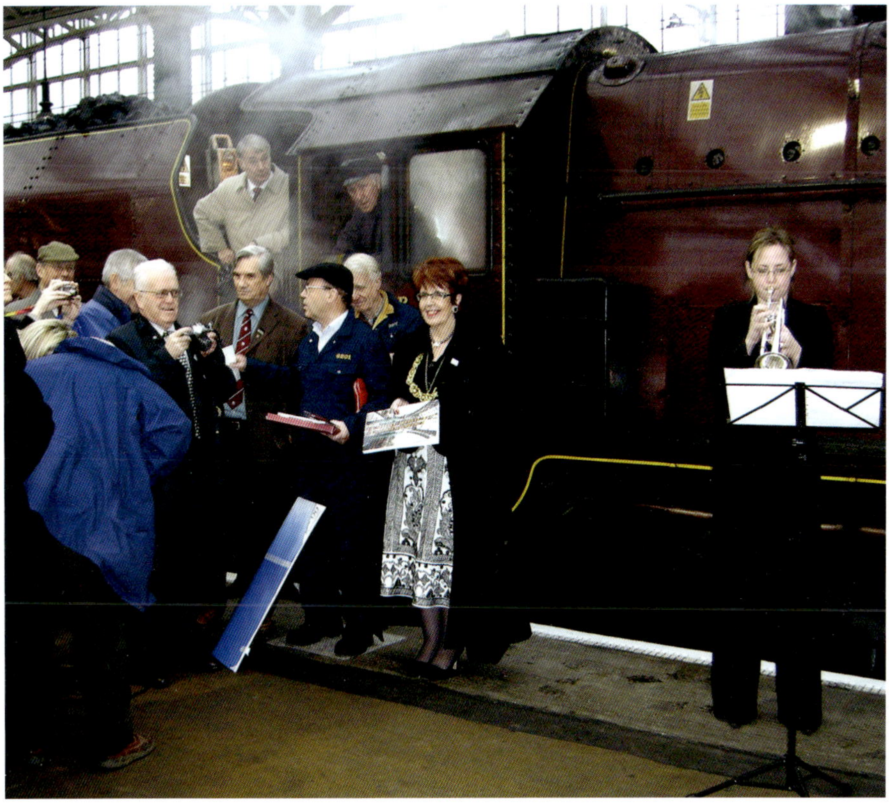

The first edition of "Central to Glasgow" was launched by the Lord Provost of the City of Glasgow, Baillie Liz Cameron, on 17th November 2006 beside No. 6201 "Princess Elizabeth". The locomotive was about to re-enact her record run to London Euston exactly 70 years previously to the day in 1936. Musical accompaniment was provided by students from the Royal Scottish Academy of Music and Drama, conducted by their Principal, John Wallace. Dugald Cameron, David Maidment and Clive Mojonnier, – Bill Ure and Bob Hart in the cab look on. A cheque to the Railway Children charity for £10,000 was also presented.

The first edition of this book, published in November 2006, sponsored by the then railway industry in Scotland quickly sold out and raised just over £10,000-00 for the Railway Children charity.

**An affectionate tribute
in the form of
facts, recollections, images and miscellanea
from some admirers of Glasgow Central,
upon the 100th anniversary
of the expansion of the station
under whose spell we have fallen.**

Railways were one of Great Britain's gifts to the world. No one and no place in this island made a greater contribution than the people and City of Glasgow. At St Rollox, the Caledonian Railway had its principal locomotive and carriage works which it established in 1856; so the year 2006 saw its 150th anniversary. Railway engineering is still being undertaken there, having undergone many changes of ownership over the years from the "Caley" to the LMS, to British Railways / BREL and now to Alstom Springburn. The year 2006 also saw the centenary of the building at St Rollox of J F McIntosh's illustrious 4-6-0 express passenger locomotive for the Caledonian Railway, No. 903 *Cardean*, forever associated with the Corridor train from Glasgow Central.

It is, though, on Glasgow Central that this book concentrates, for the year 2006 saw also the centenary of its ambitious expansion into an institution which is truly Central to Glasgow.

This second edition has been generously supported by the Institutuion of Civil Engineers whose Glasgow and West of Scotland Branch celebrated its 125th Anniversary in 2009. They have done so in commemoration of their illustrious member, the late Donald Matheson, chief engineer and general manger of the Caledonian Railway whose creation, Glasgow Central station, provides an enduring, practical, monument.

Dedicated to railway men and women, of the old railway and the new.

First published 2006
Second enlarged edition 2009
ISBN 1-905276-36-2
978-1-905276-36-3

Published by Strathwood Ltd
Glenavon House
Kinchurdy Road
Boat of Garten
Inverness-shire
PH24 3BP
Tel: 01479 831 139
info@strathwood.co.uk

ice | glasgow & west of scotland
125 years
ice
Institution of Civil Engineers

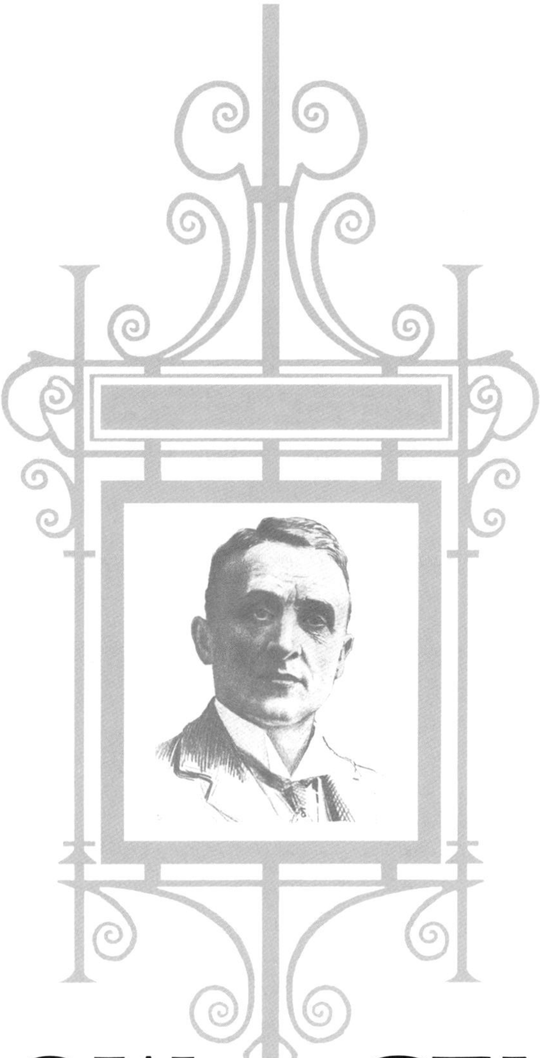

GLASGOW CENTRAL
CENTRAL to GLASGOW

Compiled by Dugald Cameron
Edited by Jim Summers
Production by Alan Carlaw

STRATHWOOD

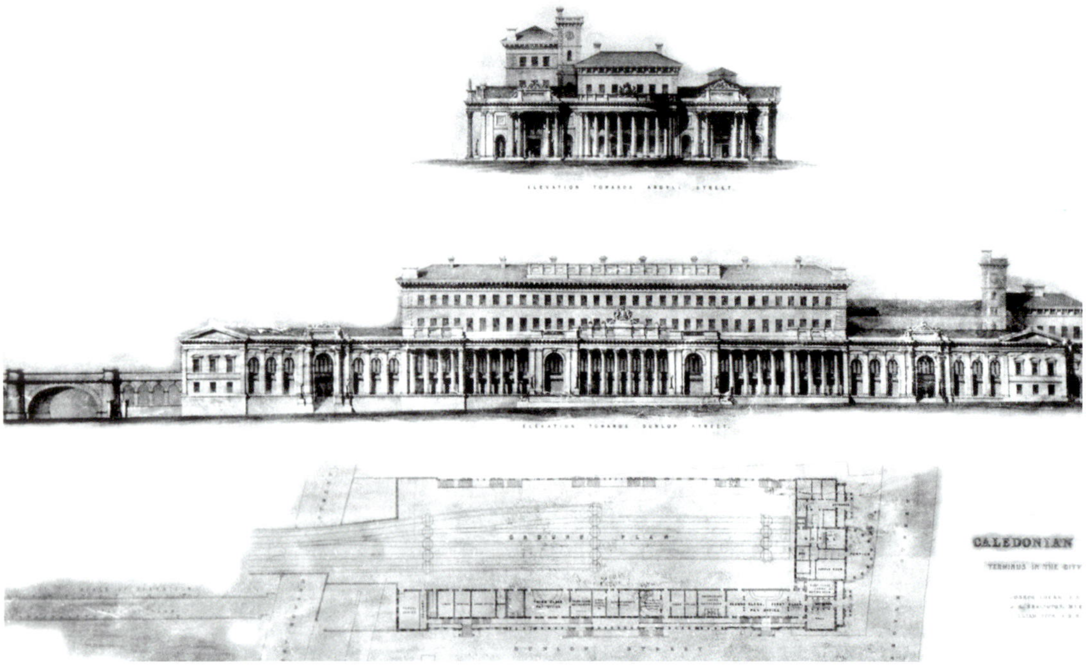

Dunlop Street Station Architect William (later Sir William) Tite's 1846 drawing of the proposed terminal for the Caledonian (Clydesdale Junction) Railway in Glasgow fronting Argyle and Dunlop Streets. It was to be connected to the main line by a branch from the Polloc & Govan Railway at Gushetfauld. Although the branch was authorised by Parliament there was a proviso that the river bridge be approved by the Admiralty. The station was abandoned and the line terminated at Southside when the Admiralty stipulated an opening span in the river bridge.

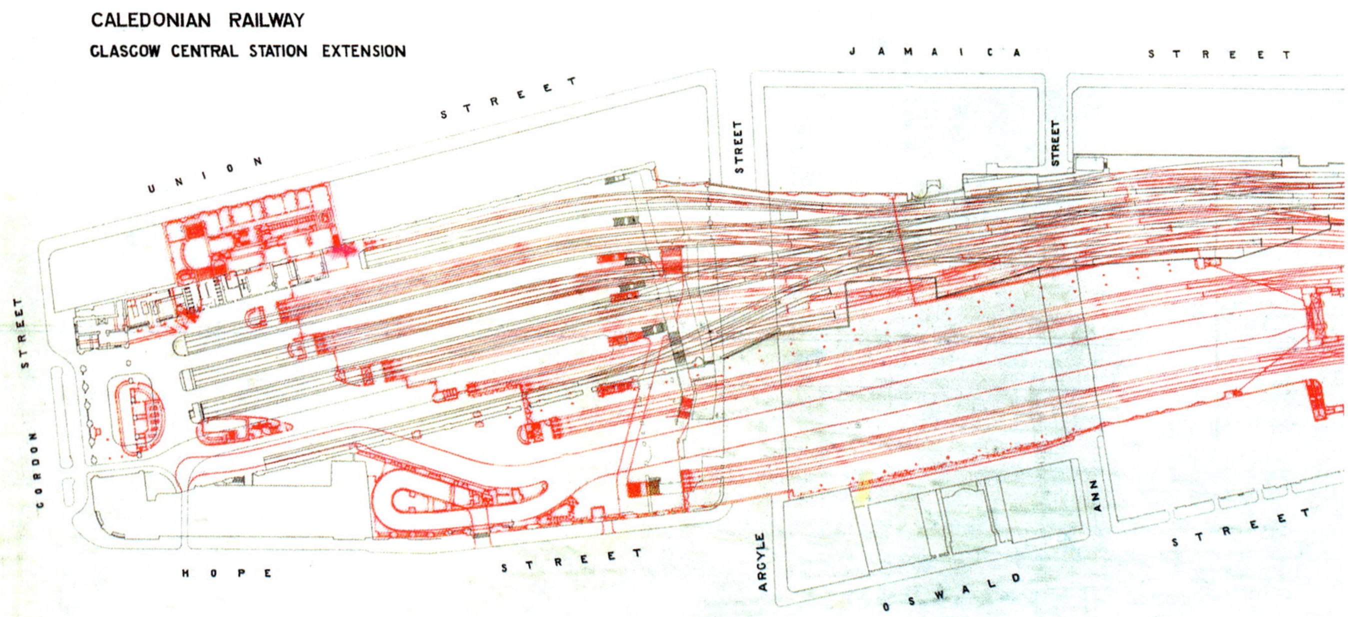

Original Bridge Street Station, on the south bank of the Clyde, with a Glasgow and South Western Railway train, probably for Ayr, on the right.

Rebuilt Bridge Street Station looking across the River Clyde towards the 1879 Central Station.

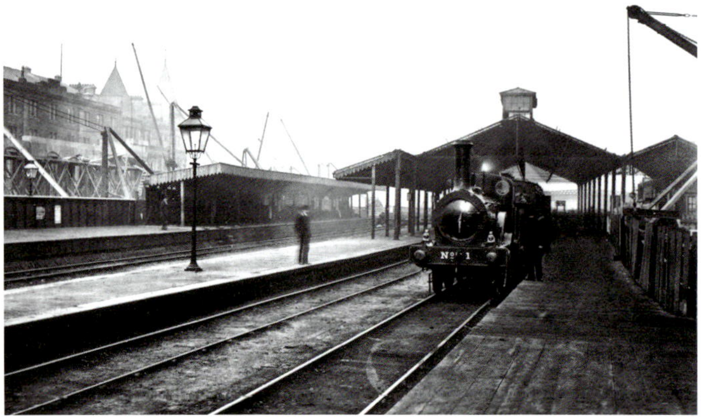

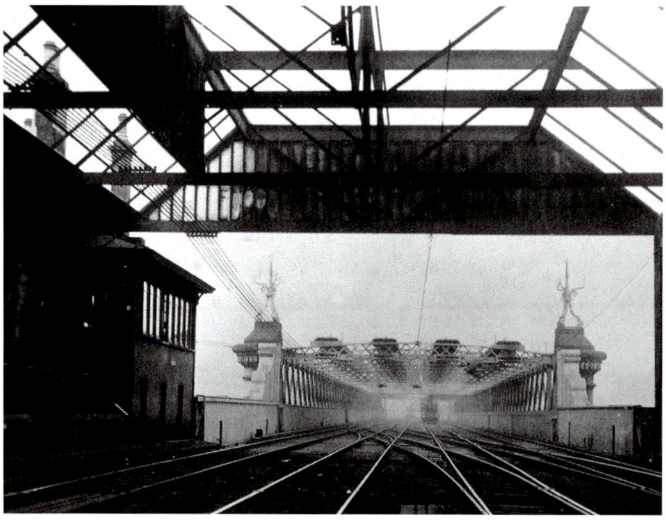

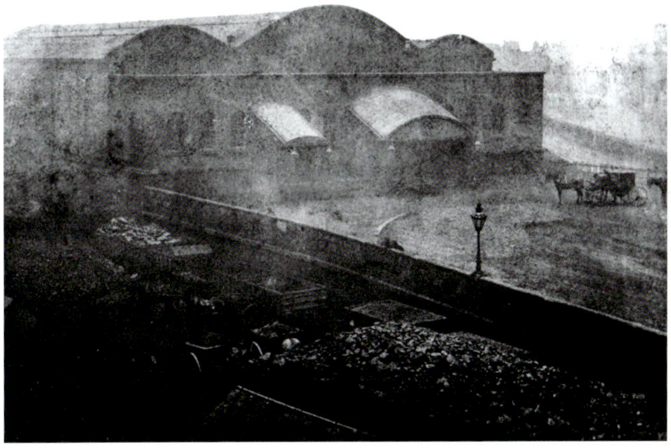

South Side Station near Gushetfaulds.

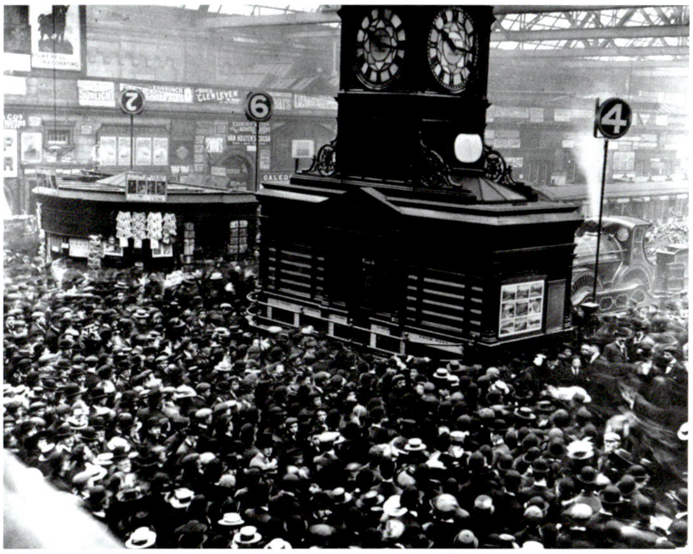

The 1879 Central Station. Platform numbers were in reverse order to what they became after the extension. Need for expansion!

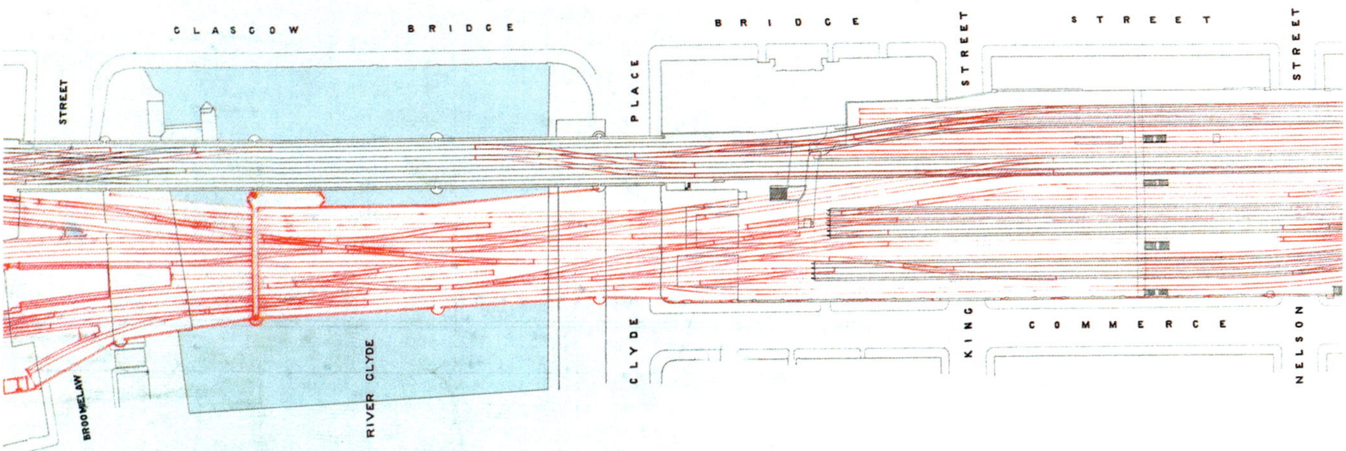

Glasgow Central Station Extension

One of a series of undated drawings illustrating the redevelopment of Glasgow Central Station. The black image represents the Central and Bridge Street stations at the start of the 1900 redevelopment and incorporates the modifications to the original 1879 layout. The red image shows the extent of the 1900 -1906 works which includes the replacement of all the original platforms. Reproduced by permission of the National Archives of Scotland (RHP124157).

The original cramped station showing on the left the inner face of the Central Hotel and a view looking out from the Hotel on the right. Note that platform 1 is on the right in the approximate position of the current platform 10.

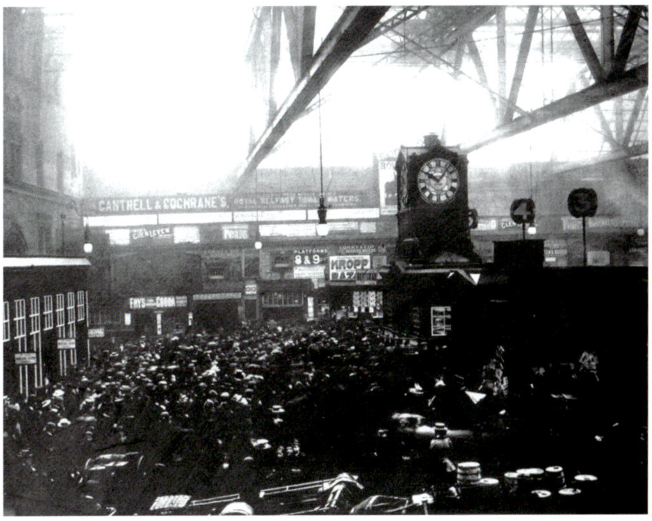

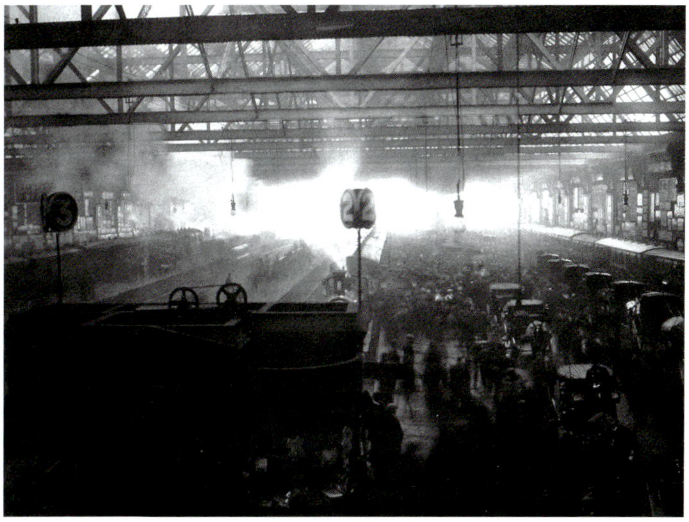

Contents

Acknowledgments

In compiling this publication I have leant shamelessly on many of my good friends to write a piece, lend some photographs, or generally advise. I have also had the great pleasure of making new acquaintances, within the railway and outside. All, without exception, have willingly acceded to my many requests and involved their friends and colleagues too. Their individual approaches, I hope, shine through. I am deeply grateful to them all, and I hope that they will feel satisfied with the result. Inevitably, with such a rich subject, much good material has reluctantly had to be left out – another volume for another time maybe! Particularly, I want to acknowledge Bill Ure's considerable contribution along with Evelyn Brown of Network Rail in looking after the finance and liaison with the industry, Jim Summers' willingness to edit – much of it done in the agreeable working environment of long-distance trains from and to the Central, and Alan Carlaw's patience and skill in preparing the raw material for production.

All of those involved hope that the Railway Children charity will truly benefit from the sales of this book. The Charity supports The Aberlour Trust, which operates the valuable "Running Other Choices" programme in Glasgow.

The following individual photographers or organisations have generously contributed their own work and items from their railway collections: Eric Aitchison, Bob Avery, Michael Beaton, Bill Brown, Morrison Bryce, Dugald Cameron, Alan Carlaw, R S Carpenter, H C Casserley (via R M Casserley), Phil Connell, Campbell Cornwell, Derek Cross (via David Cross), Kevin V Crowe, M Anne Dick, Ian Dyce, John Edgington, Niall Ferguson collection, First ScotRail, A E Glen, Ann Glen, GM+AD Architects, Vic Gilchrist, Norrie Gilliland, Guthrie Aerial Photography, Tom Heavyside, David Horne, Jim Howie, Douglas Hume, John R Hume, Jack Kernahan, C Lawson Kerr, Charles McCrossan, Jim MacIntosh, Ken MacKay, Willie McKnight, Donald Macleod, LCGB (Ken Nunn Collection), Colin Marsden, Brian Morrison, Network Rail, the NRM, Robin Nelson, Irving Nicol, Tom Noble, Bob Osborne, Steven Parkes, John Paton, Bruce Peter, Brian Stephenson (RAS), Rail News, Robin Ralston, G H Robin, W Stuart Sellar, Montague Smith, Virgin Trains, W A C Smith, J L Stevenson, Hamish Stevenson, Jim Summers, John Thomas, Colin Whitbread, John Young, and the 6201 Society.

Graham Todd, Fred Landery, and David Maidment have been diligent in uncovering some of the arcane aspects of the Central, supplementing the researches of the various authors.

In addition, for the use of some of their images, I am grateful to the valuable collections of Scottish life and times, such as the "Herald" Archive, the National Archives of Scotland, the National Library of Scotland, and to the indispensable transport collection from the photographers of Colour Rail, as well as to that respected authority the Railway Gazette International. Then there are the train crews and engineering staff who supplied wit, wisdom and professional expertise. Some are based at the Central itself and others at those essential adjuncts, the historic Motive Power Depots of Polmadie, Corkerhill and more recently Shields. Phil Connell, in addition to contributing his own photographs, introduced me to those recently retired stalwarts from Polmadie, Jack Laughlin, Davie Sweeney and the former Inspector Willie McLaggan. All these staunch railwaymen, like so many others from so many railway grades, have their own stories for another time.

To all those who have contributed, whether to this book itself or to that whole experience which is Glasgow Central, but who remain unknown by name, I offer my thanks and respect. *Dugald Cameron*

Without the financial support of the following organisations associated with the great city of Glasgow and the railway industry this book could not have been published. Grateful thanks are therefore due to –

Arup Engineering
Chief Executive's Department, Glasgow City Council
First Engineering
First ScotRail
Glasgow City Council
Gordon Murray + Alan Dunlop, Architects

GNER
Network Rail
Plan It Contracts Ltd.
The Railway Heritage Trust
Strathclyde Partnerships in Transport
Virgin Trains

This Second edition has been generously supported by the
Glasgow & West of Scotland Branch of the Instution of Civil Engineers
&
FP Commercial Print of Stranraer

Introduction

John McNaught, Chairman Glasgow & the West of Scotland ICE

The Institution of Civil Engineers, Glasgow & the West of Scotland, and the Railways all have a gloriously inter-twined history.

Prior to the nineteenth century, Civil Engineering as a profession barely existed: there was no identifiable profession, although many civil engineering works of significance had been carried out. These works had been undertaken almost exclusively by military men. From the earliest days of the Roman occupation up to the eighteenth century, roads and bridges were constructed throughout Scotland by the likes of General Wade. It was not until 1771 that, on the initiative of John Smeaton, the Smeatonian Society of Civil Engineers was formed, with a group of leaders of the profession meeting over dinner to discuss the relevant topics and developments of the day. From these informal beginnings the Institution of Civil Engineers was born, with Smeaton universally regarded as the founding father of the profession.

Founded in 1818, the first meetings of the Institution were reputedly held at Kendal's coffee house, in Fleet Street, London, before a more permanent location was found. The Institution (or ICE as it is commonly known) is now headquartered at One Great George Street, in the heart of Westminster. This splendid building was designed by the renowned Glasgow architect James Miller, who was better known for his work for the Caledonian Railway on magnificent railway buildings and grand hotels (Glasgow's Central Hotel amongst them), to which extensive references are made throughout this book.

The first ICE President was one Thomas Telford, a West of Scotland man, born of humble origins at Westerkirk in Dumfriesshire. From his early career as an apprentice stonemason, the largely self-taught Telford developed and extended his talents to the design and management of significant construction projects. With an impressive portfolio of major civil engineering works behind him, he was an obvious choice to be the first President of ICE. Telford himself was never particularly enthusiastic about railways and is remembered more for his bridges and canals. He did however have contacts and knew many within the profession personally, regularly introducing new members. Most important of all, it was under his leadership in 1828 that the Royal Charter was granted, which further enhanced the Institution's claim to its status as the leader of the profession.

From this association with the first President, Glasgow and the West of Scotland has continued to influence the development of ICE. On 16th October 1884 a meeting was convened at the Institution Rooms, 207 Bath Street, Glasgow, for the purpose of forming a "Local Centre for the benefit of Student Members residing in and around Glasgow". From such beginnings ICE's Glasgow & West of Scotland Local Association was born – the first such Local Association of the ICE outside London. An entirely appropriate choice, as the University of Glasgow was the first university school of engineering in the United Kingdom to establish a chair in civil engineering. Its Regius Chair of Civil Engineering and Mechanics was established in 1840 on the appointment of Professor Lewis Gordon and many distinguished engineers have held this post since.

In those early days it was actually called The Glasgow Association of Students of the Institution of Civil Engineers, with the objective of "participating in the education of students of Civil Engineering". This was achieved through the practice, which continues to this day, of arranging an annual programme of technical meetings at which a paper is presented followed by debate, discussion and questions. However, 1884 was seen by many, for many years, as a false start, with poorly attended meetings and questions raised over the sustainability of the Association. In 1888 the organisation was widened to include all grades of membership, and for a number of years, this was regarded as the year of establishment. Such controversy was finally laid to rest when, in session 1933-34, the Association decided to celebrate its Jubilee and in doing so, 1884 was confirmed as the year of its formation!

One of the long-standing traditions of ICE Glasgow & West of Scotland (ICE G&WoS) has been the Chairman's Address. Every year at the Annual General Meeting, after transacting the business of the day including the election

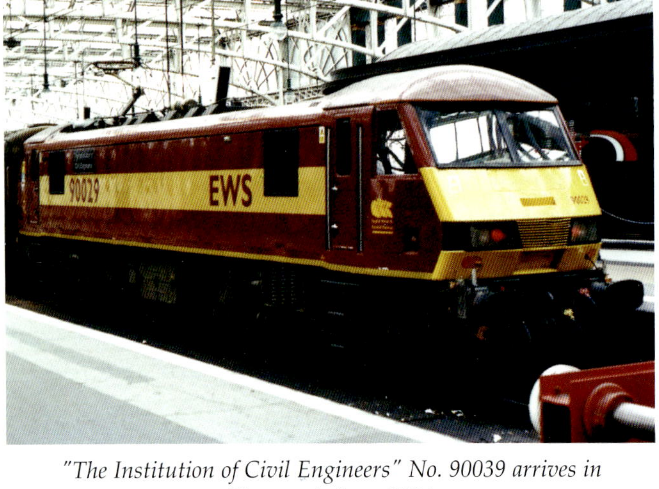

"The Institution of Civil Engineers" No. 90039 arrives in Glasgow in June 2004.

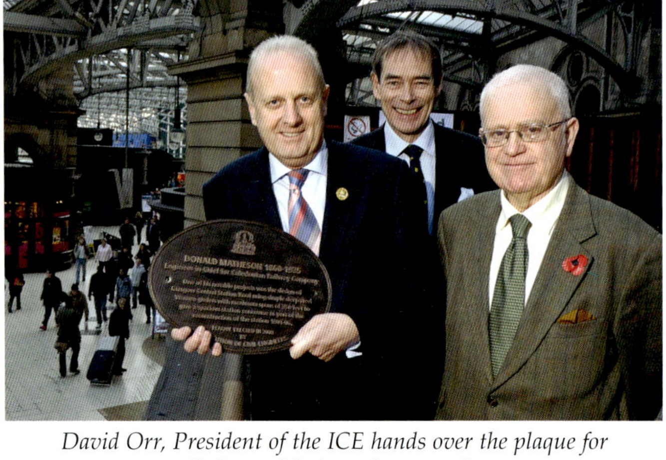

David Orr, President of the ICE hands over the plaque for affixing to Matheson's masterpiece while John McNaught and Dugald Cameron look on.

of the new committee, the incoming chairman is invited to deliver his Chairman's Address to the assembled company. Upon completion, a formal request is then made of the newly elected chairman, for permission to publish his address. Once printed (providing that the Chairman's permission has been granted!), this modest booklet has then been circulated to the membership. Thus, within the archives of ICE G&WoS (lodged for safe keeping in the Mitchell Library, Glasgow), exists a fascinating record of Addresses stretching back over a hundred years. These provide a remarkable insight into the issues and topics which have affected and been of interest to the civil engineering profession over the years.

There is no blue-print to follow, and newly-elected chairmen over the years have had a pretty free rein to address the members in whichever way they choose. Some have given a résumé of their careers or detailed their involvement in a particularly prestigious project, whilst others have delivered a state-of-the-nation type address.

Donald Matheson M.Inst.C.E; M.Am.Soc.C.E; having been duly elected as President (as it was styled in those days), delivered his address to the Glasgow & West of Scotland Association of Students of the Institution of Civil Engineers on the 20th November 1905. In it, Matheson refers to his previous spell as Vice-President when he had "the great privilege of serving under George Graham, George Cunningham and Charles Forman…..men whom I would describe as three of the "Old Masters" in Scottish railway engineering". George Graham in particular was a 'Caley' man through and through. President of the Association in 1893, his death occurred at the age of 76 on 30th June 1898 – the very day he retired.

What is clear is that, the railway engineers of that time played a particularly prominent role in the fledgling local affairs of ICE during the first twenty-odd years of its existence. This reflected the importance of railway engineering at that time, even although many thought that by 1884, the railway heyday was well and truly over, with the basic pattern of lines already well established throughout the country.

Indeed, Matheson's own career might have followed a quite different path as he recalled in his Address. When his father was endeavouring to have the young Matheson placed in an apprenticeship he was advised by more than one of the well-know railway engineers of the time, that so far as new railways were concerned, the days of the railway engineer were numbered, and that the "necessary railways had all been made"! History however refutes this theory as befuddled thinking, with over 7500 miles of new track constructed and some £550m of capital invested in the railways throughout Britain over the last quarter of the nineteenth century. In those days, road construction techniques and the motor car were still in their infancy. Hardly surprising, perhaps, when you consider that the regulations requiring a motor vehicle on the public highway to be preceded by a man bearing a red flag were only withdrawn in 1896!

At around the same time another young man entered the profession and could later recount that of four contemporaries, one had gone on the become Chairman of Sir William Arrol, the great railway bridge builder, another was Chief Engineer of the Great Indian Peninsular Railway, while the third had "held an important appointment with the railway system in Siam". The young man himself was John Hogg, who was elected Chairman of ICE Glasgow & West of Scotland in 1936. So whilst "all the necessary railways" might indeed have been "made" by this time, there was still scope for the railway engineer to ply his trade for many years to come. This is evidenced by the many landmark buildings and other structures associated with the railway engineers over the years, not to mention the track and infrastructure improvements which are still on-going today.

The continuing importance of this sector of the Civil Engineering profession is reflected in some of the papers which have been delivered at ICE Glasgow & West of Scotland technical meetings in the most recent of times. These have included the West Coast Mainline Modernisation and the Glasgow Airport Rail Link, and it has been an unusual year if at least one railway paper has not featured in the syllabus.

In the early days, the Glasgow & West of Scotland Association effectively covered the whole of Scotland, with many members travelling from far and wide to attend. References were made in committee minutes of changes in the timing of some technical meetings to suit the train timetables. In 1928, however, the Chairman suggested that some meetings should be held in Edinburgh, to reflect the increasing numbers of members who lived and worked in the east., but it was 1938 before a separate Association was founded in the east. For the ensuing seventy years Scotland has been well served by the two 'Local Associations'. Times move on, and ICE members have recently decided to form a single region, ICE Scotland, coming into being in 2009. ICE Glasgow & West of Scotland will however remain as an active Branch member of the umbrella organisation, and thus a long local tradition will not only be maintained, but the G&WoS will play a prominent role within the new national body.

The activities of the Institution are of course not restricted to arranging technical meetings, and ICE Glasgow & West of Scotland, through a busy structure of sub-committees undertakes a wide and varied range of activities. An active programme of events exists to interest the youngsters of today in a career in Civil Engineering. Here once again, G&WoS led the way with its ambitious "Bridges to Schools" project, whereby primary children experience the thrill of building their own bridge – and there is always a clamour to be the first to test their construction skills by walking across the completed structure. Developed in Glasgow, this programme has been copied and is now undertaken by many other ICE regions across the UK.

In conjunction with colleagues in the East of Scotland, the Saltire Society Awards for Civil Engineering were established in 1981. This annual competition recognises excellence in civil engineering and is open to all projects completed throughout Scotland. Railways projects have featured regularly at the annual commendations and awards ceremony. Most recently, the Waverley Station Regeneration project received a commendation, and it can only be a matter of conjecture how Matheson's Central Station project might have been received, had such awards existed over a hundred years ago. The spacious concourse, round-edged buildings for ease of pedestrian traffic flow, the mighty roof structure and the bright airy feel of spaciousness would all have scored highly in the adjudicators' markings.

As well as recognising current works of note, ICE Glasgow and West of Scotland has a programme of erecting plaques to notable Civil Engineers of the past. Most recent of these is the one erected in Central Station in 2008, located on the left-hand pillar of the easterly entrance from Gordon Street. Bearing the inscription, "Donald Matheson (1860-1935), Engineer-in-Chief of the Caledonian Railway Company", it is a tribute to Matheson's direction of the redevelopment and expansion of Central Station in the earliest years of the last century. Of the eight plaques erected thus far, four have marked Civil Engineers associated with railway works. A plaque in St Enoch Subway Station celebrates Alexander Simpson, Chairman of The Glasgow and District Subway Company from 1905 to 1921, while at Oban Station one commemorates John Strain, pioneer of the Oban to Dalmally line.

Another ICE initiative is the publication of leaflets for walking tours which take in Civil Engineering works of general interest. The first of these covered the Clyde Bridges throughout Glasgow, and prominent amongst them, are the Dalbeattie-granite piers, which are all remaining of the original, four-track, first Caledonian Railway Bridge built in 1878, and alongside which is the 1905, 'New Clyde Viaduct' of 1905. These gave a total of 13 tracks into Central Station. At one time it was the widest railway-over-river bridge in the country. The bridge cost £275,000 which included compensation payments to the River Clyde Trustees and before opening it was load tested with nineteen locomotives!

The 'social' side of ICE Glasgow and West of Scotland has largely revolved around the Annual Dinner which in 2008 was the 105th such occasion. With its reputation for being a "lively" affair over the years, ICE members and their guests have looked to be well fed and watered, before being entertained by humorous and informed guest speakers. Woe betides the ill-informed or not-so-entertaining guest who on a few occasions has been less than well received! In recent years this annual event has regularly attracted attendances of around nine hundred people, making it one of the largest Dinners of its kind in the country. Nowadays, the guests are treated to a good quality four-course meal followed by three or four speeches, mercifully adopting a slightly more modest approach to things than our forebears – a menu card from1895 sets out a seven-course meal followed by nine toasts! Interestingly the toast list (each with a reply) included:

The Queen,
The Prince and Princess of Wales,
The Institution,
The Glasgow Association,
Past Presidents,
Our Scottish Railway Companies,
The Visitors,
Contractors,
The Chairman.

That the Railway Companies are the only sector of Civil Engineering to merit a toast is yet another example of the importance in which the Railways and the Railway Engineer were held in ICE Glasgow & West of Scotland at that time.

Throughout its 125 years, ICE Glasgow & West of Scotland had always sought to educate and inform. From the early days as an Association of Students, right up to the current days' activities which focus not only on ICE members, but also on the general public. There are few areas of the 'civilised' society that we all enjoy today that does not bear the mark of the work of the Civil Engineer. From our water supply and sanitation in our public health, our roads and bridges, railways and canals, docks and harbours which all transport goods, materials and people in the upwardly-mobile, consumer-led society in which we all live, and our power supplies in all their various forms – all things that we take for granted in our everyday lives. Something to think about the next time we stride purposefully through Glasgow Central.

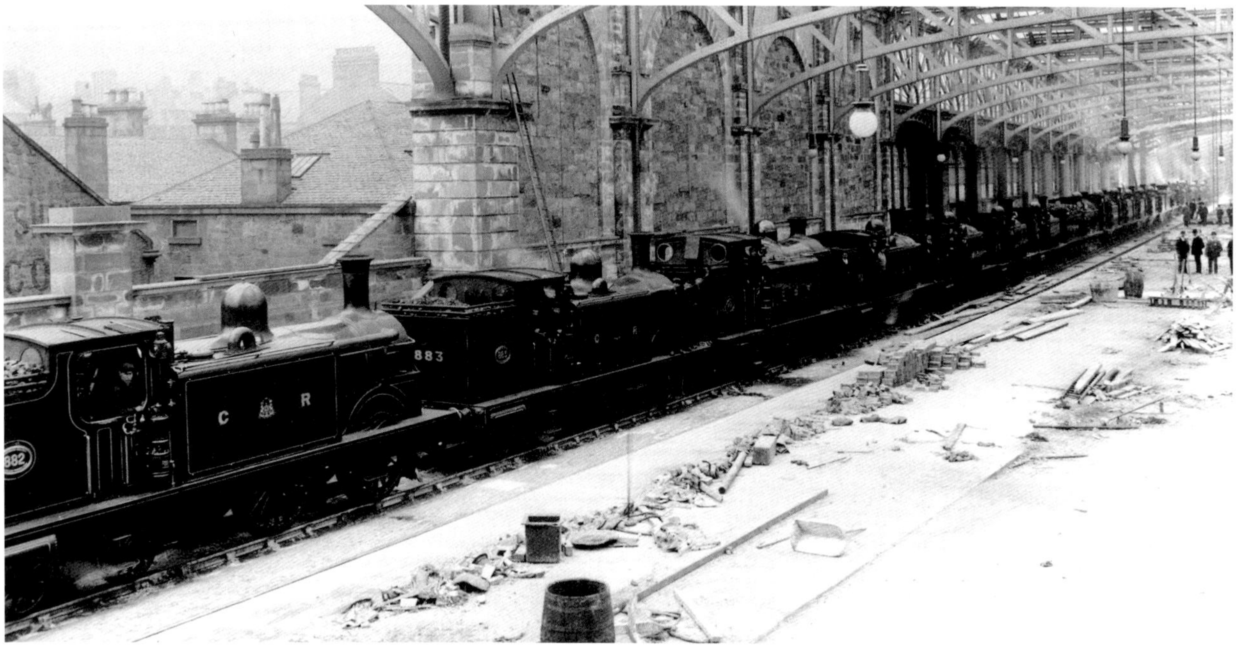

Nineteen locomotives – nae bother!

Prologue

Dugald Cameron

From "The Railway Engineer", January 1906:

The work of enlarging the Caledonian Railway's Central Station, Glasgow is proceeding rapidly. The new approach and six additional lines are in use, but the works in the station will not be completed before next spring. The station will have thirteen platforms instead of nine, and new ones will be broader and therefore much more commodious than the old ones. When the station is complete, the Caledonian Company will have a splendid terminus, and Glasgow a valuable addition to its architectural greatness.

November 2006 at Glasgow Central station in the company of "Princess Elizabeth". Also known as Pacific steam locomotive Number 6201 of the former LMS Railway and 46201 of British Railways, she had arrived the previous day, on a special train celebrating the 70th anniversary of her epic return trip from and to London Euston, which took place precisely on those days in 1936.

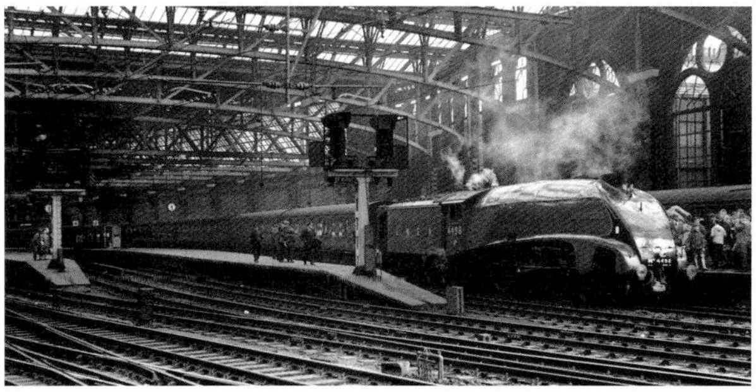

Restored LNER A4 No. 4498 "Sir Nigel Gresley" in Platform 2.

That the locomotive is not only still in existence, but fully certificated to all the required current main line running standards, is truly wonderful and a great tribute to the 6201 Society. Her regal presence, and the enthusiasm of a gifted brass ensemble from the Royal Scottish Academy of Music and Drama, conducted by their Principal, Professor John Wallace, combined to make the launch of the book a memorable occasion. That the book quickly sold out, earning over £10,000 for the Railway Children charity, was a great satisfaction to all concerned. That first edition was generously supported by the railway industry in Scotland, The Railway Historical Trust and Glasgow City Council.

This second edition too has been generously supported, and our gratitude this time is for the Institution of Civil Engineers, through their Scottish Branch: its 25th Anniversary falls in this year, 2009.

The art of engineering combines human creativity with technology in the service of us all, and there are no better examples than the railways of the world. This is as much true today, as it was in the Victorian era. Now and in the future, the need is ever more pressing for environmentally efficient transport, such as railways provide.

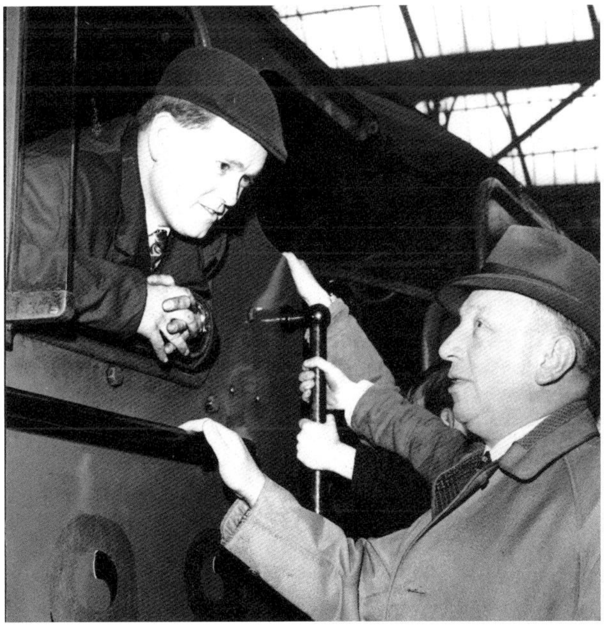

On Saturday, 20 May 1967 a special run to Aberdeen and back was made by newly restored A4, No. 4498 "Sir Nigel Gresley". Dugald Cameron (with bunnet) is seen trying to convince BR's Jim Hewitson that it is a good idea!

Nowhere is that great art of engineering better expressed than in the railway works of civil engineers. They wrought an iron road which presents a confident and reassuring course through the landscape by way of wonderful bridges, viaducts and tunnels. But the railway needs the skills of other engineers too, mechanical, electrical, signalling, telecommunications, architectural, in the last case often delightfully at its finest in modest country stations as much as in great termini.

The railway they made is a dynamic industry, and Glasgow Central is a constantly changing business – particularly so post-privatisation. In the relatively short time between the two editions of this book, train operators have changed, platform numbering has been altered, new information systems have appeared, toilets have been refurbished, new shops have enticed more folk to linger in this remarkable place. Further developments will occur. They always do at Central. One sight not available when the first edition was being produced was that of a Cessna seaplane flying over the station approaches preparatory to landing on the river Clyde – on a service to Oban.

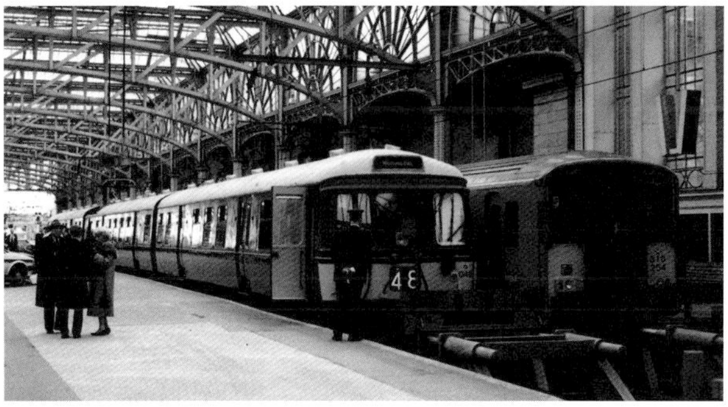

To celebrate the completion of the refurbishment of Wemyss Bay Station, the official party was transported by restored Class 303 'Blue Train' EMU No. 303048 – 25 March 1994.

Nonetheless, some things don't need to change, for they remain eternally right, and at heart this great Glaswegian institution is the same as it always has been – a remarkable tribute to the planning genius of Donald Matheson. Now in its second century, its ability still to satisfy and adapt to changing traffic needs is eloquent testimony to the foresight and skill of that great engineer and manager.

A society which is ignorant of its past is unlikely to understand its present; and thus may not know with any degree of certainty where it might go, could go, or is going. Perhaps this book, composed by many people as a "collective memory", will therefore serve as a valuable repository of knowledge and experience, for these things can be too lightly dismissed, even determinedly dismissed, in our modern age. But may the book also bring amusement, delight, and affection, as the Central itself has always done.

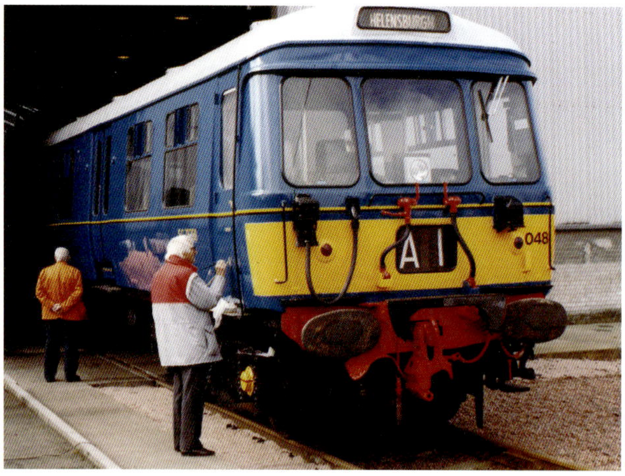

The man who inspired the compiler, the incomparable Terence Cuneo painting his personal mouse on the newly restored 'Blue Train' at Shields Depot on 28 March 1991.

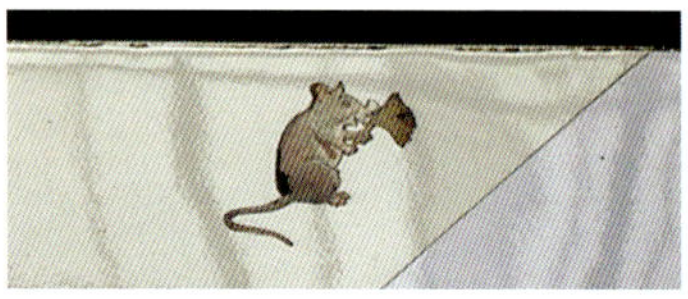

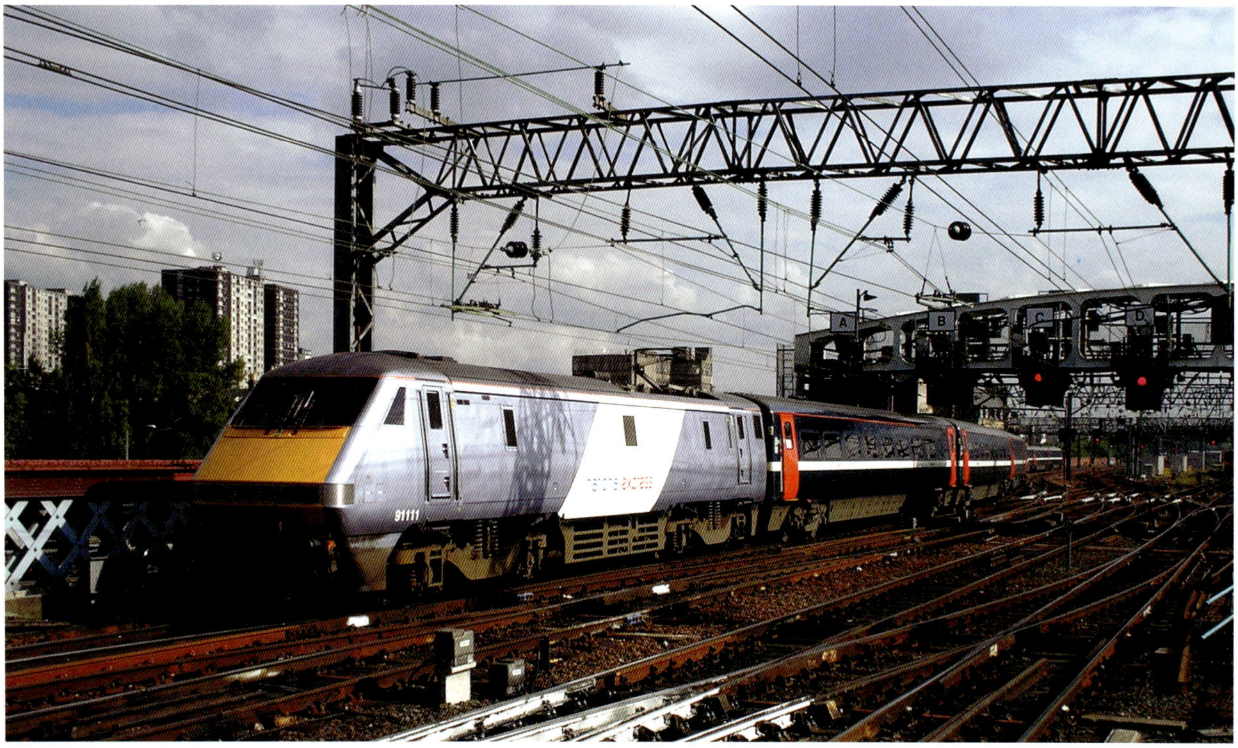

No. 91111, the erstwhile "Terence Cuneo", seen leaving on 30 June 2009, was the only Class 91 to get the new National Express livery. It may no longer bear the artist's name, but his mouse still goes along for the ride!

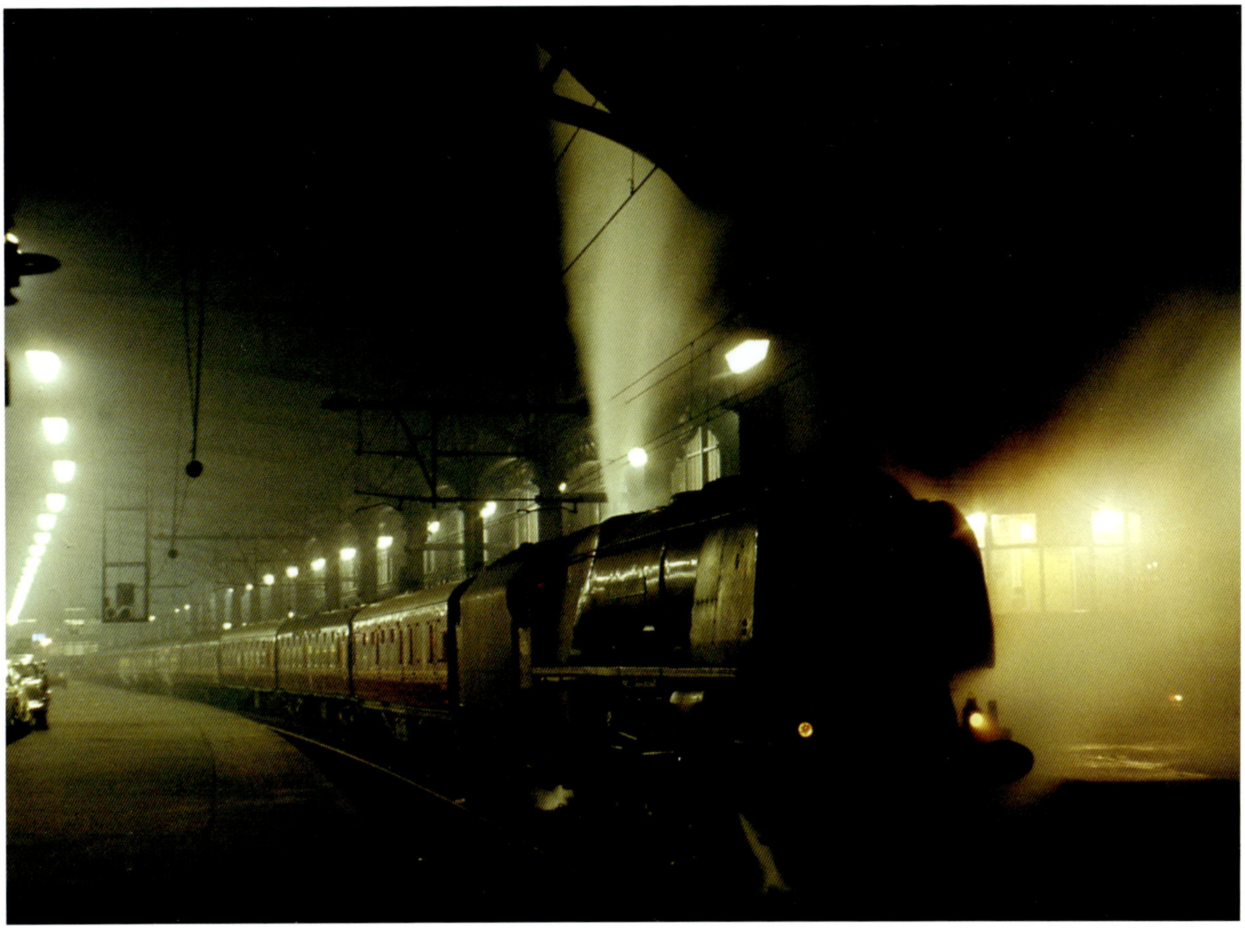

Stanier Pacific No. 46256 "Sir Willian Stanier FRS" awaits departure with a return Football International Special in April 1964 during the twilight months of the class.

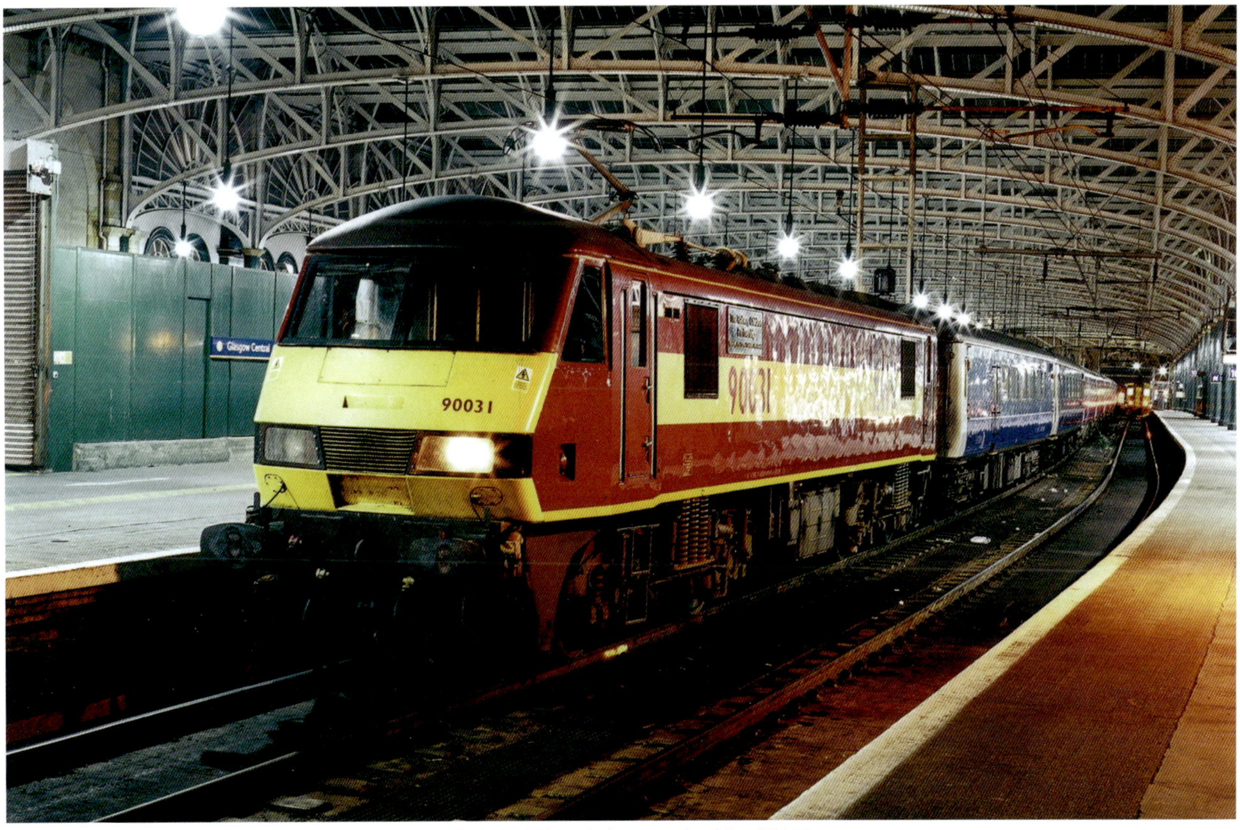

Class 90 Electric locomotive No. 90031
"The Railway Children Partnership Working For Street Children Worldwide"
warms the berths of the overnight FirstScotrail Caledonian Sleeper bound for London Euston.

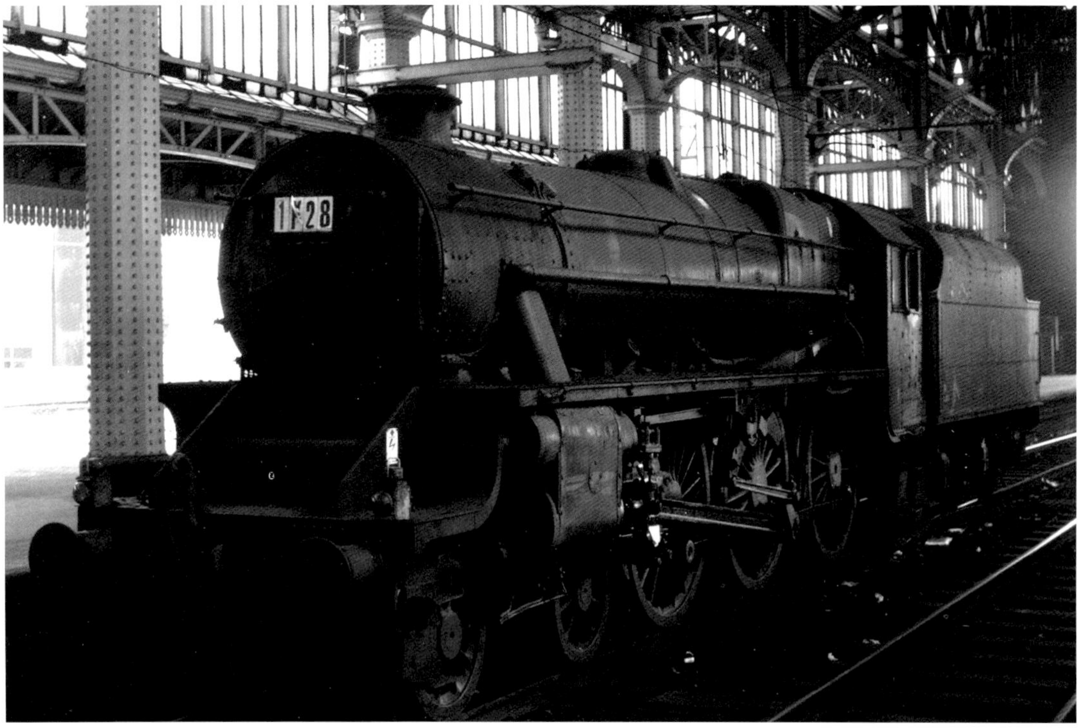

A Stanier masterpiece Class 5MT 4-6-0 awaits its turn to go to Polmadie – one of the many unremunerative movements eliminated by the coming of the multiple unit train and push-pull working.

Now preserved Jubilee Class 5XP 4-6-0 No. 45593 "Kolhapur" pauses briefly before backing out to Polmadie for servicing.

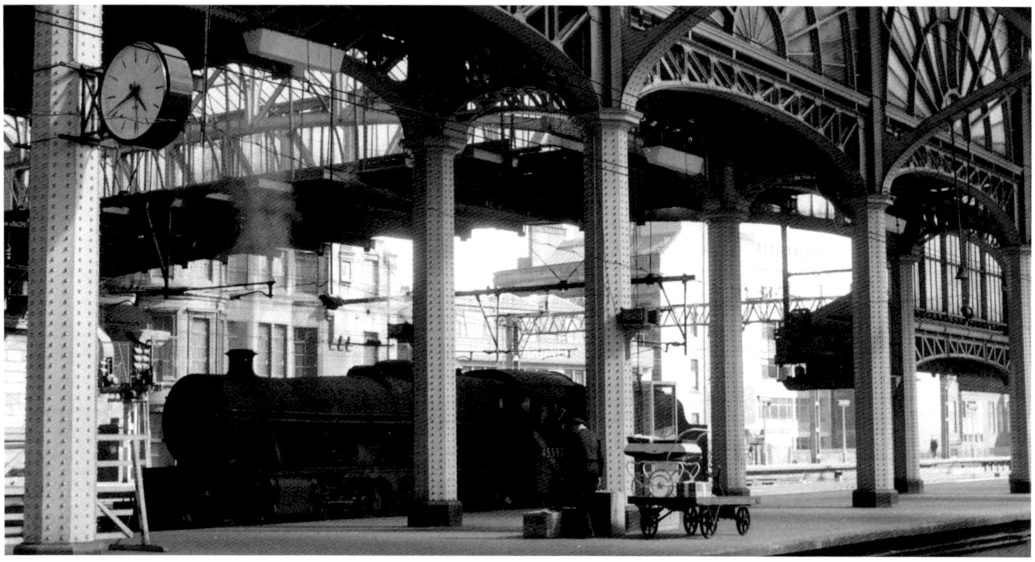

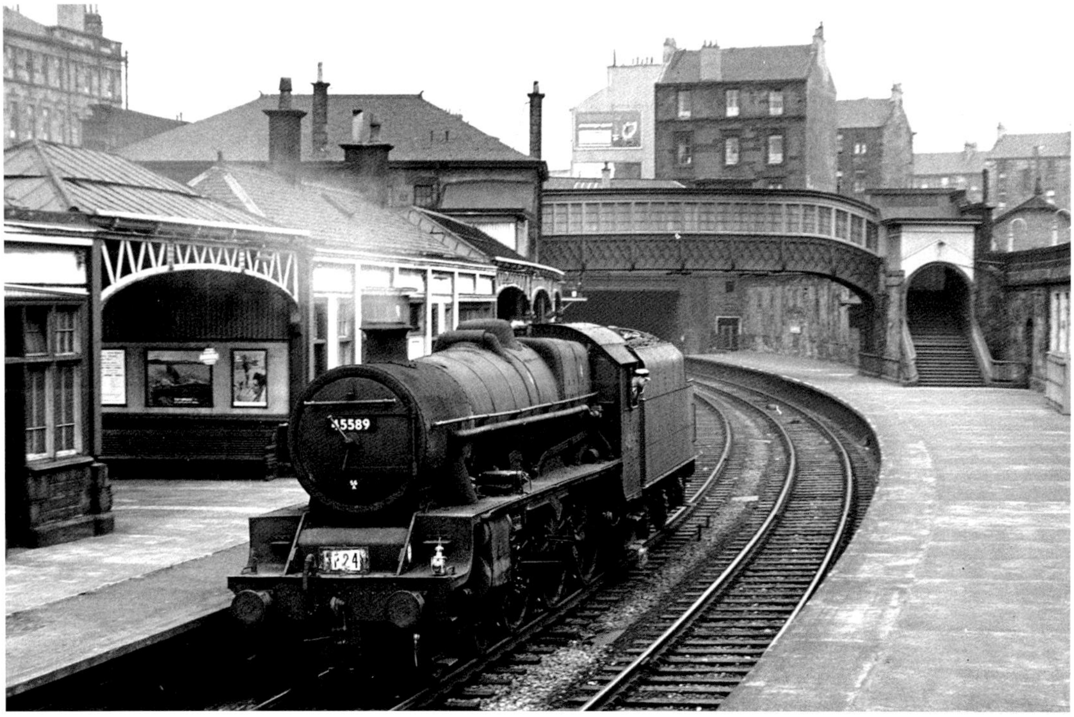

Jubilee Class 5XP 4-6-0 No. 45589 "Gwalior" passes through Eglinton Street Station on its way to Polmadie MPD after arriving at Central with a train from the south in 1965.

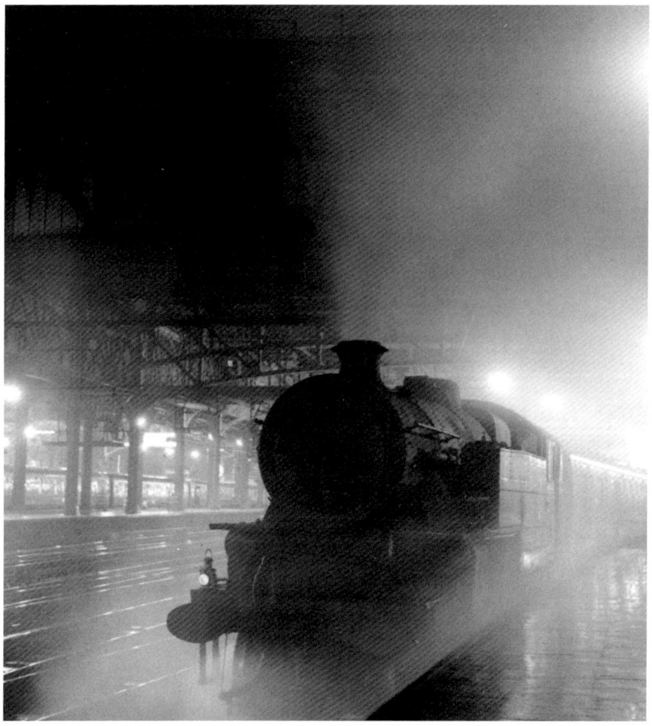

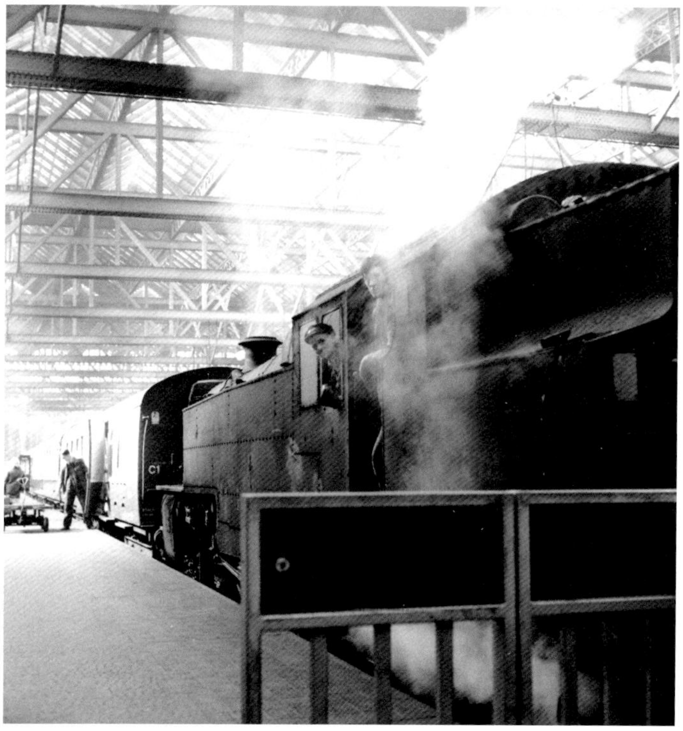

Fairburn 2-6-4 tanks on empty stock duties near the end of steam.

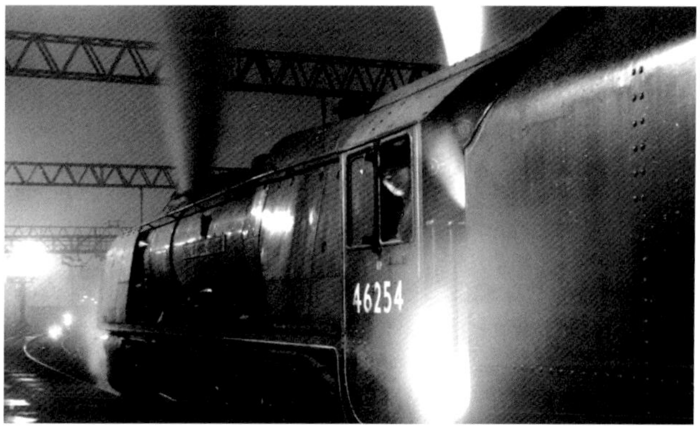

Ahead lies Craigenhill, Beattock and Shap for these Crewe North enginemen on a wet, cold and foggy January evening in 1964 bound for London Marylebone.

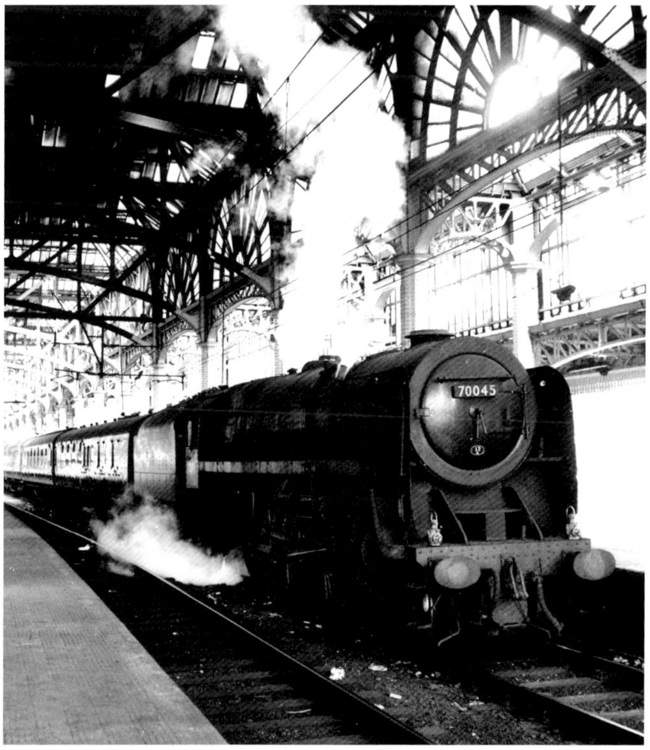

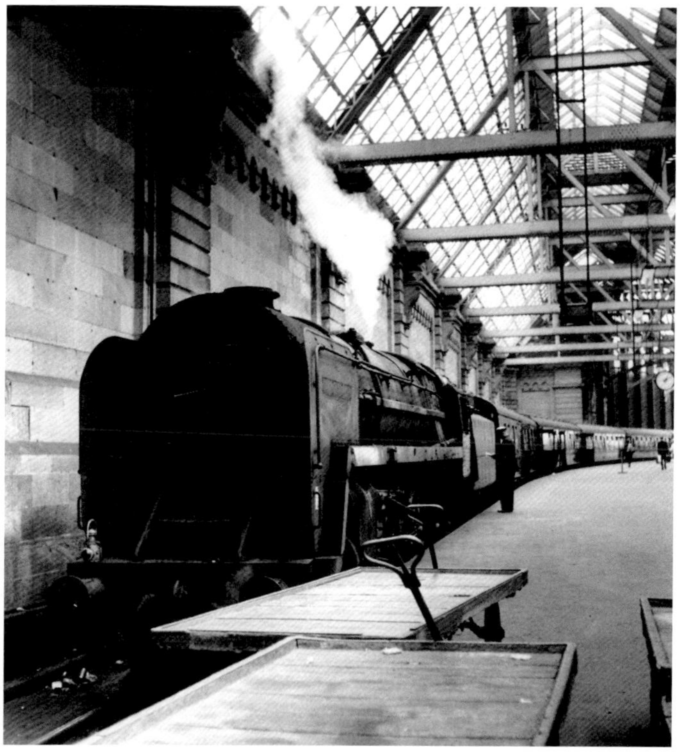

Britannias rule OK!

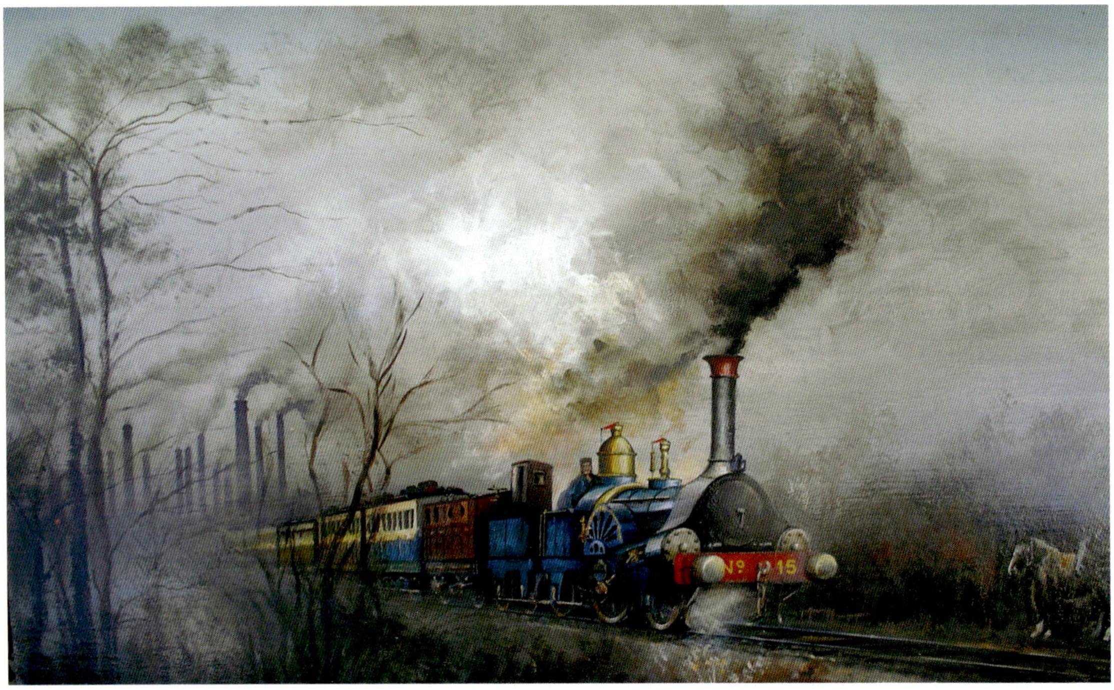

"In the beginning" – Train to the south 1848 hauled by Allan 2-2-2 Single.

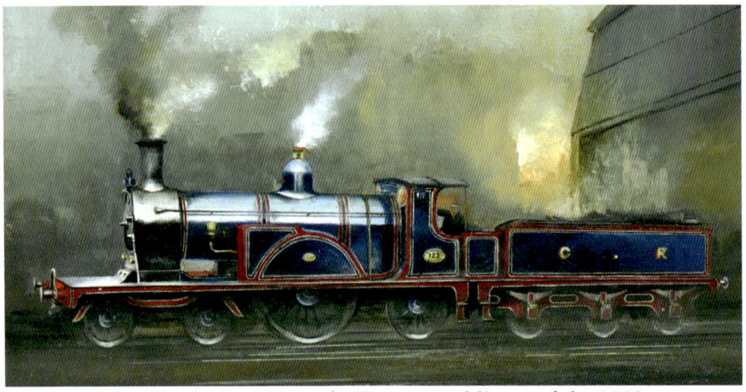

Caley Single No. 123 in the Drummond livery of the 1880s,
still on view preserved in Glasgow's Museum of Transport.

The original Glasgow Central Station of 1879 with Conner 2-2-2 Single and Britain 4-4-0 awaiting departure.

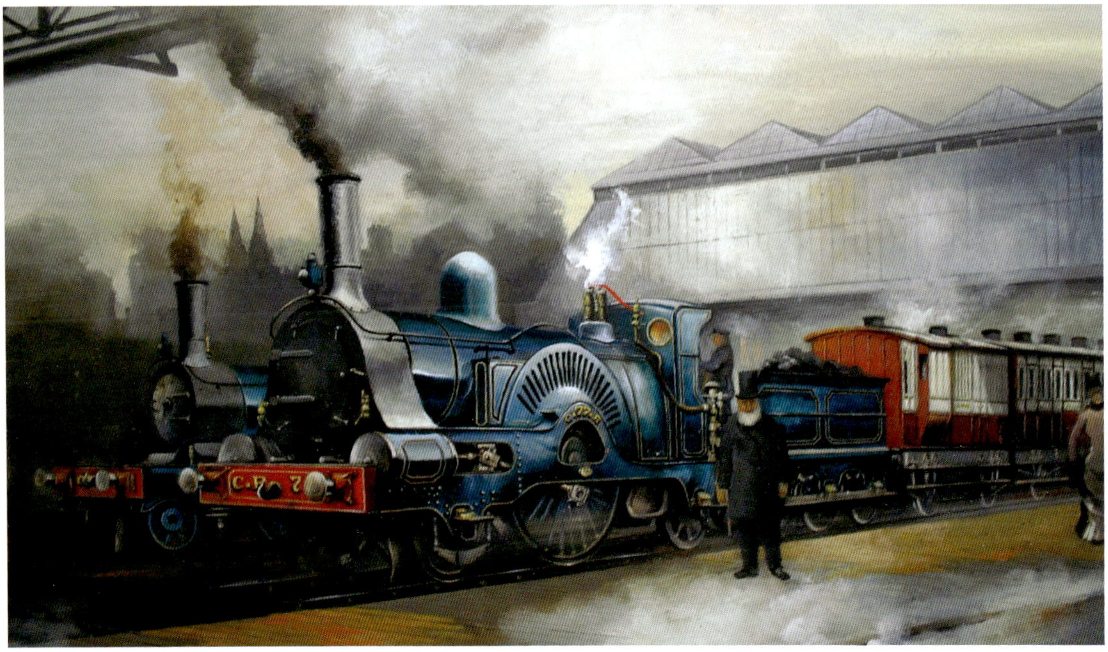

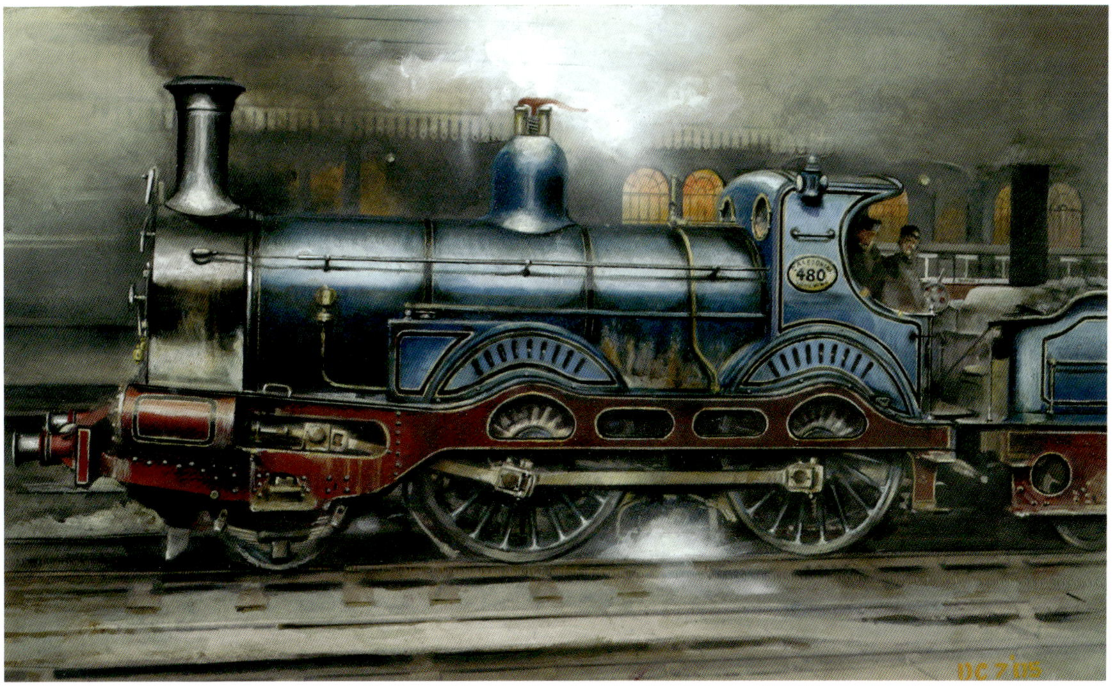

Station pilot – Conner 2-4-0 No. 480 1906.

Becoming Central to Glasgow

J F McIntosh's masterpiece – Dunalastair II No. 766 set against Donald Matheson's masterpiece - c1906.

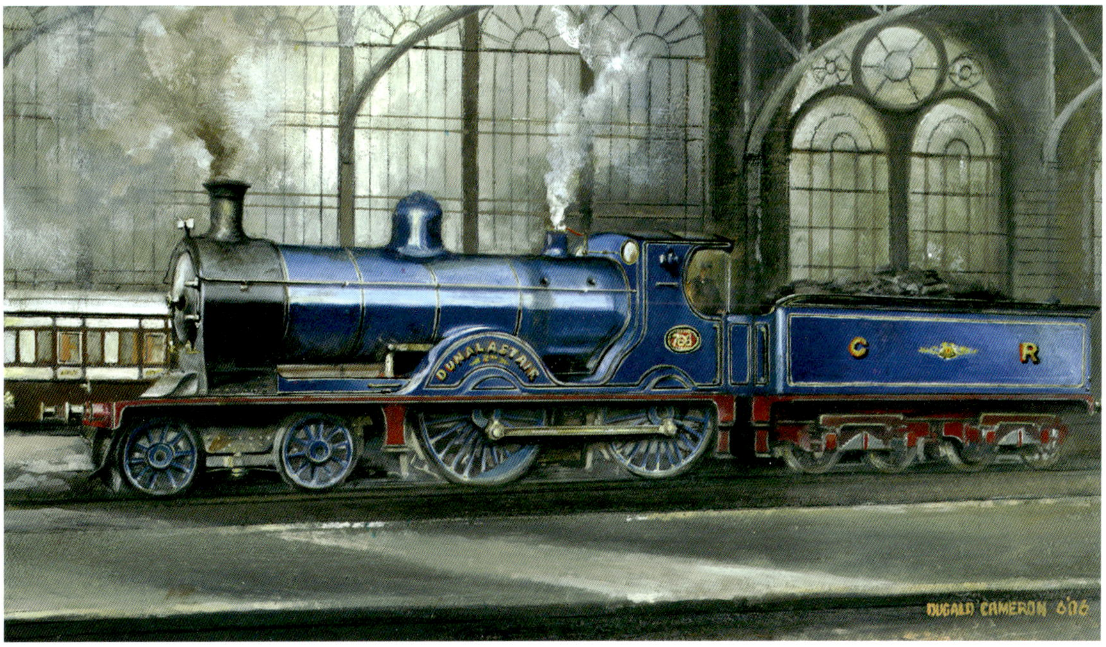

1 Railways and the city

John R Hume

Railways were crucial to the evolution of the European city from the 1830s until the mid 20th century, and are still critical to the life of most large cities. The railway developed in England as transport for fuel, and this has remained a primary role of railways. Today, the supply of coal by rail to Longannet and Cockenzie power stations, and the movement of nuclear flasks to and from Hunterston and Torness, make urban life in lowland Scotland possible. This ability of railways to move heavy materials efficiently was also central to urban growth from the mid 19th century, as building materials were needed in increasing quantities. When locally available building stones were exhausted, new sources were exploited, notably red sandstone from Ayrshire and Dumfries-shire. Stone for road-making also came in by rail. Bricks, tiles, timber, slates, cast-iron goods (and the pig-iron to make such goods) all came into Glasgow by rail. The suburban goods yards, developed from the 1880s, handled the materials to build the suburbs they were designed to serve. Canals and coastal shipping were also important in this trade, but railways became increasingly dominant until mechanised road transport developed.

In Glasgow, the opening of the Garnkirk and Glasgow, primarily a coal line, was followed by the development of passenger traffic and the use of the railway as a means of communication and trade in foodstuffs, raw materials and manufactured goods. Large grain warehouses were features of Buchanan Street and Queen Street goods stations by the 1870s. From the 1880s, fish from North East Scotland also came by rail, as did dairy products from Ayrshire and Galloway. More importantly, livestock came into Glasgow in quantity, much of it from Scottish sources, but also from North America and from Ireland, the cattle being imported through the docks, and moved by rail for slaughtering at Bellgrove. Other foodstuffs and beverages which came in by rail included fruit, vegetables, biscuits, beer, whisky and wine. The importance of Glasgow as a centre of the whisky trade was dependent on railways. Though the city did have its own distilleries, most of the whisky which was blended and bottled in Glasgow came in by rail, and much of it went to market in railway vehicles.

Apart from food, drink, fuel and shelter, the other essentials for life in Scotland are clothing and footwear. Until the 1860s, the cotton used in the mills of the west of Scotland was imported into Clyde ports, but later most came from Liverpool by rail. For the Scottish woollen industries, however, much of the wool used was imported through Glasgow and distributed by rail. From the late 19th century, ready-made clothing came into Glasgow from Leeds and from the hosiery industry in the Borders. Cloth was also bought in from Yorkshire and from the Borders tweed industry by Glasgow tailors. Boots and shoes came from Ayrshire and the English Midlands.

As the 19th century wore on, the range of goods demanded by urban society expanded enormously. Many were made in Glasgow, but more were brought in by rail. Focus for this trade were the large goods stations, but these were also tranship depots, where goods for onward shipment were transferred from van to van without ever leaving railway premises. Much of this was parcels traffic, involving sharing of vans and wagons. Dominant though the railways were, they depended on short-haul road transport for linking goods and mineral depots with individual commercial and domestic customers. Until the 1950s this system was largely horse-hauled. The maintenance of Glasgow's enormous population of horses, used to pull trams, buses, hackney and private carriages and delivery vehicles, was largely the task of the railways, which brought in fodder and bedding, and removed the by-products for use in improving Scotland's farmlands.

Railways became part of urban life, as well as serving it. Glasgow had the headquarters of two of Scotland's four major railways, the Caledonian and the Glasgow and South Western, and the principal workshops of the Caledonian and North British railways. Large numbers of staff were also employed at stations, as train crew, as Signalmen and as locomotive and carriage-shed workers. The railway service was structured: all employees knew where they were in the system, helping to give stability and cohesion to Glasgow society. Railway employment was generally secure, whereas industrial employment was often precarious. The companies engendered loyalty: a Caley or NB man would be just as fiercely proud of his company as a modern football supporter is of his team. Few women were employed on the railways until the First World War.

Railways were also critical to the siting, growth and character of urban industry. From the earliest days there were locomotive workshops in Glasgow. Private locomotive-building preceded building by the railway companies themselves, and in Glasgow this private locomotive-building developed dramatically. The North British Locomotive Co. Ltd. was the largest concern of its kind in Europe. Rolling-stock was built and repaired alongside the locomotive workshops in the city. From the 1860s, many industrial concerns either developed rail links, or moved to rail-served premises. Railway routes became industrial corridors, and some new lines were planned to serve industry, notably the Lanarkshire and Dumbartonshire route, which served harbour facilities, shipyards and engineering works. The willingness of the railway companies to service private premises gave Glasgow one of the highest concentrations of private sidings in the United Kingdom. Even where industrial premises could not be linked directly by rail, the network of goods and mineral depots served both industry and private householders.

The railways were also integral to the development of efficient postal services. Rowland Hill's "penny post" was from the start dependent on the railways, and the railways also handled their own parcels trade, as well as that of the Post Office. This was vital to the development of newspaper publication, and it is significant that Glasgow Central was closely ringed by newspaper offices. When the electric telegraph was introduced in the

1830s, it was the linear routes of the railway lineside that were used to create a network of telegraphic communication.

The first railways were designed to minimise disruption to existing buildings and roads. Apart from Queen Street, all the early terminals were built on the edges of the city centre. When, however, the goods stations in the High Street were constructed, and St Enoch and Central stations were built in the city centre, the extent of demolition was considerable. Their expansion between 1895 and 1906 resulted in even more disruption. The areas demolished were densely settled, so the human cost was high. By the 1880s and 90s, when cross-city lines were built, tunnelling was the only possibility. More positively, competition between railways resulted in the construction of grand hotels, much improving the standard of hotel accommodation in the city. The success of the St Enoch Hotel forced the Caledonian to convert their planned new offices at Central Station into an even grander hotel. The North British economically revamped an existing hotel beside Queen Street.

The Glasgow railways had, as well as the functions mentioned above, several highly specific traffics. These included: holiday excursions; high-class tourism, particularly on the Highland lines; the movement of workers from old industrial areas to new (of which the workers' trains from Bridgeton to the Singer sewing machine works at Kilbowie were the most important); boat trains, run in connection with Clyde Coast and Loch Lomond steamers; trains to take upper middle class sportsmen to golf courses; and trains to convey working men in vast numbers to football matches.

The railways were intensively used during both world wars, but the inter-war trade depression meant that investment was minimal after 1914. Users of the railway system in the late 1940s and early 1950s would have found little changed from before the First World War. Decline in the basic industries, exhaustion of coal seams, and the apparently inexorable rise in the use of motor vehicles all contributed to the problem. By the mid 1950s it was apparent that the nationalised rail system was in urgent need of modernisation.

Dr Beeching's initial proposals would have eliminated most of the Scottish railway system, but they were mitigated by Government. The rationalised system, with its new diesel and electric trains, generally offered faster, more frequent services, and many stations were modernised. In Glasgow this involved phased electrification of most of the city's inner and outer suburban network, and ultimately of the West Coast and East Coast main lines.

In the late 1970s the value of railways as a complement to motor transport began to be recognised. A century after the end of railway expansion, the Glasgow railways have recovered much of the ground they lost in the interval. The First Class traffic, the excursion traffic and transport to sporting events have almost completely gone, as have freight services, and manufacturing industry. But travel to work has, if anything, increased, and on some lines is nearing capacity. Services have become more frequent, cleaner, and in many cases faster. Where railways go from here is by no means clear, but they continue to shape urban change in Glasgow, as they have done for more than 170 years.

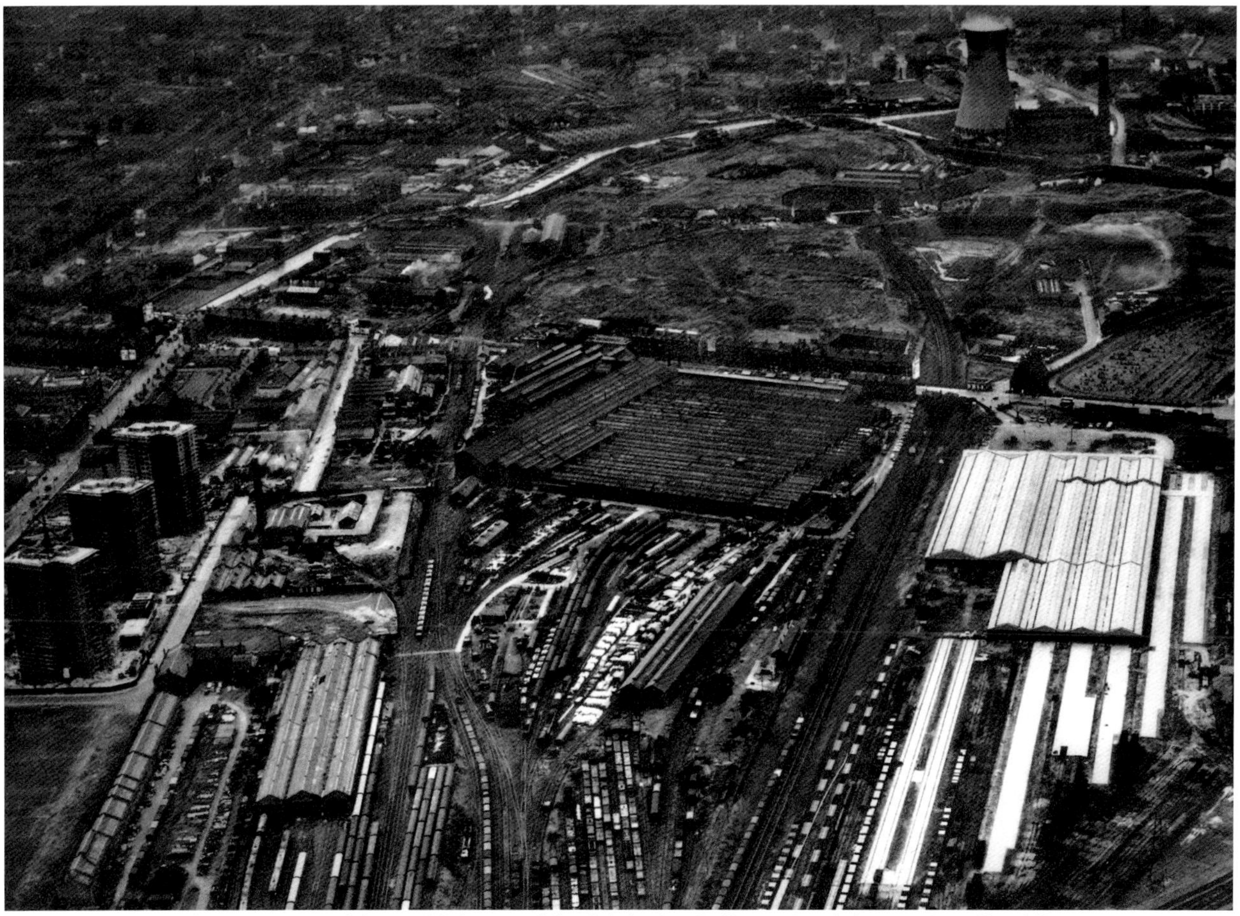

The 150th anniversary of the establishment of the Caledonian Railway's Workshops at St Rollox fell in 2006. This is the site in its later years with the original Garnkirk and Glasgow Railway line on the left.

2 Glasgow and the Caledonian Railway

Jim MacIntosh

As the 19th Century progressed, railway development in the Glasgow area was based on the local deposits of coal and iron. The canal boom of the 1790s had done little to help most Scottish coalmasters, with only the Monkland Canal (engineered by James Watt) serving the coal-producing areas and helping to supply coal to the city of Glasgow, which by 1820 was using half a million tons a year for domestic fuel and industries from cotton mills to steam boats. By 1835, 31 different industries had installed 355 steam engines, and Glasgow had 13 firms manufacturing them. Blackband iron stone, a low grade ferrous ore, is found in most coal measures, but around Airdrie and Monklands it was particularly rich in iron. James B Neilson, (whose son Walter went on to establish Hyde Park Locomotive Works), invented the hot-blast process in 1828, when he was manager of the Glasgow Gas Works. This development worked particularly well with the local splint or hard coal, which could be used without first being coked, and so by 1833 a ton of iron could be made with one-third of the amount of coal and limestone for flux previously thought necessary, making Scottish iron the cheapest in the country.

This gave the West of Scotland a decisive advantage and heralded an explosion in the production of pig-iron from 25,000 tons in 1825 to 564,000 tons in 1848. The developing railways across the world were a major consumer, and in 1846 a total of 377,000 tons of Scottish iron was shipped down the Clyde. The growth of iron production created an expanding demand for coal and encouraged the construction of new railways across the Lanarkshire coalfields. These two commodities, and the engineering products manufactured from them, would form what has been called "the Bread and Butter" of the commercial success of the Caledonian Railway. In 1912 the receipts per train mile were 51.33d for Passenger/Coaching traffic and 104.36d for Goods/Mineral Traffic, which also accounted for 58% of the total receipts. But before the Caledonian Railway reached the heart of Glasgow in a fitting terminus, much persistence was to be needed. And that early network which began in the Monklands was to play the major role in its entry into the city.

Waggonways as a form of transport linking the coal mines to the waterways, were first superseded in Scotland when the Monklands & Kirkintilloch (M&K) Railway was authorised in 1824 and opened in 1826. Although this railway subsequently became part of the North British company, the Caledonian retained running rights between Gartsherrie and Garnqueen South Junction, a distance of 52 chains, as part of the route to meet the Scottish Central at Greenhill. From Gartsherrie, the Garnkirk & Glasgow (G&G), authorised in 1826 and opened in 1831, ran westwards to the terminus in the Townhead District at St Rollox on the northern fringe of the city, where Charles Tennant's factory, a major consumer of coal and the largest chemical plant in Europe, was also sited. Although the railway linked with the Monkland Canal at St Rollox, the G&G, unlike the previous railways of the area, was built to be in competition with the canals (rather than simply to feed them) and to be operated from the outset by locomotives. The G&G was followed by the Wishaw & Coltness (W&C), opened progressively from 1833 to 1844, which ran south from the M&K to Wishaw and Chapel. Although these early railways were primarily built for coal traffic, passenger services started as early as 1830 on sections of them.

Glasgow's first "passenger railways", however, were the Glasgow, Paisley & Greenock (GP&G) and the Glasgow, Paisley, Kilmarnock & Ayr (GPK&A), both authorised in 1837 and opened between Glasgow and Paisley in 1840 – a section of the line which was to remain jointly-owned up until the Grouping of Britain's railways in 1923. Both railways were opened throughout in 1841 and shared the Glasgow terminus of Bridge Street, near the city centre but separated from it by the river Clyde. The other early passenger railway was the Edinburgh & Glasgow Railway (E&G), authorised in 1838 and opened in 1842 with a city centre terminus at Queen Street (originally called Dundas Street). The traffic potential for these passenger lines was great. In 1830 half of the 7-mile journeys between Paisley and Glasgow were still on foot, and the canal companies transported some 400,000 passengers from Paisley and 200,000 from Edinburgh to Glasgow per year.

Grand designs

A potential railway linking Central Scotland with the English centres of Lancashire and the West Midlands first emerged in 1836. A trunk line was opened from London to Birmingham, and the Grand Junction Railway was under construction from Birmingham to Warrington, with the North Union projected as far as Preston. The directors of the Grand Junction instructed their engineer, Joseph Locke, to survey a route which would extend the line of railway from Preston to Carlisle, and on to Glasgow and Edinburgh. In his 1842 report he refers to the line between Lancaster and Carlisle as "Caledonian Railway Part 1" and the line north from Carlisle as "Part 2". Locke was no stranger to Scotland, having engineered the Glasgow Paisley & Greenock Railway and modernised Greenock Harbour, his greatest work of civil engineering other than railways.

Whilst the alternative routes for the line of the railway between Preston and Carlisle were quickly resolved, the "Battle of the Dales" raged for a number of years, as two potential routes from Carlisle to Glasgow were fought over. Locke's first report proposed the route from Carlisle to Glasgow via Dumfries and through Nithsdale, having found that to follow Thomas Telford's direct mail-coach route through Annandale would involve a ten-mile stretch near Beattock with a gradient of 1 in 75. The resulting in-fighting and political manoeuvring has been extensively documented, showing the Glasgow interests preferring Nithsdale, to meet the proposed GPK&A Railway, but local landowners and early promoters striving for Annandale. A second survey by Locke, in 1837, admitted the possibilities of Annandale but proposed that a Royal Commission be held to decide on the chosen route, on the assumption that there would be only traffic for one cross-border railway, and there were already other competing proposals, in particular an east coast line from Edinburgh to Berwick and a second line from Edinburgh to Carlisle via Hawick.

The shortage of potential subscription capital resulted in the Government not acting on the proposal until 1839. The eventual outcome of the Smith-Barlow Commission favoured Annandale over the more lightly-graded Nithsdale route, which, although serving more populated areas, necessitated an additional 20 miles to Glasgow and 50 miles to Edinburgh. Further surveys and increasingly bitter arguments ensued, leading to an alliance of the east coast and Nithsdale routes aimed at stopping the Annandale (Caledonian) project. This was consummated in March 1844 with an agreement for mutual co-operation, signed by John Learmouth of the North British and John Leadbetter of the Glasgow, Dumfries and Carlisle (later to be the Glasgow and South Western Railway, the G&SWR), an alliance which was to frustrate the Caledonian throughout the Company's existence.

Meantime, Parliament required that the Lancaster and Carlisle line had a guarantee of completion before the Annandale line could be started, so it was not until February 1844 that the title Caledonian Railway Company was formally adopted and the prospectus issued on 27 March. In spite of, or perhaps because of, the English

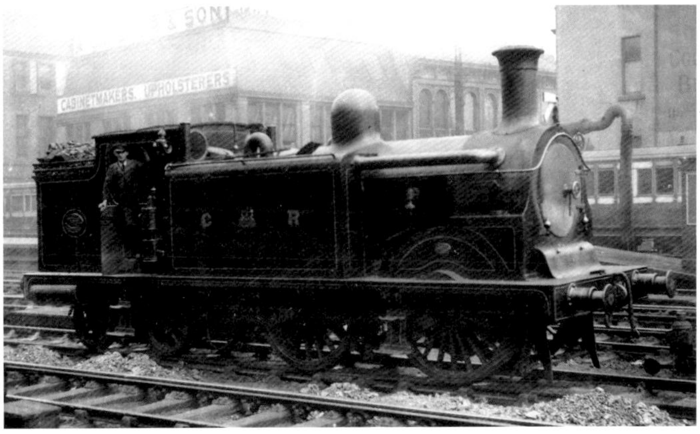

CR '92' Class 0-4-4 tank No. 100, in black livery with condensing apparatus for working underground lines.

parentage – some 80% of the capital was raised in England – the Caledonian Railway from the outset promoted a fiercely Scottish identity, calling itself the National Line and annexing as its own the ancient Scottish Arms and the motto, Nemo me impune lacessit (No one provokes me with impunity), and completed the image by painting the passenger locomotives the colour of the Saltire.

Onwards to Glasgow

The natural approach to Glasgow, as envisaged by Locke and Errington in their 1842/3 surveys into the best and cheapest route, was to follow the south bank of the Clyde into Hamilton, but the opposition of the tenth Duke of Hamilton and possible difficulties with Parliamentary approval made them recommend a junction with the Wishaw and Coltness (W&C) and the use of these early connecting lines on the north side of the river, as the route into Glasgow and towards Aberdeen.

The Act of 1845 authorised the line from Carlisle to a junction at Garriongill, with a branch from Carstairs to Edinburgh. Beyond Garriongill, Glasgow was to be reached over the lines of the W&C and the Garnkirk and Glasgow, now known as Glasgow, Garnkirk and Coatbridge, both of which were re-gauged, having originally been built to the Scottish gauge of 4 feet 6 inches. The GG&C was sold to the Caledonian in 1846 and the W&C amalgamated with the CR in 1849. Also included in the Act was provision for the Caledonian to acquire the Clydesdale Junction Railway (CJR), also authorised in 1845, which extended to Motherwell the Pollok & Govan Railway (P&G) owned by coalmaster William Dixon, which had been authorised in 1830 but was based on an eighteenth century waggonway from the Govan Collieries to the Clyde. The CJR, P&G and the Caledonian were amalgamated in 1846. This line of railway gave access to the Glasgow, Paisley and Greenock Railway (GP&G) by a connecting line authorised in 1846. The GP&G amalgamation with the Caledonian was first authorised in 1847, but it was to take until the 1880's to finalise the financial arrangements. The Greenock workshops built some of the locomotives and rolling stock for the opening of the Caledonian Railway and served as the locomotive department until St Rollox was established in 1856. A total of 97 locomotives were built at Greenock for the Greenock and Caledonian Companies.

The final part of the 1845 Caledonian Act was a line from Garnqueen, on the Monklands & Kirkintilloch Railway, to Greenhill where it would meet the Scottish Central Railway, which in turn met at Perth, the Scottish Midland

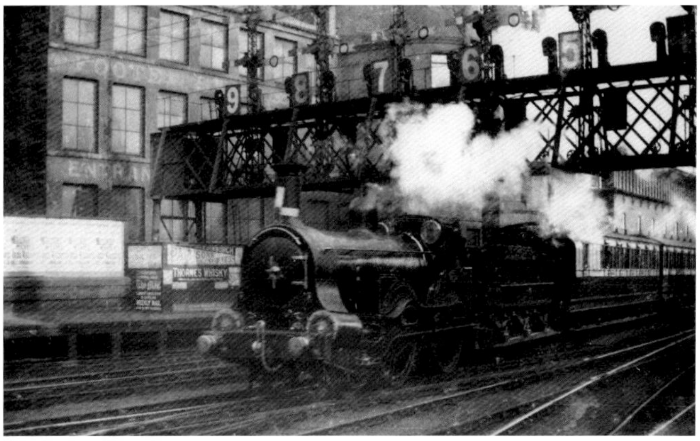

Caley '288' Class, Conner 2-4-0 as rebuilt in 1886 entering the original station.

Junction (SMJ), which included a number of local lines originally built to link Dundee with Strathmore. The SMJ would then meet the Aberdeen Railway at Guthrie. The Scottish Midland Junction and the Aberdeen Railway were to amalgamate to form the Scottish North Eastern Railway in 1856.

The various Acts for all of these lines were incorporated on the same day, all had been surveyed by Joseph Locke and in 1865 and 1866 were absorbed by the Caledonian Railway as the trunk route from Carlisle to Aberdeen. Prophetically, the Board of Trade, as early as 1842, had referred to this network as the "Caledonian System".

Teething troubles

While the use of the existing lines as the route into Glasgow reduced the initial costs of construction, tolls payable for running powers were to prove a steady drain on the Company's resources and were a contributory factor in the early financial crisis. "The Times" leading article on 30 September 1850 commented, "The Caledonian Railway Company, the work neither of

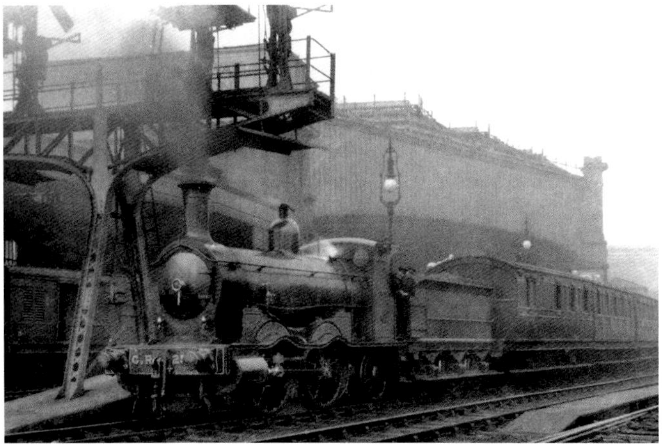

CR 0-4-2 No. 253 as station pilot in 1920
Note the milk van in next platform!

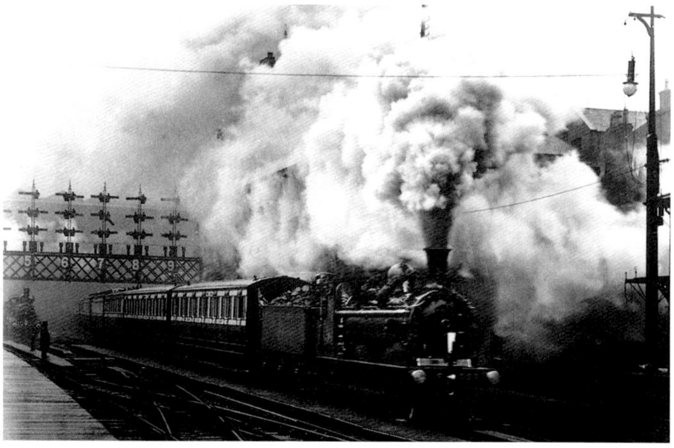

Decorated 'Jumbo' CR '709' Class 0-6-0 No. 587,
a condensing locomotive leaving the original 1879 station.

lawyers, nor old women, nor spendthrifts, but of shrewd middle-aged mercantile men, is just such a tangle as one might dream of after supping on lobster salad and champagne." The "Arrangement Act" of 1851 was an attempt to establish better financial terms between the Caledonian and what were to become the five "Guaranteed Companies", Garnkirk, Clydesdale Junction, Greenock, Wishaw and the Glasgow, Barrhead and Neilson Railway.

That financial crisis with the "Guaranteed Companies" and the resultant clear-out of directors in 1850 was also the culmination of a period of poor operational management, so bad that Brassey and Locke had been approached to run the railway on contract. The directors had neither business experience nor ability, and were preoccupied with the expansion of the sphere of influence of the Company rather than successfully operating what was already built or authorised. Accusations of using shareholders funds to invest in new companies led to a revolt by the "English" shareholders. The first step to recovery was the purchase of a large number of shares by James Baird, the multimillionaire ironmaster, re-establishing sufficient confidence in the Caledonian Company as an investment. A large slice of Scottish capital was thus introduced and prevented an "English" takeover. Many of the Directors, who had been the original promoters, resigned, including eventually Hope-Johnstone, the man whose vision and dogged persistence had secured the adoption of the Annandale route and the establishment of the Caledonian Railway Company.

The new board instituted strict cost controls on the operation and suspended negotiations on the proposed amalgamation with the Edinburgh and Glasgow Railway and the current fares war between the two railways and the canal companies for the intercity traffic. From the brink of disaster the Caledonian began an unsteady climb to prosperity, but how different might the history of Scotland's railways have been if the amalgamation had gone ahead. The Caledonian made further attempts to absorb the E&G in 1860, 1861 and 1864 and the ruinous competition with the North British almost brought about the collapse of both companies in 1860. The Company papers record that a "Peace Agreement" was signed with the NB on 31 October 1891, but it did not stop the intense competition.

Central eventually

The line from Carlisle to Beattock had opened on 10 September 1847, through to Glasgow and Edinburgh on 15 February 1848 and to Greenhill on 7 August 1848. The first direct horse-drawn coach from London to Glasgow arrived at the Saracen's Head in the Gallowgate in 1788, and the journey time for this service was gradually reduced from 63 to 48 hours. By 1841 Euston to Glasgow was accomplished in 24 hours with the train from Euston to Fleetwood via Preston, a steamer to Ardrossan and a train to Glasgow. With the completion of the Caledonian Railway the journey was timetabled as 13 hours from 1st March 1848 and from the 10th of that month the Post Office transferred the London to Edinburgh mails to the West Coast Route. By the time Glasgow Central Station was opened in 1879 the express was timetabled for 10 hours, and when the station rebuilding was complete in 1906 the journey time was 8 hours 20 minutes. A century later the journey time is now 4 hours 24 minutes for the fastest train, with more savings to come.

An appropriate terminal for Glasgow was a difficult problem to resolve. By the end of the 17th century the city of Glasgow occupied a strip of land sloping from the cathedral down to the north bank of the river Clyde at the Broomielaw. By the 1840s the city had expanded to the east and west and to a smaller extent south across the river, which was to become one of the barriers to the development of a central railway terminus for the city. Besides London, Glasgow was the only 19th Century city to have a Royal Commission to analyse the multiplicity of railway projects, but the city still ended up with four separate terminals, within a mile of each other, no through station and only one cross city link between the northern and southern railway networks.

A cross-city link, the West of Scotland Junction Railway, had been proposed as early as 1846, which was to link the Edinburgh & Glasgow with the Glasgow & Paisley Joint and connect with the Caledonian via the Polloc & Govan. Included in the proposal was a major through station at Blythswood. A similar scheme was proposed in the early 1860's with the intention that this "Central Station" would be available to all the lines serving the city with the Caledonian Railway acting as the leading agent. However the G&SWR and Edinburgh & Glasgow companies were discussing a link between their networks which would bridge the river but would not be able to use the station because of the geographical layout. As ties between these two companies with the Midland and North British Railways were being strengthened, interest in the joint station for Glasgow was withheld. The

Caledonian went as far as buying land, from the Blythswoodholm estate, which extended from Hope Street through to Pitt Street and was bounded by Waterloo and Bothwell Streets. "The Engineer", 5 January 1866, reported that

the Caledonian Company is about to ask Parliament for power to raise £6.6 million of new capital for a great station (£2 million) and several miles of underground railway with viaducts over and tunnels under the Clyde and with suburban circuits of the most costly kind.

The scheme foundered and the Blythswoodholm land was eventually sold.

Turning specifically to the Caledonian stations in Glasgow, the proposed 1846 station, the terminus of the Clydesdale Junction Railway, to be located facing later Argyle and Dunlop Streets failed because the other railway companies and the Clyde Trustees objected and the Admiralty required that the river bridge immediately outside the station should have an opening span to allow the passage of shipping. This was unacceptable to the railway company and the scheme was abandoned. The first trains from the south, therefore, terminated at Townhead, the original Glebe Street terminus of the Garnkirk and Glasgow Railway situated on the northern fringe of the city, requiring all passengers and goods for the city to pass through a toll-gate before being transferred through the already crowded streets to the city centre.

South Side station at the southern end of Main Street, Gorbals, on the opposite bank of the river and a mile from the city centre was opened 27 September 1848, as the terminal of the Glasgow, Barrhead and Neilson Direct Railway, authorised in 1845. The Caledonian leased it, and reached it over the rails of the Clydesdale Junction. For a brief period, Anglo-Scottish traffic was handled at South Side, until Buchanan Street Station was opened in 1849. This was reached by a line off the original Glasgow, Garnkirk & Coatbridge Railway at Milton Junction and a tunnel under the Forth & Clyde Canal and over the Cowlairs Tunnel, bringing the northern terminus closer to the city centre. Unfortunately the wooden shed originally constructed by Joseph Locke for Buchanan Street station, although developed and extended, was never replaced by a more fitting structure and that station was perhaps the poorest legacy left by the Caledonian Railway.

From the opening of the Scottish Central Railway, traffic from the north used the Edinburgh & Glasgow from Greenhill to Queen Street station, (where the Caledonian had a booking office), to avoid reversing at Gartsherrie or Coatbridge. With the completion of the Gartcosh to Garnqueen North Junction fork, or Hayhill Branch, northern traffic started using Buchanan Street in January 1870. Part of the early sharing of facilities involved the North British trains from Coatbridge and Airdrie terminating at Buchanan Street.

The continued development of Glasgow, "the second city of the Empire", as a major industrial and trading city with the ever-increasing passenger numbers, demanded that additional station capacity be at last addressed. Caledonian carryings rose from 2.7 million in 1863 to 5.5 million per annum in 1873. Opposition from River Trustees, the City Corporation, Bridge Trustees, and the railway companies themselves blocking each other's proposals, had delayed progress for some 25 years.

Bridge Street station on the south bank of the river, had been shared by the Greenock and Ayrshire lines since the railways opened, but by the late 1860s when the Wemyss Bay (CR) and Bridge of Weir (G&SW) lines had opened, the overcrowding of the station and the deteriorating relationship between the Caledonian and the Glasgow & South Western over the use of Bridge Street led to the latter planning a new station in the city centre, at St Enoch's Square and in conjunction with the North British they established the City of Glasgow Union Railway linking their two networks north and south of the river. Bridge Street Station would, as part of this development, become the sole property of the Caledonian Railway and the land at South Side would be re-distributed between the companies.

The Caledonian Railway finally obtained the Act to bridge the river and build Gordon Street Station, soon to be known as Glasgow Central Station in 1873. The original plan was to build a top deck for the railway over a widened Glasgow Bridge, as in Newcastle's High Level Bridge. But by 1875 an Amendment Act had been passed for a separate river crossing and some re-alignment of the line. The Caledonian paid the City £25,000 towards the cost of widening Glasgow or Jamaica Bridge and £70,500 in compensation to the Clyde Trustees for loss of quay frontage. The 1899 enlargement would cost a further £75,000 for the Clyde Trustees and £30,000 for the City Corporation.

The new Central and its predecessors

The new Central Station was planned to share traffic with Bridge Street, which now became a through station with bay platforms for the suburban traffic. The new station was opened in 1879, and the Edinburgh and Carlisle trains moved to the Central from 1 September 1879. Southside ceased to handle passengers from that date.

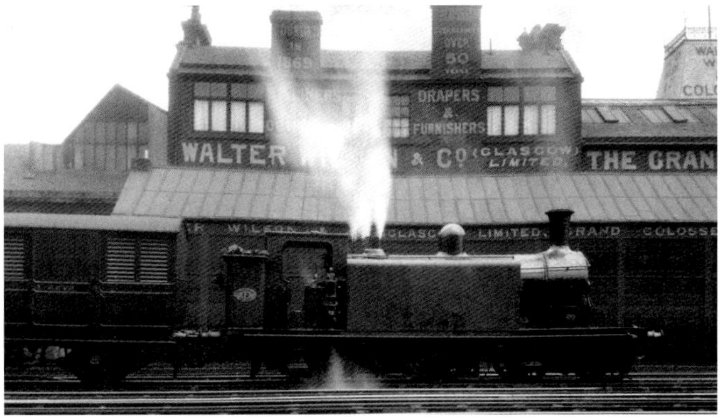

CR Lambie '1' Class 4-4-0 tank No. 12.

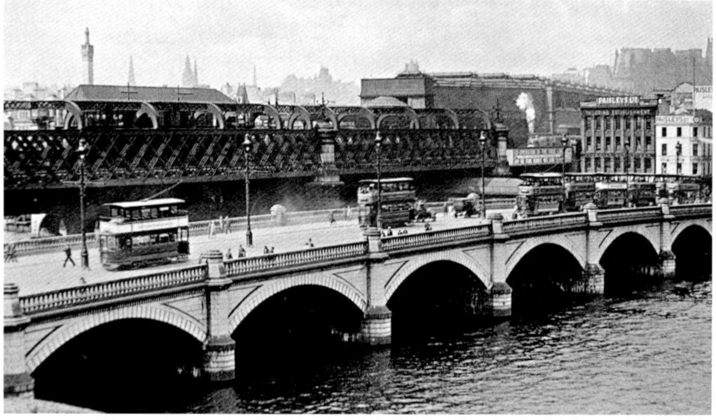

Jamaica Bridge with Central Bridge behind.

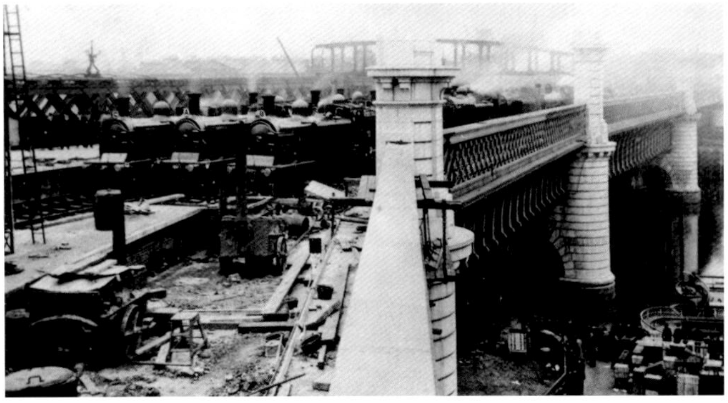

Testing the new bridge.

Previous histories have stated that all the Clyde Coast traffic continued to start and terminate at Bridge Street, but the timetable for December 1879 gives 17 of the 18 trains from Greenock stopping at Bridge Street but then running on to terminate at Central. The 9 am from Greenock was the exception and did not stop at Bridge Street. However the five daily trains on the Wemyss Bay service all started and terminated at Bridge Street, and this was the only service so timetabled. The Greenock & Wemyss Bay Railway did not amalgamate with the Caledonian until 1893, so was this the reason for the exception?

With only an odd exception, all the Anglo-Scottish services to and from Central also stopped at Bridge Street and Eglinton Street Stations, as did the local trains for Carlisle. The opening of Central Station appears in simple terms to have increased by one the stops on most journeys. The new station also turned out to have been badly planned, underestimating the traffic volume that would be generated from lines under construction. The capacity of the eight platforms was soon outstripped and still proved inadequate even after an early extension to the circulating area and the addition of a ninth platform. The 134 trains handled in a day in 1880 had risen to over 300 by 1887.

Among the elegance of the West Coast trains, the Boat Trains and the intercity services using Central Station was the equally renowned, if less elegant, Cathcart Circle suburban service. The suburban railways of Glasgow, unlike other British cities, had a much smaller influence on the expansion of the suburbs. All three railway companies were late in starting to develop their lines, their competitive zeal produced much duplication, and their timing overlapped with introduction of the trams, firstly horse drawn and later the famous electric "Caurs". Glasgow suburban traffic had a feature unique in the UK, a "reverse" or outward flow of commuters, with the city as the dormitory and the workmen's trains delivering their passengers to, among other destinations, the industrial centres of Singer at Clydebank, and the steel works of Newton and Coatbridge. The most successful suburban line was the Cathcart District Railway authorised in 1880 as a line from Pollokshields East to Cathcart which was opened in 1886. The line was extended back to Glasgow Central via Langside, Shawlands, Maxwell Park and Pollokshields West and 2 April 1894 saw the start of the service of 89 trains daily on the two 8 mile concentric circles. At Central Station they had dedicated platforms 7 & 8, their ornamental gates inscribed "Outer and Inner Circle" and an approach stairwell direct from Argyle Street.

Success and Leadership

Increasing traffic necessitated the complete remodelling of Central station and the approach lines and in 1899, the year in which the Act authorising reconstruction was passed, 17 million passengers passed through the High Level and six million through the Low Level platforms. Work started in 1901 and, in addition to enlarging the actual station area, involved the demolition of Bridge Street Station, the construction of a new bridge across the Clyde, and the raising the original bridge by 30 inches, all achieved while continuing to operate a full timetable. The hotel was also extended. The final outcome was one of the finest and best laid out stations in the UK, the 13 main platforms and 11A (originally one of the Fish Fruit & Milk platforms) still serving today's rail passengers in an overall form little changed since opening in September 1906.

Glasgow was the home of the Company Head Office at Buchanan Street and of the Locomotive Works at St Rollox, built close to the original terminal of the Garnkirk Railway, which had included repair facilities for locomotives. It was from these two establishments that so many of the aspects emanated for which the Caledonian Railway is remembered. For a company whose commercial success was very largely due to the mineral and heavy engineering traffics, it developed a standing among both early enthusiasts and the travelling public as one of the foremost railway companies of the pre-grouping era renowned for the quality of both the trains and services.

The General Manager who guided the Caledonian during the expansion of the Central and made the company one of, if not the best of, the pre-grouping railways was James Thomson (the first Scottish Railway Knight), for whom locomotive CR 50 was named. He was a lifelong employee, starting as a lad at Kirtlebridge in 1848 and becoming General Manager in 1882, and then Chairman of the Company between 1901 and his death on 8 June 1906. The last General Manager was Donald Matheson who, as Chief Engineer, was responsible for the final 1901—1906 redevelopment of the Glasgow Central Station.

Matheson, a native of Perth, had come to the attention of the Caledonian Railway as an employee of contractor Robert McAlpine on the Lanarkshire and Ayrshire Railway project. Afterwards he was appointed engineer responsible for the demanding task of building, largely below the streets of the City, Glasgow Central Railway, being promoted to Caledonian Chief Engineer in 1899. In 1902 he was part of a Caledonian Railway delegation to the USA, subsequently describing how his experiences there influenced his design of the Central Station reconstruction. The rebuilding of Wemyss Bay Station with the spectacular covered walkway to the steamer pier is a further testament to Matheson the Engineer. His paper on the rebuilding of Glasgow Central read to the Institute of Civil Engineering is still highly regarded. He was appointed General Manager on 1 October 1910 and became Deputy General Manager for Scotland under the LMS at the Grouping and as such saw the completion of the Gleneagles Hotel and Golf Courses, which he had started before the outbreak of WW1.

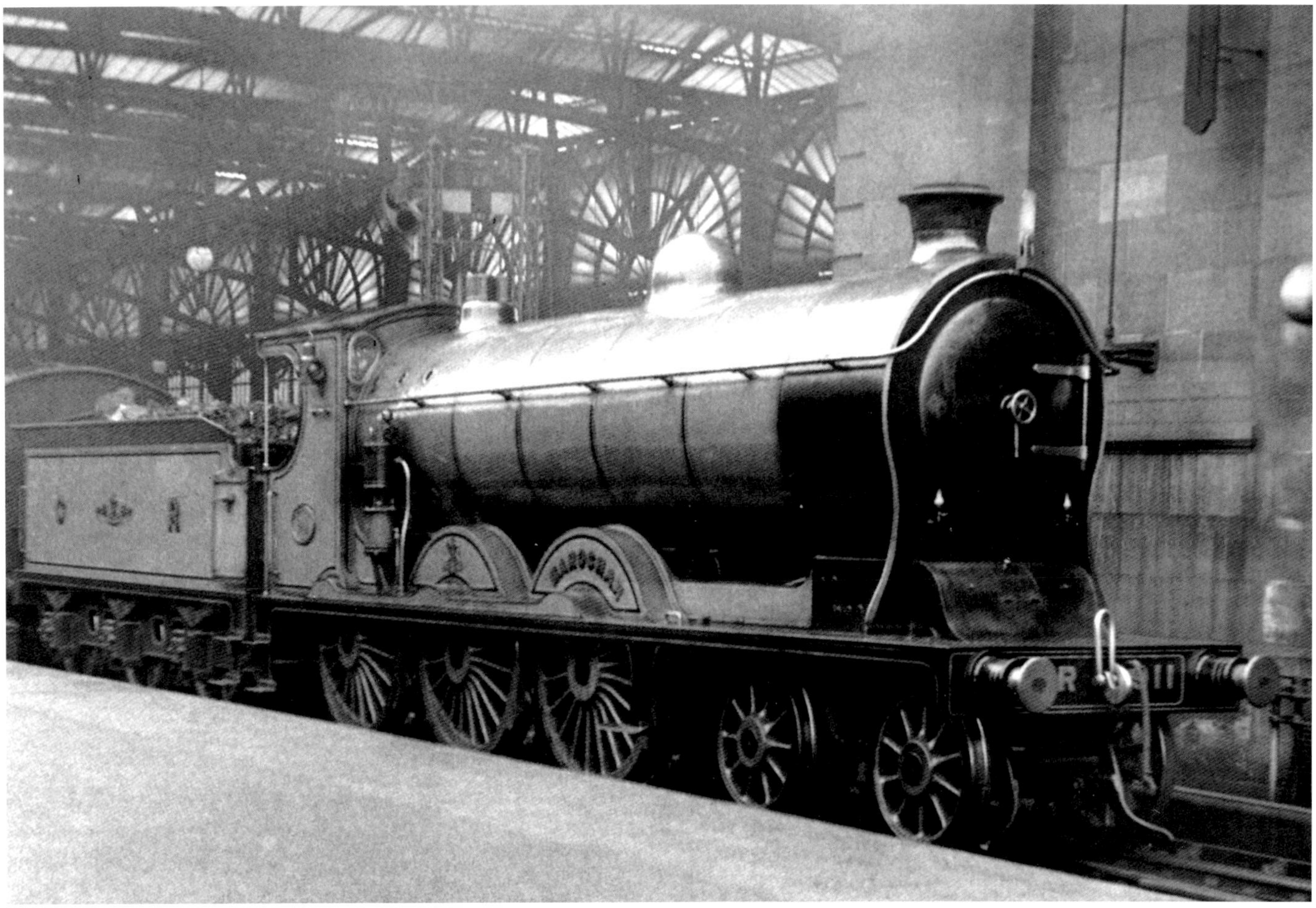

CR '908' Class 4-6-0 No.911 "Barochan" on a Clyde Coast train – 1911.

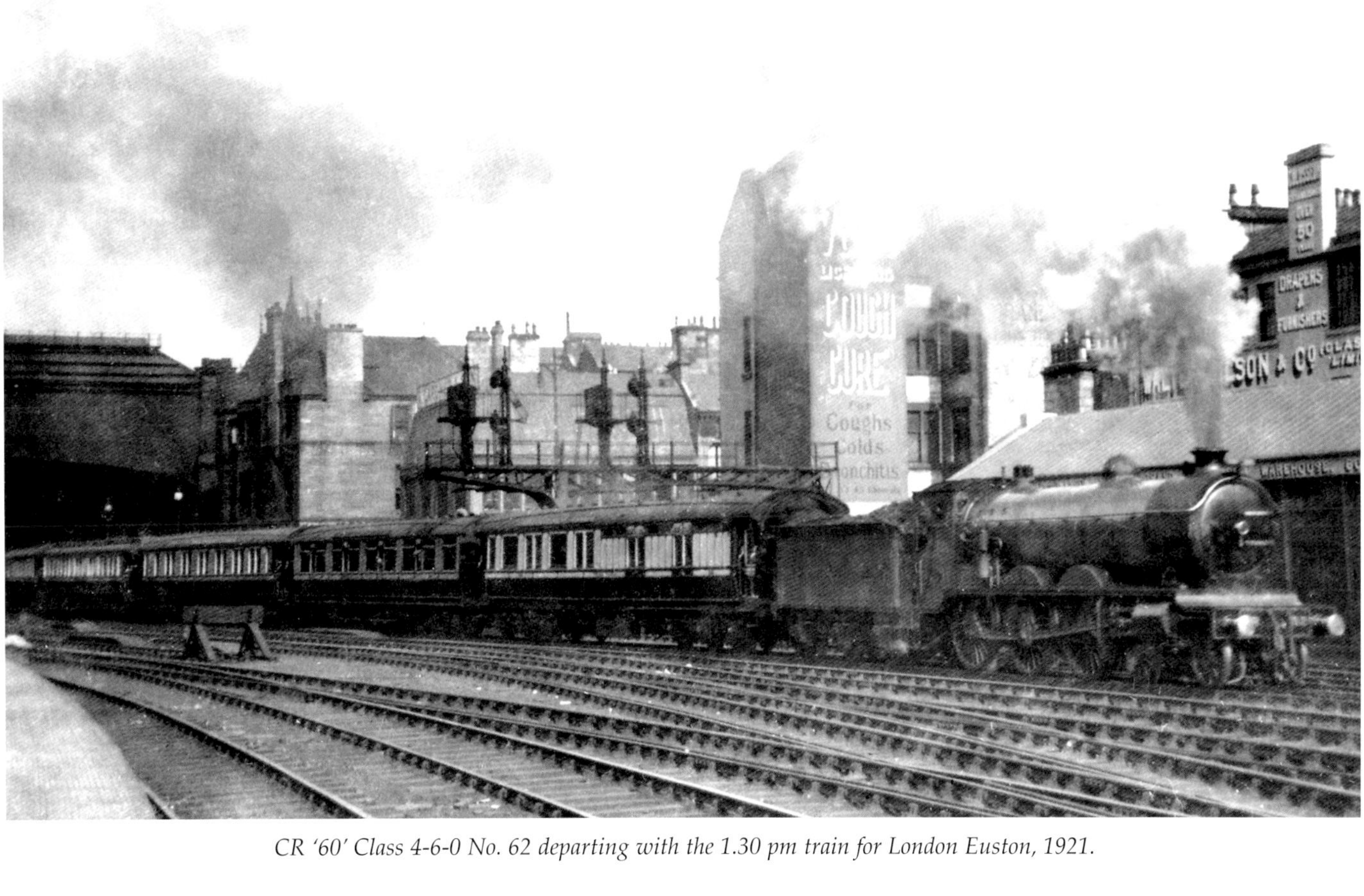

CR '60' Class 4-6-0 No. 62 departing with the 1.30 pm train for London Euston, 1921.

3 Grahamston, Glasgow's Forgotten Village

Norrie Gilliland

An enduring myth about Glasgow Central Station is that there lies, somewhere beneath the platforms and railway tracks, the abandoned village of Grahamston. Appealing though this notion may be, it has about as much basis in fact as the Loch Ness Monster. Should this news disappoint you, let me assure you that the truth is far more interesting.

Grahamston first appeared on the map of Glasgow around 1680, as a row of cottages running along the north side of Argyle Street where the Central Station Bridge currently stands. It was to grow from a huddle of dwellings, housing no more than a hundred people, to become an important commercial and residential centre at the heart of Glasgow. It seems odd that it has been forgotten, given that it occupied such an important location – at the crossroads of the main east–west route from Glasgow to Dumbarton and the north–south route between the Forth and Clyde Canal, the Broomielaw, and the towns south of the Clyde – and was to play such a significant role in the development of Glasgow.

The plans for the first phase of the station required the demolition of roughly two thirds of Grahamston, from Argyle Street up to Gordon Street, and from Union Street, through Alston Street and almost across to Hope Street. When the first phase of the station opened, several significant Grahamston buildings remained, not least St Columba's Gaelic Church, which stood where the station car park entrance is located on Hope Street. But, their reprieve was to be short, for when it quickly became obvious that the first phase of the station could not accommodate the rapid growth of passengers, the remainder of Grahamston was pulled down to allow for the extension to be built.

Grahamston had a varied and interesting life. In the mid-1700s, it had six market gardens, and it was here that the 'first theatre in Glasgow' was located from 1764 to 1780. The theatre was not actually in Glasgow – the city magistrates would not allow 'the house of the devil' to be built within the city boundary (at that time the St Enoch Burn, which now runs underground between Mitchell Street and Buchanan Street). A group of local business people defied this edict, got some money together and opened the theatre, just yards outside the city, in 1764. It was to have a rough passage, ransacked on its opening night by a mob urged on by a firebrand preacher, and completely destroyed a mere 16 years later in an arson attack.

The opening of the Royal Exchange in 1829/30 and the Corn Exchange in Grahamston in 1843 ushered in a new era in Glasgow's confidence. The city continued to march westward, and there was stiff competition for the best sites to the west of Union Street. Grahamston began to change rapidly. A panorama view of Glasgow in 1853 shows Grahamston to be a bustling place, with many businesses and tenement houses. St Columba's Gaelic Church is prominent and the tall chimney of the sugar house belches black smoke.

By the mid 1870s, as the demolishers' hammers were being wielded in the prelude to building the first phase of the station, Grahamston had become a bustling place, home to just under 2000 people and almost 300 businesses, mirroring the dramatic growth of Glasgow itself. There were merchants, agents, tobacconists, chemists, writers, brass-founders, tailors, ironmongers and pubs, as well as the offices of the Calcutta Line, the Bombay Line and numerous shipbrokers. Gone were the market gardens, and the only remaining echoes of Grahamston's rural past were the numerous corn factors and grain merchants located in Hope Street and Alston Street.

To return to the opening theme, the myth is that Grahamston lies to this day beneath the platforms and running lines of the station. There have been many 'sightings' and stories from those who claim to have seen it, but with no evidence to show. There may be odd bits and pieces of the village hidden behind some of the shop fronts on Argyle Street, but these are inaccessible. What has been overlooked for many years is that two original Grahamston buildings do remain – the Duncan's Hotel building on Union Street (currently the Rennie Mackintosh Hotel) and the Grant Arms public house, just round the corner on Argyle Street. Grahamston's most enduring legacy is the odd lie of Mitchell Street, Union Street, and Hope Street, which lie at an odd angle and interrupt the famous Glasgow grid, due to the original Grahamston boundaries. So, Grahamston has not entirely disappeared, and perhaps this particular urban myth can finally be laid to rest.

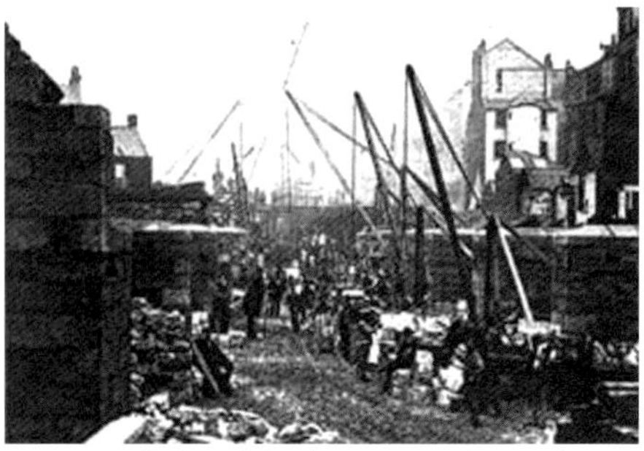

Demolition of Grahamston prior to the building of Central Station (1879).

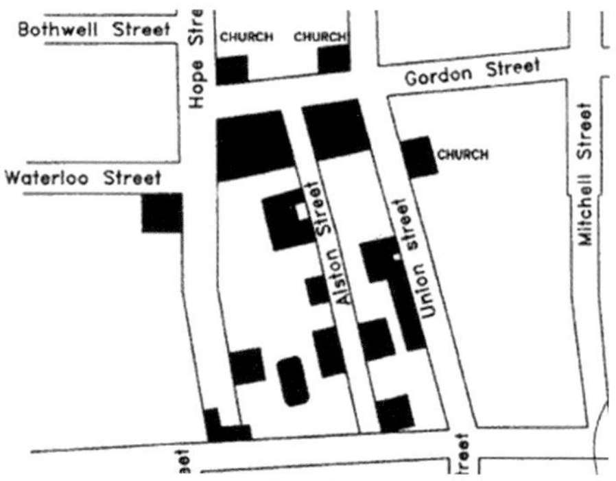

Plan of Grahamston.

4 Design worthy of the city

John Paton

As has been described earlier, the origins of the railway network in Glasgow lay in the transportation of freight. The early railways were not, therefore, conceived with passenger transport in mind: at that time the vast majority of the population had no need for travel to destinations beyond walking distance. Housing and employment lay cheek-by-jowl, and the concept of paid holidays lay well in the future.

The considerable demand for passenger travel which these early railways did experience – initially from novelty value, but in most cases sustained in the long-term – required the companies to turn their attention to the provision of booking, waiting and staff facilities. Initially, passenger facilities were tagged on to or built into staff houses or other buildings. As the system expanded, the art and science of station design evolved, and the new status of the railway station as the place in town for state-of-the-art passenger transportation began to be recognised by company boards. The promoters, investors and officials wanted to celebrate their terminals with a standard of architecture commensurate with other high-status civic buildings: the town hall, the court-house, the church, the bank headquarters or the chief office of a major company; and therefore station design embraced the avant-garde styles of the time seen in these buildings, adapted by the early designers to their best-guess of the requirements of a railway station. Nevertheless an outward show of style and exuberance was not always matched by equivalent attention to the internal passenger environment – simple iron roofs, overcrowding and awkward intermingling of passengers, luggage, cabs and freight resulted in almost all the major stations designed before the 1890s, requiring major expansion and in some cases complete rebuilding. Elsewhere on the early network, the vast majority of station buildings were the product of local builders adaptations of cottages, villas, or agricultural buildings. Until the 20th Century, architects were normally involved in only the more prestigious projects such as town or city stations.

In the 19th Century, horizontally-laid dressed sandstone ("ashlar") was the predominant building material in Scotland. An abundance of easily quarried building stone was available in most parts of central and southern Scotland within carting distance of towns and cities. No better example of this is Glasgow, where the expanding city up to the early 19th Century is characterised by local grey stone quarried in the Dundas Street area (part of Queen Street station occupies the site of one such quarry). Later road system improvements enabled better yellow sandstone to be carted from the Giffnock area to the expanding city, but, as these quarries were worked out, the railway network allowed red sandstone to be transported to the City from Dumfries-shire and Ayrshire – thereby radically changing the appearance of the city. Rail transportation of stone by the Caledonian Railway far beyond its indigenous localities is well illustrated by the Company's use of Dumfries-shire red sandstone in the reconstruction of Edinburgh's Princes Street station and hotel in a City where that material was and still is totally alien; and its use of yellow sandstone for rebuilding the Joint station in the "Granite City" of Aberdeen.

Bridge Street Station

The first proper passenger terminus built in the City served two new lines which, from the start, sought to attract passengers as a major element of their traffic: the Glasgow, Paisley, Kilmarnock, and Ayr, and the Glasgow, Paisley and Greenock railways. They shared a new terminus at Bridge Street, immediately south of the river Clyde, which opened in 1841. This station certainly heralded the arrival of the railway as close to the City Centre as it had dared yet to progress. The architect, James Collie, was commissioned by the line's engineer John Errington to design the station. Its most distinctive feature was the main entrance: a classical Greek portico with four Doric columns supporting an entablature and pediment. Choice of the Doric order was significant: it symbolised strength and masculinity – expressing the triumph of the railway and traits easily associated with by those who promoted, built and invested money in Victorian railways. The architecture of the Greek temple and classical frontage remained very much in fashion at that time and could be seen on major contemporary city buildings. Indeed, the style was to become most closely associated with the City at this time and in the ensuing decades in the architecture of Alexander "Greek" Thomson. Contrasting markedly with the grandeur of the frontage of Bridge Street, on a viaduct behind the main building and out of sight of the street, lay the operational part of the station: two extremely cramped platforms under a low iron-truss roof, and a goods warehouse alongside. The station underwent various phases of enlargement which saw removal of all non-passenger

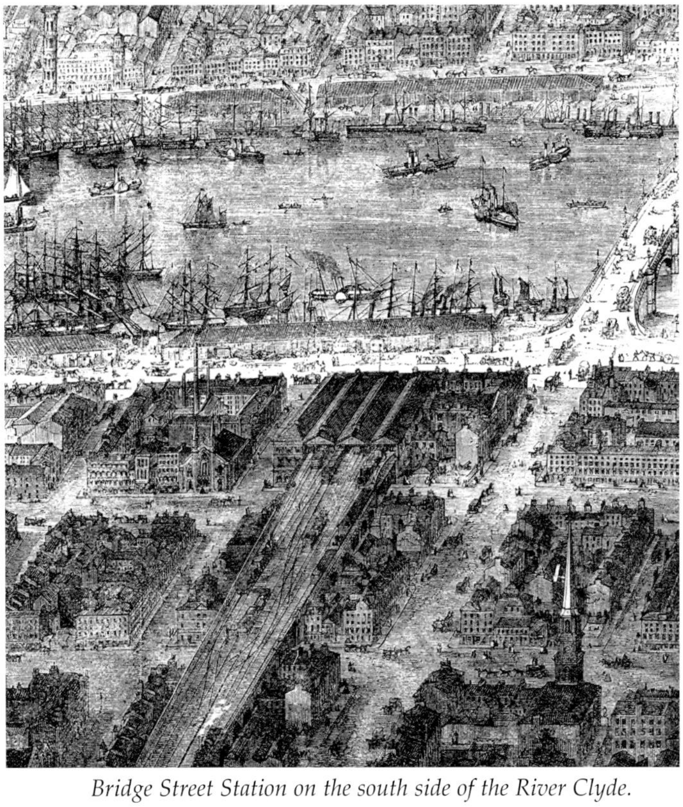

Bridge Street Station on the south side of the River Clyde.

The Caledonian Railway Crest

"The ruddy lion ramping in his field of tressured gold" has been the Royal Arms of Scotland since at least the days when Alexander II (1214 – 1249) bore it on his shield, it may however date from his father William the Lion (1165 – 1214). How the unicorn came to be taken as a Scottish royal beast is still to be explained but they had attained that position by the reign of James I (1406 – 37). It was not, however, until the latter part of the 16th century, that two unicorns were adopted as the regular supporters of the Scottish Royal Arms.

The motto Nemo me impune lacessit, "No one provokes me with impunity", is better known in the Scots tongue as "Wha daur meddle wi' me?"

The Union of Crowns (1603) brought about significant change to the Royal Arms, as used in Scotland, including the right hand Unicorn being replaced by a Lion.

The Caledonian Railway adopted the ancient Royal Arms of Scotland and not the current sovereign's arms as is often stated.

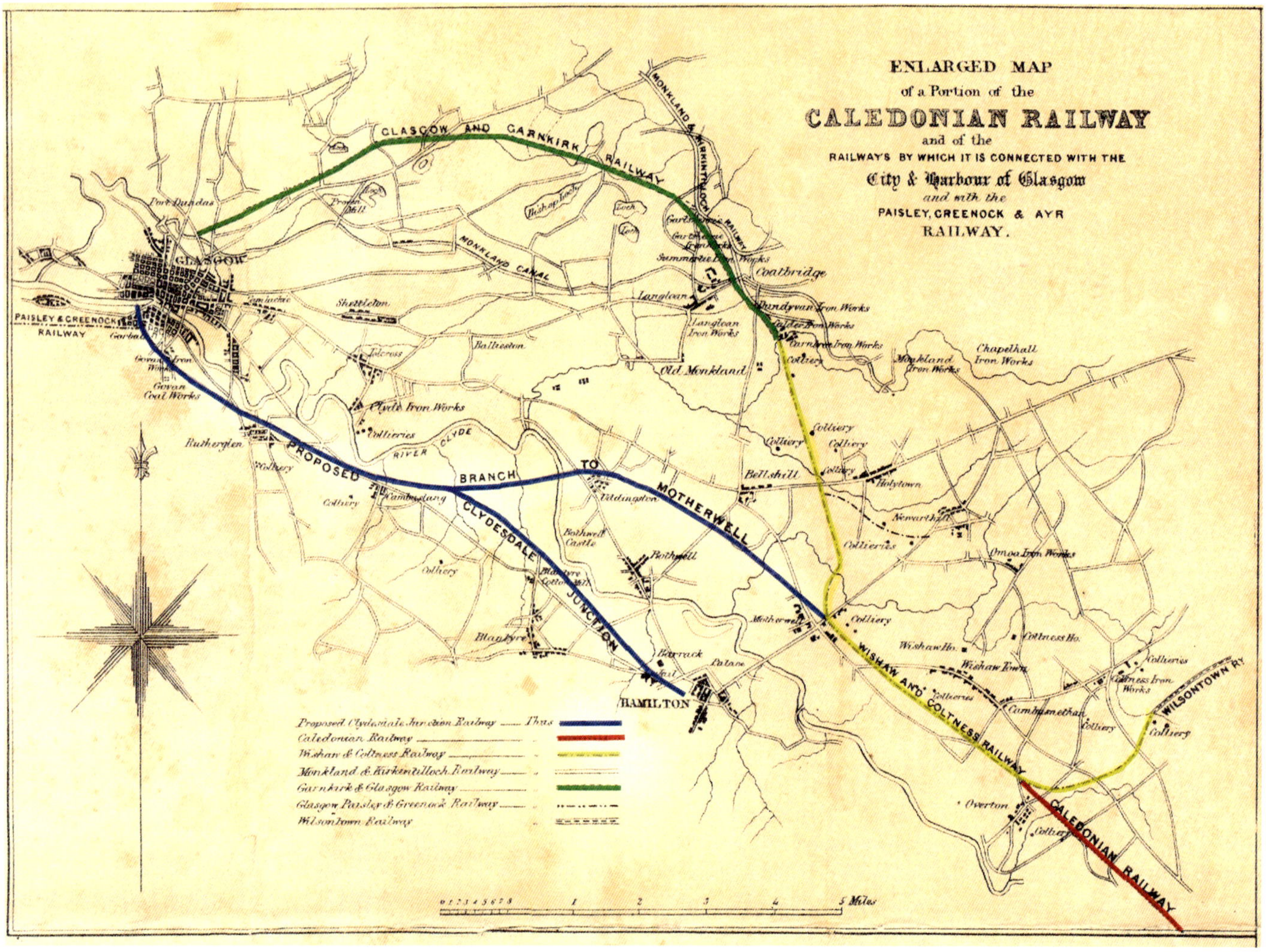

1844 Map of Caledonian Railway "Shewing its Connection with other Railways in England and Scotland", by Vacher & Sons 29 Parliament St London, includes this insert to show how the City and Harbour of Glasgow were to be reached over the existing and proposed lines which would later become part of the Caledonian System. The branch from Gartsherrie to meet the Scottish Central Railway, missing from this insert is shown on the full map. Reproduced by permission of the Trustees of the National Library of Scotland (EMS.s.81).

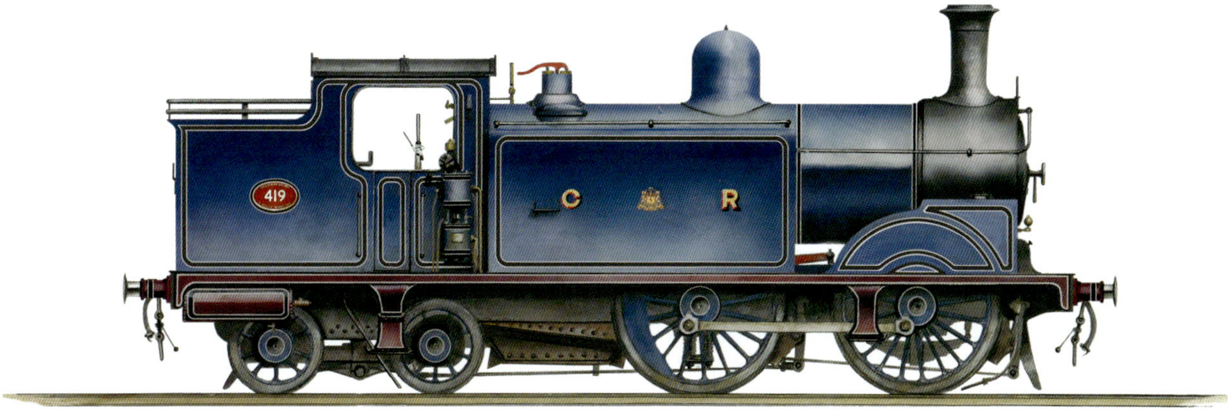

CR McIntosh '439' Class No. 419 built at St Rollox in 1907, acquired by the Scottish Railway Preservation Society Fund in 1963, restored to working order and now based on the Bo'ness and Kinneil Railway at Bo'ness. The illustration depicts the locomotive in the condition as built.

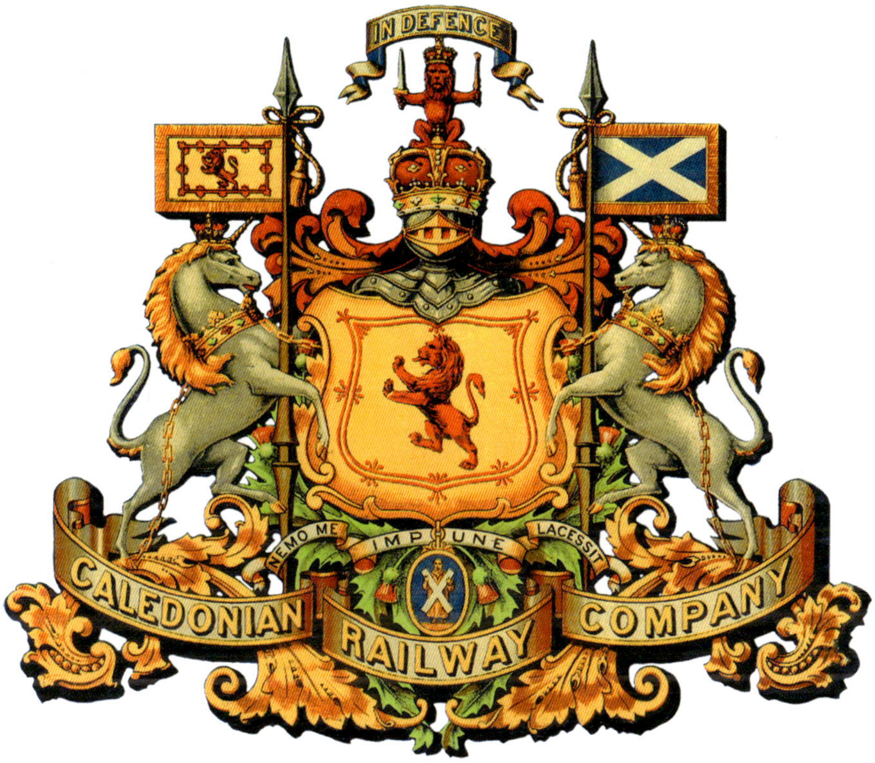

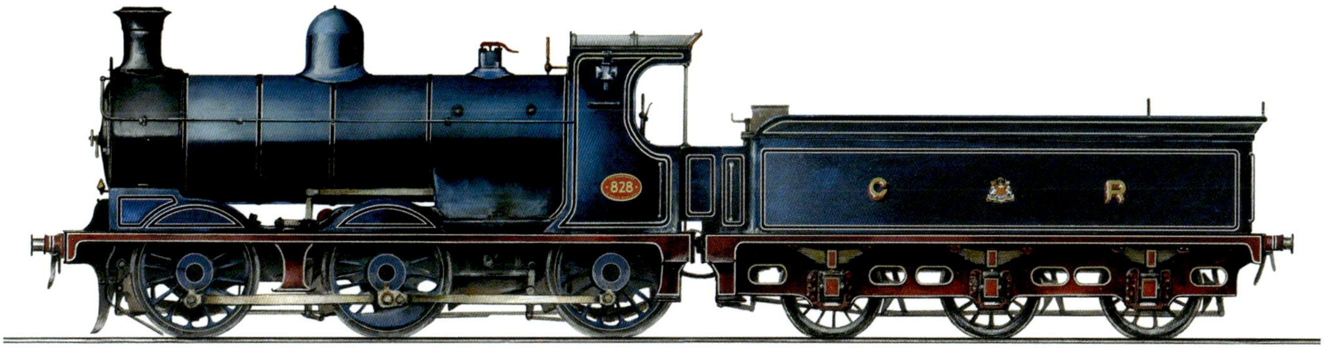

CR McIntosh '812' Class No. 828 built at St Rollox in 1899, acquired by the Scottish Locomotive Preservation Trust Fund in 1963, restored to working order and now based on the Strathspey Railway at Aviemore. The illustration depicts the locomotive in the condition as built.

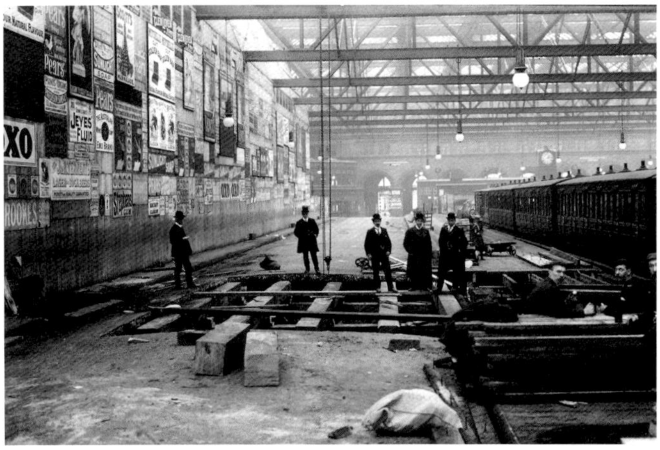

The start of the extension; dated 3 May 1903
Note the extensive advertising on the west wall of the original 1879 Central Station and also the 'hats' – topper and bowlers!

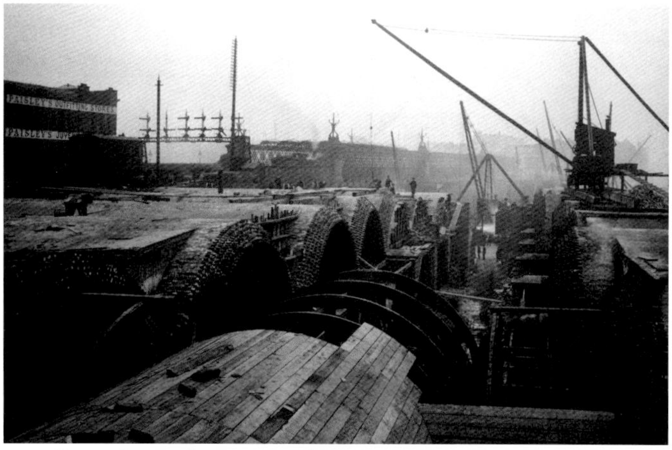

Extension under construction, Paisley's building on the left and original Clyde Bridge.

activities and piecemeal extensions to the roof structure. In about 1885, the station was rebuilt and extended throughout. A new frontage was created facing the river, a vast truss roof was erected covering the entire station, and new four-storey sandstone station offices in French Renaissance style were designed by James Miller. The columns and entablature on Collie's building were removed in the early 1950s and the remains survived in slum condition into the early 1970s.

South Side Station

A further station opened on the south side of the City in 1848 when the Glasgow, Barrhead and Neilston Direct Railway opened. This was South Side, a station situated a considerable distance from the City Centre in Main Street, Gorbals. Its status was considerably enhanced the following year when the opening of the Clydesdale Junction Railway connected it to what by then was the Caledonian main line to Motherwell. Nevertheless the station had no architectural pretensions, and by 1849 tenders were out for the construction of a new building. Johnstone and Hume in Glasgow Stations, advise that the winning design was by Sir William Tite, a well-known English station architect, who also designed Perth and possibly Paisley Gilmour Street stations in Scotland. They include a drawing of the station showing a very simple façade with a triple-span overall roof. The station was demolished in 1873 to allow the construction of new lines.

Glasgow Central née Gordon Street

The Caledonian Railway finally made it across the Clyde in 1879. The connection was made by a new bridge over the Clyde, which took four-tracks directly onward from under the overall-roof of Bridge Street. Once over the Clyde, the new line ran behind the existing buildings in Jamaica Street, and not until Argyle Street had been crossed was the new station entered. This was Glasgow Central in its first incarnation, with eight platform faces, two of which were short docks. The building which welcomed passengers for the first time was however incomplete, and photographs taken the following year showing the station offices still under construction. The drawbacks of opening a new station, which should have been a triumphant achievement, with an on-going major construction project occupying the main passenger entrance and exit routes are easy to see. Indeed, Central Hotel did not finally open until 1883. The station roof was designed by the Edinburgh-based engineering consultancy Blyth & Cunningham in their typical style of the time: immense truss-girders, which spanned across the entire station, resting at either side on massive stone walls. The Company had already installed a similar roof at Bridge Street and, in time, stations at Edinburgh Waverley, Leith Central, Dundee West and Perth all received similar Blyth & Cunningham roofs. Ground levels, and the need to avoid a descending gradient on the tracks, resulted in the buffer-stops being higher than the Gordon Street entrance. A narrow, steep concourse, which became very overcrowded, was the result.

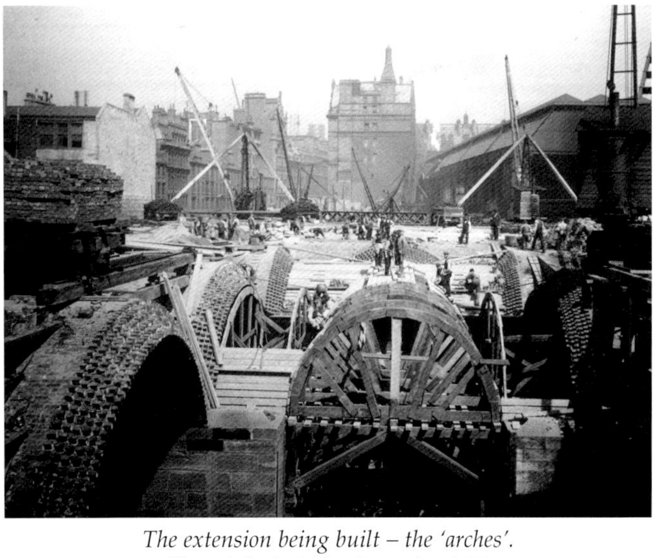

The extension being built – the 'arches'.
The original station is on the right.

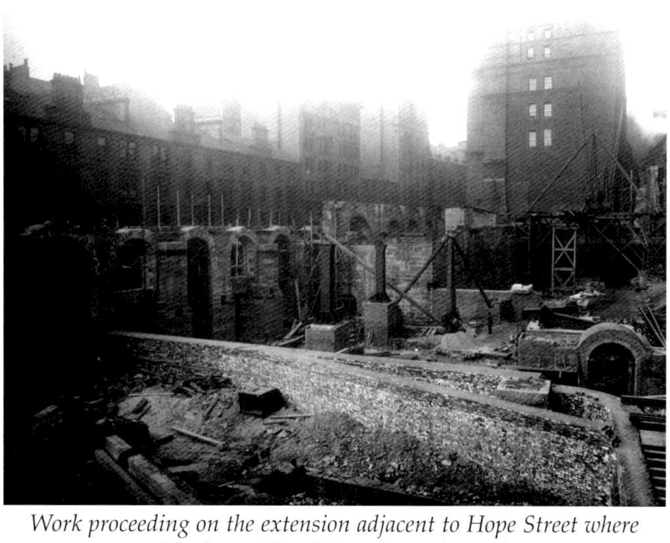

Work proceeding on the extension adjacent to Hope Street where Platforms 14 and 15 are now located.

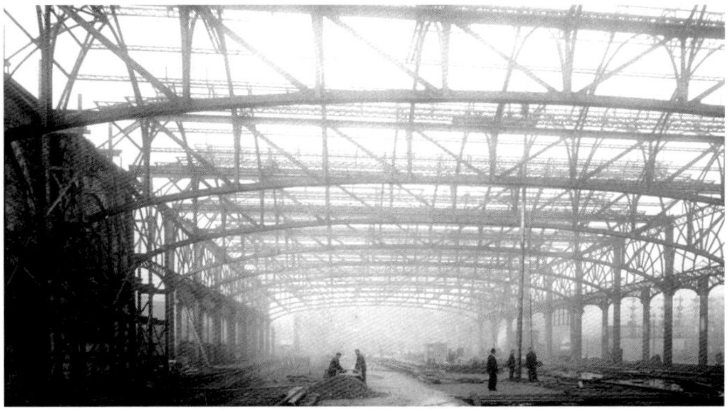

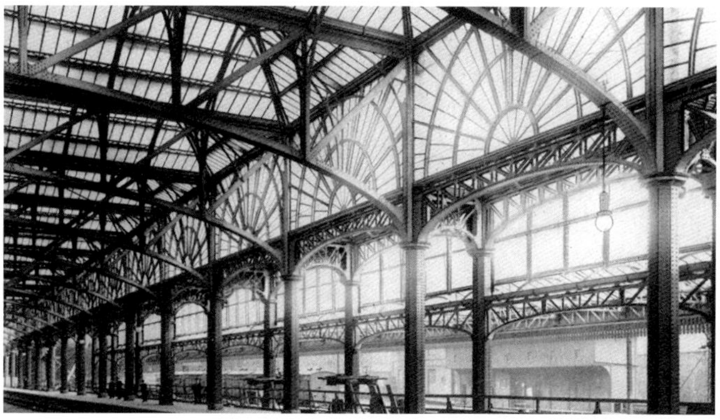

The extension included a large section on new roofing with supporting columns. The roof span was 136 feet and the contract also included the steelwork for hotel extension and administrative buildings, the steelwork at rail and platform level, and the renewal and widening of Argyle Street Bridge. The weight of steelwork was approximately 10,000 tons.

Inside Story of the Bridge Pillars

When the Motherwell Bridge company constructed vast sections of Glasgow Central Station, including the Hielanman's Umbrella over Argyle Street, welding was unknown. Fabrications were held together by rivets. The rivets were also used as a form of ornamentation on the giant pillars reaching up to the huge glass and steel canopy above the concourse and platforms. Riveting squads worked in three-man teams – the heater (who made rivets red-hot in a small portable furnace), the catcher or picker-up, who was usually a young boy of 14 or 15, and the riveter. On the Central Station contract, to achieve the required almost Art Deco finish to the pillars, it is said the catchers were lowered down inside the pillars. There they caught in a bucket the red-hot rivets dropped down, and rammed them through the holes, at which point, as they held them in place, the riveter would hammer the pliant metal into position. Riveting squads could be a source of friction, particularly if the men were on piece-work. There was an art in ensuring that the right number of rivets reached the proper temperatures just in time for use, and a clumsy catcher could slow down the pace of a job. With red and white hot pieces of metal flying around, the scope for trouble was considerable.

The station buildings, variously described as Queen Anne style or "an amalgam of Italian, Jacobean and northern European" were designed by the Edinburgh architect Robert Rowand Anderson (1831-1921). Anderson was trained in the office of Sir George Gilbert Scott who had designed Glasgow University and St Pancras Station in London, leaving to set up his own practice in 1860. His best-known buildings include the Scottish National Portrait Gallery, McEwan Hall and the University Medical School in Edinburgh; the Old Parish Church and the Pearce Institute in Govan; Pollokshaws Burgh Buildings; and "Mount Stuart" house on the Isle of Bute. His architecture has been described as "eclectic" – ranging over many different styles. He was considered by many to be Scotland's leading architect of the late 19th Century and was knighted in 1902. Anderson's original drawings for Central Station assumed that the upper floors would accommodate offices for the Caledonian Railway company, accessed by a main entrance on the Hope Street/Gordon Street corner leading to a spiral staircase to the floors above. However, following the success of the Glasgow & South Western Railway's St Enoch hotel, a late decision was taken to use this accommodation as a hotel, and the existing entrance corner – which had already been constructed – was found to be unsuitable for this new use and had to be demolished. The re-built corner did not differ significantly from the original in appearance except for having more and larger windows, but no doubt its interior was markedly different, as the grand staircase seen today in the hotel was not likely to have been provided for mere offices.

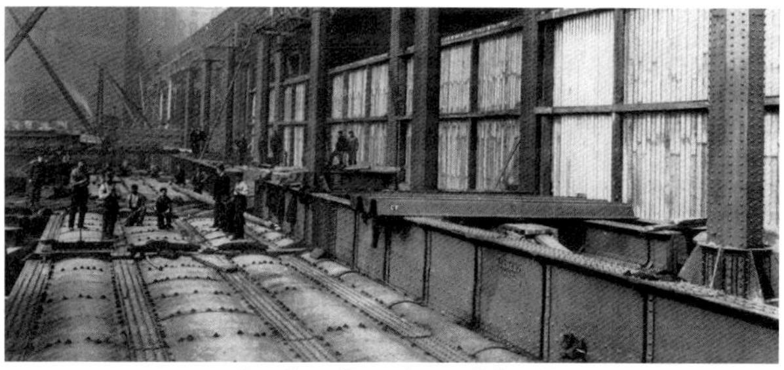

Steelwork under rail level

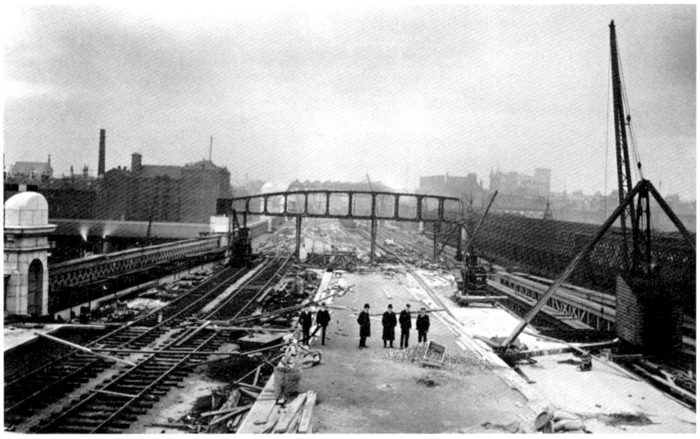

Looking north from Bridge Street over the Clyde with the Central approaches being remodelled before the erection of the new signal box.

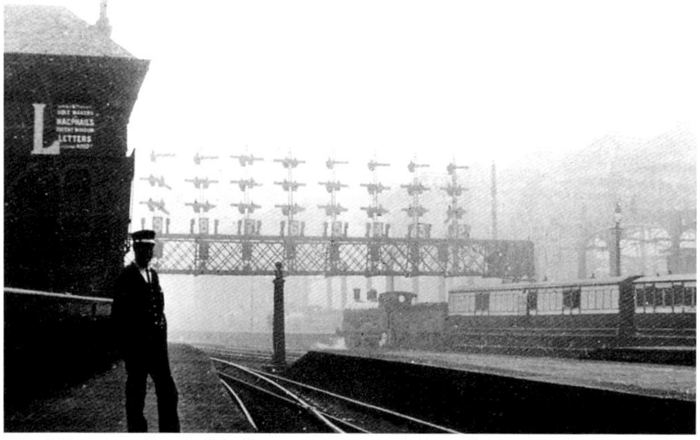

Glasgow Central before reconstruction of the original station and extension of the original roof.

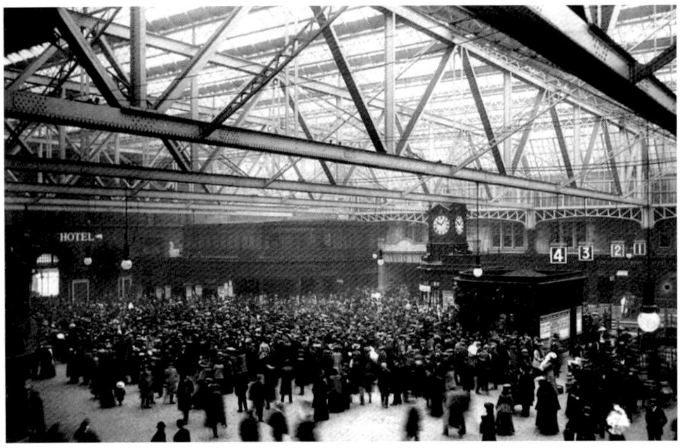

Concourse – Early days of the extended station – c1910.

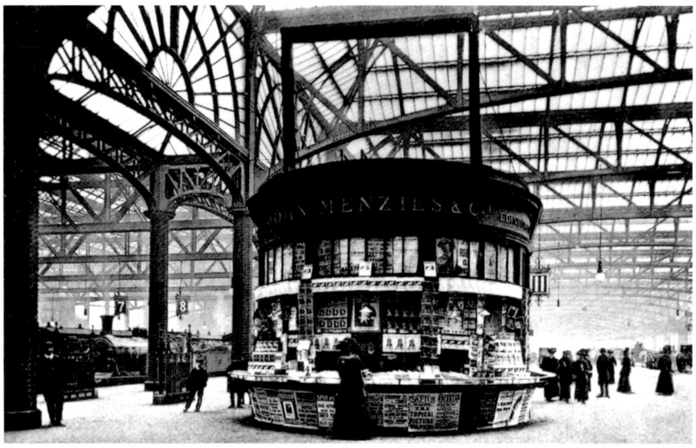

The John Menzies bookstall in the extension.

A separate station down below

In the late 1880s, railway companies within the Caledonian sphere of influence started to plan and promote a suburban railway network to the north and west of the City, and to exploit the freight traffic to and from the expanding dock and shipyard developments on the north bank. Notable amongst these was the Glasgow Central & Suburban Railway which was to pass from east to west through the City Centre. Its most distinctive feature was that it was to be an elevated railway, of the type then spreading a web of steelwork above the city streets of New York and Chicago. The appeal of this system was its cheapness: no tunnelling or underpinning, but the downside would be its noise and visual impact on the City – especially when steam-worked. The line was going to run above Argyle Street and pass through Central Station: a feat which was easily achieved by designers of US elevated railroads, who constructed double-deck "ELs" within the confines of narrow tenement-lined streets in downtown Manhattan. Nevertheless the City authorities and business interests rightly forced abandonment of the plans. In its place came the Glasgow Central Railway which ran under Argyle Street, and which opened in 1896. This resulted in the addition of a low-level station beside Central, initially situated outside the main station on the west side of the Hope Street/Argyle Street junction.

It is reputed that the well-known Glasgow architect Sir John James Burnett was commissioned to design the low-level platform buildings, which were, like all the interior walls and roof structure in the station, clad in white glazed brick. They certainly were to the same design as those at the adjacent Anderston Cross and Glasgow Cross stations which were Burnett's work.

Central expanded

Piecemeal additions to the high level station failed to address its problems, such as inadequate number of access tracks and lack of platform capacity. Many trains from the south still had to terminate at Bridge Street where passengers either walked across Glasgow Bridge to the City Centre, or changed to doubtless already crowded trains for the last stage of their journey to Central. In recognition of the folly of previous small-scale enlargements, perhaps as a result of the Company's prosperity in the early years of the new Century and, possibly, of the vigour of the management team, a radical re-think took place, leading to a fundamental reconstruction of the station. Central to that management team was the Company's Chief Engineer, Donald Matheson.

There were two important parts of the station rebuild: a new Clyde bridge accommodating eight tracks alongside the original, and expansion of the station westwards to Hope Street and south to the Clyde. In the expanded station the original buildings and roof were retained, but new roofs extended the covered area southwards across Argyle Street together, with an entirely new roofed section westwards to Hope Street and down to the new Clyde bridge. As part of the works, the low-level station was wholly integrated into the main station by a warren of underground passageways which linked to many of the high-level platforms and to new station entrances at either end of the "Hielandman's Umbrella" – the now roofed-over and extended bridge over Argyle Street.

Matheson designed the station interior to smooth out the opposing flows of passengers moving to and from the trains by avoiding sharp corners on the interior buildings.

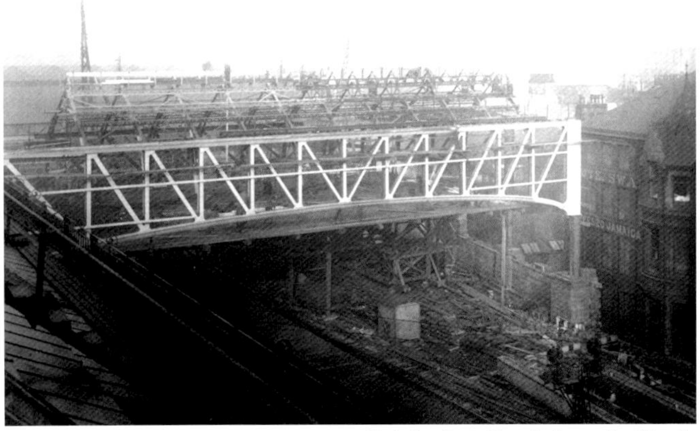

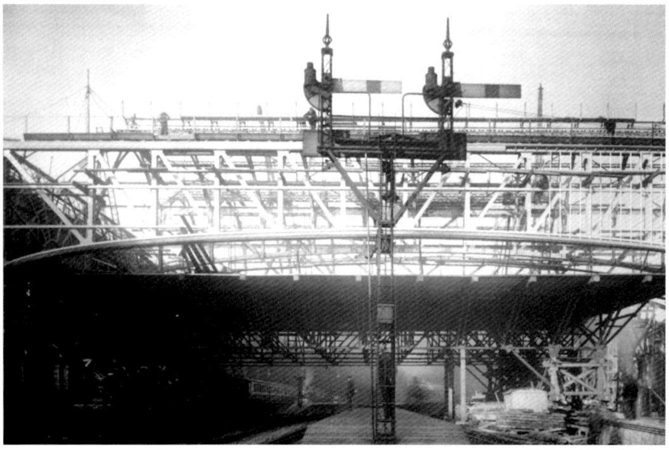

Original station being rebuilt after completion of the extension – c1905.

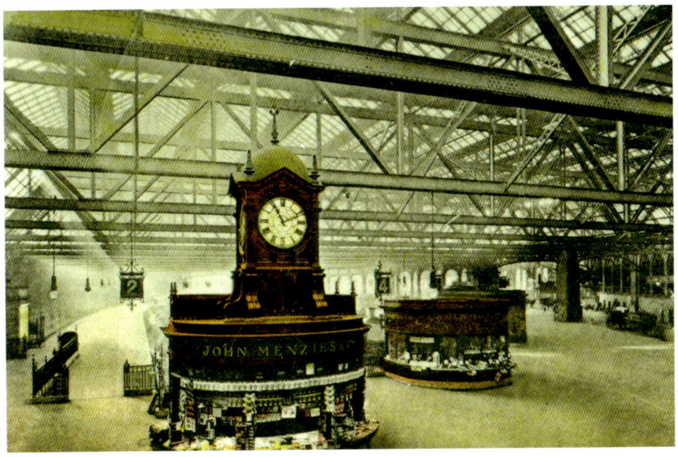

Concourse of extended station in Caledonian days with John Menzies and Malcolm Campbell stalls.

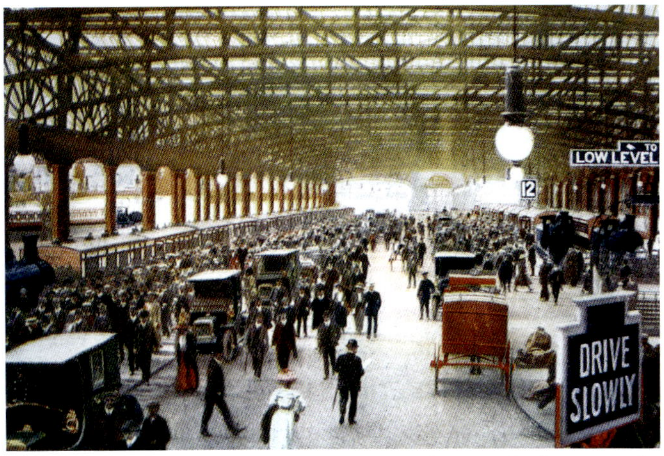

In designing the extension, the Caledonian foresaw the future needs of road traffic by including a generous carriageway between platforms 11 and 12.

The thirteen platform-ends were staggered along a broad pedestrian way from the main Gordon Street entrance right to the highest platforms at Hope Street. A new route for road vehicles was introduced, entering from Hope Street by a twisting slope then turning behind the new "torpedo" building and leaving by an existing arch near the hotel entrance. Buildings in the extension were designed by the architect James Miller (1860–1947), a contemporary of Matheson at Perth Academy, who early in his career had joined the Caledonian Railway engineering department. In 1888 he had set up his own practice and subsequently designed many of Scotland's most distinctive railway stations (Wemyss Bay, Stirling, Greenock Princes Pier, Gleneagles, Glasgow Botanic Gardens, St Enoch Underground, the West Highland Line), hotels (Gleneagles, Turnberry, Peebles Hydro), a significant portfolio of major commercial buildings in Glasgow; houses, factories and hospitals. Miller's contributions to Central were an extension to the hotel in Hope Street lying south of Robert Rowand Anderson's original, the distinctive timber buildings within the station, and "Caledonian Chambers" – the large office building in Union Street which forms the eastern side of the station concourse.

The overall impression of the rebuilt station was of opulence, style and size. Ornament was everywhere: most entrances to the station were fitted with large canopies including the new iron porte-cochere over the cab rank in Gordon Street, a canopy bracketed far out over the pavement at the Union Street entrance which including stained glass panels, a wrought-iron canopy over the hotel entrance, and a long canopy over the high level/low level entrance at the bottom of Hope Street. Inside was decorative stonework, ornate wood panelling of the buildings, and extensive ornate ironwork, signs, railings and large platform numerals. The Royal Arms of Scotland – mis-appropriated by the Company as its own Coat of Arms – appears carved in the stonework, and the rampant lion was woven into other stone and iron details.

Whilst lacking the drama of the barrel roofs of Queen Street and St Enoch, the ridge-and-furrow roofs give an airy and spacious impression, with the added excitement of the colonnade of pillars that mark the joint between the old and new roofs. Dramatic, though, was the vast west wall of the station in Hope Street, with windows of cathedral-like proportions. The numerous accesses from all surrounding streets made the station a meeting place, a shopping centre, a place to eat, drink, or somewhere to find toilets or a shower. In short, a social centre for countless numbers of people who may never have boarded a train. Indeed it is claimed to be the largest covered indoor space in the City.

The main concourse was where people met, overlooked by the Station Master from his curved-window office. Other features of the concourse included a large clock in an ornate wooden pagoda, which sat on top of the bookstall in front of the platform 2/3 bufferstops, and the manually-operated station departure indicators located in the upper floors of the building later to be known as the "torpedo building". Then there were the news-stands, refreshment rooms (all originally along the east side), and the "Shell" collecting box, used as a "sweethearts'" meeting place.

Elsewhere, the extensive network of underground passageways leading down to Argyle Street and the low-level station – significantly curtailed and altered today – had an atmosphere quite different from the station above. Curved like the buildings upstairs, they were however gloomily-lit and were lined in off-white and green glazed tiling. Outwith rush hours they, like the low-level station itself, seemed eerily quiet. There were ticket offices at each end of the "Hielandman's Umbrella" linked together and to the low-level station by various passageways and by individual staircases to most high-level platforms. At the west end was an underground booking office for the low-level station, with its own small concourse and train departure boards, from which passengers passed through expanding metal gates and further corridors to the final smoky descent by staircase to the low-level platforms. Users of today's low level station have no inkling of the atmosphere of the old station: smoke in the air, soot on all surfaces, poor lighting, the massive black roof, walls and columns – in fact, blackness everywhere. There was an awesome effect as an approaching train was inevitably preceded into the station by an almighty wall of smoke, which the train pushed in front of it, and which then enveloped the whole cavernous space and the waiting passengers. The enormous black engine and train then charged out from this maelstrom of smoke, soot and darkness. To provide some passenger comfort (!), central heating radiators were installed around the platform buildings.

The low-level station closed in October 1964, and the

underground network of passageways was sealed up, except for one route out to the Hope Street / Argyle Street corner. As it lay below the level of the river Clyde, and pumps needed to operate continuously to keep it and the basements of the main station water-free, access for staff nevertheless had to be maintained. The Low Level station did re-open in 1979 and a ticket office was opened amongst re-designed and narrowed underground passageways to the low-level station, although it has since been relocated to street level.

Upstairs, the station remained virtually unchanged until preparatory works started for the South Side suburban electrification. A new modern main ticket office was opened along the Gordon Street frontage, a distinctive feature of which was a very large mural, a birds-eye view of the Clyde Coast painted by William C. Nicholson, chief artist of the McCorquodale Studios in St Enoch Square. In about 1966 the high level station was comprehensively "modernised", with the loss of most ornamental items that were removable. The big station clock was dismantled for no other reason than it was old-fashioned (the bookstall on which it had sat remained for many years), wrought-iron railings were replaced with white plastic panelling, the ornate platform numerals were torn down, and a similar fate met the balustrades along the top of the glass screens at either end of the "Hielandman's Umbrella". In the1980s, further alterations to the main station saw replacement of the manually-operated train departure indicators by a vast dot-matrix screen, together with removal of some of the wooden bookstall buildings at the platform-ends. At this time the "torpedo building" was attractively refurbished as a restaurant, and a new shopping centre built alongside it in a similar style.

In the 1990s, a comprehensive refurbishment of the station was commissioned by Railtrack, with architectural work by Gordon Murray + Alan Dunlop architects, as described later. Significant improvements were refurbishment of the entire roof structure, re-instatement of the balustrades over Argyle Street and the restoration of the glazed screens, to their original design featuring the station name, the addition of new interior buildings which were designed as exact matches for the James Miller originals, rebuilding of all shopfronts under the "Hielandman's Umbrella" in traditional style, and the reworking of the stone supports of a long-removed water tank at the southern extremity of the roof into an impressive stone portico bearing the station name.

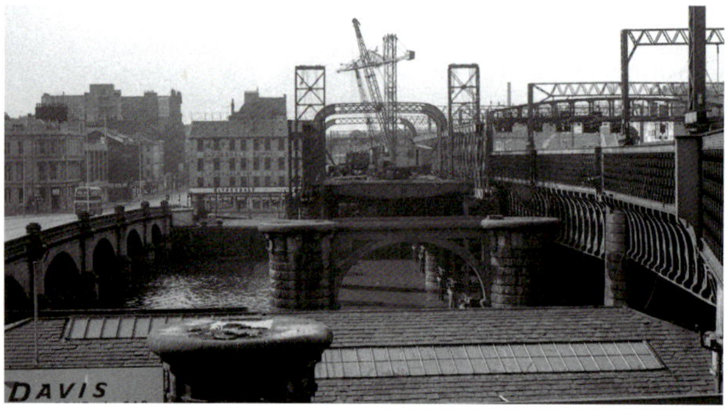

The original Clyde Railway Bridge into Central Station was removed in 1967. The stone piers however remain to this day.

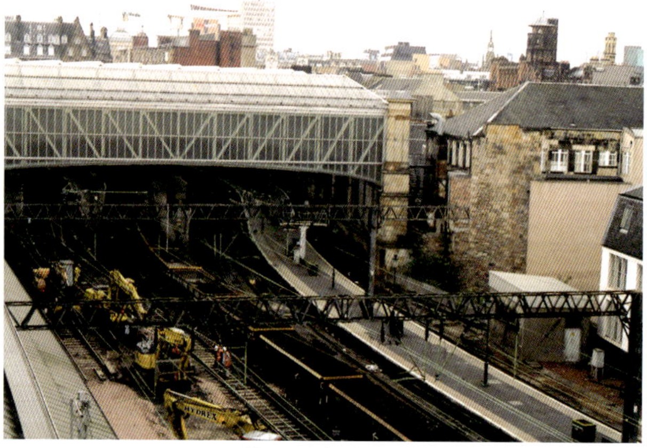

Renewals, 2006

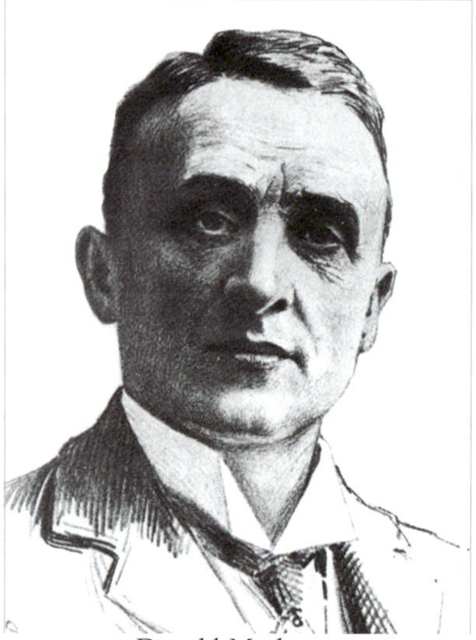

Donald Matheson
Chief Engineer later General Manager of the Caledonian Railway.

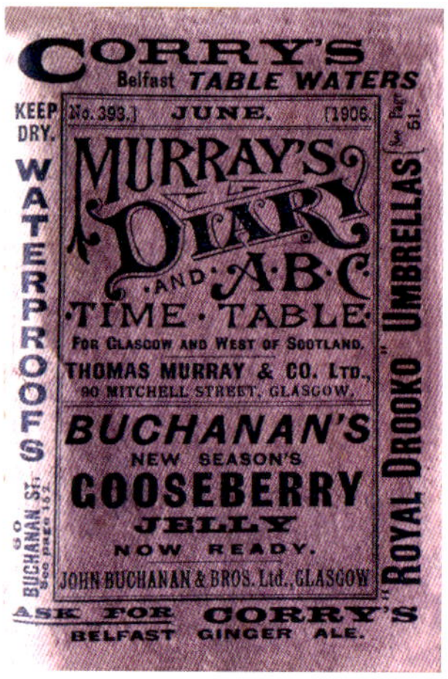

"Murray's Diary"
Everyone's railway timetable
June 1906

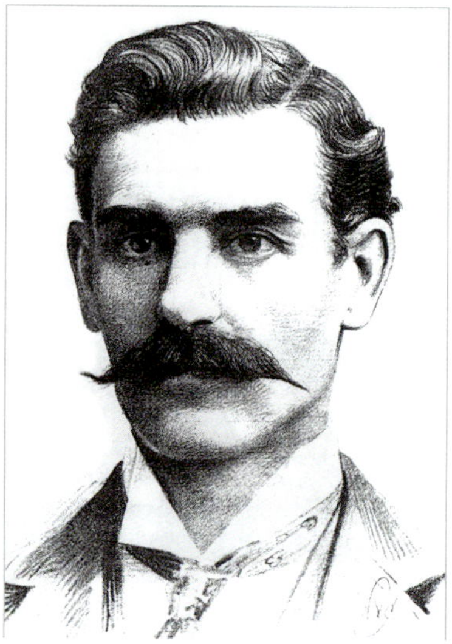

James Miller
Architect to the Caledonian Railway.

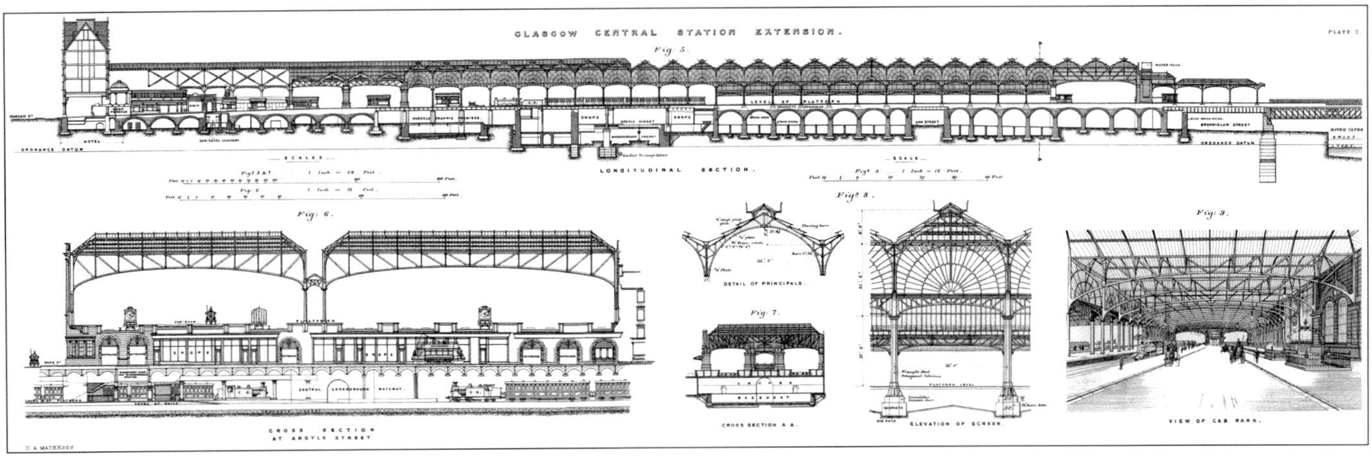

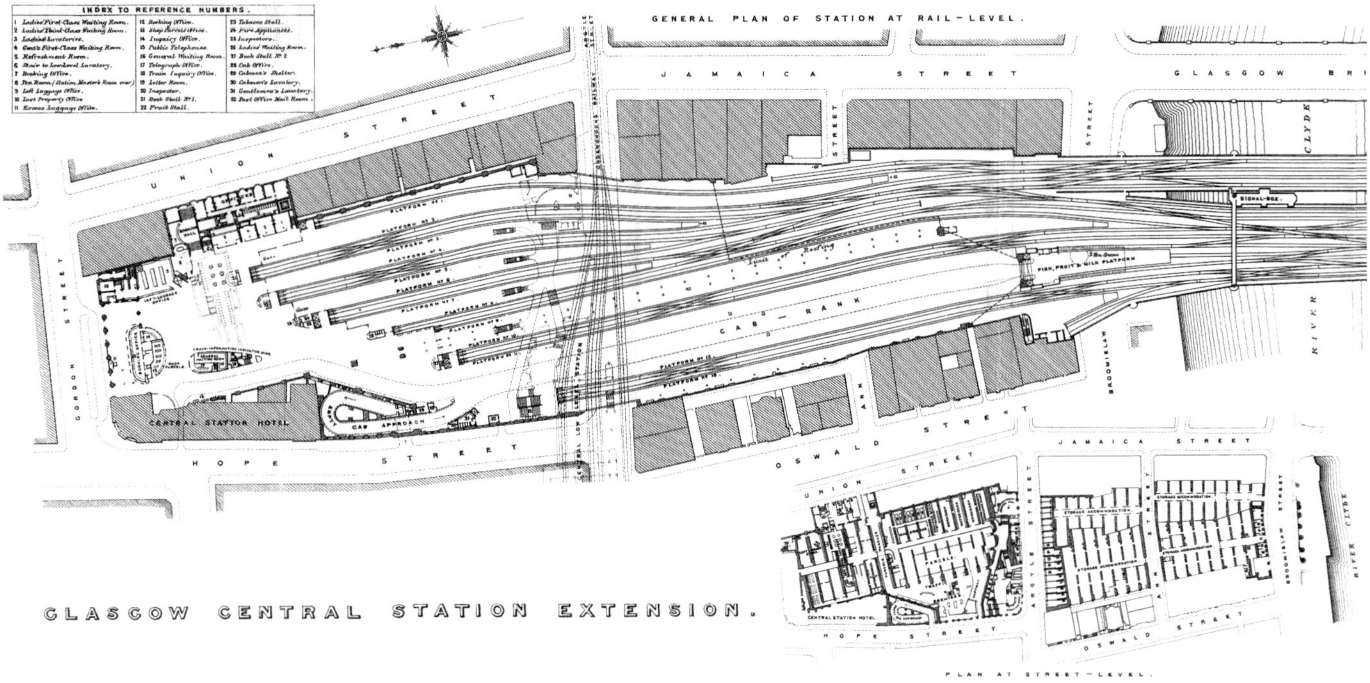

Diagrams from Donald Matheson's Paper – c1908 Institution of Civil Engineers.

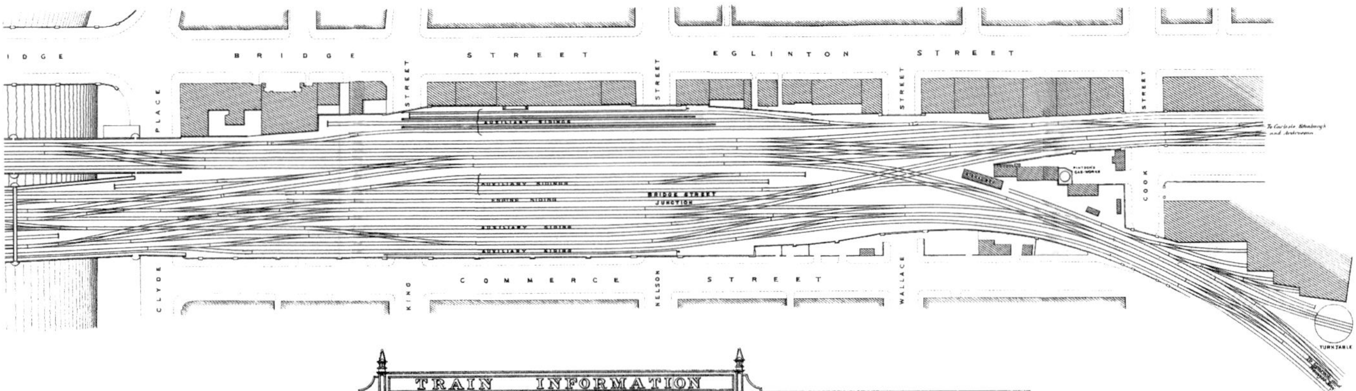

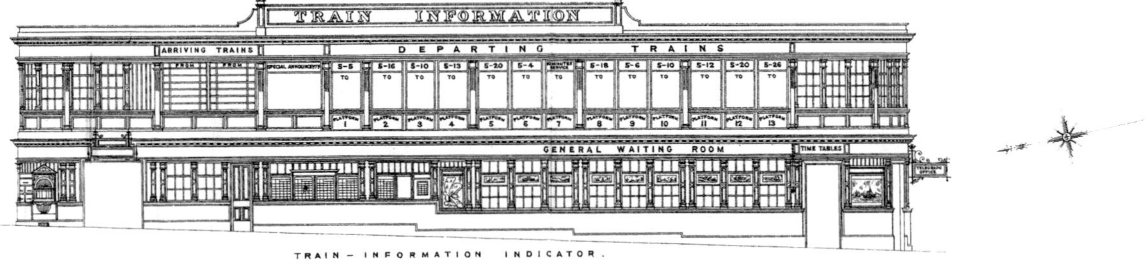

5 Which Platform?

Jim MacIntosh

The extent of the 1879 station can be discerned today by glancing at the roof and distinguishing the original rectangular pattern of girders from the elliptical pattern used in the extension. The east wall carrying these girders can also be clearly seen.

The dividing line between old and new is generally regarded as the double row of columns between today's Platforms 9 and 10, more precisely, by the eastern row. Both rows were erected as part of the extension completed in 1906, but the eastern row replaced the west wall of the original station and assumed its role of supporting its roof girders. This line of columns was continued southwards to accommodate the extension of the station. The 1879 station had originally eight platforms, numbered from west to east. A ninth was subsequently put in by converting the single line on the east side to a double track, about 1890, when the bridge over Argyle Street was widened for the first time and some of the platforms were extended. Platform 9, as it then was numbered, lay along the east wall of the station, where the track that serves today's Platform 1 now is. Central Station was supplied with gas from the Company's own works at Cook Street, and this was piped along the track bed to gassing points at a number of the platforms.

In the great extension of 1906 none of the original platforms were retained. After the completion of the new platforms in the extension, the platforms of 1879 were realigned and rebuilt. Additionally, the original Clyde bridge was raised by some 30 inches before being incorporated into the new layout of the original site – which explains the time between opening the new platforms in the summer of 1904 and the completion of the redevelopment in 1906.

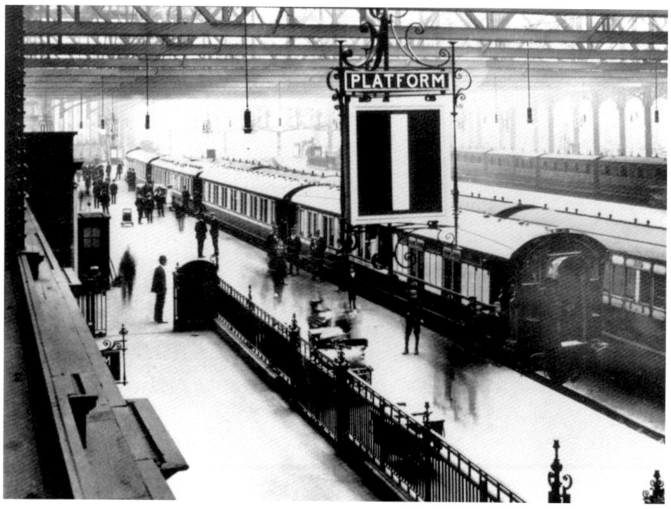

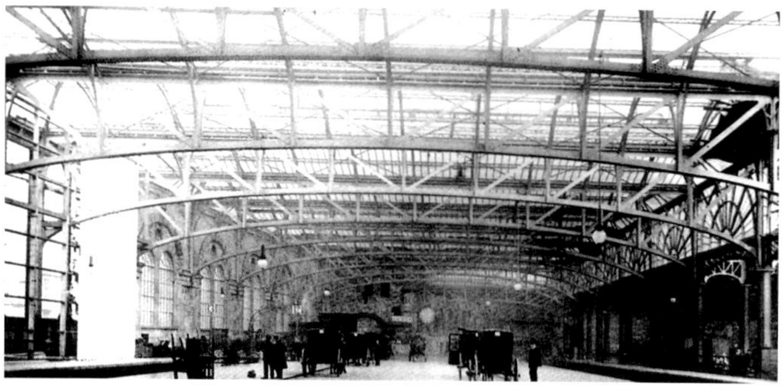

The extended Station in Caledonian days showing the farsighted provision for vehicular traffic

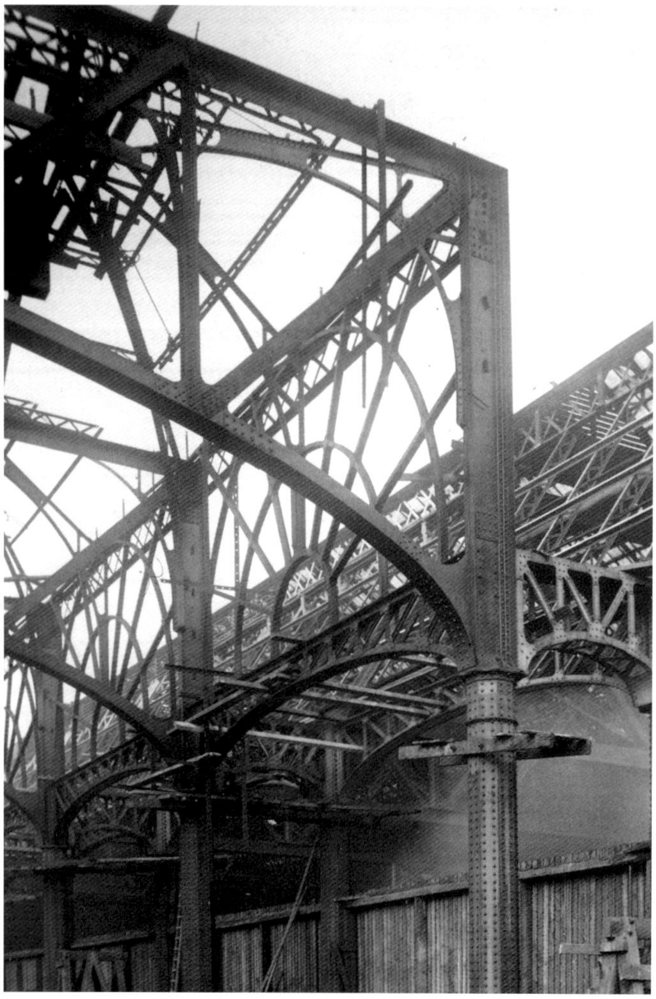

The 'new' extension on the left being joined to the original station

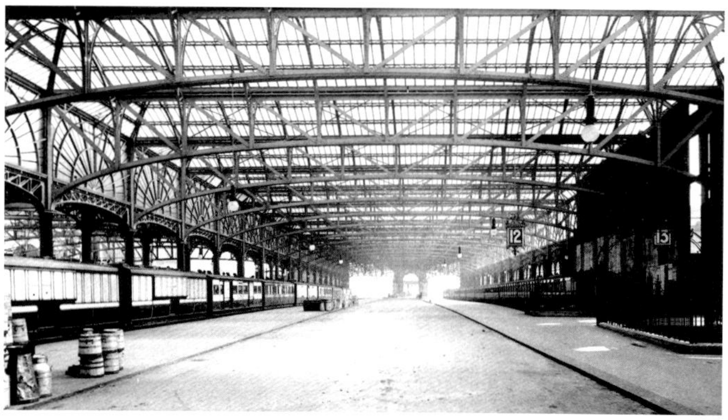

In Platform 11, West Coast Joint Stock Postal pre 1923

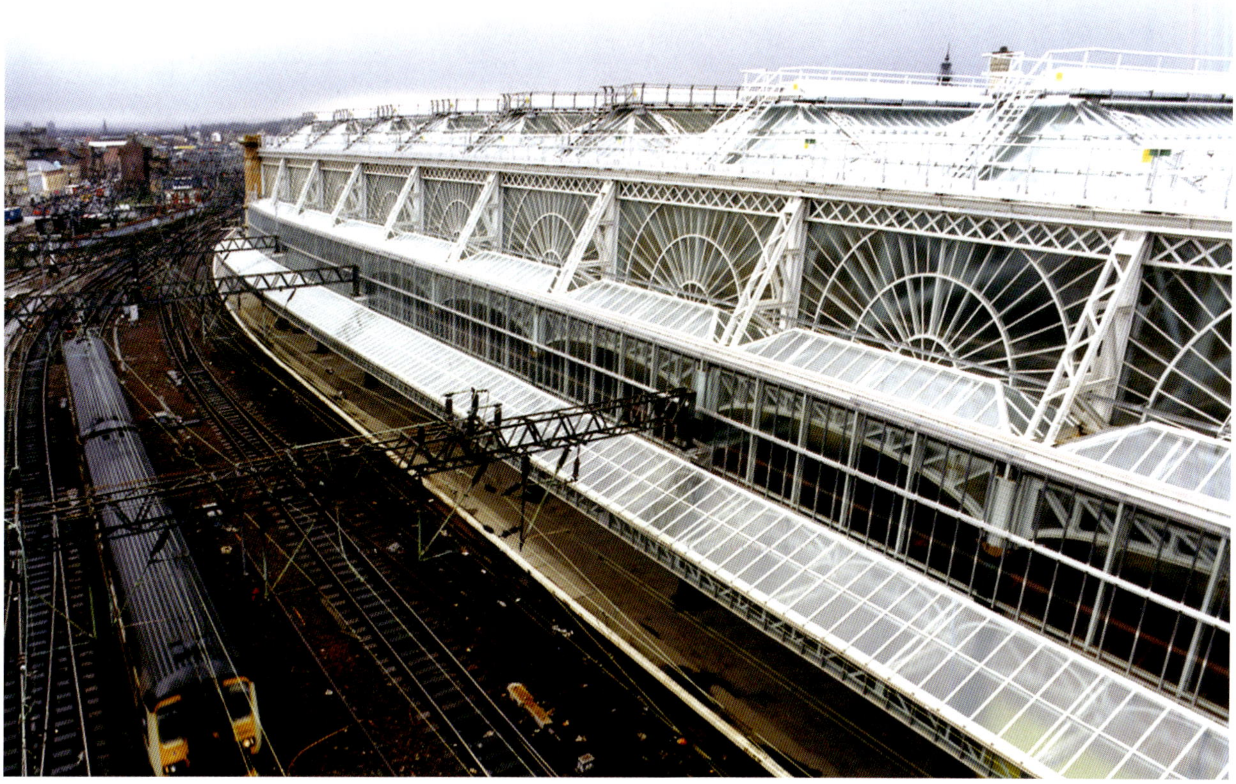

Fit for the 21st Century.

Central Experiences

"The Hielandman's Umbrella"

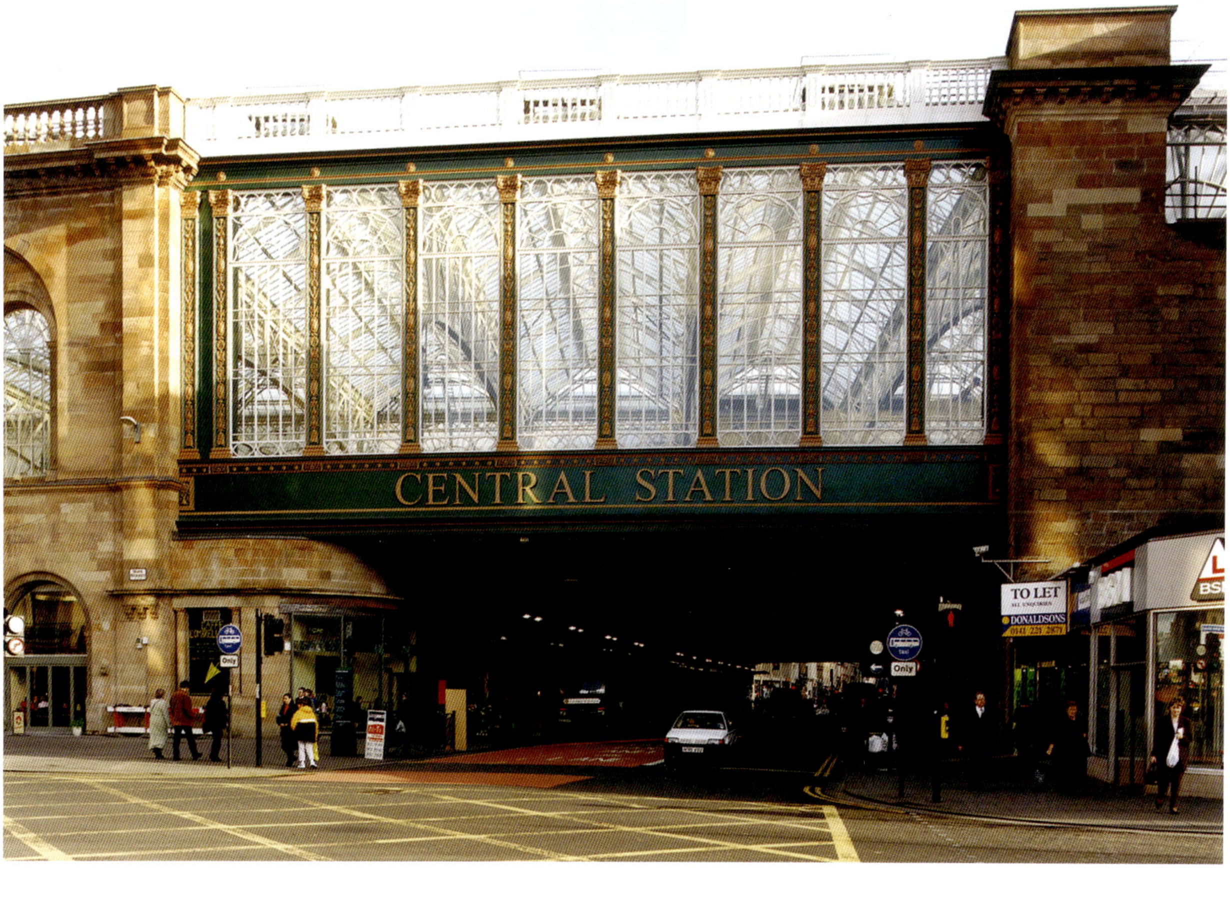

6 Better to travel......Easter 1935

Bill Brown

"Porter Sir?"

Hardly had the taxi come to a standstill before one of the lads separated himself from the group and, his barrow nearby, opened the passenger door. Our heavy leather suitcases with their locked brass latches were given over to his care. Our train was identified for him – The Royal Scot – then the class and preferred seat; alternatively if we had a pre-booked seat ticket, price one shilling (5p), then this would have given him this information.

Now in a vast edifice, exceeding the proportions of some great medieval cathedral, we pause. No peace or reverential silence, but an almost pagan din: noise, clatter, hails and farewells, and a swirling rush of people. The holy incense here is a pale bluish-grey, soot-laden atmosphere, with the fragrance of smoke and hot oil so dear to a railway enthusiast. No organ voluntary either, but an inspiring anthem of rattling luggage barrows, hissing steam, the rhythm of Westinghouse pumps, and the rising throb of a departing locomotive's exhaust reaching a crescendo – the clarion hoot of a former Caledonian Railway 'whistle'.

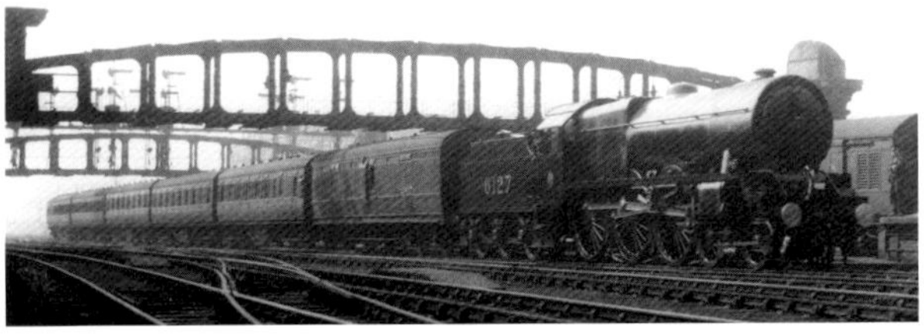

'Royal Scot' No. 6127, the first built by Glasgow's NB Loco in August 1927, approaches Central later that month.

A strict ritual had to be followed, one quite different from the casual happening of today. So, the next move was to a small confessional-like window guarded by a substantial rail, for our ticket. Glasgow or Edinburgh to London was £5 or £3 return, depending on the class, with the option of returning north on the rival The Flying Scotsman. The small stout cardboard ticket was pressed into a fixture to impress the date, accompanied by a characteristic somewhat metallic chump-chump sound. Then to the bookstall (Menzies, of course). A newspaper – a penny ha'penny (0.6p) – its headline being the text for the day, a copy of "Punch" perhaps, and one of the newfangled Penguin paperback novels – sixpence each (2.5p) – were purchased. The habit of "being seen off" was part of the ceremony. After all, this was an event rarely repeated. So with friends to a tall red painted machine with a fine brass handle which, after inserting one penny each (0.4p), produced their platform tickets. Once through the chancel-like rail of the ticket barrier, in place of an aisle lined by finely masoned stone pillars and stained glass windows, we proceed along a platform lined with immaculate maroon LMS passenger coaches. Our porter awaits, to show us to our seats and to receive a small silver coin towards the day's collection. Vending trolleys of refreshments, sweets, fruit and papers supply forgetful travellers. The Stationmaster, attired in his full regalia, including a top hat and morning coat for the departure of his premier service, supervises over all with the omnipotence of a bishop.

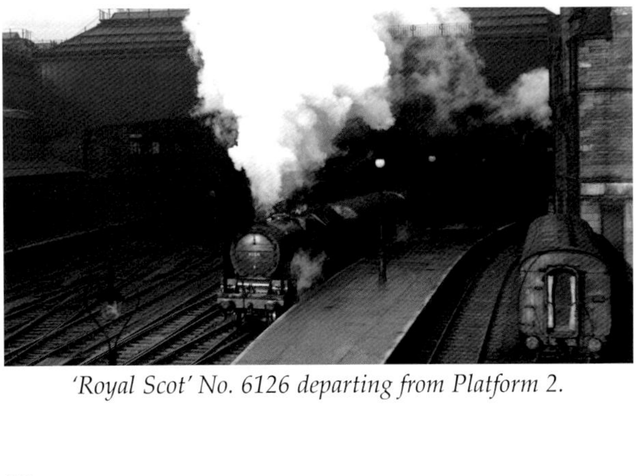

'Royal Scot' No. 6126 departing from Platform 2.

One last pleasure remains: a walk up the train to "see the engine" and glance respectfully at those who could be regarded as high priests in their cab-cum-pulpit. With little time left, we hurry back to the privacy of our warm, comfortable First Class compartment: only corner seats here. Shortly, the doors are slammed shut, a whistle is blown, a green flag is unfurled, a hoot is heard from the

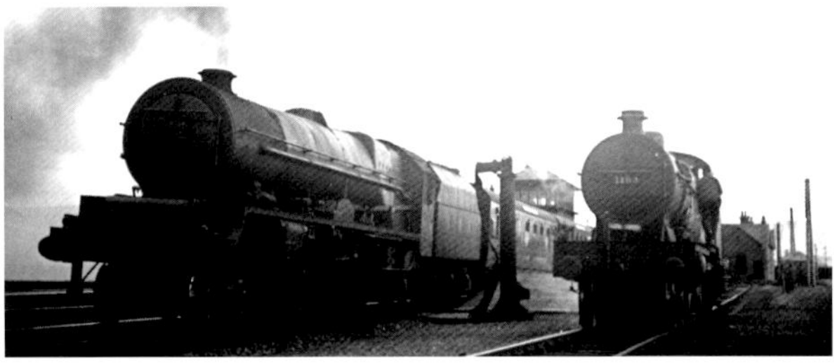

The Royal Scot train divided at Symington into portions for Glasgow and Edinburgh. LMS No. 6208 "Princess Helena Victoria" continues to Glasgow while Compound 4-4-0 No. 1183 waits to head for Edinburgh.

locomotive, hats are doffed, handkerchiefs waved and, with a gentle tug, our pilgrimage begins, 10 am sharp. The platform slips away to the clatter of wheels negotiating the pointwork. Soon, but before coffee is served, an Attendant brings us our individual hand-towel, a small cake of soap, and a brochure describing the route and timings.

A stop is made at Symington where the Edinburgh portion, with its own dining car joins the main Glasgow coaches bringing the load to fifteen or so vehicles. The Glasgow locomotive, which takes this formation forward, is one of the "Royal Scot" class. The publicity-minded LMS was proud of their "Scots" when new and exhibited one in Glasgow Central and in other major stations. As a youngster, I was taken to see the great new red giant. In the corner of the cab sat the driver with, I seem to remember, a pipe in his hand. Thinking nothing of it, I enquired as to the number of cylinders the locomotive had. The Driver turned on my father: "Whit? What does he ken aboot cylunders? Are you an engineer?" Father was far from such a profession. I have reason to believe that this was my only encounter with the redoubtable Driver Davie Gibson of the Caledonian Railway and its celebrated locomotive Cardean.

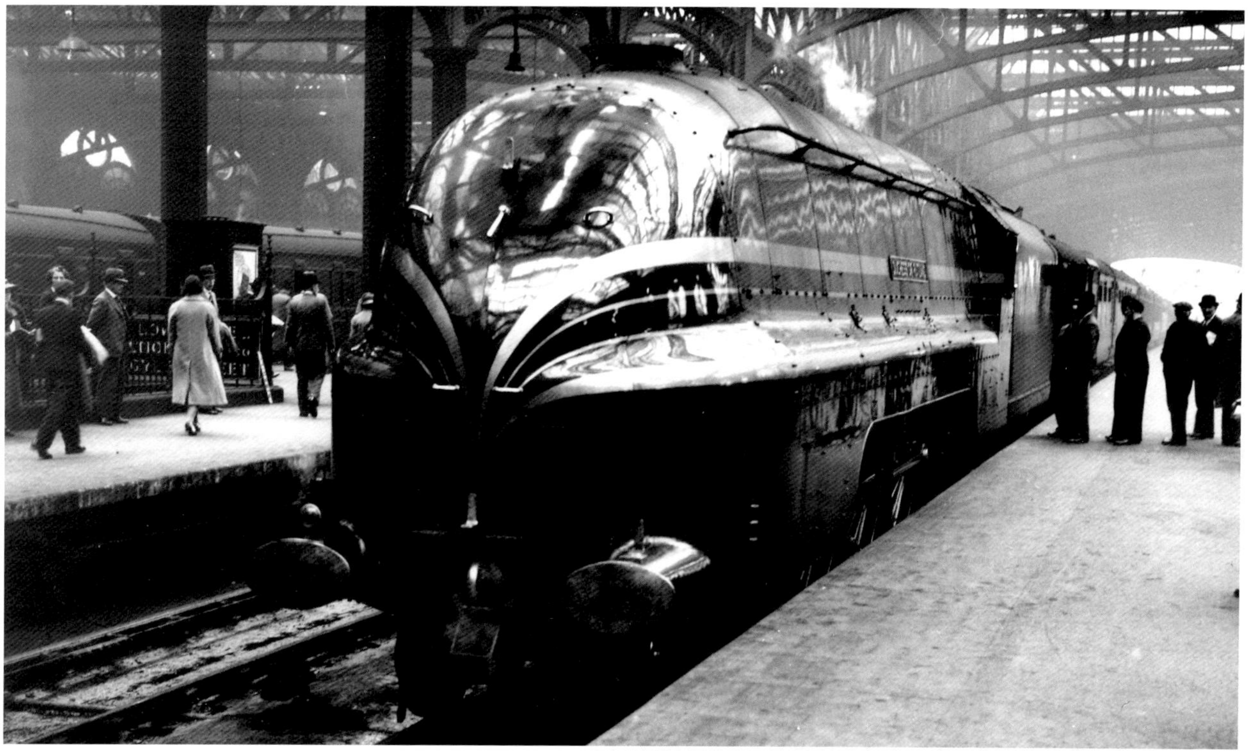

On 12 July 1938 the down 'Royal Scot' train arrives in Platform 11 on 12 July 1938 behind streamlined No. 6228 "Duchess of Rutland" resplendent in LMS red and gold livery.

But today's trip south is the matter in hand. Immediately on leaving Symington, the Chief Steward visits each compartment taking bookings for lunch and issuing reservation tickets. Usually there are two sittings, the first of which is served after leaving Carlisle, the next stop.

According to Bradshaw's Guide for 1938 (and the timings in 1935 would not have differed materially), the three long through platforms of the Citadel Station at Carlisle coped with the arrival at 12.02 pm. of the Thames – Clyde Express, followed by The Royal Scot, the Glasgow and Edinburgh to Birmingham train, the Thames – Forth Express, and finally the Perth to London train, which departed at 12.46 pm. Locomotives were changed, and carriage cisterns were topped up, while wheeltappers walked along the trains, their long-handled hammers producing a metallic chime from the coach wheels. They checked the pipes and couplings between the coaches. All round was the hubbub of passengers, either greeting friends or, often with the aid of porters, finding their seats. If we travelled at the front of the train there was time to stretch our legs and watch our new locomotive buffering up and the coupling being tightened. This would be another "Royal Scot" for, at Easter 1935 only two "Princess" Pacifics had been built, with both being employed on the Euston-Liverpool services (other "Princesses" entered service from June 1935 onwards). One could, however, enjoy the comings and goings of such pre-group locomotives as ex-LNWR "Claughtons", ex-L &Y "Dreadnaughts", ex-NBR "Atlantics", with Midland Compounds galore and the occasional LNER Pacific, besides smaller locomotives from various old companies. No "ABC" lists compiled by Ian Allan for guidance in those days, although the Locomotive Club of Great Britain did produce a Locomotive Stock Book in 1935 – a rare commodity.

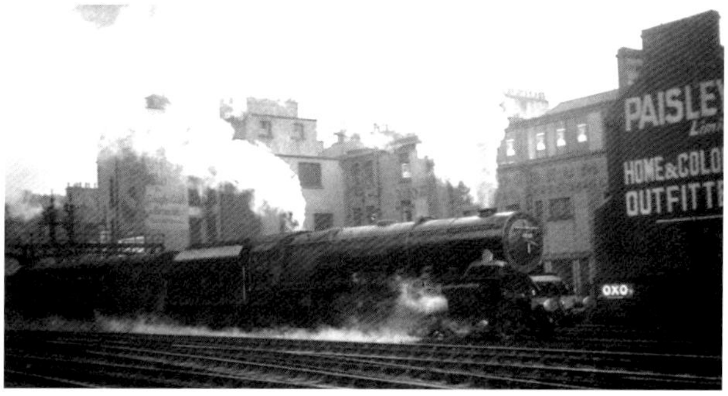

Newly introduced, unstreamlined Stanier Pacific No. 6232 "Duchess of Montrose" departs in the summer of 1938.

A call to lunch, and passing through to the dining car we are shown to our seats. Snow-white tablecloths, lightly starched, fanned-out napkins, polished cutlery and shining glasswear have been carefully laid out (Gleneagles Hotel could not have done better). A choice of two dishes is offered for each of the three courses on the menu, and served with great panache from deep tureens or large ashets, without a drip falling out of place despite the swaying of the coach. The meal, of excellent quality and beautifully presented, costs three and sixpence (17.5p), the same as on the 2 p.m. "Corridor" Express in 1906. (Once, in 1939, the writer travelled in a school party on this train. The menu card was printed with the name of the school, the occasion and the date. How I regret not keeping a copy; but such touches were then taken for granted.)

So back to our compartment to snooze or dream away the afternoon to the dum-de-dum of bogies passing over rail joints. Not even in our nightmares could we have imagined the miseries of what travelling would be like only a few years later, in war-time conditions. I once made the journey from the Central to Liverpool overnight about 1942 or 3. It was summer, so one did not stumble about the station in black-out conditions with the aid of a torch, the light of which had to be partly obscured. The queue for the train extended from the barrier nearly to the Gordon Street entrance to the station. To ensure a seat, a First Class ticket had been obtained: no booking seats in

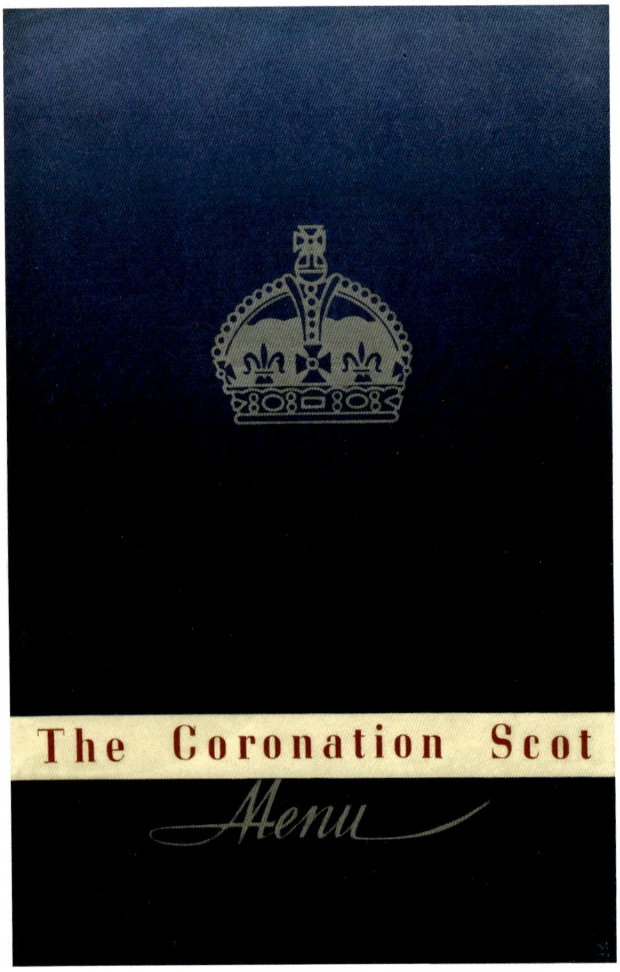

Luncheon

3/6

Mulligatawny

—

Grilled Cod Maitre d'Hôtel

—

Roast Mutton Red Currant Jelly
Baked & Boiled Potatoes
Green Vegetables
or
Assorted Cold Meats
Salad

—

Apricot Trifle
or
Vanilla Ice

—

Biscuits Cheese Salad

—

Coffee, per Cup, 4d.

—

THIRD CLASS AFTERNOON TEA, 1/3 14/9/38. b

The L M S Official Time Table and the A. B. C. Railway Guide can be consulted and Writing Paper and Envelopes obtained on application to the Conductor.

In the general interest Passengers are requested to refrain from smoking immediately prior to and during the service of meals. Passengers are requested to see that their bills are written out in their presence, and not to pay any money until the bill has been presented.

Wines

	CHAMPAGNE	Bot. s. d.	½ Bot. s. d.
365	Perrier Jouët, Finest Extra Quality	17 6	9 6
318	Lanson, Extra Quality, Extra Dry ...	18 6	10 0
315	Veuve Clicquot, Dry...	19 6	10 6
351	G.H. Mumm, Cordon Rouge, Très Sec	19 6	10 6
345a	Geo. Goulet, Ex. Qual., Ex. Dry, 1928	21 0	11 0
	SPARKLING MUSCATEL		
259	"Golden Guinea"	15 0	8 0
	BORDEAUX RED		
30	Bordeaux Supérieur	4 0	2 3
31	Médoc	4 6	2 6
32	Margaux	6 0	3 6
	BORDEAUX WHITE		
52	Graves	4 0	2 3
252	Clos du Gravier, Extra Dry	4 6	2 6
54	Haut Sauternes	5 6	3 0
179	Graves Dry Royal, 1st Growth Podensac	7 0	4 0
185	Château Carbonnieux Château Bottled	10 0	5 6
	BURGUNDY RED		
56	Macon	5 0	3 0
59	Beaune	7 0	4 0
61	Pommard Supérieur, 1923	8 6	4 6
	BURGUNDY WHITE		
74	Chablis	5 0	3 0
	BRITISH EMPIRE WHITE		
762	South African Hock Type, Paarl Amber	5 0	3 0
757	Australian Highercombe Amber ...	6 0	3 6
760	South African, Dry Dominion Sparkling	12 6	7 0
	HOCK		
598	Laubenheim	5 0	3 0
615	Nierstein	7 6	4 0
603	Liebfraumilch	7 6	4 0
	MOSELLE		
599	Cueser-Berncasteler	5 0	3 0
661	Zeltinger	7 0	4 0
	SHERRY		
4	Amontillado, Pale Dry per glass	1/-	
1	Fine Rich ... ... ,, ,,	1/-	
	PORT		
15	Ruby ... ... ,, ,,	1/-	
400	Vintage Character ... ,, ,,	1/3	5 0
401	Finest Old Tawny ... ,, ,,	1/3	5 0

	GORDON'S "SHAKER-BOTTLE" COCKTAILS	s. d.
	Bronx, Dry Martini, Martini, Manhattan Piccadilly, ...	1 6
	WHISKY	
138	"ROYAL SCOT" finest procurable	- 10
	Other Proprietary Brands	1 0
	GIN	
	Finest Dry	- 10
	Proprietary	1 0
	Gin and Bitters	1 0
	Gin and Vermouth	1 0
	Vermouth French or Italian	1 0
	COGNAC	
	Fine Old Cognac	1 6
	liqueur glass	
134	Cognac Vieux Maison, 40 years old	1 6
207	Hine's Grande Champagne, 25 years old ...	2 0
	LIQUEURS, &C.	
	Drambuie "Scotland's Own Liqueur" ...	1 0
	Crême de Menthe; Curaçao; Cherry Brandy	1 0
	Kümmel; Bénédictine; Grand Marnier ...	1 6
	Cointreau	1 6
	BEER, CIDER, AERATED WATERS, &C.	
	Bass' No. 1 Barley Wine ... *per nip*	1 0
	Bass' or Worthington's Pale Ale, *per bottle*	- 11
	Guinness' Stout ... ... ,, ,,	- 11
	Graham's Golden Lager ... ,, ,,	- 11
	"Red Tower" Lager ... ... ,, ,,	- 11
	Barclay's "London" Lager ... ,, ,,	- 11
	Pilsner Urquell ... ... ,, ,,	1 6
	Cider ... ... ,, ,,	1 0
	Bulmer's "Pomagne" per bot. 4/-, per ½ bot.	2 6
	Ross's The Belfast Ginger Ale *per bottle*	- 8
	Schweppes' Sparkling Grape Fruit ,, ,,	- 8
	,, Sparkling Lime ... ,, ,,	- 8
	,, Aerated Waters ... ,, ,,	- 8
	,, Soda Water ... *small bottle*	- 5
	Sparkling Buxton ... *per bottle*, 8d., *split*	- 5
	Apollinaris ... ... *per bottle* 1/-, *split*	- 6
	Perrier ... ... ,, ,, 1/-, ,,	- 6
	Still Malvern ... ... *per bottle*	- 8
	Vichy Celestins ... ... ,, ,,	1 6

QUARTER BOTTLES

CHAMPAGNE G. H. Mumm, Cordon Rouge, 5/-

OTHER WINES

Bordeaux Supérieur 1/3 - Graves 1/3 - Haut Sauternes 1/9 - Hock 1/9
Moselle 1/9 - Macon 1/9 - Chablis 1/9
Sherry No. 1 & 4 2/9 Port No. 400 & 401 3/-

LIGHT REFRESHMENTS
AVAILABLE WHEN TABLE D'HOTE MEALS ARE NOT BEING SERVED

Tea or Coffee, 2 Poached or Boiled Eggs, Bread and Butter, &c.	2 6
Tea or Coffee, Fish or Plate of Cold Meat, Salad, &c.	3 6
Meat Sandwiches ... each – 6 Glass of Hot or Cold Milk	– 3

It will be appreciated if patrons will report any unusual service or attention on the part of Dining Car Attendants to Arthur Towle, Controller, L M S Hotel Services, St. Pancras Chambers, Euston Road, London, N.W.1. This will enable the management to recognize exceptional efficiency, which they desire to encourage in their services.

SOME FACTS ABOUT THE CORONATION SCOT

THE ENGINES

4-6-2 Streamlined Locomotives:
No. 6220 Coronation
No. 6221 Queen Elizabeth
No. 6222 Queen Mary
No. 6223 Princess Alice
No. 6224 Princess Alexandra

Boiler Pressure 250 lbs. sq. in.
Heating Surface 2807 sq. ft.
Superheater 856 sq. ft.
Total Weight, Engine and Tender, 164 tons 9 cwt.
Grate Area 50 sq. ft.
Cylinders (4) 16½" × 28"
Coupled Wheels 6 ft. 9 ins.
Tractive effort 40,000 lbs.

THE TRAIN

Seating Capacity:
82 First Class; 150 Third Class
Total Weight 297 tons
The formation is as follows:
Corridor Third Class Brake
Third Class Vestibule Dining Car
Kitchen Car
Third Class Vestibule Dining Car
Third Class Vestibule Dining Car
Kitchen Car
First Class Vestibule Dining Car
Corridor First
Corridor First Class Brake

THE EUSTON HOTEL, LONDON, N.W.1., AND THE CENTRAL HOTEL, GLASGOW, ARE TWO OF THE 28 FAMOUS L M S HOTELS IN GREAT BRITAIN AND IRELAND

Menu from the Dining Car on the "Coronation Scot" train.

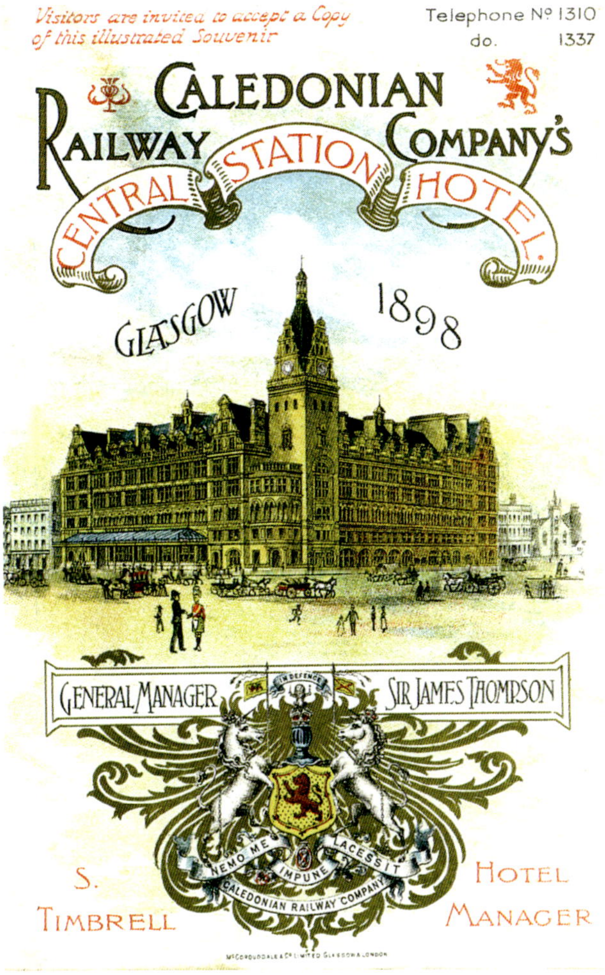

Cover of the 1898 Hotel brochure.
The Hotel closed in 2008 but will reopen in 2010.

war-time. By the time I found a compartment, all corner seats were occupied. Soon I was told to raise the arm rests, and the three-aside seats were converted to four-aside, the armrest digging into one side of my back for the next many hours. Soon darkness descended; the blind was drawn and the only miserable light came through a slit in the shade covering a puny weak bulb. Attempts at reading were futile. The enormous train filled up. Latecomers sat in the corridors on upturned suitcases. Service personnel sprawled over their kitbags. Even if one could get to the lavatory, it was likely to be occupied by at least one sleeping passenger.

No dining cars ran except on certain long distance trains, and the production of a meal sorely tested the skill and ingenuity of the staff. Sleeping cars were only available to the very V.I.P.s. Trains were stopped out in the country if the next town was suffering from an air-raid. Rarely, but

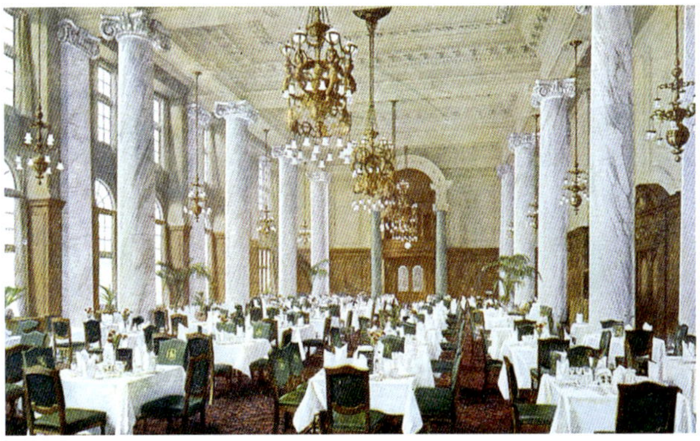

The main dining room in the Central Hotel.

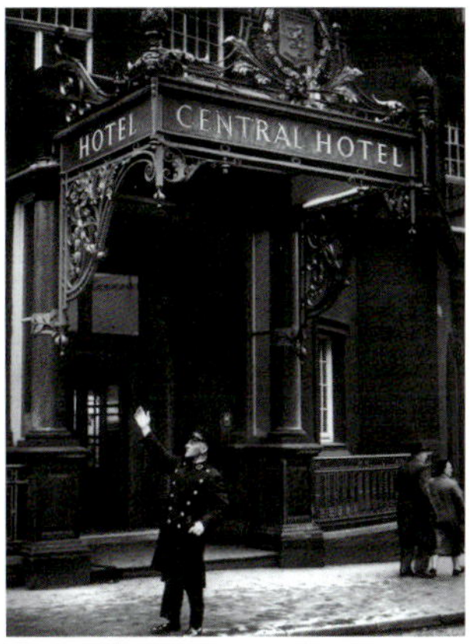

Taxi!

it did occur, a train might be attacked by machine gun fire from enemy aircraft, especially near the coast. Instead of posters exhorting holidaymakers to come to this or that resort and displaying beaches and pretty girls in bathing costumes, simple notices demanded, "Is your journey really necessary?" Complaints were met with "Don't you know there's a war on?" On one occasion, when I was travelling from an isolated part of the country, known to be a landing ground for spies, either by parachute or submarine and dinghy, the train was stopped between stations. Immediately, police and soldiers boarded and inspected our tickets, identity cards and enquired as to the reason for our journeys. Eventually, their duties completed, they left without explanation, and we were on our way again. Apparently this was not an unusual event in the area.

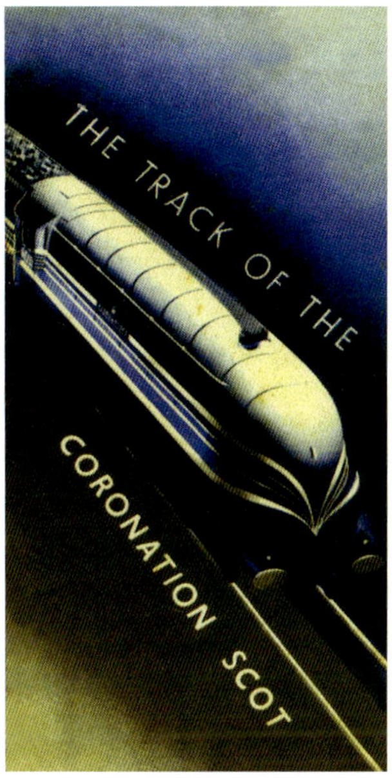

But in 1935, these were things still to come. We are well on our way south now. The afternoon passes, till our reverie is disturbed by a respectful call by a dining car Attendant to afternoon tea. But not the plastic cups of tea at £1.20 and cellophane-covered sandwiches at £2.30 of the future. On this journey, there are toasted tea-buns dripping with melted butter, sandwiches, scones, butter, jam, slabs of rich fruit cake and tea unlimited: a schoolboy's feast, for one shilling (5p).

Outside, from time to time advertisements pass by in the fields: "Carters Little Liver Pills", and, in smaller letters "43 miles to London", then two painters in outline carrying a plank of wood between them, recommending "Halls Distemper", and soon "25 miles to London". We pass an occasional line-side factory or a prim village served by the Watford electric trains from Euston, before reaching the smoky outskirts of London. Speed drops down, a tunnel, then, to the right, Camden sheds, overflowing with express locomotives. Brakes are squealing intermittently as we reach the last remaining mile and the cautious descent down Camden Bank. Coats and hats are collected, as travellers anticipate the rush for onward transport. Euston is upon us, and we glide into a platform lined by porters' faces, searching and upturned. The final application of the brakes, a slight shudder, a sigh of steam from our engine and the vacuum brake. Doors are flung open wide.

"Porter Sir?"

7 Of ticket queues and loos

Ronnie McIntyre

In updating the Central from 1956 onwards, British Railways desired to retain the character of the original Donald Matheson station. So our new cadre of architects quickly established a rule (supported by the then despotic General Manager James Ness) that the timber facia and the structures above would remain inviolate, and modernisation, where required, would take place below. Where this rule had already been breached, as at the Enquiry Office, the facia would be restored. Total preservation could not march with the changing needs of the railway, however; and the Ticket Office had to be rebuilt to create a better working environment for the ticket clerks and to allow an extension to the Hotel above. So we architects learned a lot about ticketing.

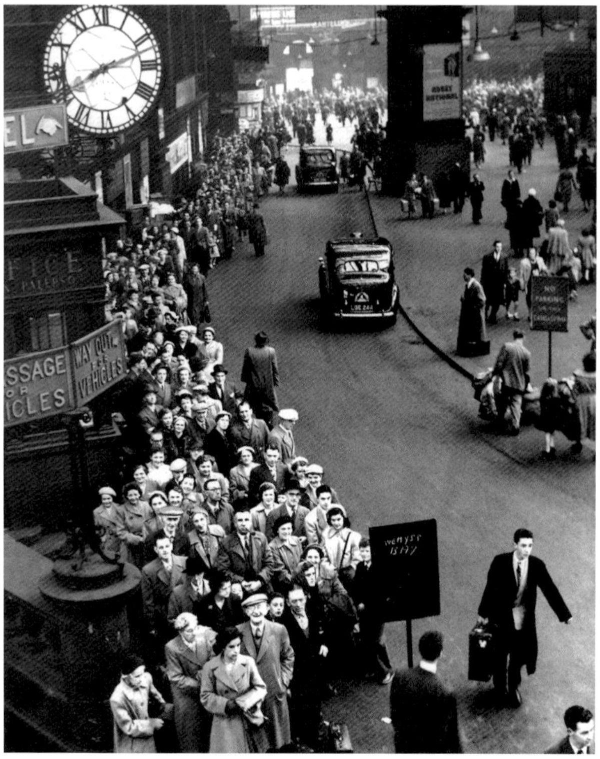

Glasgow 'Fair' traffic queueing for the Wemyss Bay train during the 1950s.

At that time, and for many years after, BR and most railways used traditional systems for selling tickets – the Edmondson card tickets, with the destination already printed on. These were the equivalent of cash, and treated as such. Their gravity-fed timber racks totally surrounded each clerk in the original booking office. As an example: in 1956 it was necessary to have 96 different Edmondson tickets for passengers to Aberdeen (singles and returns, half fares, Forces tickets, dogs, bikes, and prams and the like, duplicated for First Class of course; and the same again for those travelling via Edinburgh). Even after we had rebuilt the office, one third of the clerk's shift was taken up in making up his final balance, for the new Belmatic ticket racks were neater, but not more efficient in accountancy.

Central required ten main ticket windows, with six more hidden in the semi-circular rear, for football days. Hidden, because wherever there was a ticket window – whether open or closed – someone would knock, seeking an enquiry. Queues formed when popular trains were about to leave, and prospective passengers were not happy to be kept waiting for a ticket and possibly missing a train. Hence the ten windows. In the late 1950s and the 1960s the Chief Booking Clerk would look out at the Glasgow weather at 7 am and decide how many Clyde Coast tickets he would date-stamp in advance, ready for quick selling. Apparently Glasgow families decided by 8 am whether to travel or not, no matter what weather prevailed later. This well-honed skill was of course frowned upon by the accountants. Under our scheme, one of the booking windows to be blanked off was that for excess luggage, and this was staffed at a cost greater than

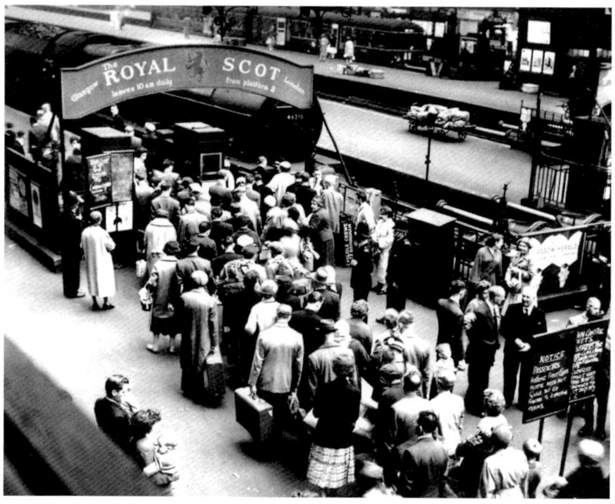

Passengers waiting to board the London train in the 1950s.

the money it took in. Willie Scott, the then Station Master, declared that, if this were to be removed, then the Clyde Coast trains in the summer would look like removal vans. As a compromise, he finally settled for a new location on the concourse.

The main claim to fame of the new Ticket Office was that it had a clear glass front, allowing good communication between the clerks and the travellers. For very many years it remained the only large Ticket Office to have this feature. Part of the rebuilding scheme in the Office was for shop windows facing Gordon Street. The price for this removal of all adverts from the frontage was that we had to concede that the windows would become commercial showcases. Most successful at first, this later proved disastrous. The canopy, however, was saved and renovated, but not until the 1970s, by which time we

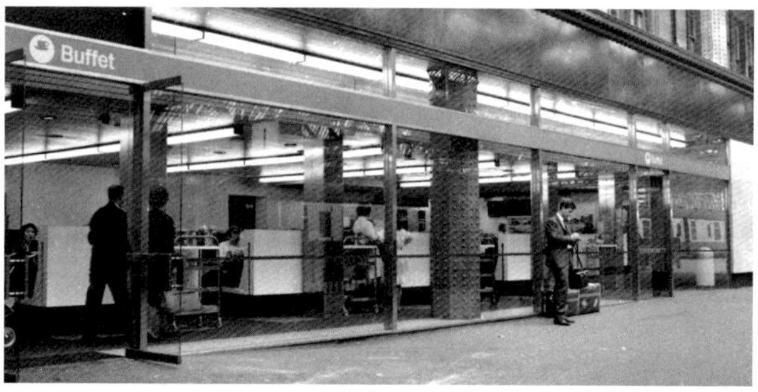

Modernisation – New Buffet.

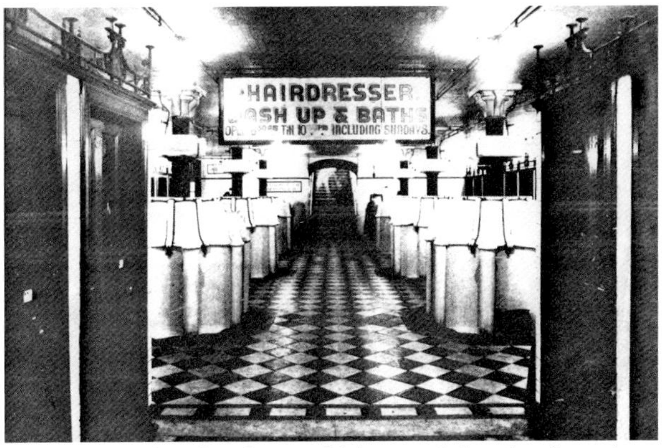

The great Victorian Gents which extended under the main concourse from side to side and included a hairdressing salon. Some of the detail drawings are shown below.

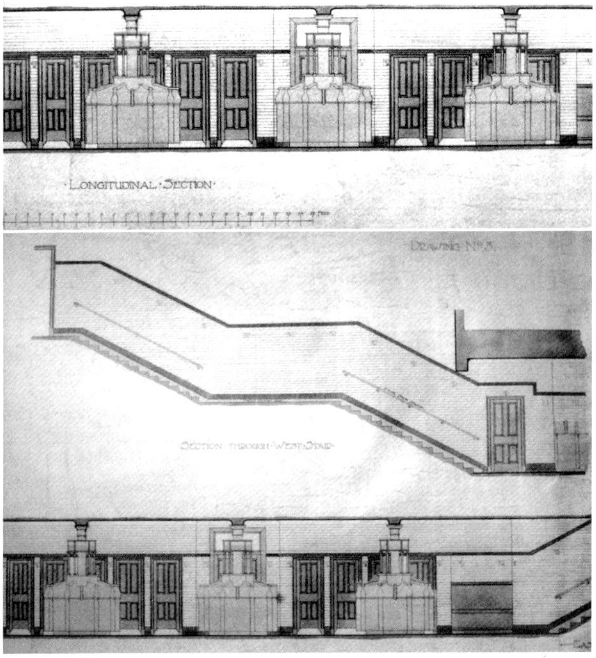

architects were organisationally a department on our own, and were powerful enough to insist that it be painted in all its glory.

In the Ticket Hall, Pirelli rubber floor tiles (as in Central's equivalent in Rome) and metal acoustic ceiling tiles were used to reduce the noise and allow normal conversation between passenger and clerk. It helped, but cleaning was a problem, and it was not until 1982, with the creation of the Travel Centre, that we got it right. On the other hand, with improved heating and summertime refrigeration of the air supply, I knew we had got it right, because the clerks addressed me as "Sir" instead of muttering "bloody architect". It took us a long time to realise that a building within a building required cooling in the summer, even in Scotland.

The end wall of the extended Kintyre Room of the hotel was to feature the crests of the former railway companies. I checked with the Lord Lyon King of Arms that these were authentic. He stated that the crests were for rolling stock only and should these be placed on a building they would be " removed and smashed." These were the exact words.

The biggest fright we had was when the joiners doing the fitting out developed a rash or bites on their arms. This was found to be cat-flea bites. A multitude of cats lived in the arches below the Central. The Vermin Extermination Officer of Glasgow recommended a humane trap, and I bought six, which were duly baited with fish. No cat looked near them: they dined on the scraps from the hotel, including the prestigious Malmaison. My panic was as nothing to that of Central Hotel management. I don't know what happened to the cats, but after the Extermination Officer blew sulphur compound through our new vent system, we had no more trouble.

The large iron gates were renovated, and the one originally at the west end was brought along to form a double entrance at the much more used east end. I was told by the Chief Architect of Boots, Central was the highest revenue-earner per square foot of all their retail outlets in the UK.

When renovating the Station Master's office, I discovered that a small area was reserved for the number of people each day, who were in some sort of trouble and required help. Usually it was a ticket to get home; and so it was for a young lady from Liverpool. The Station Master told me she had arrived off the train from the south with "a fella"; but he had gone to use the toilet via the stairs down from the Union St. end of the concourse, never to be seen again and leaving the poor girl without even a penny to spend. The toilets of course had an alternative way out via the stairs at the Torpedo Building on the other side of the wide concourse. We stopped that with the "Superloo".

By 1964 that massive Gents' lavatory had got into a very poor state and was subject to vandalism wherever its robust structure would allow. The ventilation, by a large fan exhausting through a vent at the rear of the bookstall, was very poor, and I cannot understand how the hairdresser's shop was able to go on for so long. At one time only nine WCs were in any sort of working order, and this figure was used to justify the massive reduction in number of WCs in the new design. The Chief Civil Engineer, at that time still the boss of us architects, insisted that any renovation should incorporate "eastern type closets", i.e. a hole in the floor. I have often wondered since why we never hear of that now. Anyway, the CCE maintained that in the factories and shipyards nobody sat on a WC seat. Indeed, we were later to discover that 98% of women do not sit on a WC seat outside their own home.

The concept of "Superloos" was entirely the brainchild of Dr Beeching. Station lavatories were highest on the list of complaints made to him, so he ordered a new concept. By a strange set of circumstances and internal politics, one of our cadre of architects, Findlay McCracken, found himself in London, where they lumbered him with this challenge. Little did they know that for years we had been researching a replacement for Glasgow Central loos. So when Findlay designed the first Superloos, for Victoria Station in London, these were awarded the maximum five stars in London's Good Loo Guide. When they were due to be officially opened, nobody wanted to have the honour. So the Public Relations Officer of BR Southern Region had to undertake the job himself. His name was Eric Merrill, except that henceforward he became known as "Clochemerrill"

The loos fulfilled Beeching's remit and proved to be very popular especially with the ladies. The press of course had a field day, because in old money the entry was 3d for men, whereas it was 6d for ladies. The first customer to use the room for nursing mothers was full of praise for the new facilities, but the second was surprised that there was no boiling water available. The first lady had taken the electric kettle!

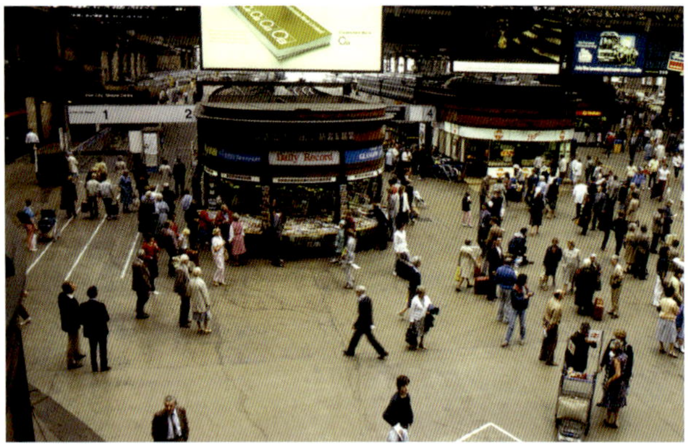

Concourse before the 1980's modernisation and the coming of the "white tiles".

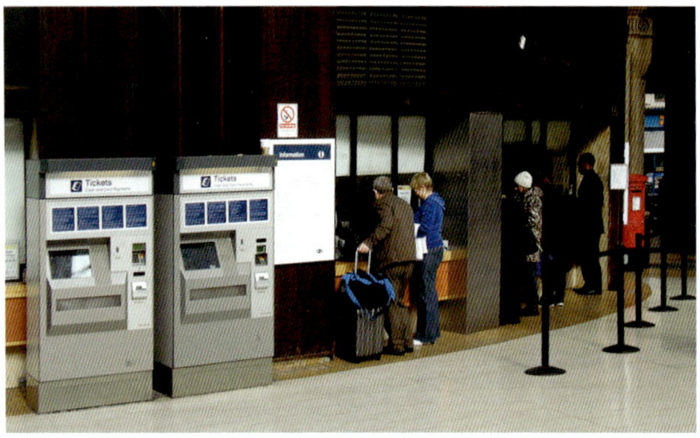

Everything is Central is curved - even the queues for tickets

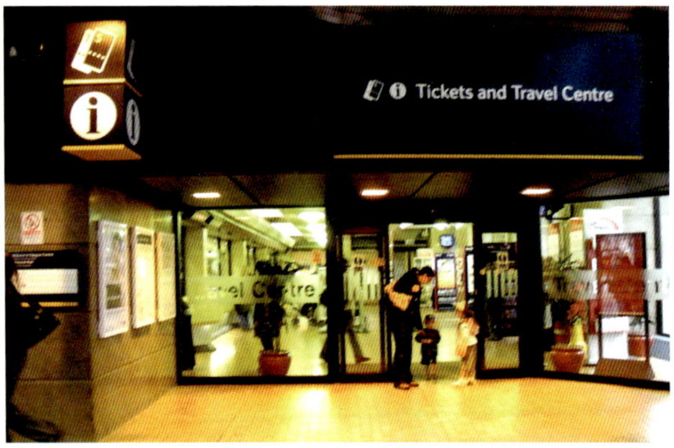

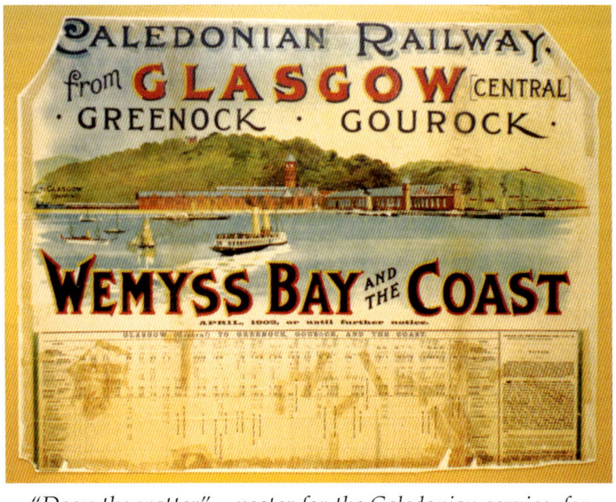

"Doon the watter" – poster for the Caledonian service for Wemyss Bay and the steamers.

Characters, human and animal

All main stations inevitably encounter problems with those who use the station for purposes other than travel. Undesirable people are rarely allowed to tarry long, but the wildlife can be trickier to deal with. Pigeons for example. One General Manager of the Scottish Region compared those at Glasgow Central with those at Newcastle Central. At the latter station, he maintained, a hierarchy dictated the ascending order and discomfort towards the apex of the entablature upon which the pigeons perched of an evening. On the other hand those at Glasgow Central, it seemed to him, were more democratic – presumably also in regard to where they emptied their bowels. In addition to the pigeons, the duty Assistant Station Masters at Glasgow Central had a dog problem. A down-and-out Labrador would hang around, and look all pathetic and appealing, and thus make a good living from scraps from sympathetic passengers. The latter did not realise that the dog regularly clocked off at four in the afternoon and set off to the affluent West End of Glasgow.

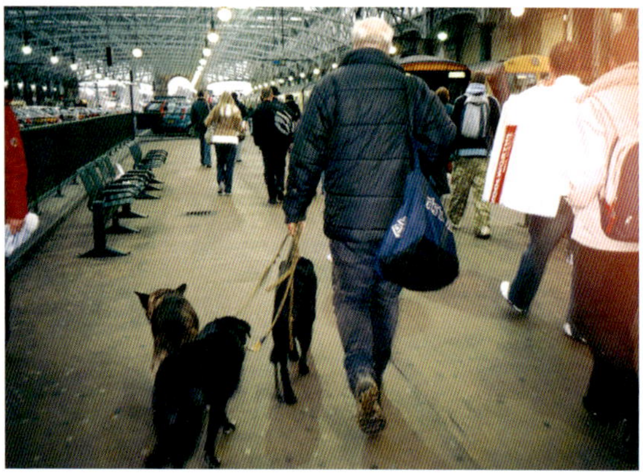

The British Transport Police, in their Force headquarters office away from the hurly-burly of the Central, were very proud of their remote control CCTV system. This had the facility to home in on a specific point and arrange for an alert to sound, if any felonious activity was subsequently seen by the camera. The railway manager visiting the police control room was suitably impressed. The proud Police Inspector decided to demonstrate the point, and identified an unattended suitcase in the middle of the concourse at Central High Level – this was before terrorism had become a major concern. The Inspector commanded the camera to keep an eye on the suitcase, while he showed the railwayman other aspects of the control room. Suddenly the alarm sounded, and they dashed back to the CCTV screen to ascertain what had occurred – in time to see a dog blissfully lifting its leg at the suitcase.

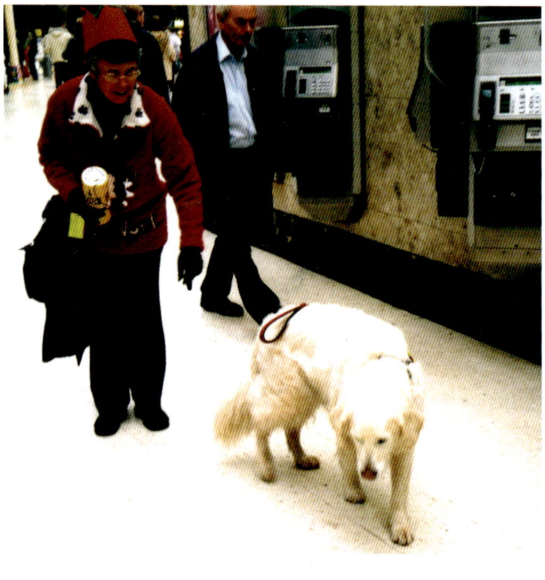

8 Conserving the Central

Murray Thomson

My first memory of Central Station was as a child of some five or six years accompanying my architect father as he safely delivered some distant relatives to a southbound train, an event made more memorable by an obliging train Driver allowing a young child to clamber on board and "toot" the whistle of the steam locomotive, as the fireman stoked the fire. But this was the early 1950s, the golden age of steam and an altogether more innocent time. Little could either of us have known that, some forty odd years later I would play a significant role in the restoration of the magnificently engineered station which our Victorian forefathers had the foresight to bestow upon the "Empire's Second City".

Fast forward forty-two years: it is 1996, and I am standing on the roof of the Station overlooking the spine of the building delineated at concourse level by the double row of octagonal columns on Platforms 9 and 10 which separate the original 1874 Station structure from the 1906 west wing extension. I am surveying for the first time the vast expanse of station roof covering an area of six and a half acres, equivalent to three and a half times the size of Hampden Football Stadium. My initial feelings, to borrow from contemporary military jargon were of "shock

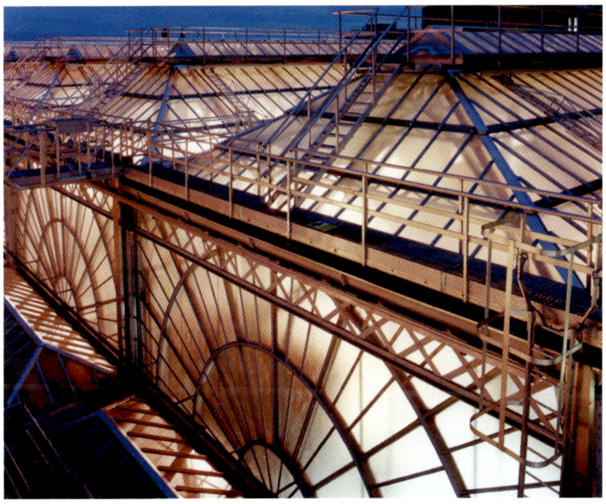

and awe". "Shock", that the custodians of such an impressive and historically significant building could have allowed it to deteriorate into such a dilapidated condition. Commuters had regularly to negotiate sheets of water cascading from defective roof glazing and from gutters overflowing as a result of blocked rainwater pipes. And "awe", at the sheer scale of the task for the construction team in the years ahead, a task burdened by the prerequisite that the station had to remain fully operational throughout the duration of the re-construction. This meant that only two platforms could be taken out of commission at any one time.

Fast forward a further seven years: it is the 9th May 2003, Europe Day, and I am seated in the Grand Hall of Mirrors in the Palais d'Egmont in the centre of Brussels, in the company of HRH Crown Prince Lorenz of Belgium and seventy fellow Laureates, gathered from 19 European countries. It is the first joint European Union Prize for Cultural Heritage/Europa Nostra Awards, and the restoration of the Central is being awarded a Diploma. It is the seventh and most prestigious award of a total of nine the Station regeneration will eventually receive. Europa Nostra, it should be explained, has no connection with the Cosa Nostra! Rather it is a pan-European federation for Heritage, bringing together over 220 non-governmental heritage organisations across 35 countries on our European Continent. Its ethos is "the Power of Example". In support of this ethos, the Diploma signed by HRH The Prince Consort of Denmark, President of Europa Nostra reads: "Awarded for the research and exemplary conservation of an important 19th century train station including important protection measures to the roof, executed with sensitivity and meticulous attention to detail". This was an accolade achieved through the efforts of a great many dedicated individuals, who had collectively expended over 850,000 man-hours in restoring the grandeur of the Station. It was no less an accolade than was befitting for perhaps the finest Victorian Railway Station in Britain – a building which embodies the very heart and soul of the City it has so faithfully served for over 125 years.

So it was with this history in mind that we developed the ethos of our approach for the restoration of the station that was to be the flagship of the Railtrack Station Regeneration Programme in Scotland. Whereas the Station Regeneration Programme had been implemented to retard deterioration of the property portfolio of Railtrack, our approach was more concerned with the conservation of the Station. There is a significant difference, as "conservation" in its truest sense means all the processes of looking after a place so as to retain its "cultural significance". This can be defined as meaning the aesthetic, historic, scientific, social or spiritual value for present and future generations. The "cultural significance" is embodied in the Station itself, in its fabric, setting, use and associations. By establishing how this cultural heritage had been managed historically, we were able to put in place multi-stranded creative processes,

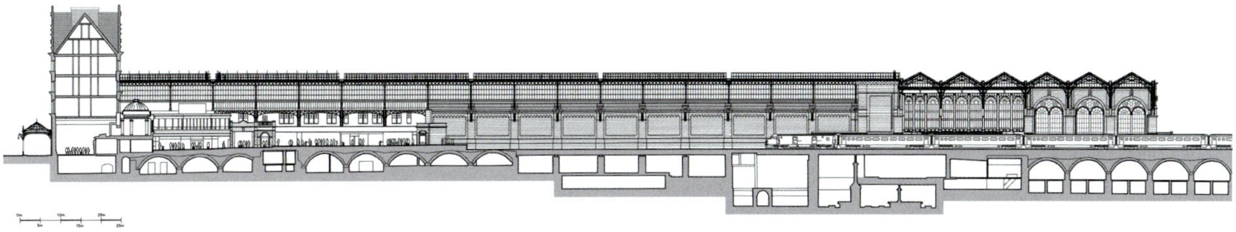

which would not only enhance the station environment but also significantly improve the management of our cultural heritage for future generations.

This approach to conservation demanded a review through critical eyes of the residue of the past that was manifest in the unchecked proliferation of decay of the station fabric. The creative processes employed in response to this decay are best demonstrated in the conservation of the screens of the "Hielandman's Umbrella": historically, for some reason, the original significant sum of £2 million. One hundred and twenty years later the conservation of the station was completed one year ahead of schedule, and 15% under budget, at an outturn cost of £28.5 million. The construction processes which led to such a positive outcome were rewarded with the Best Practice Award at the 2000 British Construction Awards. Judges commented that "Outstanding teamwork and performance in every department brought this project a year ahead of programme and significantly below budget. This must become the client's benchmark for future schemes". Praise indeed. However, we must

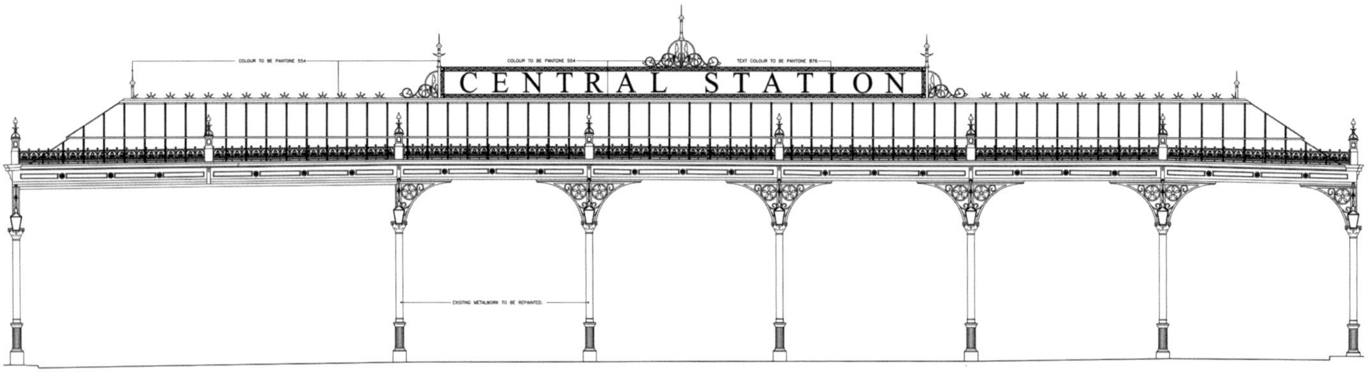

AL(0)016
GORDON STREET ELEVATION 1:50

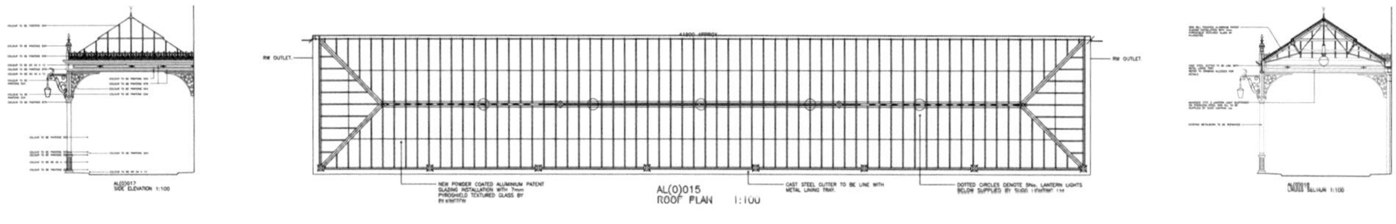

frieze, cornice and parapet castings had been removed from both sides of the bridge and subsequently destroyed. Experience determined that it was unlikely that the cast iron cladding would have failed, as the life cycle of the material far exceeded the 100 years during which the bridge cladding had been in place. In any event, the lower castings had largely survived intact. Research had revealed that water ingress over a sustained period of time had corroded the mild steel fixing brackets supporting the castings, and this had necessitated their removal. This focused our attention on the detailing of the replacement parapet and fascia, once their profile had been established, so as to replicate as closely as possible the original castings, as determined from surviving archive photographs, but subject to modifications to eliminate the water ingress that had resulted in their removal in the first place.

Similarly, the failure of the glass roof and the subsequent corrosion of the steelwork of the roof support had remained unchecked for so long due in part to the absence of a system to gain access to the roof and to the fact that, where the original access provision had been installed, it had been removed historically, again through failure of the support framework. Evidence of this had survived at the high level lantern lights on the west wing of the station. The replacement of the roof, subsequent to conservation of the steelwork, allowed the integration of the "important roof protection measures", referred to in the Europa Nostra citation.

The original 1879 station was constructed for the then not lose sight of the fact that we were conserving the works of our pioneering forefathers who in creating their "cathedral of transport" were working at the cutting edge of the architechtonic capabilities of their day. We relied heavily on computer technology for the analysis of the existing structure to determine loadings for the crash deck that was installed above the concourse and tracks to facilitate safe execution of roof works. That technology was equally important too for the preparation of the hundred or so architectural drawings, just as it was for the financial management and programming which had undoubtedly contributed to the expeditious delivery of the project.

How would we have fared had the roles been reversed and our project team charged with the delivery of the original station – without the reliance on computer technology? We can never know – it is pondering the imponderable. We can only marvel at the ingenuity of those pioneers of modern station design who had been responsible for what is undoubtedly Glasgow's finest building. For that, we must raise our hats to Sir Robert Rowand Anderson (1834-1921), architect for the original station building, Donald Alexander Matheson (1860-1935), the Caledonian Railway's engineer-in-chief responsible for the design of the Station extension and James Miller (1860-1947), the celebrated Glasgow architect and consultant to the 'Caley', who had designed the façade of the Hope Street train hall and the early renaissance façade of the Hielandman's Umbrella, with its huge vertical windows articulated by colourful cast iron pilasters and capitals.

9 Assignations of one sort......

When I was a medical student in the 50s, one of the Professors of Surgery at the Royal Infirmary was J A G Burton, who was always referred to affectionately as 'Pop'. He was an older man, a bachelor who lived for his work, and he was often to be seen around the hospital at all kinds of ungodly hours. A kindly man, he was much liked by his students and colleagues, but he had an impish sense of humour. Being a bachelor, there was always the thought that he might eventually get married, and no doubt he knew about this speculation. And he played on it. One of his ploys was to slip up to a nurse in the hospital corridor and ask her if she would like to go to the theatre with him? "Of course", she would delightedly agree, and no doubt would think to herself that she had netted a professor. "Well then," he would say, "meet me at the Shell at the Central Station tomorrow evening at seven".

The next evening, full of expectations and all dolled up for the occasion she would get to the Shell: there was no Professor Burton, but by five-past-seven there were another half-dozen nurses, who had all been lured in the same way. By ten-past, when they had decided that a rotten trick had been played on them, up would sail "Pop" with a huge box of chocolates under his arm and a handful of theatre tickets, and he would cheerfully escort the whole group of young ladies to a show at the King's or the Alhambra.
Despite his gallantry he remained a bachelor to the end.

Alastair Munro, M.D. Halifax, Nova Scotia

......and another

Tommy (Cupid) Love flew Spitfires as a sergeant pilot in 602(City of Glasgow) Squadron late in the war. He was a very wee Glaswegian. After being shot down over the Channel, he was to get some leave in Glasgow. Passing through the Central, he was apprehended by the Military Police in Central station – for impersonating a pilot.

As related by the late Tommy Love

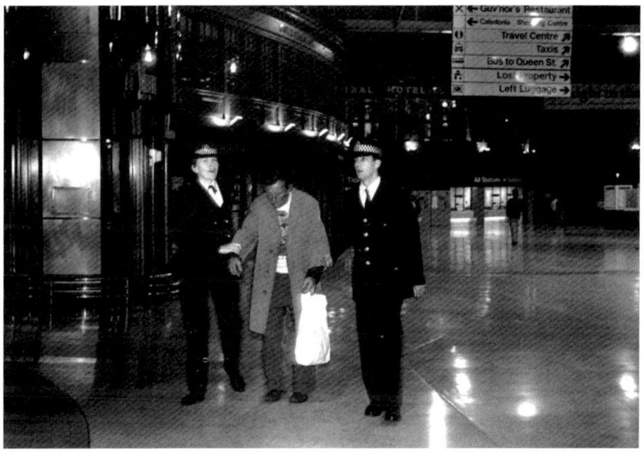

Show me the way to go home – a helping hand from the British Transport Police on "Glasgow Fair" Friday 1988.

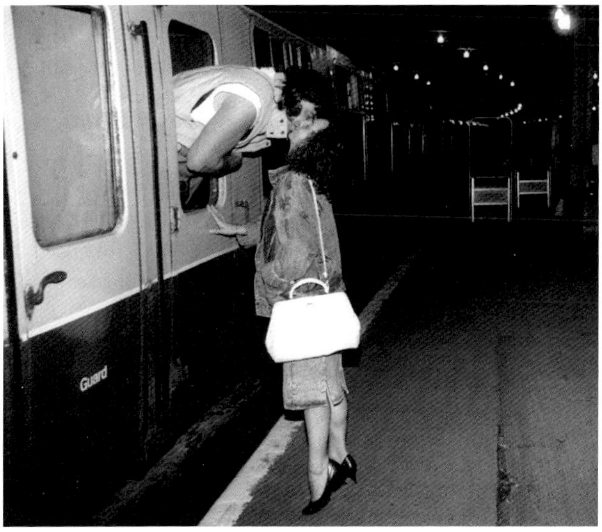

"Ae fond kiss...... "

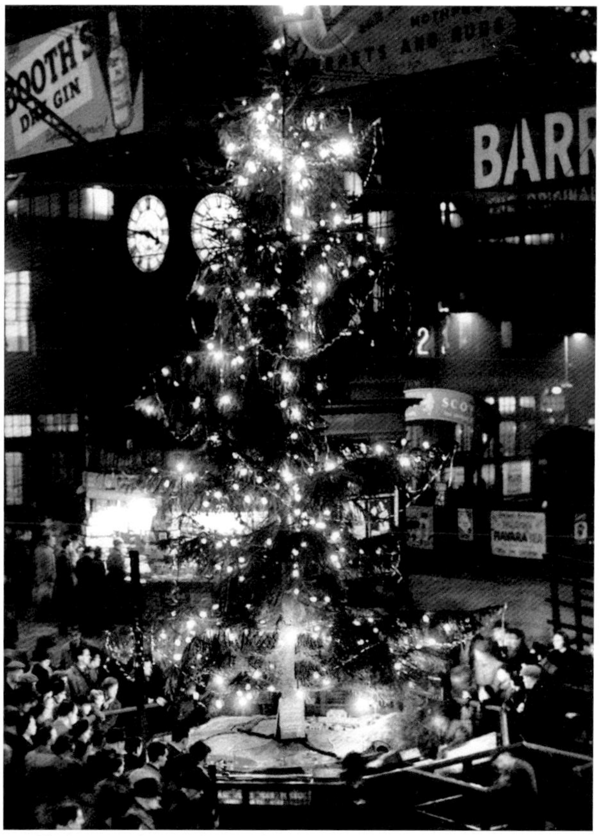

Christmas decorations when running your own train cost one old penny to 'wheech' round the tree. Proceeds to charity.

10 "A refined amalgam" - an architectural comment

George Horspool

In the early 1950s, when I travelled up and down to Ayrshire as an architectural student, my point of arrival in Glasgow was St Enoch Station. It was only much later that I learned that the creation of St Enoch was the spur which impelled the Caledonian Railway to leap across the River Clyde from its Bridge Street outpost, to create Glasgow Central station in its present location. The Glasgow and South Western Railway had refused the Caledonian running rights into its station at St Enoch. So the Caledonian, and its ally the London and North Western, had no choice but to cross the river likewise, and acquire all of the land and property from Bridge Street, across the river up Alston Street to Gordon Street.

Central Station and Hotel was to be an awesome project. The station built in 1876-9 was designed by the Edinburgh engineers Blyth and Cunningham. The architect Sir Rowand Anderson was commissioned to include in his proposal a magnificent headquarters office block, the necessary hotel accommodation being provided opposite at 91-115 Hope Street. The Caledonian thereafter had second thoughts, and instructed him to convert the proposed offices into a hotel. Anderson's brief was to produce such a hotel as would outclass St Enoch's. Instead of a twelve-month contract period, the project took three years.

The five-storey facade of the structure contained "a refined amalgam of early Italian, Jacobean and northern European influences – notably at the tall, somewhat Teutonic pyramid-roofed clock tower". In 1901-6, the station was doubled in size on the western side and the hotel considerably extended down Hope Street. Donald Mathieson was the engineer and James Miller the architect. Amongst Mathieson's contributions to the design were the semi-elliptically arched roof girders, a feature much more elegant in its solution than those used by Blyth and Cunningham in the original scheme. Miller contributed the very large early Italian fenestration on Hope Street and the early renaissance details of its extension over Argyle Street. The station concourse rejoices in the stylish well-detailed oval timber building, formerly the waiting room and indicator screen where destination boards rattled as the many changes to destinations were effected with unbelievable speed and efficiency. The interiors are still fairly complete: notably at the domed lounge area, with glass by Oscar Paterson.

Much is obviously changed but, equally, the greater part of the splendid scheme remains, offering a fitting tribute to the wonderfully robust architecture of a bygone age and a lasting memorial to Scotland's foremost independent railway company, the Caledonian Railway.

As this second edition was being prepared, the good news came that the Central Hotel, which closed in February 2009, was to reopen after a £20 million refurbishment.

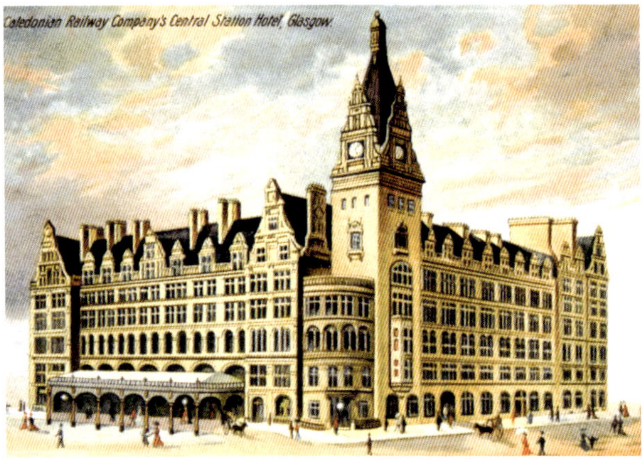

An early image of the Hotel from a Caledonian Railway postcard.

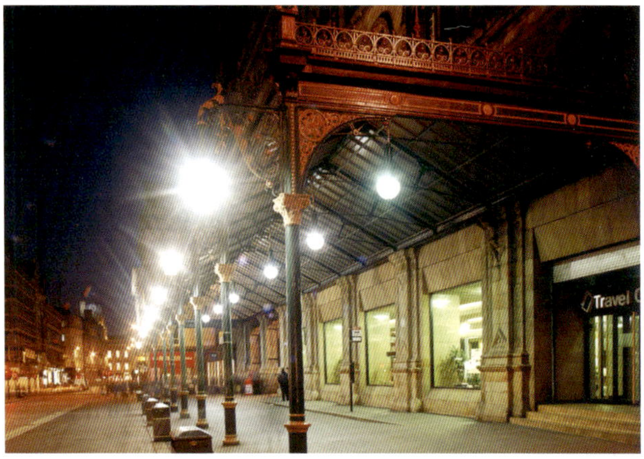

The Gordon Street Canopy Victorian architecture at its best!

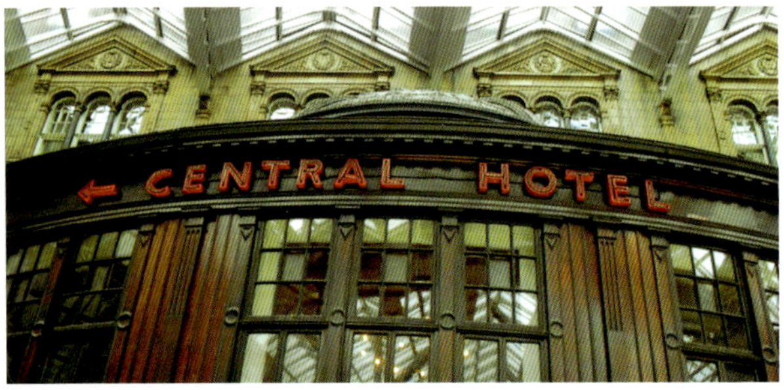

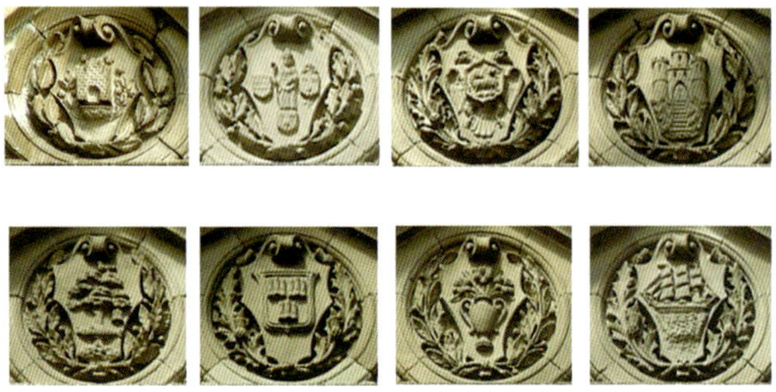

The Hotel seen from the Station Concourse with stone carvings showing the arms of various towns and cities in the frieze above the upper windows shown here in greater detail.

11 Underground activities

Charles Weir

Trains hauled by steam engines can still be regularly found in Central in 2006, somewhere between the main line and low level stations. Unfortunately they are only one forty-third of the size of the real thing and powered by electricity.

In the mid-1980s, a group of a dozen or so railway modellers – some professional railwaymen, some from diverse other walks of life – obtained from the then British Railways the tenancy of a disused storage area beneath the station concourse, as a place to re-create in miniature the imagined perfect railways of their youth. Much time and effort was expended in the initial clearing and decoration of the premises and in the construction of a detailed scenic layout, until disaster struck in the 1990s, in the form of a constant inflow through the entire ceiling from a burst in a water pipe beneath the concourse, which could not be traced.

This resulted in the premises being continuously under a foot of water for many months and being unfit for occupation for some two years. Fortunately, parts of the layout were able to be salvaged and are incorporated in the group's present layout, which is now substantially complete (it is a cliché among railway modellers that a layout is never finished) and extends to roughly 30 feet by 20 feet. It is a "Gauge O" layout, built to the somewhat curious but well-established scale of 7mm. to one foot, set in the 1930s and inspired by the Callander and Oban section of the Caledonian Railway with its Ballachulish Branch, although it does also play host to models of locomotives and rolling stock from other times and places.

The group also has a much more compact, portable layout portraying a small urban passenger station and goods yard somewhere in Lowland Scotland, and over the past three or four years members have taken this to various model railway exhibitions in both England and Scotland, principally under the banner of the Gauge O Guild (a very active association of over 5000 modellers in the United Kingdom and elsewhere). The object has been to show that it is possible to have an interesting layout in this larger scale even in a modest space, and to demonstrate techniques to achieve this at reasonable cost. Plans are in hand to create a link between the two layouts in such a way that they can be operated together or still as two separate units.

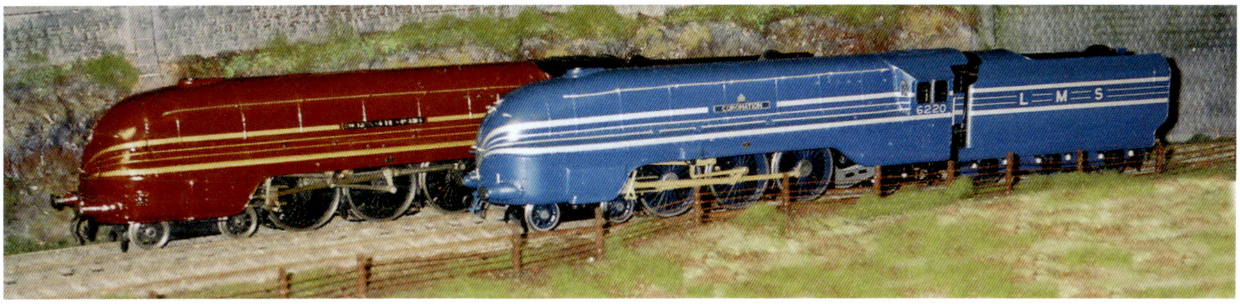

"Underneath the arches" – two scale model 'Duchesses' as they once graced the Station above on the Strathclyde '0' Gauge Group's model railway (7mm to the foot) which is housed beneath the Station.

Tiles below ground

"The Central's just the place for the annual Trip", said the Sunday School Superintendent emerging from the marble halls of the subterranean Gents. "Plenty trains for the kids to watch – and endless toilets".

Tiles above ground

The white tiles certainly brightened the concourse, but there was upheaval while they were laid, and, initially anyway, they could become slippery when wet. The cynical old railway Inspector had been sceptical as the work progressed with all its inconvenience. "Now it's finished, and you can see the whole effect, what do you think?", asked the enthusiastic manager. Back came the dispiriting reply, "Fastest part of the journey from Euston now is slipping on your backside from the platform out into Gordon Street".

Not what it seemed

Until the accommodation for traincrew was moved into Caledonian Chambers on the west of the Central, a bothy for drivers was situated below ground level, with the exit facing the celebrated departure boards of the Torpedo Building. It was natural, as you emerged, to glance up at the board displayed for your train. There was a risk, however, if you thought that the board was a valid substitute for the Working Timetable. A number of Anglo-Scottish trains called at Motherwell to pick up only, and thus were not shown as a calling point on the board at Central for those trains – which may have explained why the odd southbound Anglo roared through Motherwell to the acute disappointment of the passengers waiting to be picked up only.

Filthy Lucre

The railway could never understand why it should pay the banks so much. After all, it was giving them money. So it set up in Glasgow Central its own banking operation, with more modern cash-handling machinery than the banks possessed, and there it gathered in the takings from all the suburban stations. It became a big operation, with even the bus companies seeking to be involved alongside many of the big department stores. But the most immediate effect was a famine of small change in the businesses of central Glasgow . . . and the banks coming to buy small change from the counting house at the Central.

12 Travelling in style

Bruce Peter

The experience of modern life in the rapidly expanding cities of the latter 19th century was one of constant flux and movement – an unprecedented maelstrom of traffic and pedestrians, mingling with the nascent signs of consumerism, represented in bold electric lighting. The shock of this new environment must have been all the more profound for populations who had hitherto been rural-dwelling. Glasgow grew rapidly during this period, and the Georgian merchant city was usurped by a Victorian commercial and industrial powerhouse. The grid-iron layout of its central business district encouraged the mass movement of people, commodities and finance. By the Edwardian era, the development of an underground railway, of an extensive tramway network and of four major railway termini had further enhanced Glasgow's reputation as a modern metropolis par excellence. Of its stations, Glasgow Central was arguably the most impressive (although the Glasgow and South Western Railway's St Enoch, nearby, possibly had the finest train shed of any in Britain).

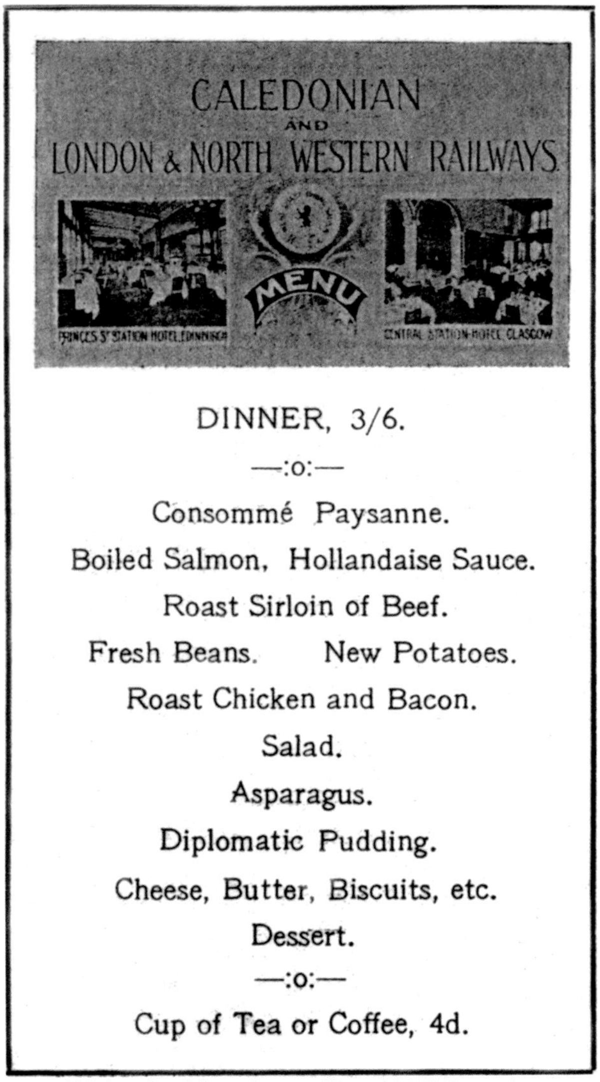
CALEDONIAN
AND
LONDON & NORTH WESTERN RAILWAYS
MENU

DINNER, 3/6.

—:o:—

Consommé Paysanne.

Boiled Salmon, Hollandaise Sauce.

Roast Sirloin of Beef.

Fresh Beans. New Potatoes.

Roast Chicken and Bacon.

Salad.

Asparagus.

Diplomatic Pudding.

Cheese, Butter, Biscuits, etc.

Dessert.

—:o:—

Cup of Tea or Coffee, 4d.

Dining Car Menu from a CR and LNWR service.

Unlike its rival, the North British, the Caledonian Railway tended to build on a grand scale, utilising the latest architectural innovations and employing progressive designers, such as Sir Rowand Anderson and James Miller. Miller, in particular, had strong views about architectural aesthetics and believed that different styles were appropriate for particular settings. In the new suburban commuting dormitories and coastal piers served by the Caledonian, an Arts and Crafts style was chosen to impart a cosy domesticity, but for the flagship station in Central Glasgow, a more ostentatious approach was required. Indeed, Glasgow Central Hotel, the station's public face to adjacent streets, is a remarkably refined amalgam of early Renaissance, Jacobean and Teutonic elements, topped off by a magnificent clock tower – which would not have looked out of place in a Prussian cityscape.

Indeed, German design was highly fashionable in the Edwardian era (as were German popular music, cuisine, consumer goods and clothing), and it is said that the Caledonian Railway and its architects looked to German termini for inspiration. For example, when extended in 1901-6, the concourse at Glasgow Central was laid in hardwood parquet, much like German stations. The most striking feature of the concourse, however, was its plan, which was intended to facilitate the easy and safe movement of large crowds. This was achieved by entirely avoiding any sharp corners: instead, the timber-clad pavilions on the station concourse were given sinuous, flowing forms, quite unlike any other major station in Britain. This ingenious and innovative design maximised the spectacular station concourse, opening up sweeping vistas and making the whole business of rail travel thrilling even for the casual observer.

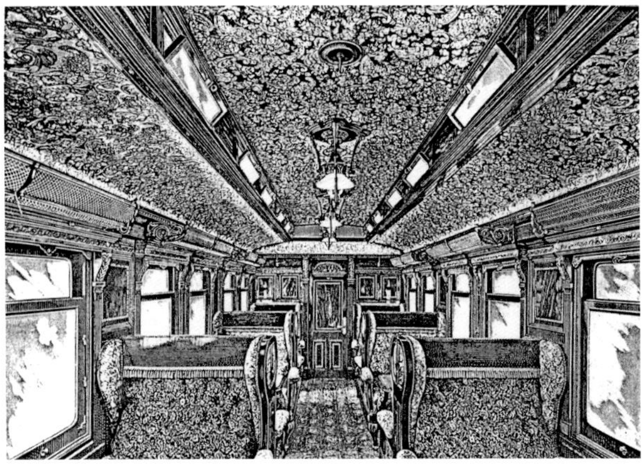

Victorian opulence on the West Coast service in 1893 West Coast Joint Stock Diner.

Not only were travellers beguiled by the atmosphere, but also passers-by were attracted to spectate – as the Caledonian Railway's crack express trains were memorable in their own right. Writing about the public's reaction to the large and powerful locomotives required to haul these over the lengthy gradient of Beattock, the distinguished railway writer O S Nock observed that:

The stately goings and comings of these engines [and the] no less than chronometer-like punctuality that they maintained, sent the prestige of the Caledonian sky high in the pre-1914 era.

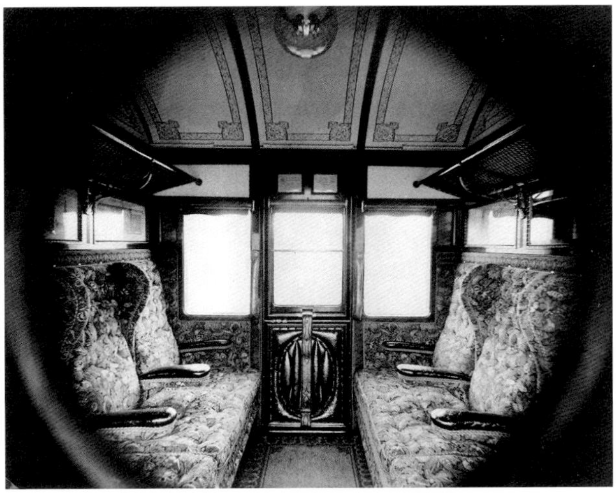

Compartment in a Caledonian Railway Grampian Stock First Class carriage – 1906.

Such locomotives were decked out in a magnificent livery of rich blue with black and white lining, with maroon frames lined out, with tomato red buffer beams, and with a great deal of elegant small scale details, such as shaded lettering and highly polished brass work. To be assigned to drive one of the Caledonian's top express locomotives was a great honour bestowed upon only the most respected and experienced of enginemen – who, in turn, took great pride in ensuring that their charges always appeared in immaculate condition and were driven punctually, as Nock observes. Besides, at that time, labour was relatively inexpensive and teenage boys were employed in large numbers as cleaners in locomotive depots – the first rung on a career ladder which might eventually lead to one becoming a driver, or even a shed foreman.

These locomotives hauled coaches that were masterpieces of design in their own right. Jointly operated by the Caledonian and the London & North Western Railway companies, and hence known as 'joint stock', they were painted in madder and white (even the roofs were white), and many had three axles on each bogie to give the smoothest possible ride. Furthermore, these twelve-wheelers had corridors throughout, with flexible vestibule connections from one to another, meaning that passengers could enjoy a visit to the restaurant car. Externally, the bodywork was highly finished with a lustrous sheen, created by the careful application of layers of paint and varnish. Within, the décor was in the fashionable Arts and Crafts style, with deeply upholstered settees and moulded glass lampshades. Small wonder, then, that the public at large went to Glasgow Central just to watch the expresses to London as they pulled away from the platform!

From 1918 onwards, there was much less progress than there had been in the pre-war Edwardian 'golden age'. New locomotive types were tried – but it was not until the later 1920s that significant advances were made. By then, the Caledonian Railway had been absorbed into the London, Midland and Scottish Railway as a consequence of the 1923 'Grouping'. Overall, the LMS acquired from its predecessors a mixed bag of often elderly locomotives and rolling stock from its constituents. Clearly, new thinking was urgently required.

The LMS's new Henry Fowler-attributed, but North British Locomotive Company-built, "Royal Scot" class of 4-6-0s, introduced in 1927, were mighty locomotives with huge boilers practically filling out the loading gauge and capable of hauling the 15-coach Royal Scot express non-stop from London Euston to Carlisle. Even so, by the 1930s, Sir Josiah Stamp, the recently appointed chairman of the LMS, believed that still more needed to be done – even although money was scarce (the Great Depression had compounded the railways' financial woes). A new Chief Mechanical Engineer, William A. Stanier, was appointed from the Great Western Railway, and he developed two new classes of 4-6-2 Pacifics – each the largest and most powerful yet seen under the train shed roof of Glasgow Central. In 1933, the first of a small batch of engines of the "Princess Royal" class made its debut, followed four years later by Coronation, the first of the streamlined 'Duchess' class – intended to haul the matching Coronation Scot train.

As the economy slowly recovered in fits and starts, there was intense competition between the LMS on the West Coast and the LNER on the East. Gresley's streamlined A4 class and the LNER Silver Jubilee train had broken all records for speed – and visual elegance; and so the LMS was obliged to respond. Of course, the latter's Coronation Scot was every bit as alluring, perhaps more so. Both engine and train were turned out in a vivid shade of blue with 'speed whiskers' on the bulbous casing covering the locomotive's smoke box door. These continued the full length of the train, making a single coherent design statement. Inside, the coaches were sumptuously appointed – but, by then, Arts and Crafts-inspired elaboration had given way to Art Deco flamboyance. There was 'jazzy' upholstery, polished veneer and chromed fittings – the height of 1930s style. Any small

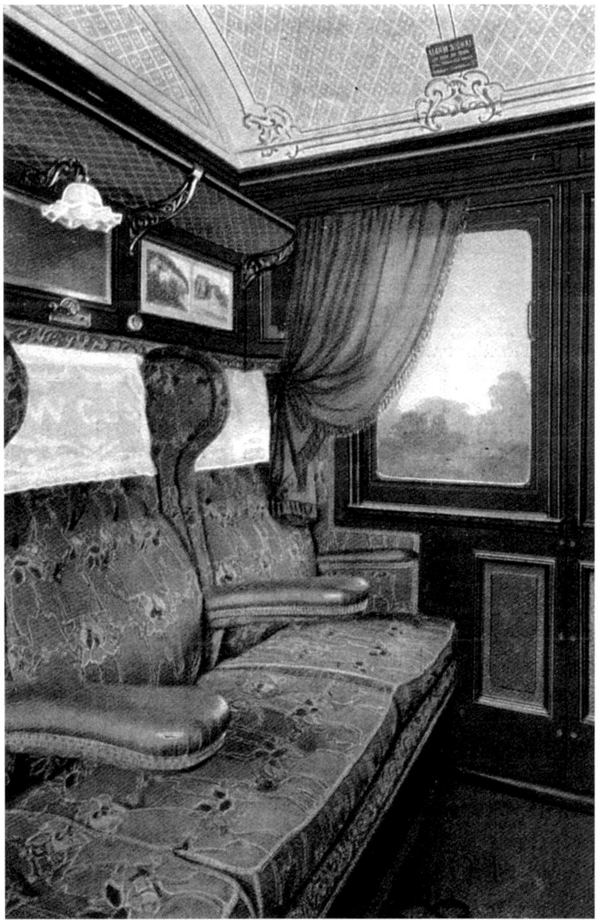

First Class Coupé compartment of the West Coast 2 pm Scotch Express.

boy setting eyes upon Coronation – or one of its sisters – would have been bound to want to become a locomotive driver when he grew up.

But the age of the glamourous streamlined train was only a brief interlude, lasting four years at most. When the Second World War was declared, the locomotives were

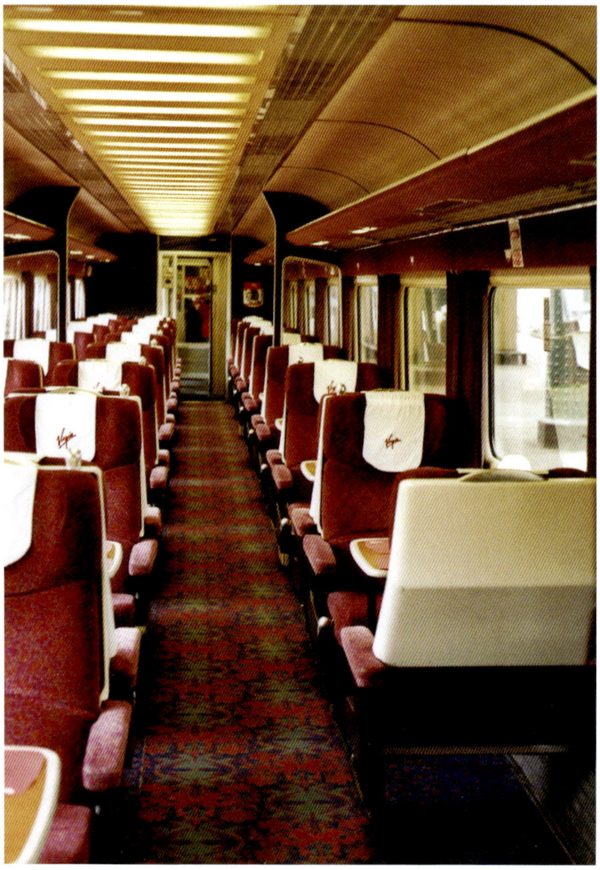

BR Mark 3 (Virgin) 1st Class Open carriage interior.

painted black, and when railway staff were called up to the forces, all non-essential work ceased and the locomotives declined quickly into decrepitude. The named expresses were withdrawn and, throughout the 1940s, style disappeared from the railways. As Britain's railways attempted to regain normality after peace returned, it seemed that nationalisation was inevitable and, indeed, this happened in 1948. In Central, however, things continued much as before. Occasionally, a "Duchess" would appear in the new British Railways experimental blue livery – itself rather like that of the old Caledonian – and from the early 1950s, the London expresses began to be formed of British Railways' Standard Mark 1 coaches, which were, by common consent, often inferior to pre-war LMS designs in terms of passenger comfort. The most prestigious named trains returned – with locomotives specially cleaned to add a little much-needed sparkle to the railway scene – and the Stationmaster would appear, dressed in his morning suit complete with tile hat, to wave them off.

At Central, diesel locomotives appeared on expresses from the later 1950s onwards. At the same time, diesel multiple unit trains of various types were introduced on suburban routes and, to great acclaim, the Cathcart Circle was electrified. The new suburban electric trains were amongst the first successes for British Railways' recently-established Design Panel, and they set new standards for passenger comfort, as well as heralding faster and more frequent services. The old Caledonian continued to make its presence felt, however, as these electrics were turned out in what was described as "Caledonian blue". Nearly all of the new commuter trains of the era had observation saloons with glazed partitions immediately behind the Driver so that passengers could view the passing scenery as they hurried along.

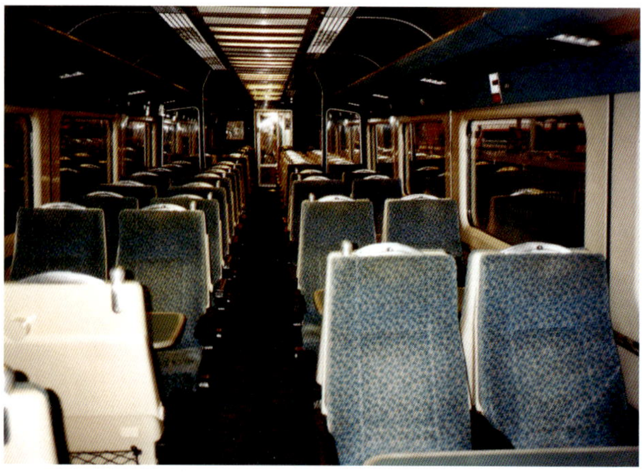

BR Mark 3 (Virgin) Standard Class carriage interior.

In 1958, the Conservative Prime Minister Harold Macmillan had opened the Preston Bypass – Britain's first motorway. Meanwhile, increasing wages and outdated work practices and infrastructure meant that, notwithstanding recent investments, the railways became ever more expensive. Dr Richard Beeching was appointed as Chairman of British Railways with a mandate to prune the network and to cut losses, but Beeching realised the value of modern design and believed that the railway needed to overhaul its image better to meet air and road competition. He instigated the British Rail corporate identity programme, with a new livery, new graphics and new brand names, of which Inter-City was the most memorable. New Mark II carriages were developed, again utilising the skills of industrial designers appointed by the Design Panel. Later versions of the Mark II were air-conditioned and, simultaneously, development work began on the Mark III – a luxurious Inter-City coach capable of travelling serenely at 125 miles an hour.

When the new electrically-hauled Inter-City trains finally reached Glasgow Central, celebration was in order. British Rail had been transformed in less than thirty years from neglected post-war dilapidation into a modern system, which could boast more air-conditioned coaches and more trains travelling at 100 mph or above than any other in the world. The Class 87 electrics were the pride of the West Coast fleet and most were given names previously carried by Fowler's "Royal Scot" class. These electrics could generate 5,000 horsepower, meaning that they could soar effortlessly up Beattock without any assistance from banking engines. Cocooned in the cool temperature-controlled comfort of a Mark III coach, gazing at the passing scene through wide, double-glazed tinted windows and seated in ergonomically designed reclining chairs, passengers using Inter-City were amazed by the transformation of the rail travel experience.

British Rail, however, wanted to go one better with a high speed tilting super train, to be known as the Advanced Passenger Train, or APT for short. In nearly every respect, this project was at the leading edge of rail technology – but the research budget was only a fraction of that set aside to develop the supersonic airliner Concorde. The concept of APT was to 'smooth out' the West Coast journey with coaches that leaned into the line's many curves, enabling higher speeds to be maintained. When it worked, the train was a wonderful experience, and some cracking performances were recorded with speeds in the 140-150 mph range. It was thrilling to 'fly' down the

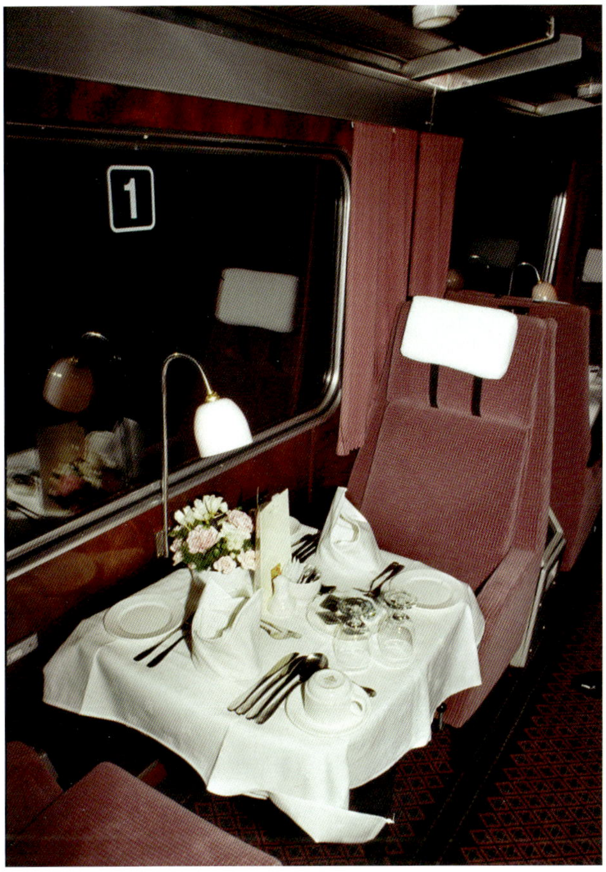

Table for two – Inter City elegance. BR Mark II Diner 1994.

Clyde Valley with its meandering river – feeling as if it might come through the window when the train tilted. After an all-too-brief period in service in the mid-1980s, all of the trains were scrapped except one, which now lies at Crewe Heritage Centre and looks over the fence there, wistfully watching the "Pendolinos" pass.

Extension of the East Coast services from Edinburgh

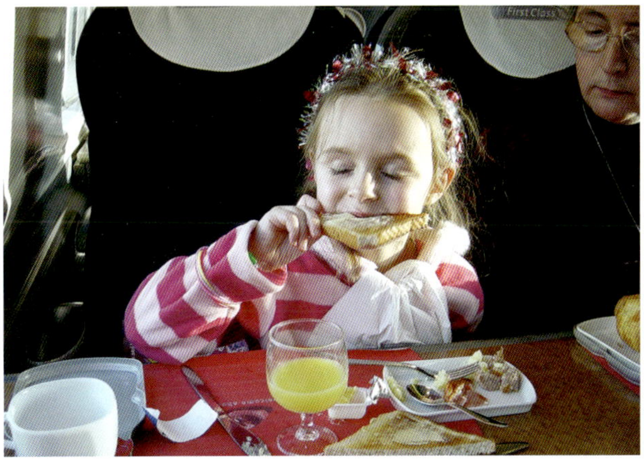

Dining in style!

introduced to Central the InterCity 225 trains, consisting of a locomotive and Mark IV coaches (designed to be retro-fitted with tilting apparatus). With consequently restricted loading gauges, these were rather less commodious than the 1970s West Coast Mark IIIs and the tight budget to which they were constructed showed in an inferior level of passenger ambience. GNER set out to bring a little more panâche to the operation – beginning with gourmet catering in the restaurant cars. Subsequently, InterCity 225 trains were refurbished to a high standard, under the Mallard branding – a reference to the famous 1930s LNER record-breaking A4 Pacific of that name. Nowadays, the East Coast franchise is operated by National Express, which is gradually introducing its own livery and more 'mass market' standards of service.

On the West Coast operation, Virgin faced the need to replace the entire existing fleet, which, without significant investment, had become unreliable. Two new train types were developed – diesel "Voyagers" for cross-country routes and electric "Pendolinos" for services from London to Manchester, Liverpool and Glasgow. Of course, the "Pendolino", like the APT before it, is a tilting train – but it makes use of Italian, rather than British, technology. As each coach of the nine-car sets is powered, a great deal of machinery needs to be packed into small volumes, meaning that the on-board ambience – particularly in Standard class – can be rather reminiscent of aircraft. In First Class, the "Pendolino" is a most attractive train.

Today, the designs of the express trains using Glasgow Central are radically different from those of the 1900s – but the station itself remains remarkably intact, showing that its ambitious design was fit for purpose from the outset.

Meticulously restored, it now looks better than it probably ever has done in the past. For travellers, its commodious concourse and expansive glazed roof give a very positive first impression of the city – an impression reinforced by the handsome commercial edifices of Gordon Street outside. Moreover, the building today is more than just a railway station, as it has become a cultural and retail hub in the city. Glasgow Central has hosted many generations of stylish trains – and is itself undoubtedly an icon of style and modernity.

Recycling reprehensibly

Glasgow Central pioneered the use of Automatic Ticket Barriers from the beginning of 1973. Although this kind of ticket inspection had been in use in London, Chicago, Philadelphia and local railways in Japan, the installation at the Central was the first in Europe to feature a stored journey system. Tickets were sold for 1, 2, 10, 20 or 50 journeys on the Gourock and Wemyss Bay lines, were read by machines at the barriers, and that journey was automatically deducted from the validity of the tickets. Reliable, if unscrupulous, sources claim to have had good results with the tickets in the equipment at Morden on the London Underground network – just about as far away as it is possible to get from Cartsdyke. It wouldn't have worked the other way, though – supposing anyone had felt like trying.

13 "Sombre, sulphurous and Plutonian"

Jim Summers

While the great of expansion of Central raised the number of platforms from 8 to 14 platforms (13 plus eventually 11A), that was only part of the station. The total became in fact 18, by virtue of including the four new platforms, which had been opened in 1896, as part of another great and ambitious enterprise of the dynamic Caledonian Railway. This was the Glasgow Central Railway, running unseen in tunnel below Argyle Street and below the extended main station. It served a station known from its inception as Glasgow Central Low Level. For the first three years of its existence, the buildings at surface level of Low Level station were a temporary structure until replaced in 1899 by facilities, which much impressed the Railway Magazine of the time: *The new building, which has a frontage of 154 feet to Argyle Street and 123 feet to Hope Street, is a one-storey structure of massive and ornamental design, with a huge dome at the corner, and canopies, carried on cantilevers, which overhang the footpath along the whole frontage.*

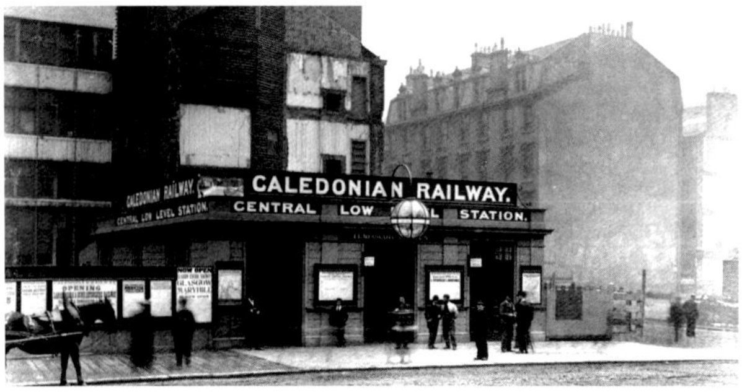

Temporary entrance to Low Level Station in Argyle Street.

Despite this grand public face, the Glasgow Central Railway (its original title) was not conceived purely as a passenger suburban line – it was a mixed traffic railway, because the Caledonian, which was behind its promotion, needed a route to the north bank for shipment and other traffic. Nevertheless, the line was laid out on exemplary principles for a modern suburban railway of high throughput: a high capacity central trunk ran through the heart of the city, the stations on it were evenly spaced at half-mile intervals, roots and branches fed and grew from that trunk, while the busiest station, Central Low Level, had facilities to be loading one train while another followed in and discharged. The entire design was well thought through and represented a major engineering triumph, with the tunnels created just above the level of the Clyde – a fact appreciated by the British Railways engineers who, when they came to add Argyle Street Station in 1979, needed to pressurise the workings in order to construct the new passenger subways at a lower level below the line.

Flooding was in fact not unknown during the closure of the Low Level line between 1964 and 1977, when the tracks had been lifted and the drains damaged. The most notable flood occurred, however, during the second incarnation of the route. Glasgow endured exceptional rainfall over two days in December 1994, which led to the overflowing waters of the River Kelvin entering the un-reopened section of tunnel at Kelvinbridge. They then flowed into the reopened route at Exhibition Centre (formerly Stobcross) and, at around 1800 on the evening of Saturday 10 December, marooned a train at Glasgow Central LL. Water rose nine feet above rail level, and halfway up the windows of the pair of Class 314 units forming the luckless train. Such extensive damage was done, that the route remained closed until 24 September 1995.

The four platform faces of the two islands were originally identified as A, B, C, D. On one island, A and B served eastbound traffic, while, on the other island, C and D served the westbound. The idea was that all trains serving particular routes should always use the same side of an island, so the waiting passengers could be automatically distributed into two groups on the appropriate sides. It may also have helped passengers with their whereabouts in the gloom. A hoist connected the platforms directly to the parcels department above. Despite being considered part of the overall Central Station, the Low Level station nevertheless enjoyed its own stationmaster and staff.

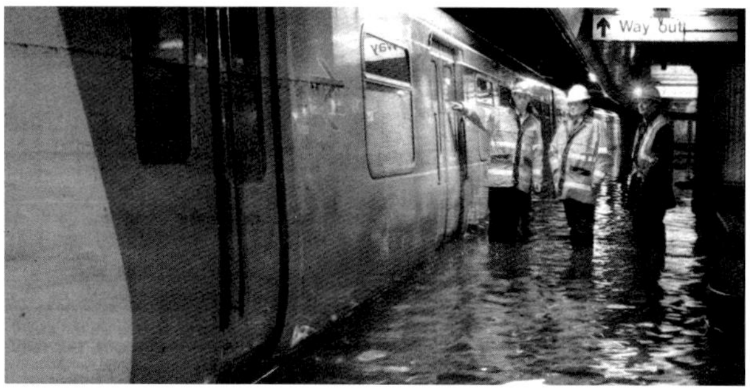

Engineers contemplate the tide mark as the waters subside.

In its heyday, 130 trains a day passed through Central Low Level, and were controlled by two signal boxes, designated East (14 levers) and West (15 levers). The passenger traffic pattern was always heavily orientated on getting people to and from work, so Saturday services looked very different from those from Monday to Friday. Fifty years ago, two core services existed: one from Dalmuir Riverside to Rutherglen, with several trains starting/terminating beyond these points, such as Balloch ; and one from Maryhill via Carmyle to Coatbridge, again with extensions. Saturday afternoon services were sparse, with the few westbound trains at 2.53 pm, 4.29 pm, 5.20 pm, finishing up with the 7.20 pm. By contrast, in the morning peak 11 trains arrived from the East, including services from Cumbernauld, Larkhall and one from Strathaven. A demonstration of how the trains met a specific commuting demand was the 0658 service from Bridgeton Cross, which ran, via Rutherglen, to Hillington and Paisley. There were no trains on Sundays.

Interesting as the Low Level station might have been, it was not a healthy, bracing place to be. Few passengers will have lamented its closure, but by October 1964 there were too few of them anyway to sustain the residual passenger service. Tracks were ripped out, and the station fell silent – but it was not forgotten. The Greater Glasgow

Transportation Survey established a role for the route, and it became part of the Clyderail proposals, developed ultimately by the Greater Glasgow Passenger Transport Executive and, on its behalf, built and operated by British Railways. At the east end of the route, beyond Bridgeton Cross, only one branch was to be re-opened, the choice falling on the direct link via Dalmarnock to Rutherglen, rather than on the leg via Carmyle and Newton. The latter was felt by some to have the potential merit of keeping the suburban service isolated from the proposed intensive occupation of the bottleneck on the main line by tilting Advanced Passenger Train, a conflict which did indeed develop with the enhanced frequency InterCity services, and remains today.

A new underground junction was envisaged at Bridgeton, linking the route to Central with the ex-North British route to Queen Street Low Level. Thus trains from the

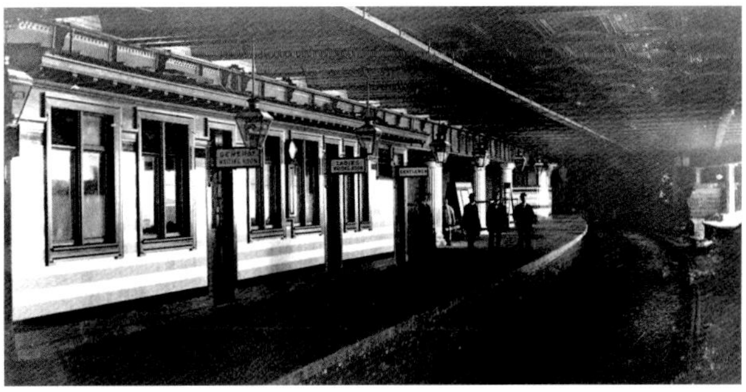

Early days of a pristine Low Level Station.

Rutherglen direction would be able to alternate between Central and Queen Street, as part of the plan to enhance public transport by offering a range of convenient city centre stations from variety of suburbs. A similar choice of routes to Queen St. LL or Central LL was envisaged from the west of the line. It too involved new construction, a link between Stobcross and a junction at Kelvinhaugh, and it did come into being. A siding was provided at Stobcross, not only as a useful turnback facility in case of trouble further west, but also as a potential terminating point for Cumbernauld services – a glint in the eye of some planners. Indeed, three trains an hour were to serve the (aborted) new town of Stonehouse. The Clyderail planners reckoned that, in the city centre, 89% of places of employment, and 98% of the retail space, would be within five minutes walk of a station.

In the event, the link at Bridgeton to the Queen Street line

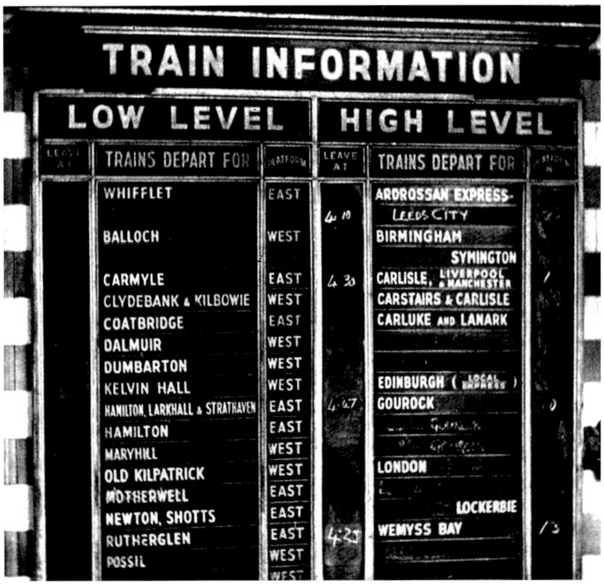

Central Low Level train indicator board.

was not authorised, and the Central Low Level line was reopened as "The Argyle Line". At Central Low Level station, the four platform faces were reduced to two for the new electric services, by elimination of the island on the north side. The platforms were now numbered as 14 and 15, in the High Level sequence, and escalators were installed from the High level station down to the circulating and booking office area at Argyle Street/Hope Street level, with a further set to the underground footbridge over the line, from which a staircase leads to the island platform. Access is available from both sides of Argyle Street, but a proposal to have an entrance on the west side of Hope Street was not adopted.

One objective, though not the main one, was to reduce the trains using the high level station, a far-sighted move, which released capacity to permit the introduction of new train services from the High Level station. The trains which were diverted to the reopened, electrified Argyle Line through the Low Level, were those of the Hamilton Circle and Lanark lines in their entirety, which had been electrified from 6 May 1974. West of the new Kelvinhaugh Jn., this Lanarkshire service was integrated with the existing North Electric services, and created a regular pattern of trains every 10 minutes. One of these paths was for a fast Lanark service, which succumbed after some years to an economy drive, resulting in a lopsided timetable with an awkward 20-minute gap. This was not rectified through the core of the route until the Larkhall line was reopened in December 2005 and directed into the Argyle Line.

The Argyle Line remains an important route, and one capable of enhancement to play an even more significant role. It is today therefore a far cry from that described so memorably by the artist/poet C. Hamilton Ellis, who wrote in the "The Railway Magazine" of January 1938:

Sombre, sulphurous and Plutonian the line may be, but to a good railwayist, to anyone, in fact, who can appreciate fine engineering, it is a most fascinating place. The locomotives which work on it do not condense, a fact which increases the Miltonesque effect of their exits and entrances. There is something very stimulating even, in the sensation of climbing into one of a long row of lighted compartments in the midst of a dim haze, and moving off, with the steamy windows tightly shut, into a darkness more profound, to the accompaniment of a deep, thudding exhaust. Heroics apart, the Glasgow Central is a notable line.

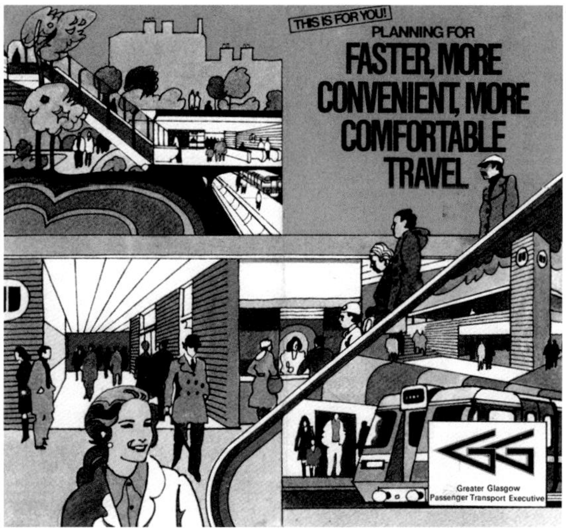

ClydeRail is presented to the public in the early 1970s.

14 Trial by heat and water

Ian Hetherwick

On first entering the Central a prospective passenger must be impressed with the scale of the structure and the 15-acre of glazing in roof above him. Yet the Civil Engineers charged with its construction and on-going maintenance have had to confront and solve challenges largely unknown to the citizens of Glasgow

At the time of the third extension, built towards the West as far as Oswald Street, obtaining foundations to the upper and low-level stations gave rise to considerable difficulties for the engineers, when water-laden running sand of considerable depth was encountered. The problem was resolved by the ingenuity of the eminent engineer of the day—Charles Forman, M Inst C E. His solution was to have large timber boards, butted together and driven to approx 30 ft. below ground level of Argyle Street, extending the length of tunnel and foundation works. Other boards, to form a grid pattern like a chessboard, subdivided the area between these piles where construction was to be undertaken. Excavation and de-watering could then be undertaken to the required depth and stone block foundations laid. Every second bay was treated in a similar manner, thereby not allowing the running sand to escape into the excavations and undermine adjacent structures

Few citizens and passengers will be aware that the renewal and new construction of miles of sewers, ranging from small domestic pipes to 5ft trunk sewers, was undertaken at the same time as the works described above. This huge undertaking was a result of the new tunnel, below Argyle St and the station extension, severing sewers in central Glasgow which had previously been laid to discharge directly into the polluted River Clyde. The rerouting of sewage to pumping stations at Partick and Dalmarnock was therefore responsible for a major improvement in the cleanliness of the River Clyde, albeit at considerable cost to the railway company

In modern times, engineers have had to act quickly to ensure safety – such as during the 1966 heatwave when, after several days of exceptional heat, the rails on the bridge over the Clyde could barely be touched. The rails, and the steel bridge below them, retained the heat, and the resulting temperature rose to some 20 degrees more than the passengers were experiencing. All expansion joints had closed up, so a quick solution was required to prevent buckling and jamming of moveable fittings. Tons of ice were acquired and packed round the rails which gave an unorthodox but effective solution!

Yet another near-disaster was avoided, after the resident plumber reported a hole in the floor of a vacant shop below the station, at the Argyle St level. An exploratory shaft was sunk some 15 feet deep; and further shafts had to be sunk in five adjacent shops, all of which showed indications of voids in the sandy material excavated. The question arose as to where the missing sand had gone, and whether the station above was itself in danger. A chance report, that surveyors working on a nearby construction site were having difficulty in establishing a stable bench- mark, made the local railway engineer recall that a similar problem had arisen in London when the London bridge was being dismantled prior to shipment to America. On that occasion, ground adjacent to the Thames was swelling and rising on each change of tide.

So investigations were put in hand, and it was found that water level in the Clyde, when at high tide, was similar to the rail level in the Argyle St tunnel. Further investigations in manholes in the tunnel found a small pipe below the concreted floor of the tunnel. Water issuing from this pipe was fed into the large 15 inch diameter pumps, which raise the water to ground level and carry it to "the cleanest sewer in the town". For over 100 years this small pipe had been leaching sand and creating voids behind the tunnel wall. Heavy expenditure had been incurred in excavation and back-filling whereas the solution was simply the provision of a bend and a short vertical length of pipe to raise the outlet above High Water Level in the Clyde!

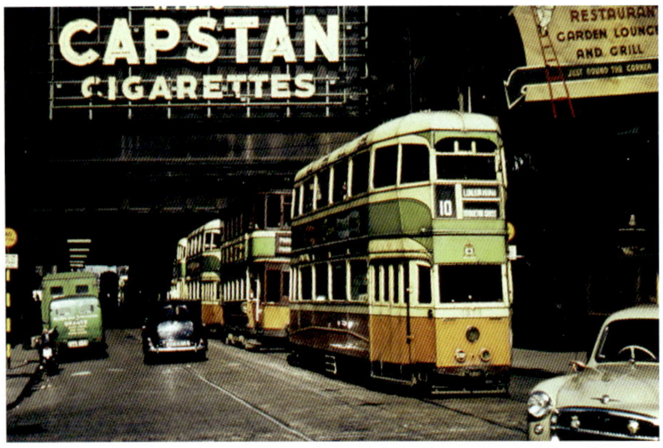

A selection of 'Glesca Caurs' emerging from the Hielandman's Umbrella – it was a continuing source of free shelter to Glaswegians as well as those who came from the 'Hielans'. The shops which lined Argyle Street were above water level.

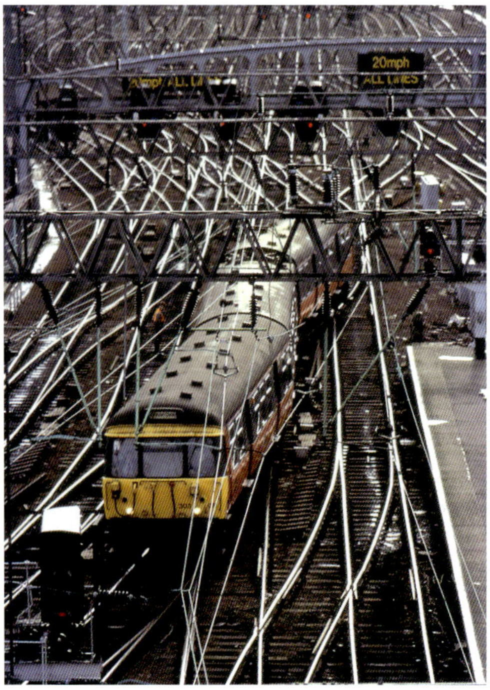

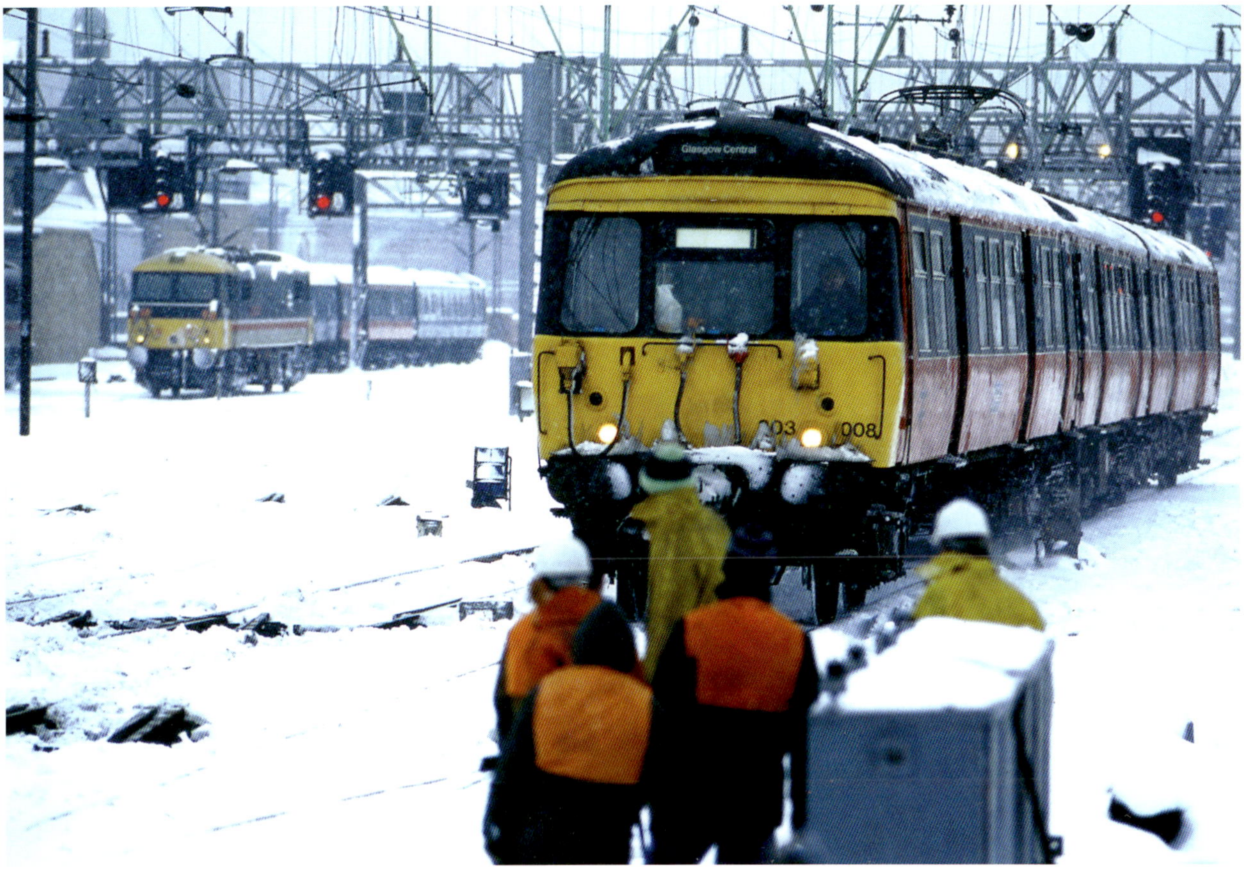

In all weathers!

Central at work

A Class "318" driver's view on approaching at night.

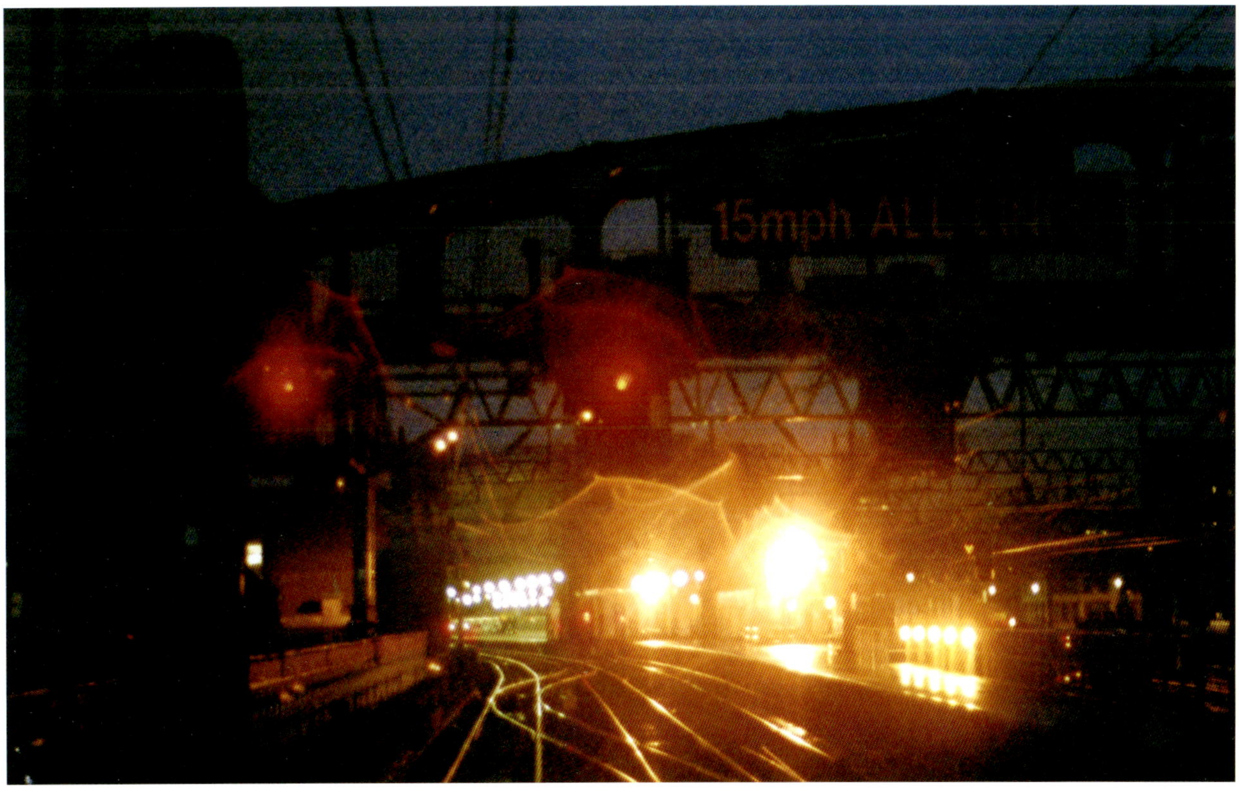

15 Going out and coming in

Alan Mackie

When Glasgow Central station was opened in 1879, it comprised four lines and eight platforms and was approached by a four-track bridge over the River Clyde. Little is known about the operation of this station today; but it can be surmised that, besides the scheduled passenger train movements to the Glasgow – Paisley Joint Line, and the Clydesdale railways, including the Caledonian main line itself and all its branches, there would have been a considerable amount of light engine and empty coaching stock working to and from the locomotive and carriage sheds at Polmadie and Larkfield. Indeed, it is known that there was considerable congestion in this area, which resulted in the creation of Eglinton Street depot to reduce the number of movements to and from the much larger sheds at Polmadie.

The expansion undertaken between 1900 and 1906 was aimed at more capacity, resulting in a total of 13 platforms and eight approach tracks. Not so immediately obvious perhaps was the significant flexibility introduced by many additional crossovers, giving the facility for simultaneous parallel movements. The new layout also provided a number of sidings on the site of the former Bridge Street station, between the Clyde bridges and Bridge Street Jn., and these allowed the stabling of any locomotives or coaching stock which did not require to go to depots for servicing between workings.

Most of the pairs of platforms were provided with crossovers at the buffer-stop ends for engine release, (and some platforms had crossovers at the top of the platform as well), to allow incoming locomotives to run round their trains. However, these were not provided between platforms 6 and 7 (the Cathcart Circle platforms), which instead were provided with connections to an engine spur in the middle of the layout. This enabled the locomotive of an incoming train to be detached at the buffers, while a second locomotive, stabled in the engine spur, would be attached at the country end and subsequently work the train away. The original locomotive at the buffers would then run into the engine spur and await the next incoming train, when the same series of manoeuvres would be performed again.

In the case of long-distance trains, the empty coaching stock for departures would be worked in from Larkfield carriage sheds with a pilot engine at each end, stopping short of the Clyde bridges to enable the leading engine to be detached and run off into an empty platform (or sometimes even on top of a train already in a platform). This allowed the rear pilot engine to propel the coaches into their planned departure platform. The pilot engine would then be detached and run off, allowing the train engine (usually from Polmadie) to be attached on the front for the journey south.

Impact of multiple units

This form of working remained relatively unchanged for many years, continuing through the Second World War and into nationalisation. The first significant change came in 1959, with the introduction of the first generation of diesel multiple unit trains, initially to some of the Lanarkshire services. The arrival of these units, based principally at a new DMU depot at Hamilton West (created from the former steam shed) significantly reduced the number of light engine movements around Central station and made the working much easier.

A further, more drastic, change came on 3 October 1960, with the modernisation of the signalling, both in the station and in the station yard area out as far as Eglinton Street, and the associated commissioning of the new Glasgow Central signal box. Despite its name, this was located at Bridge Street Jn. in the "vee" between the main lines and the Ayr/Gourock lines. At the time of its commissioning, this installation by Westinghouse was the largest route relay interlocking in the world, although it did not hold this honour for long. Controlled by a One Control Switch (OCS) control panel on the top floor of the new building, it required four Signalmen to operate it, but allowed the elimination of the signal boxes at Glasgow Central, Bridge Street Jn., Eglinton Street Jn. and Eglinton Street Station. Significantly, it allowed the removal of the original Clyde bridge, as the new signalling provided bi-directional working over the tracks of the "new" bridge of 1906, as well as over a number of lines out as far as Eglinton Street Jn. Moreover, it brought the benefits of co-ordinated control of the entire area.

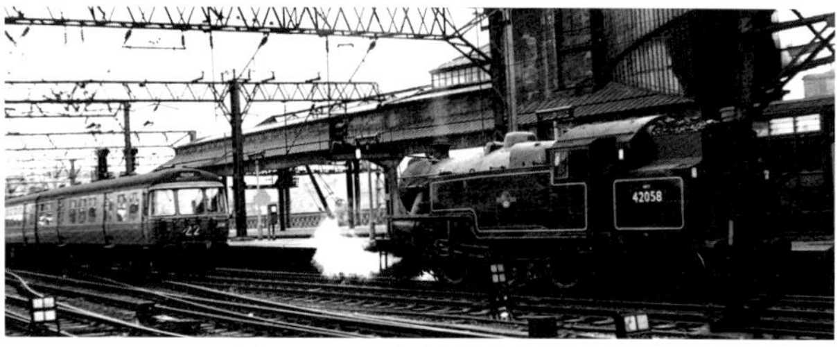

The new and the old – 1964.

The re-signalling heralded the introduction of electric traction on the Cathcart Circle, Neilston and Kirkhill lines. For the new services, wiring was installed on: Lines No. 1 Down, 3, 4, 5 and 6; Lines W, X, Y and Z on the Clyde bridge; and Platforms 6 to 11, as well as the Centre sidings, Engine Loop and No.7 Carriage siding. The two running lines on the Paisley route were also wired, as far as Cook Street, together with certain parts of Smithy Lye carriage sidings, where the new electric trains were to be stabled. Again, the use of electric multiple unit trains reduced the number of light engine movements in the

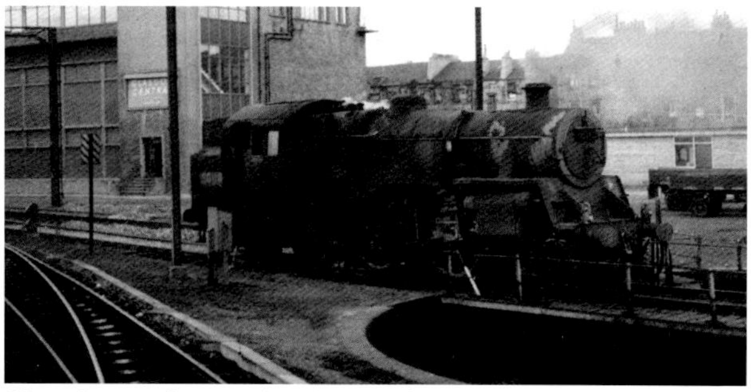
Use of steam locomotives involved much to-ing and fro-ing for servicing and turning such as at Cook Street.

station and, as the new trains were stabled either in the Centre Sidings between the Clyde Bridge and Bridge Street Jn. or at Smithy Lye, the number of empty stock workings was also reduced.

In parallel with all these changes, steam traction was gradually superseded by main line diesel locomotives on the one significant group of services still loco-hauled – the Anglo-Scottish expresses to London and the other English destinations. After 136 years, steam traction on the Scottish Region of British Railways ended on Friday 28 April 1967, with the arrival at 1807 of the 1703 from Gourock, hauled by Fairburn tank 42274. The locomotive then propelled its train out to Smithy Lye sidings, which now lie redundant in a railway operated today almost completely by multiple units.

Elbow room

The capacity of the station had been gradually increased by all these changes and there began to be room to spare. A key policy of the Beeching era – not always achieved – was to have only a single terminal in each major city. In Glasgow, practicalities dictated that two of the four main terminals would remain. On the south side, it was considered that there was now sufficient spare capacity at Central to accommodate the former G&SW traffic currently at St. Enoch. Accordingly, a new connection was formed at Shields Jn. to divert the Canal lines to a new junction with the "Joint" lines to/from Paisley Gilmour Street; and a new NX panel (Panel 5) in Glasgow Central signalbox took over control of the area between Cook Street and Hillington. The alterations at Shields Jn. allowed the transfer of the services operating out of St. Enoch to be transferred to Central on 7 June 1966, resulting in a significant increase in traffic in Central station. In particular, the two tracks (Branch 1 and Branch 2) between Bridge Street Jn. and Shields Jn.) became a very busy section of railway, and this has continued to this day.

One noticeable change in the station however, was the removal of the three loading bank sidings at the top of platform 11 and the creation of a new platform 11A. This

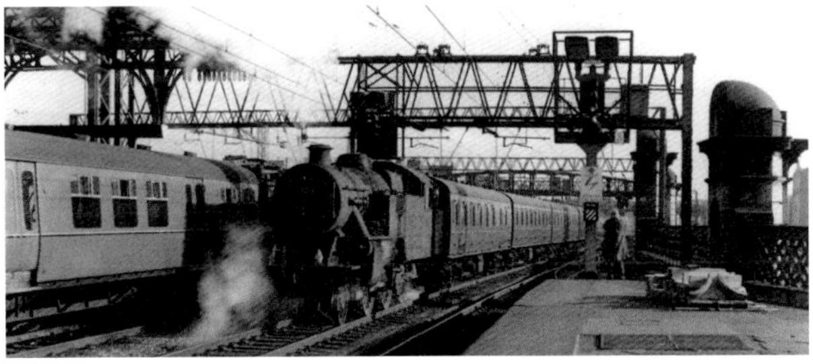

Steam bows out! 28 April 1967 saw the end of steam passenger working by BR Scottish Region. No. 42274 backs out of Central after bringing in the 1703 from Gourock.

new platform, wired for electric traction and capable of holding a six-car electric set, was provided as an emergency facility, should the station become congested for any reason, and was not initially intended for regular use on account of its extended walking distance from the main concourse. An enhanced role is envisaged with the proposed Airport link.

All of this was a prelude to the inauguration of electric traction on the South Bank of the River Clyde, and in October 1967 the services to Gourock and Wemyss Bay were taken over by three-car electric multiple unit trains of Class 311. The removal of the Canal lines at Pollokshields had also created space for a new depot (Shields Depot), which opened in 1967 to service all the electric rolling stock located south of the river. Previously, sets requiring other than basic day-to-day maintenance had been hauled by a locomotive across the City Union lines to Hyndland depot on the north bank. Cleaning and stabling of the electric sets continued to be carried out at Smithy Lye. The new connection at Shields Jn. also gave access to extensive sidings at Bellahouston, where the "Swindon" Intercity DMUs operating the Glasgow/Ayr/Stranraer services were cleaned and stabled, as well as to Corkerhill depot, which provided mechanical servicing for the units operating the other services transferred from St. Enoch. This further expansion of electrified working also saw Platforms 12 and 13, together with No.8 Loop and No.8 Loop Siding being wired, together with the remaining sidings at Smithy Lye.

There were no significant changes over the next few years, save for the removal of a number of under-utilised connections outside the station, and the replacement of a number of diamond crossings by tandem crossovers in the interests of simplifying track maintenance, since it reduced the number of custom-built components in favour of "off the shelf" items. This work culminated in 1972 with the replacement of the 1961 OCS control panel in the signal box by a NX style Henry Williams/ Integra domino control panel. This was significantly smaller, and released space, which was immediately utilised for two new panels of similar type to control the area south to Cambuslang, as part of the forthcoming scheme of route modernisation and electrification for the West Coast Main Line. As part of this scheme, Line 1 Down, as between Eglinton St and Bridge St., and Line 1 Up from Clyde Bridge to Eglinton St. plus Nos. 2 and 3 Carriage Loops in the station area were wired, along with the remaining un-wired Platforms Nos. 1 to 5.

The inauguration of electric traction between Weaver Jn. and Glasgow Central saw the commencement of public electrically hauled services on 6 May 1974, most trains being formed of new Mark II rolling stock and hauled by electric locomotives. Initially, the train sets working these services were hauled by diesel pilot locomotives out to Larkfield for servicing, but soon pressures to increase utilisation resulted in most incoming trains being turned around in the station to form outwards services. The electric locomotives, after being released by the removal of the inbound coaching stock, were generally stabled in Nos. 2 and 3 Carriage Sidings, but often were simply transferred to outbound departures, so that it was not uncommon for a locomotive to be southbound again in an hour or less after its arrival in Glasgow. Indeed, it soon became nothing unusual for an individual locomotive to have been twice to London in little over 24 hours, a far cry from utilisation in steam days.

The universal use of diesel and electric traction for locomotive-hauled trains soon led to the elimination of steam heating. From 1906 there had been facilities for heating sets of coaches stabled in the station platforms without being attached to a locomotive. This was achieved by steam connections, provided at the buffer stops of all except the suburban platforms, fed from a boiler plant at the top of Platform 13. In earlier days the plant had a very short siding (No.14) for delivery of coal for the plant, which also provided heating and hot water for the Central Hotel. Latterly, this plant had been converted to oil firing and the siding was removed in the late 1960s. With the advent of WCML electrification, the steam heating facilities at the buffer stops were discontinued and electric "shore" supplies were provided at the platforms used by main line stock. The electricity supply was taken from the 25 kV overhead line equipment by means of a transformer at the bottom of Platforms 7/8.

At the same time as the inauguration of the WCML electric services, electrification of the Hamilton Circle line, both via Blantyre and Bellshill, together with the Lanark branch took place. Over the years, the rolling stock diagrams on the Cathcart Circle and South Bank service groups had been tightened up to the extent that it was possible to replace the DMU fleet currently operating the Lanarkshire services by surplus class 303 and 311 units. This meant that the platforms on the east side of the station became very intensively used indeed, as the Hamilton Circle service was given a half hourly frequency in both directions and an hourly service ran to Lanark via the West Coast Main Line.

It had also become apparent that the existing main line carriage servicing facility at Larkfield was inadequate for the standards of servicing required on a modern Inter-City operation, with rolling stock now having increasingly sophisticated electrical equipment on board, such as air conditioning. Steam traction had ceased to operate at Polmadie from May 1967, and a very considerable reduction had taken place in the main line diesel fleet at Polmadie with the change to electric traction, so the freight loco fleet, which had remained at the depot, was transferred to Motherwell. That part of the site formerly occupied by the main running shed was cleared and a new purpose-built Carriage Servicing Depot was created there, with three reception tracks, a carriage washing plant, a shed with six through tracks (each capable of holding a full- length train set), and four departure tracks. Most of the track in the depot was wired for electric traction. On the depot being commissioned in 1977, the depot at Larkfield was closed.

Routing the trains

Signallers are skilled decision-makers. In the most modern signalling centres, they are assisted by computers, which can evaluate the optimum order of precedence of trains through complex junction areas in an Automatic Route Setting system. The pioneering installation, known as Junction Optimisation Technique (JOT), was tried out in the busy Glasgow Central area in the 1970s. In due course it had to learn that trains with passengers holding the experimental tickets under the "stored journey scheme" needed to be routed into platforms equipped with electronic turnstiles, in the interests of preserving revenue.

What was probably the busiest period for traffic in the life of Central station (1974-1979) came to an end on 5 November 1979, with the re-opening of Glasgow Central Low Level and the diversion of the Lanarkshire electric services to the Argyle lines which served it. This made significant capacity available once again on the east side of the station. A further slight reduction in use of Central station took place on 10 January 1983, when services to Kilmacolm on the Canal line were withdrawn. Some of the slack capacity at Central was later taken up again, by the reinstatement of that Canal line as far as Paisley, by the re-opening of the Rutherglen-Coatbridge line (the R&C) to passenger traffic on 4 October 1993, and by increased Anglo-Scottish services.

On 29 September 1986 electrification was extended from Paisley to Ayr, Ardrossan and Largs. Corkerhill depot, which had maintained the sadly-ageing fleet of "Swindon" diesel multiple units, was converted fully to a Carriage Servicing Depot, involving complete modernisation, part re-building, and provision of a new track layout. The new tracks were equipped for electric

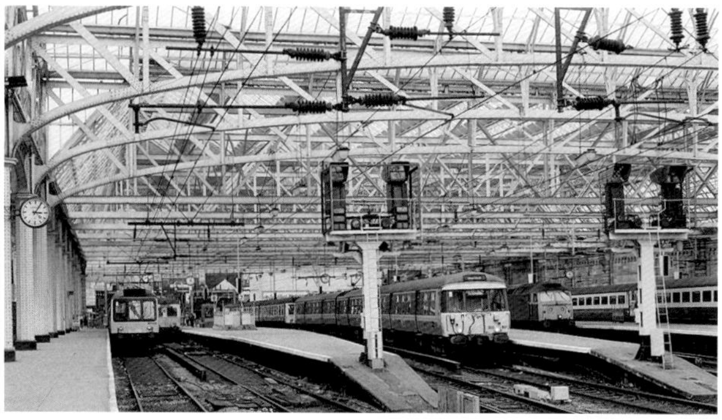

June 1986 with DMUs, 'Blue Train' and Class 47.

traction, and the task of cleaning electric multiple units was transferred from Shields Depot to Corkerhill, which in addition retains its ability to service and refuel diesel sets for the East Kilbride, GB&K/G&SW and Glasgow/Whifflet services).

Over the years, many of the "traditional" activities at Glasgow Central have fallen victim to changing trends and modern practices. There was always a fair amount of shunting of parcels vans, strengthening coaches etc. which was carried out by the station pilots, of which there were usually at least three at all times. Gradually, the need for these facilities diminished, resulting in the disappearance of the short sidings at the top of Platform 11. The trend towards fixed-formation trains, and the practice of turn-rounds in the station, led to the reduction of the numbers of station pilot engines and shunting staff. Their total elimination in the mid-1990s was made possible by the introduction of push-pull working on WCML services to London, and the replacement of locomotive-hauled trains on Anglo-Scottish Cross Country services by Class 254 High Speed Trains ("InterCity 125").

The ever-changing operational scene at Glasgow Central saw the arrival of the sleek nine-car class 391 "Pendolino" electric sets in 2004 and of the Class 220/221 four and five-car "Voyager" high speed DMUs. The continued squeezing of the Class 318 EMU fleet for greater utilisation enabled them to replace the familiar old "Blue Trains", the Class 303/311 EMU fleet, from most of the South Bank services. The final nail in the coffin of the "Blue Trains" was the advent of the Class 334 "Juniper" EMUs – though only after a long period of "teething troubles". The "Junipers" also had the effect of elevating the Class 314 trains from the Low Level and its Lanarkshire services up to the High Level and its Cathcart Circle and Neilston lines.

The trains and operations at Central never stay the same for long!

16 Of PLA and TBCF – Glasgow Central Parcels

W Stuart Sellar

When the crowds flowed through the Central at Glasgow Fair, much of their luggage was already on its way under the Passengers Luggage in Advance (PLA) arrangements by the railway. This aspect was handled by the Parcels Department, and "Parcels" was far from a seasonal trade. All year long, and largely hidden from view, Central handled the parcels traffic, which was essential to the vitality of the city. "Parcels" was part of an activity known within the railway as "coaching traffic", and this also embraced milk, newspapers, mails, scenery for theatrical shows, and sometimes even circuses.

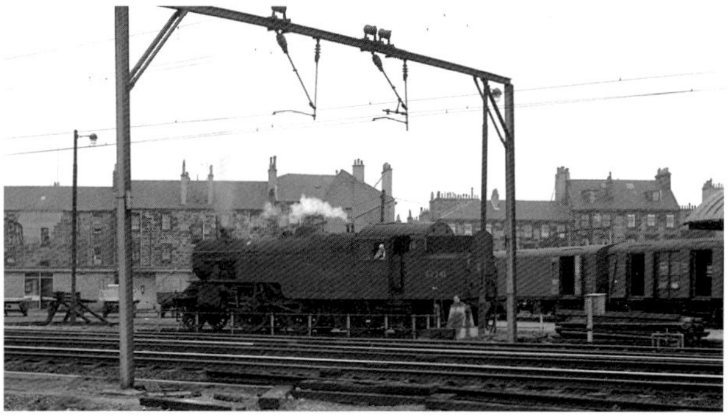

Parcel trailers and rail vans form a backdrop to an engine on the Cook Street turntable.

Prior to the Fair Saturday of 1959, horses and carts, and subsequently articulated "mechanical horses" and trailers, had negotiated the narrow entrance to and from Central station in Hope Street. Access to and from the platform level was then via hoists. The GPO parcel and letter mails shared these access and hoist facilities. Behind the Hope Street level, the handling areas could only be described as cavernous, with most of the handling and sorting activities being situated within the arches supporting the platforms above. Not only parcels were located within the bowels of the station: there too were the Lost Property stores, and temporary storage for odd things like safes.

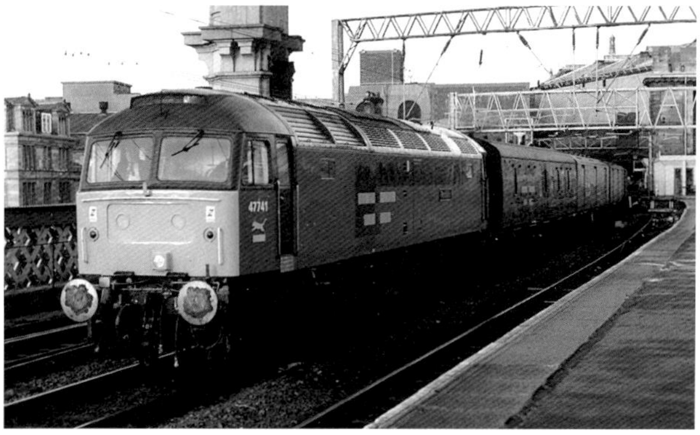

Class "47" No. 47741 "Resilient" on the 1410 Parcels/Mail train - 15 November 1994.

Much of this activity ended on that Fair Saturday, for the handling of all forwarded and delivered parcels, as well as "To Be Called For" traffic, was then transferred to Glasgow Parcels Station, situated in Salkeld Street and originally the Eglinton Street Goods Depot built by the G & S W Railway. Parcels "forwarded" and "delivered" traffic was transferred from Queen St, Buchanan St. and St. Enoch at the same time to the new concentration point.

Until the inauguration of the Glasgow Parcels Station, rail vehicles containing full loads of "coaching traffic", such as milk and newspapers (as well as GPO letter and parcel mail traffic), were handled at Glasgow Central, usually in platform 11A. The GPO Parcel Mail element was transferred to the Parcels Station, but the letter mail and newspapers remained at Central for a while longer. As BR developed its InterCity network, the use of passenger trains to convey high-value parcels at high speed emerged as a valuable service. This specialised segment of the parcels business was marketed as "Red Star", and a public office was established at Central to deal with it, until it was privatised, finishing in 1995.

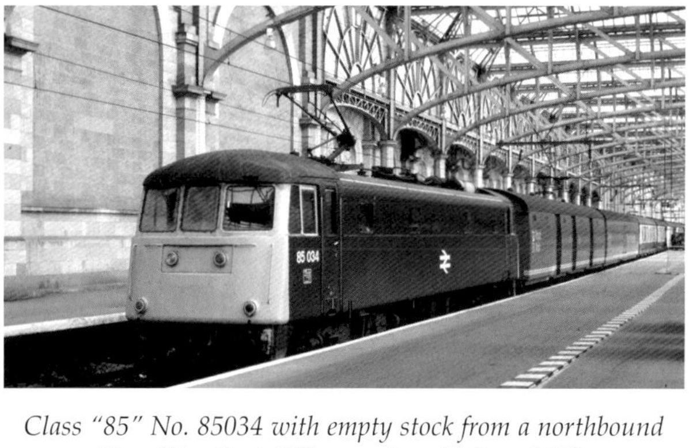

Class "85" No. 85034 with empty stock from a northbound Travelling Post Office service - 30 June 1989.

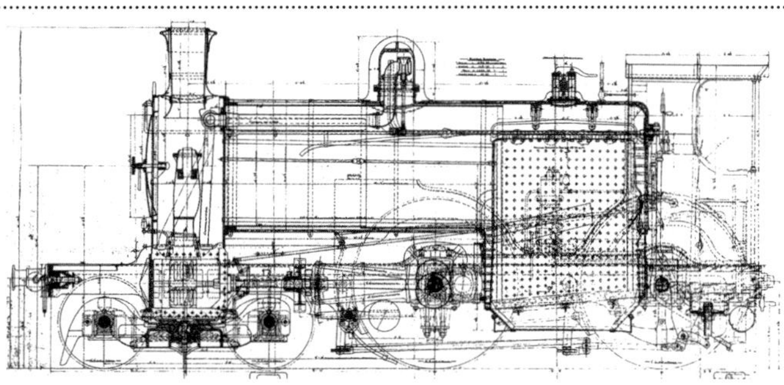

Part of a general arrangement drawing of a Caledonian Railway "Dunalastair" 4-4-0. An elegant reminder of the days when locomotives were designed and built in Glasgow.

17 Signal box with a view

Robin Nelson

The plan by the Caledonian Railway to enlarge Glasgow Central would create one of the largest stations in the country. In America, however, a station the size of Glasgow Central would have been reckoned a modest affair. A rapid increase in the population of the USA had resulted in many small towns becoming large cities. Rail transport was the principal means of transport and, to cater for the volume of passenger traffic, city-centre terminals of impressive dimensions were constructed. St Louis had a train shed that covered thirty-two platforms; sixteen pairs of

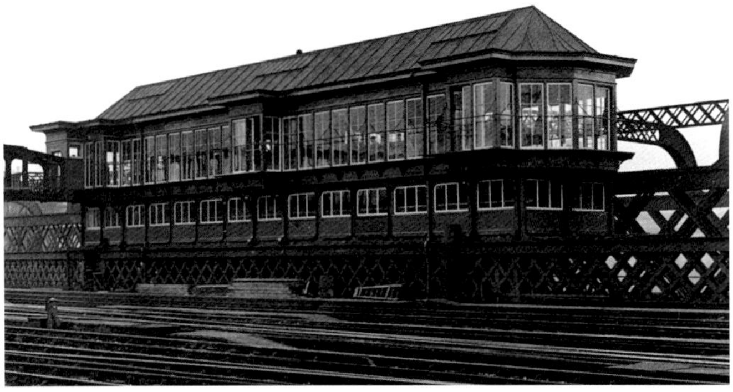

Exterior of Glasgow Central Signal Box as built in 1908.

approach lines were needed to cope with the train service; and the signalling system was equally impressive.

Railway signal engineering practice in Britain differed from American practice in many respects. By 1900, all lines in Britain had been equipped with mechanical signalling. Semaphore signal arms and point blades were operated by levers, and levers required strong men. Little effort was needed to lower a signal arm, but point blade movement really did need muscles. Signal boxes came in all sizes, with the smallest having less than ten levers, whereas a main line station box could have over two hundred levers. The first signal box at Glasgow Central was constructed on the east side of the station, above the present-day Midland Street bridge. The box, which was commissioned in 1889, had 167 levers, yet was by no means the longest lever frame in Britain. York Yard South signal box had 295 levers and Edinburgh Waverley West had 290 levers. In America, in contrast, power signalling systems were essential for major terminals. Power, of course, eliminated the physical labour of signalmen and significantly extended the control range of a signal box. A set of points could be upwards of a mile from the signal box compared with the 300 yards limit on mechanically-operated points. With power, one signal box structure would suffice for the control of large and complex layouts.

George Westinghouse, an American engineer made power-operated signalling possible, and his methods were eventually to be applied world-wide. He was born in New York State in 1846 into a family of agricultural engineers. After military service in the American civil war, he set up his own engineering business in Pittsburgh. He had that rare combination of a flair for innovation, engineering ability and an astute business mind. Problems were there to be solved and to make money in the process. Westinghouse is best remembered for his eponymous automatic air braking system for trains, which he patented in 1869. Following that, he turned his attention to the complexities of signalling trains at large stations. If the power of compressed air could stop a train by the simple act of turning a small handle, then surely the same idea could be applied to points and signals.

Thus inspired, Westinghouse set up the Union Switch and Signal Company in Pittsburgh in 1881 for the design and manufacture of the components of a pneumatic power

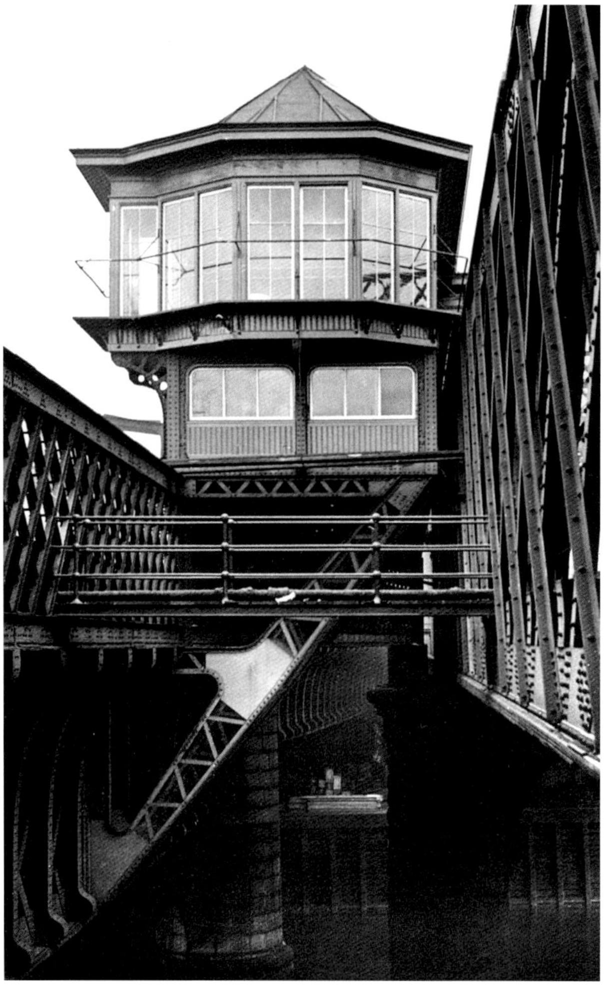

The Signal Box between the tracks cantilevered from the new bridge. Stone piers from the old and new bridges can be seen emerging from the River Clyde.

signalling system. He developed a compact interlocking machine that was controlled by small handles. Movement of the handles opened valves, which admitted air to a pipe leading directly from the interlocking machine to the trackside. Small cylinders were fitted to the point blades and to the signal arms. Compressed air from the signal box provided the driving force to move the points and signal arms. The system was known as the "low pressure pneumatic signalling. In 1892, the Union Switch and Signal Company introduced the "Electro-pneumatic" system, better known as EP. This had electrical circuits to link the control handles in the signal box with the points and signals. Electric cables are easier to install and maintain than the piping for compressed air. An electrically controlled valve at each set of points and each signal arm controlled the admission of air at high pressure to the operating cylinder.

Mechanical Britain

By 1900, there were some 150 power operated signalling systems controlling the major passenger stations in the USA. In Britain there were but two examples, both of which controlled freight-only lines. The British were a cautious lot. However, attitudes changed in the first years of the 20th century. Railways were a growth industry, both in passenger and freight. Larger stations and freight yards along with connecting lines were required and – as American engineers had realised twenty years before – mechanical signalling was not up to the task. There was little on offer in the British railway signal engineering industry, and hence attention turned to America.

In England, the Great Central Railway and the London and South Western Railway opted for Westinghouse low-pressure all-air systems. In London, the District and Metropolitan lines selected the Westinghouse EP system, as did the North Eastern Railway for the Tyneside area. The London and North Western Railway was one of the few companies to have in-house signalling capability, and their engineers designed an all-electric system with small electric motors to drive points and operate signal arms. Sykes, a British company, developed a part mechanical, part electrical system with their first customer being the Glasgow and South Western Railway at St Enoch in 1902.

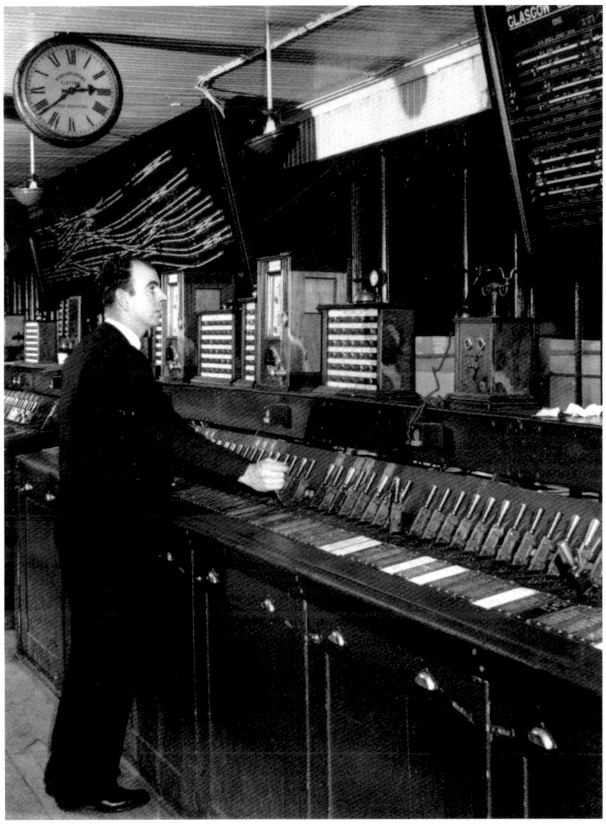

Internal view of the Box with block instruments above the long row of miniature levers. Track diagrams are mounted above and on the roof.

The Directors of the Caledonian Railway wished to take advantage of these developments, but needed to be better informed before making a decision on which of the available systems would best suit the circumstances of the new station at Glasgow Central. There was no in-house capacity to design and install a signalling system of this magnitude, and a contract would have to be placed for the work. It was decided that the signal contractors should be invited to demonstrate their products. Unfortunately, no records of the process have survived but it seems that the low-pressure pneumatic, the electro-pneumatic, the electro-mechanical and the LNWR all electric systems were assessed. The outcome was a contract to Messrs McKenzie & Holland for the design, manufacture and installation of a Westinghouse EP system.

McKenzie & Holland was a Worcester–based signal engineering company with a world-wide reputation for mechanical signalling systems. In 1895, the company entered into an agreement with the Westinghouse Brake and Signal Company in London to market and install Union Switch and Signal power equipment in the UK. McKenzie & Holland had experience of the EP system, with installations at Bolton and Newcastle and, shortly after being awarded the Glasgow Central contract, the company combined with Westinghouse to become the McKenzie, Holland & Westinghouse Power Signalling Company.

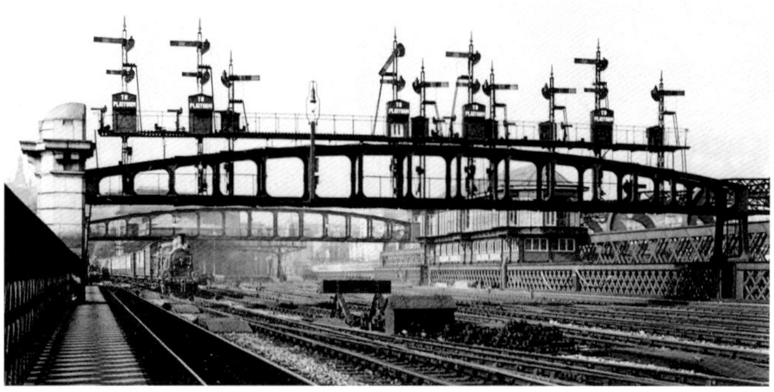

Looking into Central over the new bridge. A is train signalled from track 4 into Platform 11 while the train departing from Platform 12 is to stop.

An operating frame of 374 levers was required to control the track layout from the platforms to the neighbouring signal box at Bridge Street Junction. Even with miniature levers at two-inch spacing, the internal dimensions of the signal box would be 106 feet in length and 16 feet in width. Locating the structure was an engineering challenge, as it would have to be mounted in a position which enabled the signalmen to observe all train movements from the windows. This requirement arose because, in common with other railways in Britain, the Caledonian was reluctant to adopt the electrical track circuit as a means of indicating train positions to the signalmen on an illuminated diagram in the signal box.

Signalling over water

No vacant land of this size was available, but an ingenious solution was found by having the signal box span the space between the original four-track bridge over the Clyde and the new six-line bridge. To provide the height necessary for visibility of the track, the front of the signal box rested on the eastern parapet girder of the new bridge. Fifteen cantilevered girders, bolted to the parapet, formed the foundation of the signal box. Additional support was provided at the north end by a girder between the old and new bridges and, at the south end, by a girder inclined at forty-five degrees from the lower side

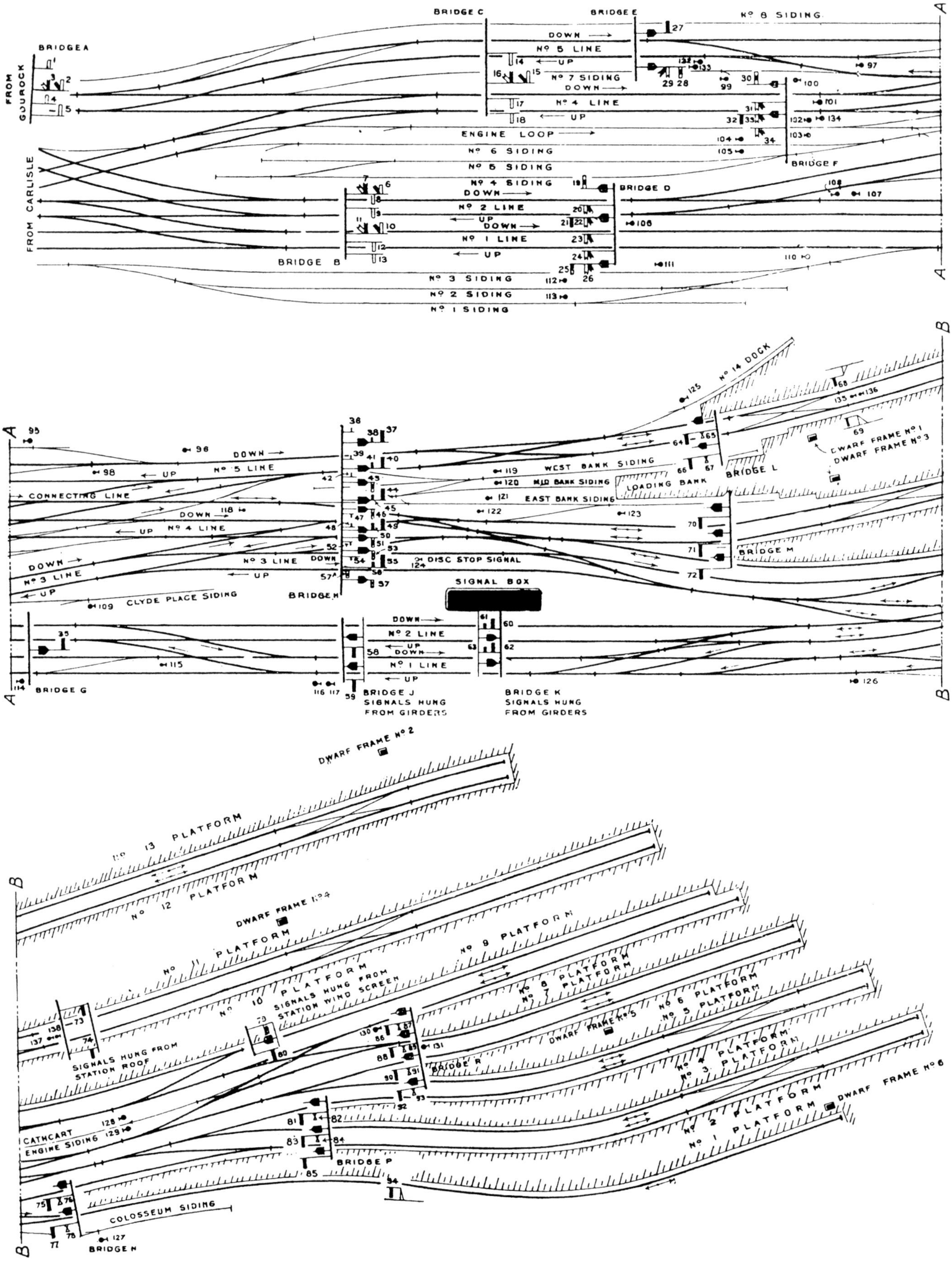

Glasgow Central track and signaling layout with old and new bridges.

of the girder of new bridge. The operating floor was constructed on top of the equipment room. There were 337 operational levers, of which 258 controlled the signals and 79 controlled the points. The remainder were spare, many of which were used in later years for enhancements to the signalling. Floor-to-ceiling windows along all four walls, combined with a hipped roof, created a building which blended with the surroundings. It was generally similar in design to the architecture of the station and was a larger version of a standard style then appearing at other major station rebuilding projects, such as those at Gleneagles and Eglinton Street.

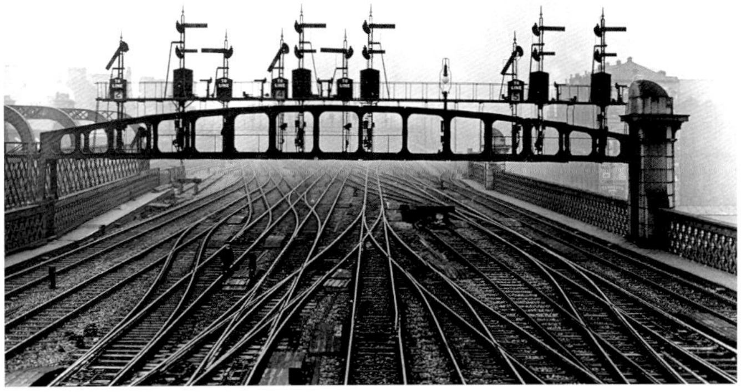

Looking south over the new bridge with the line indicator boxes clearly seen below the various signal arms. Trains are signalled to lines 4 and 5 but that to line 2 is for a calling-on or shunting operation shown by the small arm within the structure of the gantry.

Since there was no room for conventional signal posts, five signal bridges, which spanned the tracks, were installed to carry short posts, to which the lower quadrant semaphore signal arms were fitted. Where more than one route was available to a train beyond the protecting signal, British practice had been to provide a separate signal arm for each of the routes. It was a cumbersome and potentially confusing way of providing a driver with information, and created design difficulties. The problem was solved at Glasgow Central by the provision of a route indicator at signals where there was more than one route. For example, if a train were signalled into Platform 13, the figure 13 would appear in the indicator box. Signal posts which carried the signal arms for the lines into the platforms also carried an additional signal arm. This arm was shorter in length, and its purpose was to indicate to the driver that there was already a train occupying the platform, and therefore it would be necessary to reduce speed to be able to stop short of the front of this train. The full-length upper arm, when lowered, indicated the line was clear right to the buffer stops.

At night, coloured spectacle glasses in front of low power lamps indicated red when the signal arm was in the horizontal position and green when the arm was lowered to the proceed indication. Unusually for Britain, the small ground mounted signals provided for shunting purposes displayed violet for the night-time stop indication. Depression bars were fitted to the point blades, to prevent the points being moved when a train was running over them. The wheel flanges pushed the bar down, this movement making up an electrical circuit that locked the points lever in the signal box. It was an unsatisfactory method, and over the following years, track circuits were installed to lock the signalling and to indicate the presence of trains to the signalmen.

Four signalmen were required on each shift to control train movements, each signalman being allocated to one of the four "line pairs" to Bridge Street Junction signal box. No. 1 and no. 2 pairs crossed the river on the original four-track bridge. No 4 and no 5 pairs were on the new bridge, enabling trains to and from the Shields direction to be able to run in parallel with trains to and from the Eglinton Street direction. Each pair of lines operated as an up line and as a down line under absolute block working regulations. No. 3 pair gave access from no. 2, on the old bridge, to no. 4 pair on the new. The interlocking frame was subdivided into four sections. The levers at the southern end of the frame controlled no. 5 line pair, the next section controlled no. 4 line pair, followed by no. 2 line pair, and finally, at the northern end of the frame, were the levers controlling no. 1 line pair. Each signalman was responsible for signalling trains from his line to and from the platforms.

Installation of the signalling commenced in October 1907, with the west side signalling being commissioned on 5 April 1908 and the remainder a month later on 3 May. The equipment had an uneventful history, as all good signalling systems should, and remained in service until 31 December 1960, when it was replaced by a route relay interlocking signalling system – designed and installed by Westinghouse. Renewal of the signalling was necessary because of age, but there were other factors that drove the decision. The South Side suburban lines were being electrified, and signalling that was compatible with an overhead high voltage traction was essential.

There was also a problem with the 1876 bridge with its four tracks, as it also was life-expired. Rather than replace it with a new bridge, the decision was taken to remove it and provide two-way signalling on the six lines over the other bridge. The cost of the signalling – and extending that signalling to include the lines controlled from Bridge Street Jn. and Eglinton St. Jn. – would be substantially less than the cost of a new bridge. A new structure, built adjacent to the former Bridge Street signal box, houses the control panel and associated electrical signalling equipment.

The 1961 re-signalling remains in service until 2008 when it will be replaced by a micro-processor based system. Once again, Westinghouse Signals of Chippenham will be the contractor for the design and installation work.

There will be no change to the track layout but there will be a major change to the location of the signal-box, or control centre as it is known nowadays. It will be at Cowlairs. The NB controlling the Caley? Who ever would have thought that would happen!

Of one Regulator Burton, a famously inscrutable senior man and tactician at the Central box of 1961, it was written:

Hail to the Box at the Central!
The Box of the wink and the nod,
Where the inmates speak only to Burton;
And Burton speaks only to God.

Anon

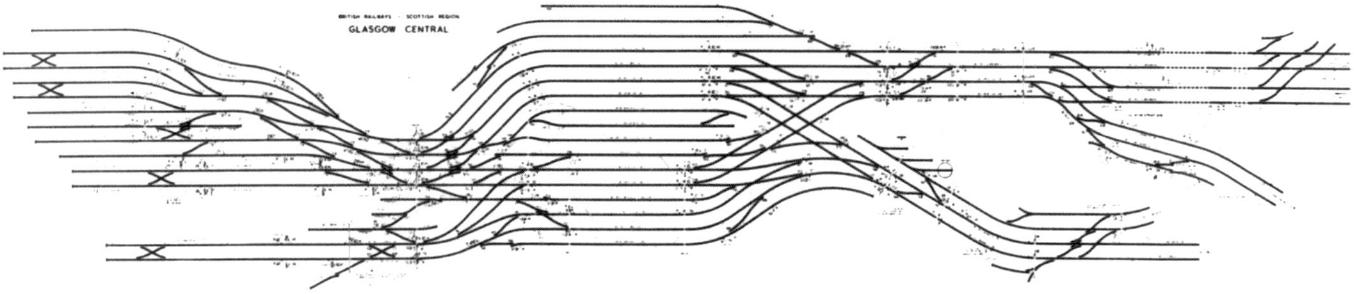

Revised track layout with only one bridge.

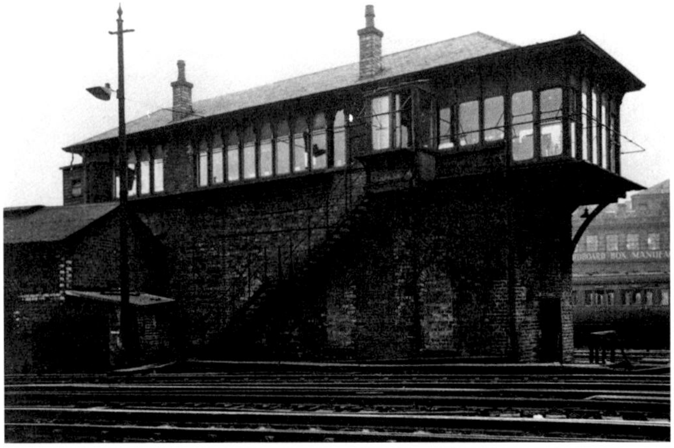

Bridge Street Junction Signal Box.

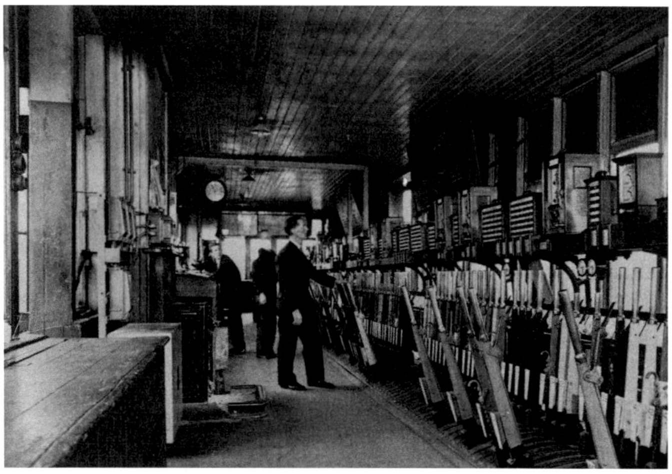

Internal view of the Bridge Street Junction Signal Box.

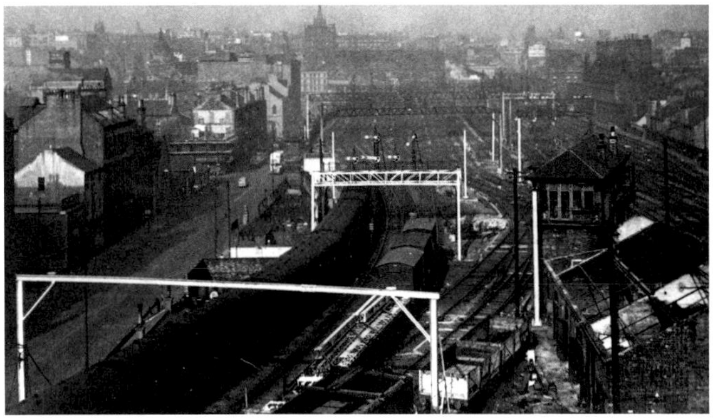

A 1960 view looking north from the new Glasgow Central Signalling Centre showing Bridge Street Junction Box and the new masts for the electrification of the Paisley lines.

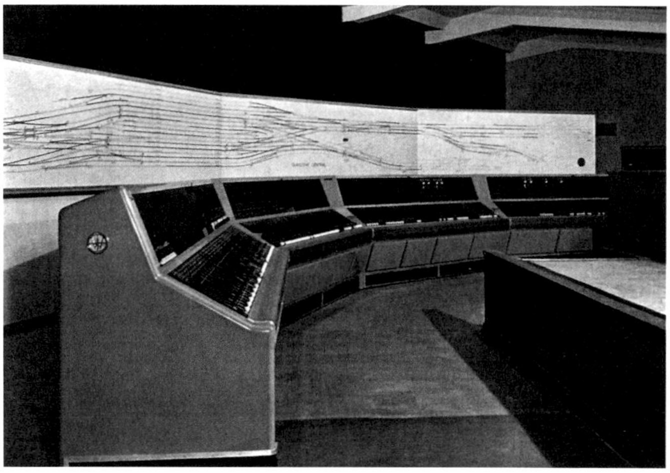

Opened in January 1961 the new Glasgow Central Box controlled over 1,000 routes and was believed to be the largest route relay interlocking in the world operated from one control desk.

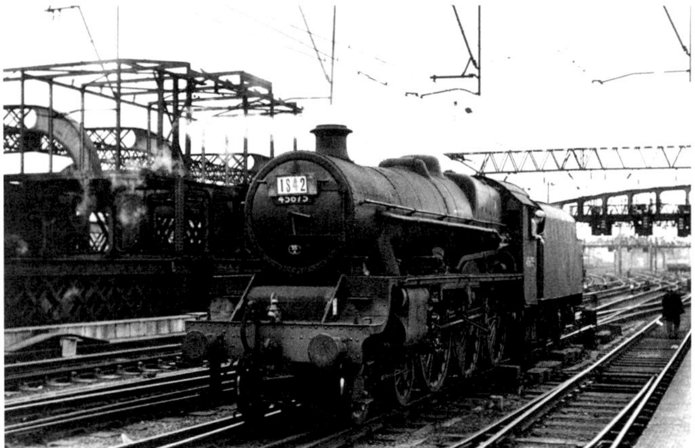

Demolition in 1964 exposes the skeleton of the original signalbox as Jubilee No. 45675 "Hardy" backs out to Polmadie.

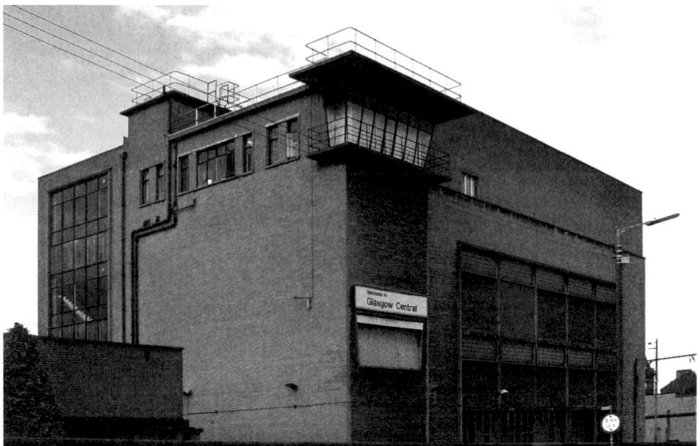

Glasgow Central Signal Box, opened in 1961, closed 24 December 2008, and replaced by the West of Scotland Control Centre at Springburn.

18 Weekend Engineering in 1908

Graham Todd

Transferring control of track and signals to a new signal box has to be a painstaking matter, as safety is at stake, the more so at an innovative and extensive installation such as that at Central. The commissioning of the new power working there took place between Sunday, 1 March 1908 and Sunday, 5 April 1908, with Central station remaining open for traffic at all times. This was achieved by installing temporary signals, and by the expedient use of Flagmen and hand signals to safeguard points and signals that were not yet operable from the signal box.

Shunting operations were conducted by verbal communication between Clyde Place (West) signalman and the shunter-in-charge. All concerned were to exercise the greatest care in ensuring that the points were properly set and that drivers did not proceed without first receiving a hand signal from the respective flagman. Speed at all times during these hand-signalling operations was not to exceed 8 mph.

From Sunday, 5 April 1908, the instructions applicable to Clyde Place (West) cabin were applied to the new Central Power Box. The new Central Power Box appeared to be fully functional from then on, as the Spring increase in Special Traffic and the normal timetabled trains appear to have been unaffected by any problems with the new system. On Sunday, 3 May 1908, Central Station old cabin and Clyde Place cabin had all the remaining locking frames and connections removed. A locomotive and brake van plus 20 wagons were provided to remove materials. Finally, Sunday, 10 May 1908 saw the removal of the redundant signal boxes within Central.

The "Railway Engineer" of October, 1909 was able to state:

" . . . nearly 18 months have now elapsed since the initial stage of the signalling was brought into use, and as yet nothing has arisen to cast doubts on the wisdom of the design"

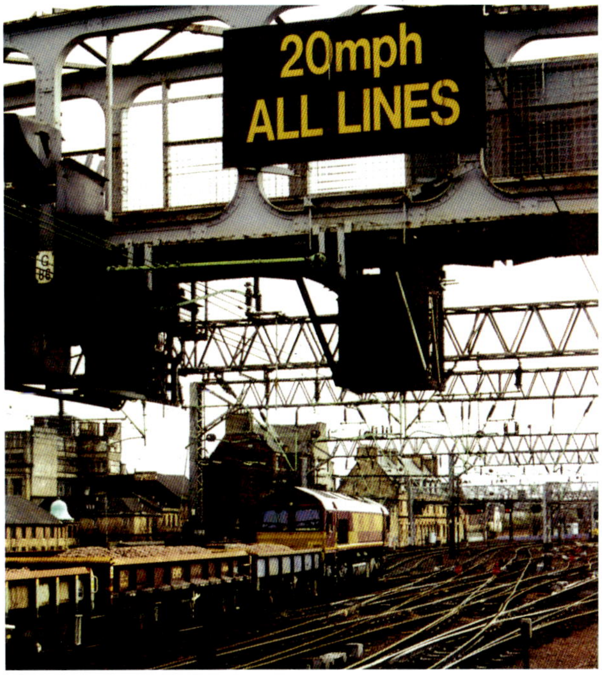

Today, in one of the busiest stations in the United Kingdom, maintenance work has to continue throughout the year both day and night. A Class '66' waits on a ballast train.

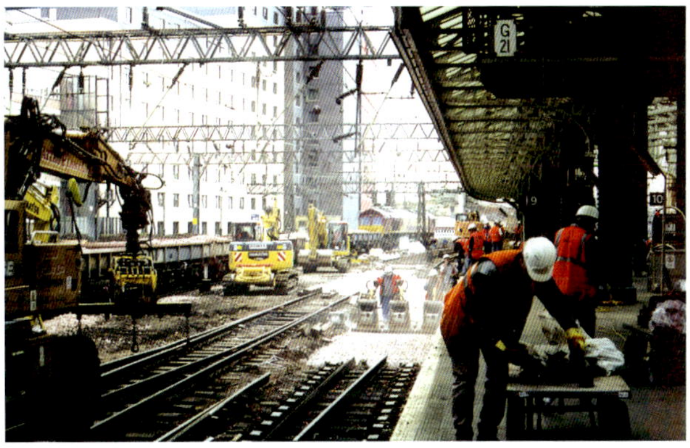

In 2006 NetworkRail and its contractors undertake weekend engineering work.

Drooping with age

The buffers at Glasgow Central High Level are fairly well concealed, but are actually pretty large and project for a few feet, ready to absorb the force from any train which might not stop just where it should. They are, or were, hydraulic, with cylinders of water providing pressure to cushion the energy of an errant train. Modern suburban trains don't have buffers like the old ones, and so for them terminal stations can be equipped with a different thing altogether. Round in the suburban platforms at Central though, the hydraulic buffers at Central remain, as a reminder of Victorian engineering. But when, a few years ago, they were observed to droop, doubtless due to age and inactivity, a consultant from the south was brought in to assess the gravity of the position. And that is why they now have a support to restrain the droop.

Pope's Visit

The visit of the Pope in 1982 was going to create huge extra traffic for the Central, as 300,000 folk made their way to Bellahouston Park. Special trains were planned frae a' the airts, and there was to be a shuttle service to and from the Central. The number of trains necessitated stacking empty trains one behind the other on the Paisley Canal line, an unusual procedure demanding almost papal absolution for the temporary suspension of some of the ingrained normal rules. The boss of the Timetabling department took up a position at the end of Platform 9 to observe the handiwork of his staff unfold with military precision. The importance of the occasion warranted the wearing of his best suit. His colleague looked on with disbelief and finally could contain his disdain no longer: "Did you really have to wear a blue suit today?"

19 Auld Enemies make up

Jim Summers

Closure of the fine, but rival, terminus of the Glasgow and South Western Railway thrust much additional work on Central, but gave it another claim to fame. It was now – or so it could be claimed by ardent supporters – busier than London's busiest terminus, Liverpool St. In fact, the number of trains was about the same, namely 1200 daily on weekdays. The achievement of Central was to handle them with only 13 platforms (excluding the distant platform 11A), as opposed to the 18 at Liverpool St. The Great Eastern Line service out of Liverpool St., incidentally, suffered the same electrical teething problems as did the Glasgow Blue Trains. In terms of the numbers of passengers, the London terminus will certainly have had the greater throughput of passengers. The daily total of passengers at Central, after the diversion of trains from St Enoch, was 83,000; 15,000 passed through in the evening peak.

A total of 20 trains had set off in the evening rush hour from St. Enoch, indicating the challenge of transferring its traffic to Central. In terms of daily train movements, 250 extra instances resulted in Central from the closure of St. Enoch – to be achieved, let it be remembered, in the absence of the four tracks of the original bridge over the Clyde. Over the remaining six-track bridge, 94 trains now arrived or departed between 1700 and 1800 (yes, 40 years ago, BR was already on the 24-hour clock). The morning peak involved 87 arrivals and departures. So, broadly speaking, each of those six lines carried a train every one and half minutes. It wasn't just as straightforward as that of course, because of varying patterns of service on the different routes, and of course there were shunting and empty stock movements.

The key to handling all these extra services was, of course, the elimination of loco-hauled workings, with their attendant need to release and re-engine inbound arrivals – though the celebrated propelling of Empty Coaching Stock to Smithy Lye was a helpful feature, hard to conceive of today. In fact, once the St Enoch trains had descended on Central, only 50 trains a day were not worked by multiple units. Most of these 50 were on Gourock and Wemyss Bay services, which were due to convert to electric multiple unit trains the following spring – and create a further 100 trains a day for Central. Operations by multiple units of course also facilitated the practice of double-docking, or even treble-docking, which still exists today, but was never a feature at the rival Liverpool St., whose lengthy trains could never share platforms. If odious comparisons are to be pursued, then it has to be said that, while both terminals had, and have, essentially six approach tracks, Central had the more complicated routing decisions and layout in the throat. And it has to be conceded that the smaller trains in Central mean some potential capacity is not used.

The transfer of trains to Central was one thing, but the transfer of passengers and parcels and mail was another. The concentration of two large terminals into one meant that investment could be concentrated more effectively too. Thus a programme valued at £250,000 (at 1966 prices) was set in hand. On the day following the closure of St Enoch, there opened at Central a women's section of a new "Superloo", with its bathroom and other luxuries, a level of indulgence which even Liverpool St. could not boast. The men's section was to follow in August, neatly – and perhaps wisely – missing the acid test of a Fair Holiday. Other enhancements included: installation of closed circuit television, the better to relay information on train running to staff and public; new train departure screens; thorough re-signing; a master clock suspended above the concourse to drive new electric clocks on every platform; modernisation of the refreshment room, and of both Hope St. and Union St. entrances; a centralised telephone enquiry bureau with a doubling of existing lines to serve the whole of Glasgow; and a new "information centre" in the former Inquiry Office. In the case of parcels and mail traffic, capacity was released at Central by transfer of most of this activity to the parcels depot at Salkeld St.

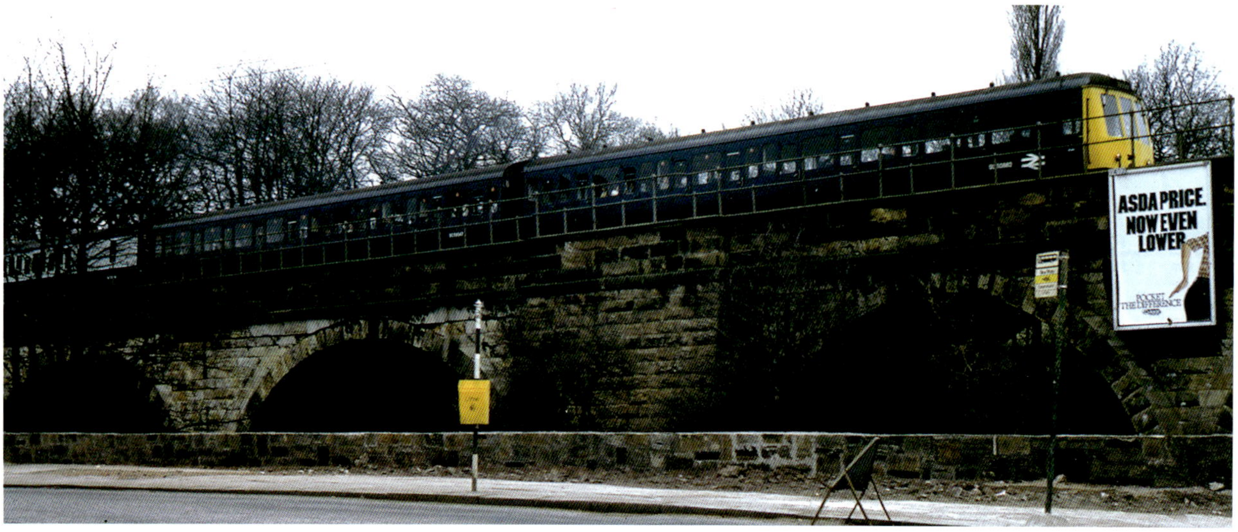

In its dying days, St Enoch still was dispatching 20 trains in the evening peak between 1700 and 1800. Working a St Enoch service over the Glasgow, Barrhead and Kilmarnock Joint Line, a DMU is seen crossing the River Cart at Pollokshaws.

20 Matchboxes and Motorail

Iain MacLean

I still have a small card which sat on the tables on the train welcoming Motorail customers to the inaugural service from Central on 17 May 1993. As InterCity began to be split up into sub-sectors, one of the casualties was The Clansman which, apart from all the other things it did, provided the day Edinburgh - London Motorail service (which had originally run from Perth, and then Stirling, but that's another story!) The split into accountancy sub-sectors separated InterCity Cross-Country services from the profit centre of InterCity West Coast, and the Clansman had ceased to be a Cross-Country operation and became a West Coast one.

Now, in the West Coast profit centre, Anglo-Scottish day trains ran to Glasgow only, so we began to look at a cunning plan, to provide both day and night Motorail, based on Glasgow Central, with the car-carrying vehicles doing a round trip in 24 hours. The problem was that, compared with the Edinburgh trains which reversed in Carstairs, the Glasgow trains were the only Anglo Sleepers which did not get involved in a reversal en route, so that what was attached at the front prior to departure from Euston would be trapped at the buffers on arrival at Glasgow and vice versa. If it was to work at all, the only solution appeared to be a side-loader – three of them in fact, one each at Euston, Carlisle and Glasgow.

After many happy hours of debate, approval was given for three freight wagons – Weltrols, for the record – to be converted into side-loading ramps, their well making it easier to load straight from the platform. Amateur timetablers will surely empathise with the "planning" that went on, consisting of shuffling the equivalent of matchboxes (though I have never smoked!) around my desk; and the dining room table, I daresay.

The resultant operation at Glasgow Central involved the Motorail vehicles arriving at the rear of the train and outside the Driving Van Trailer (it will be recalled that these passenger trains were operated as Push-Pulls with the engine at the Glasgow end and the Driving Van Trailer at the Euston end). So getting authorisation for that unique marshalling was another bit of fun. The 0840 from Euston arrived in Platform 11 at 1358 with the covered car-carrying vehicles – GUVs for the record – on the rear, with the cars facing southward. The side-loader was propelled on to the GUVs, and the cars unloaded in the wide area outside the arch. The cars were then driven down to the end of the car park to be handed over to the customers. The side-loader and GUVs were then detached and taken to 11A, so that the train could return to Euston that afternoon. The GUVs would return to Euston on an overnight train.

For the equivalent daytime southbound journey, the cars were loaded facing northwards at Central into the GUVs, which had arrived off the sleeper. This was achieved through the side loader, in the middle of Platform 11, and the GUVs were then pushed to the buffers. When the coaches arrived in that platform on a train from Euston and all the passengers were off, the loco drew its train forward to attach to the vans.

The train then headed south at 1340, with the vans on the rear, behind the loco, ready to be detached and offloaded at Euston, where the side loader was attached to the rear. The same principles applied to the sleeper trains, although they were conventionally-hauled rather than push-pulled. It did mean that the coaches for the Up sleeper had to be propelled into Platform 11, and I seem to remember something about having the GUVs fitted with brake valves and windows at the end for shunters to see out. Needless to say the windows got covered with brake dust and were rarely used.

All Motorail services ceased with the start of the May 1995 timetable, so the day service lasted for only two years.

The overnight Glasgow — London Motorail service had an even shorter history, starting as recently as May 1994.

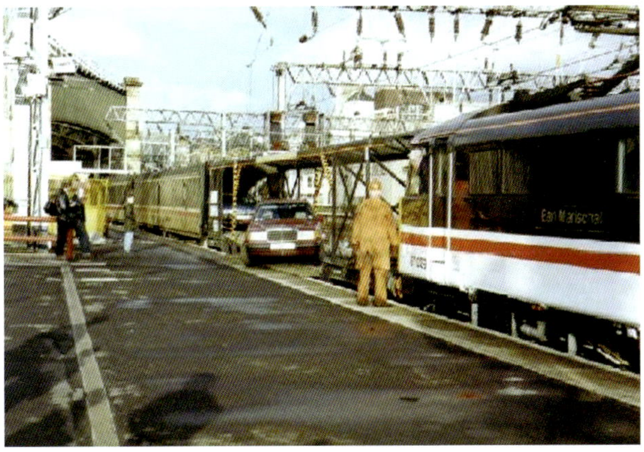

400 miles without turning a wheel!
Cars from Euston drive onto Scottish soil at Central.

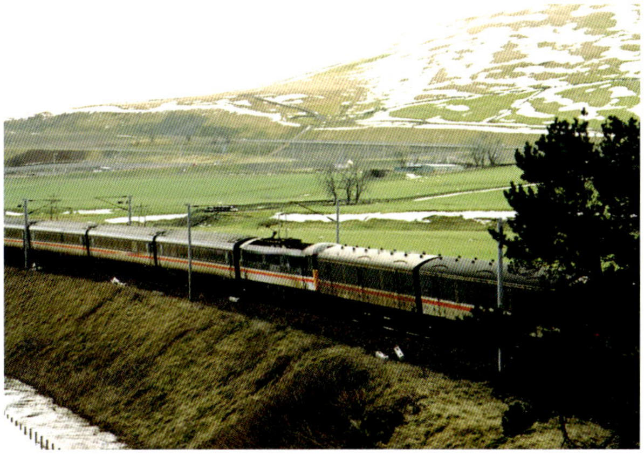

Class "87" locomotive No. 87020 "North Briton" in the centre of the train, the 13.38 from Central to Euston with Motorail wagons attached, passes Crawford on 11 March 1995.

21 Mail by Rail

I P V Jones

A sight now gone from Britain's passenger railway is the mailbag. Yet mails were a common sight on almost every station platform in the country until the advent in the 1980s of the "Sprinter" diesel multiple unit trains, which provided no baggage space. The Parcel Post was handled contractually by railway staff, whilst Letter mails were handled by Postmen. That was the common face of mails by rail.

But there was another aspect to the carriage of letters, which was not generally known or appreciated by the recipient – a nationwide network of inter-connecting Travelling Post Offices, ranging from Helmsdale in the north to Penzance in the south, and from West Wales to East Anglia. At its peak, before the World War II, this network numbered some 77 Travelling Post Offices (TPOs); after 1945, there was a maximum of 44. To railway staff, all such trains were usually just known as "The Postal", but to Postmen, to philatelists, and to some more informed railway enthusiasts, each of these trains carried a distinctive name. Many wore the names of the old pre-grouping railway companies on whose lines they first ran; others bore the name of towns or cities between which they operated, or the name of the region through which they ran. The name of each TPO was identified in the date-stamps used to frank items posted in the letter boxes on the side of the carriage. Only one train had an official Post Office name that did not conform to this practice – this was the pair of trains known as the *Up/Down Special TPOs.*

On the TPOs, letter mails and packets were sorted, loaded and unloaded at key stations en route, and in some cases set down and picked up without stopping, by means of special lineside and on-train apparatus. Often the TPO was a single sorting carriage (in railway rolling stock terms, a POS) attached to a regular passenger or parcels train, sometimes accompanied by a stowage tender (POT), or even up to four vehicles. In some cases on the major routes the TPO would be a complete Post Office train in its own right. On the railway, the TPO was identified as a Class 1 train (essentially an Express Passenger), but nevertheless had precedence over any other Express Passenger train – except a Royal Train.

The TPOs were little known, as they operated at night, in

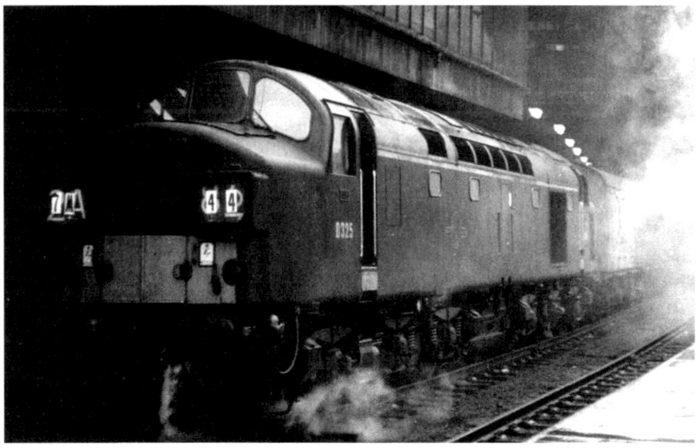

D325 with 1M44 TPO, the "Up Special" in 1964.

a few cases in the late evening, or very rarely and because of distance, in the late afternoon. They had no bodyside windows – only a line of shallow fanlights below the roof – but where the windows would have been, ROYAL MAIL was emblazoned in large gold letters. The later BR corporate livery of blue and grey relegated this logo to small print in the corner. Only when BR built a series of Mk I carriages and introduced the colour of Post Office red did these TPO trains begin to advertise themselves, and in the 1990s they finally shouted out in yellow ROYAL MAIL TRAVELLING POST OFFICE.

On the rare occasions when one caught a glimpse inside through an open door, one might see a narrow bench table the length of one side of the carriage, above which extended to the roof a sorting frame with hundreds of pigeon holes. Like the trains, the Postmen themselves were a rare breed. These were the elite of Posties, volunteering for the job, working constant night shift and lodging away from home every second day. They had a geographical knowledge of Britain's towns and streets which was second to none.

Although not widely appreciated by the general population, the TPOs offered a service which, to some, could prove vital. Long after Post Offices had closed, or the last collections from pillar boxes had been made, it

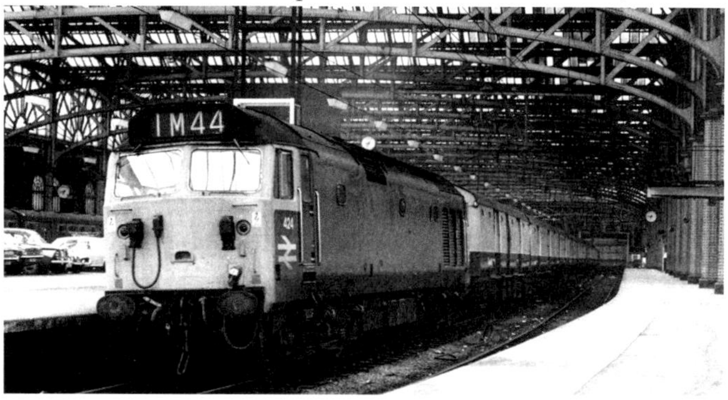

Class 50 No. 424 with the "Up Special" TPO on 9 May 1972.

was still possible to use a posting facility on a TPO. For this, a small "late posting" fee was charged (in practice, an additional stamp). In 1860 it was 2d, reduced in 1880 to ½d, at which level it remained until 1969, when it was raised to 1d. On decimalisation in 1971, it became ½p, becoming 1p in 1974 when the ½p coin was discontinued. In 1976 it was finally abolished. Later, when First and

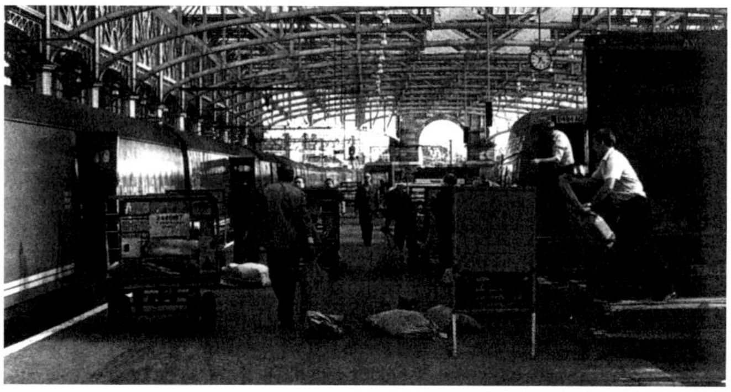

The broad carriageway between Platforms 11 and 12 is used to advantage for transfer from road to rail.

Second Class mail were introduced, late posting was restricted to First Class.

The connection of the TPO with Glasgow Central spanned nearly 150 years, beginning with the Caledonian Railway Night Mail on 10 March 1848, between Glasgow and

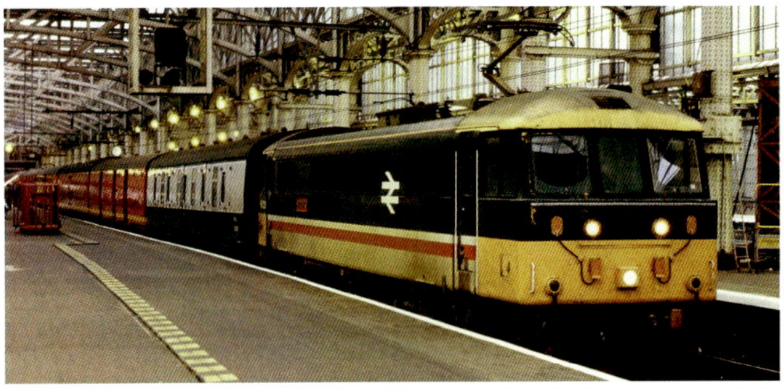

No. 86225 "Hardwicke" stands at Platform 11 with the 1930 hrs TPO service on 2 July 1988, the "Up Special" in its last days from Central.

Carlisle. Its first postal carriage was built in October that year. In time this train evolved into the *Caledonian Night TPO,* which, in conjunction with the *North Western TPO,* became a dedicated train operating between Euston and Glasgow, and on to Aberdeen. After the First World War it was re-designated the *Up/Down Special TPO.* The *Down Special* left Euston at 2030 and became immortalised in the legendary 1936 film *Night Mail* and also in W H Auden's famous poem. In steam days, it reached Glasgow at 5.22 am, in time for the morning delivery. The *Up Special* left Central in steam days at 1845, later moving to 1930. This train – better known as the *West Coast Postal* and latterly as 1M44 in non-Post Office parlance – gained notoriety in August 1963 as the subject of the Great Mail Train Robbery. Strictly speaking, the Post Office designation of *Up Special* was actually carried by the four vehicles, which started in Aberdeen at 1530; the larger Glasgow section, which joined them at Carstairs, carried the date-stamp *Up Special TPO (GW Sect).* Another TPO which served Glasgow, between 1951 and 1977, was the *Manchester - Glasgow SC,* which was conveyed on the 2320 Manchester to Glasgow newspaper train.

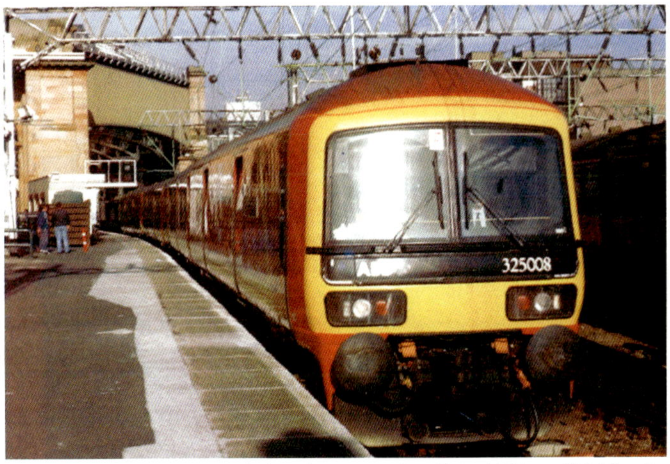

Class 325 Mail Train just before the move of mail, in 1998, to Shieldmuir.

One less well-known aspect of the workings of the *Up and Down Specials* was the requirement for the whole train to be turned on arrival at Glasgow, after unloading. This operation was necessary to ensure that the pick-up nets and traductor arms for setting down mails were on the correct side of the train. Even after the use of lineside apparatus had been discontinued, on 1 October 1971, the turning of the train was continued, to maximise use of the two door positions on which existed on one side only of the carriages. The turning movement was carried out via Shields and Strathbungo Junctions before the empty train was stabled at Larkfield Carriage Sidings.

Although the name of the *Caledonian Night TPOs* had long since disappeared, the name of the *Caledonian Day TPOs* had not. There were four sections of this TPO, three southbound to Carlisle and one northbound from Carlisle, all single POSs, starting their journeys in the late evening and reaching their destinations before or just after midnight. The *Caledonian TPO Day Up* was formerly on the rear of the 2015 Perth to Euston sleeper train, the *Caledonian TPO Day Up (GW Sect)* on the 2125 Glasgow to Euston sleeper, and the *Caledonian TPO Day Up (EH Sect)* as the 2105 train (two vans only) to Carstairs. The three POSs and a BG formed their own train forward from Carstairs to Carlisle.

There were no return *Caledonian* workings from Carlisle to Edinburgh or Glasgow. Instead, both carriages were attached to the Down Special between Carlisle and Carstairs, thence to Edinburgh, as the Carlisle-Edinburgh SC (Sorting Carriage). One was then returned empty during the day to Glasgow for the next night's working. When the above-mentioned sleeper trains from Perth and Glasgow were withdrawn, the TPO workings remained as postal trains until 30 September 1988, when they were withdrawn under a Post Office rationalisation.

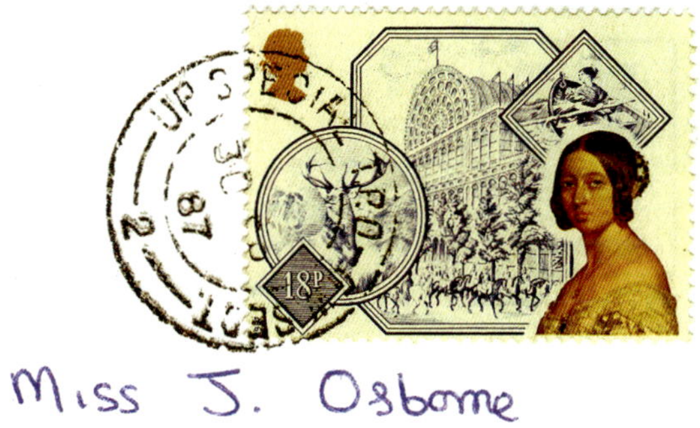

Franked on the "Up Special" TPO.

As part of the September 1988 changes, the *Up/Down Special* working between Aberdeen and Carstairs was also withdrawn and the vehicles transferred to the Glasgow Section. Further changes were effected by Royal Mail less than five years later, when the names of the *Up and Down Specials* finally disappeared on 14 May 1993. On Monday 17 May, however, 1M44, was reborn as the *Glasgow - Birmingham TPO* and was now increased to 15 vehicles from Glasgow, the rear half of which proceeded separately from Crewe to Euston as a new *North Western TPO Up.* Further rationalisation of the already much-reduced TPO network came in October 1995, prior to which only 22 trains remained. The *Glasgow - Birmingham TPO* was diverted to Cardiff, becoming 1V68, with a corresponding Down working. Change came again 2½ years later when, on Friday 13 February 1998, the *Glasgow - Cardiff TPO* pulled out of Glasgow Central Station at 1915 for the last time, and called at Motherwell for the last time, before transfer of operations to the new Royal Mail depot at Shieldmuir on Monday 16 February.

Thereafter the train, still using its Glasgow date-stamp, ran non-stop to Carlisle, so heralding the end not only of practically 150 years of TPO operation from Glasgow's central terminus, but also the last TPO to serve a Scottish passenger station.

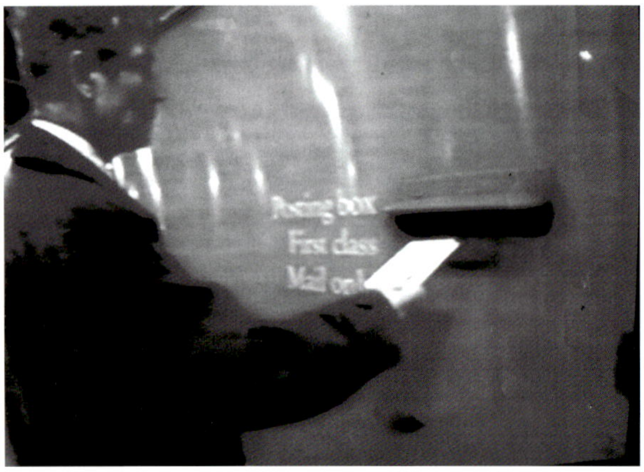

Last letter to be posted from Glasgow Central on the "Up Special".

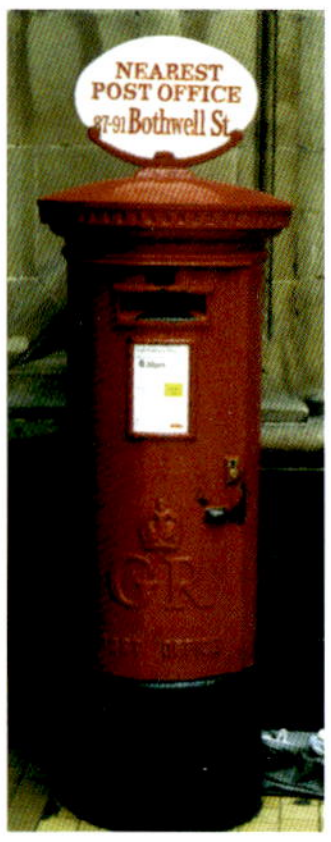

Letter box in the Station

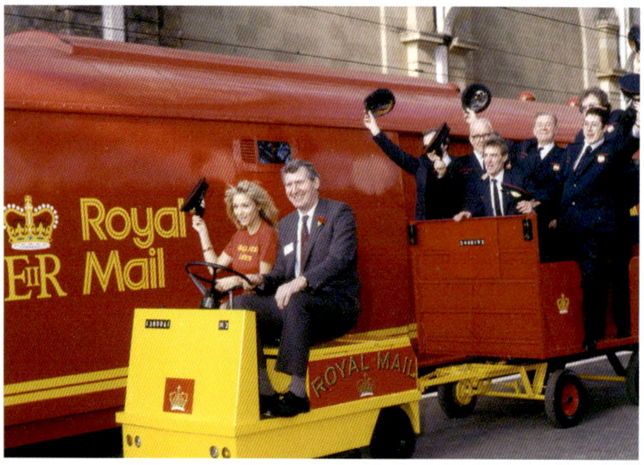

Males by Rail!

One for all, and all for one

The Central Hotel was built by hard-headed businessmen who led the Caledonian Railway, presumably because they, and the public, saw hotels as a valuable part of the total travel experience, as it would be described nowadays. But back in the 1980s hotels were not deemed to be "core activities" for the railway. The dogma was that hotels were not something by which a transport concern should be diverted from its main purpose. Thus the railway hotels were sold off. In the case of the North British Hotel at Queen Street, this meant it was ultimately was bought by Scandinavian Airlines System – a transport concern, which of course ought not to have been diverted by a non-core activities . . .

Anyway, the Central Hotel was sold off too, and suddenly it became apparent just how integral it was with the railway, from telephones to heating. It took quite a wee while to discover that the electricity bill for Central Station had not reduced to match this removal of a non-core activity, and it took a bit longer to convince the new owners that core activities for them really included paying their own light bill.

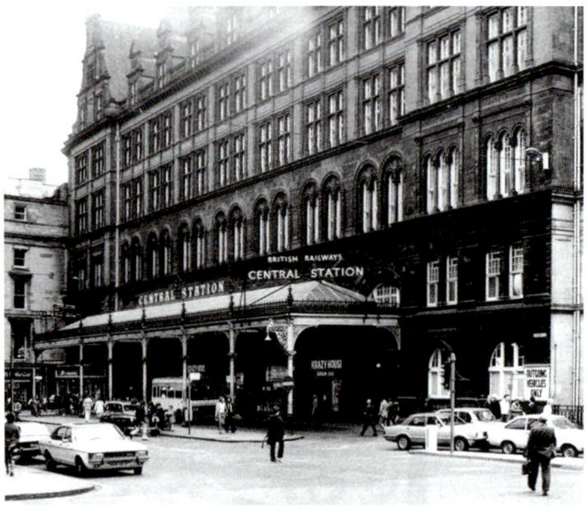

Come fly with me

The fall-out of privatisation of the railways had bizarre effects, none more so than with poster advertising. The British Transport Advertising company, which worked for the nationalised buses, trains and ships, had to be sold off, as – incredibly – a non-core activity. And Railtrack, which inherited Glasgow Central, was not greatly worried about getting passengers on the trains, that not being a core activity for its shareholders. So the valuable poster sites on Central passed from the control of the industry. Which explains, sort of, why the passengers for the rail-sea service to Ireland passed beneath a huge revolving advertisement exhorting them to take the competing budget airline easyJet to Ireland. And if they were too downcast at the prospect of leaving Scotland to look up at that, well there were large signs, with the same seductive message, laid upon the floor tiles of the concourse.

Recycling

Leaving Platform 1 in the 1980s and 90s, perceptive passengers might have wondered if their coach had "flats" on the wheels, such was the regular slight bang as the wheels revolved. In fact it was the other way round. The rails had been recovered from a portion of line over Beattock, which had been damaged by a flat wheel on a steel-carrying wagon. This had been acquired when it skidded severely when a brake became jammed on.

An American in Glasgow

The Caledonian top brass visited the USA to inform themselves on developments, and were much influenced. Somewhat later, in 1916, an American described the European aspects of universal railway operating problems in the classic work on Passenger Terminals and Trains. This was compiled by John A. Droege, the General Superintendent of the New York, New Haven and Hartford Railroad, and, like many professionals, was clearly fascinated by the complexity of railways. He had much to say on European practice (for example, that the Prussian railways had fewer accidents than the American ones, because the railwaymen were really soldiers). In the chapter discussing methods of conveying train departure information, he illustrates the well-loved arrangement at Glasgow Central High Level and says:

Foreign practice with relation to the proper indicating of trains is interesting. . . [My] illustration . . . shows the train information office in the train shed of the Caledonian Railway station in Glasgow, Scotland. This office is to the right as one enters the station from the street and in its second storey there are 13 windows, one for each of the station tracks. A reasonable time before the train leaves, a placard is placed in the proper window, showing at what time the next train will leave from the platform concerned and the stations at which it will stop. It is usually possible to insert the placard about the time the cars are placed; thereby the indicating arrangement is made to serve a two-fold purpose. Inside the little two-storey information office, one man works at posting the placards in the windows for arriving and departing trains. The time of incoming trains and the platforms at which they will arrive are shown on a series of boards with painted letters, to the left of the placard windows on which is chalked up the information about important long-distance trains, such as whether they are on time or a number of minutes late.

He was perhaps unaware that jobs in this location were much sought after by the young men of the station. After all, it was a grandstand view of the young ladies who passed through the station on their way to and from their work.

22 A berth of your own

Harry Knox

Late evening in the Central was a busy time, and posed a particular headache for the operators, since the Sleeping car trains were docked in their platforms early on, for the convenience of those travelling. This was unlike Waverley, where the trains were held out and only run in to the main platforms for loading a short time before booked departure. Central had an intensive service of trains conveying sleeping cars southwards every night of the week (including Saturday nights until the early 1980s). In 1953, for example, 140,000 sleeping berths were reserved (compared with 35,000 seat reservations) at Central. So, Late Shift in the station was always an interesting experience.

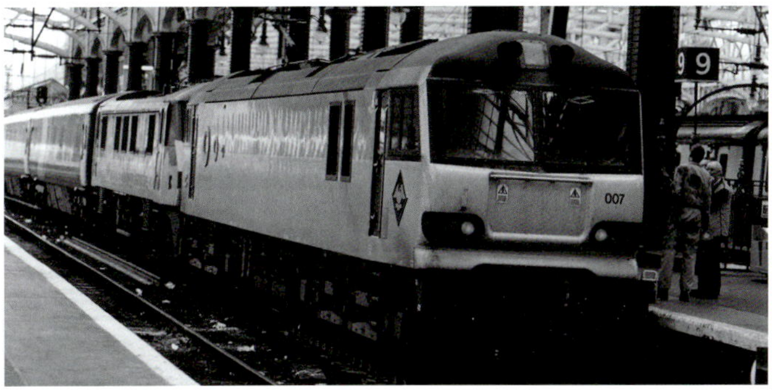

Class 92 locomotives were intended to haul the aborted overnight trains from Glasgow through the Channel Tunnel to Paris and Brussels. More mundanely, No. 92007 "Schubert", arrives in Central on 25 September 2004 having rescued a failed Class 90 on the Caledonian Sleeper.

The services were (times changed slightly over the years) as follows in the late 1950s/early 60s:

9.25pm London Euston
10.00pm London Euston (SX) conveyed second class sleeping accommodation only and also took forward the through sleeping cars from Oban (6.00pm)
10.20pm London Euston via the Sou' West
10.25pm London Euston (SX)
11.15pm Birmingham New Street
11.30pm Liverpool & Manchester

The sleepers were heavily used throughout the year, but were particularly busy over the summer period. In 1962, as Relief Station Master (RSM), Glasgow South, I was covering the Operating Clerk's position on the Fair Friday late shift (indeed, there were seven RSMs on duty in the Central that evening, the regular staff having taken leave to avoid the Fair Friday chaos). Due to seriously irregular acceptance of telephone bookings by the then Chief Clerk and Station Master – whereby these bookings did not go through the regular booking system in the Reservation Office – gross overbooking of berths loomed on the night. It fell to the staff at the Carriage Depot at Larkfield to find and prepare a total of 57 sleeping coaches for the London services (over and above the regular Liverpool and Birmingham coaches) that Friday night, and some of the old four-berth coaches had to be pressed back into service. All berths were occupied, and all trains got a Right Time departure – but it was a close-run thing and led to some searching questions from the then District Passenger Manager, Robert Reid, later of course to become Chairman of the British Railways Board.

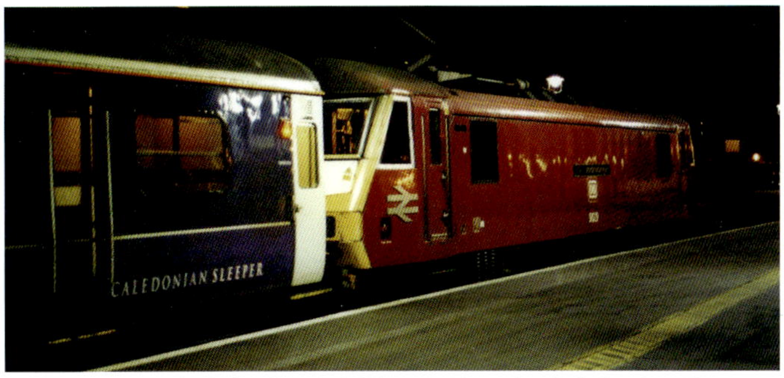

Deutche Bundesbahn liveried Class '90' on the Caledonian Sleeper.

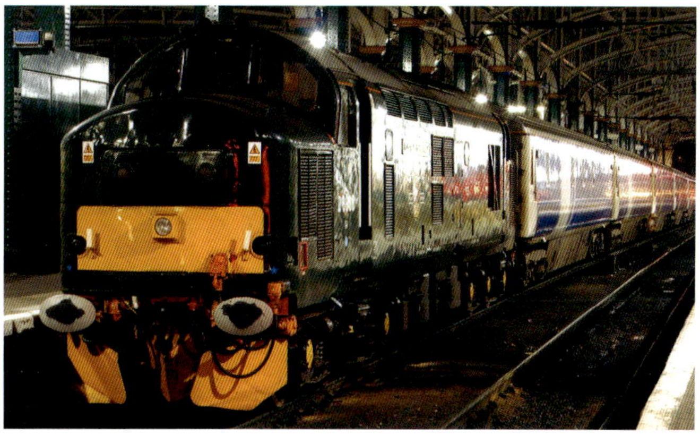

Green liveried Class 37 No. D6998 brings a train load of freshly made warm beds on a winter's night into Platform 10 – 20 December 2005.

This incident, of course, has to be looked at in the context of the regular users of the sleepers at this period, and these included the big engineering firms, such as John Brown's, Weir's, Colvilles, Stewart & Lloyds, and the like. All of these had accounts with BR and expected, and were duly given, preferential treatment.

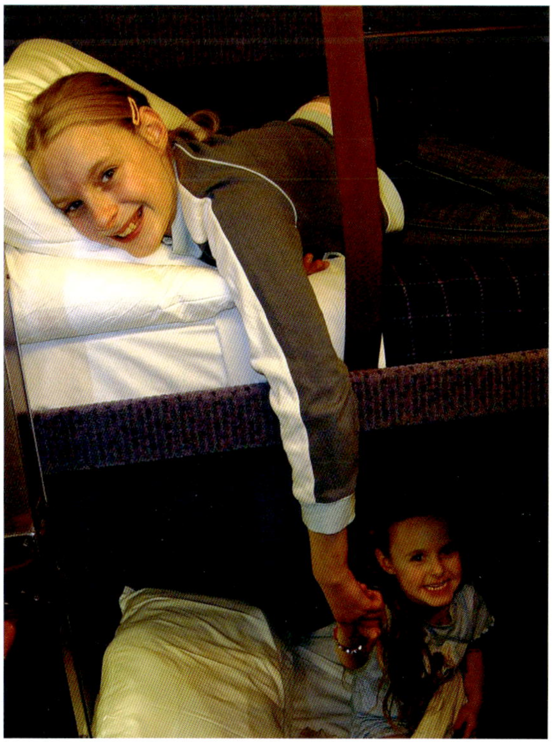

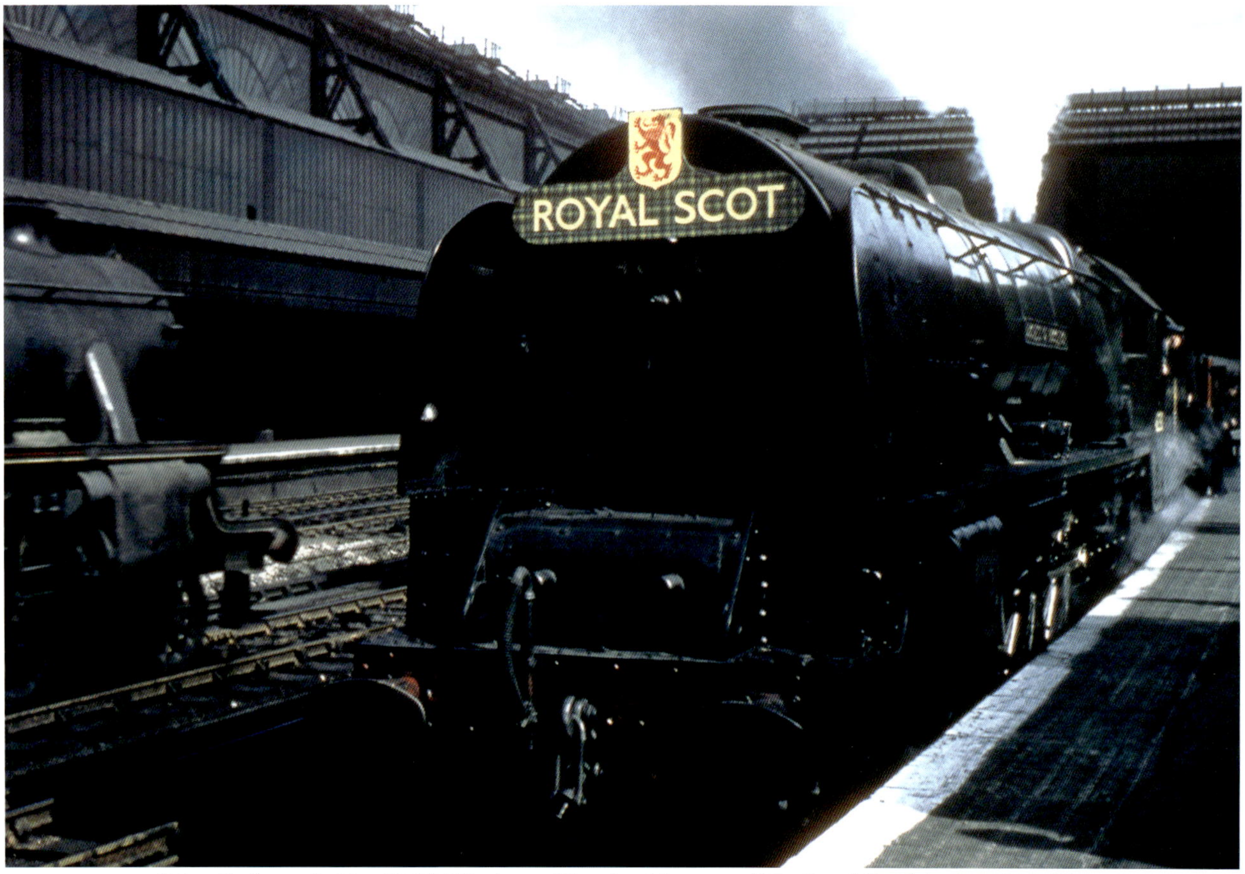

Polmadie favourite No. 46230 "Duchess of Buccleuch" powers "The Royal Scot" in the mid-1950s.

Trains of Central

"I belong to Glasgow"
A Class 390 "Pendolino" No. 390033 awaits Lord Provost Liz Cameron and its name "City of Glasgow".

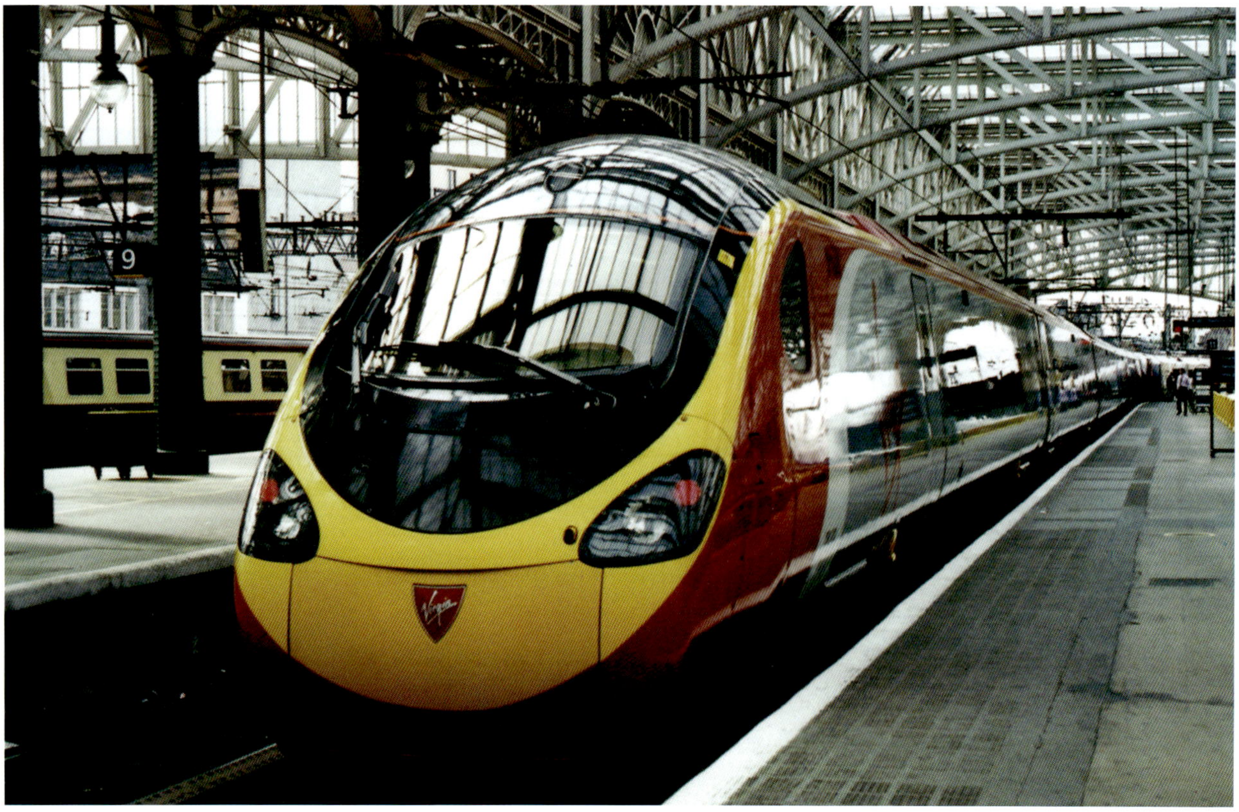

23 Steam days

Campbell Cornwell

The year 1906 saw not only the enlargement of Glasgow Central station but also the introduction of the five engines of the "903" Class. No. 903, named *Cardean* after the estate of the Deputy Chairman Edward Cox, was arguably the most famous and prestigious locomotive ever built for a Scottish railway and was undoubtedly the star of Glasgow Central for at least ten years. In her beautiful blue livery, with name and company initials CR emblazoned in letters of gold and carrying a former royal coat-of-arms on her tender, she was the epitome of Edwardian elegance, a national gem, which attracted crowds to the station and quickly became a household name. Indeed, such was her prestige that 30,000 tinplate clockwork models of her were ordered by the company from Bassett-Lowke for sale to the public at half a crown each. She was the only engine of the class based in Glasgow (Polmadie) and, with Driver James Currie (later replaced by David Gibson) in charge, was responsible for working the most famous of all trains using the station in pre-grouping years, the 2 pm *Corridor* to London Euston. This she hauled as far as Carlisle and later returned north with the corresponding train from Euston, the 8.13 pm from Carlisle.

Two other members of the "903" Class, Nos. 906-7, were based in Carlisle. One of these ran the 4.22 am down West Coast Postal to Glasgow and returned to Carlisle with the 10 am London train, while the other brought the 5.15 am "sleeper" from Carlisle to Glasgow and took back the 10.10 am Glasgow to Liverpool and Manchester express. This latter duty was subsequently allocated to a superheated 4-4-0, with the 4-6-0 then taking the 3.55 pm Carlisle to Glasgow (the 10 am from Euston) and the 10 pm London "sleeper" from the Central. *Cardean's* predecessor, the pioneer McIntosh express passenger 4-6-0 No. 49 could also be found in the Central at this time, on the heavy afternoon Liverpool and Manchester workings.

Two other named 4-6-0s could be seen in the Central between 1906 and World War 1. These were Nos. 909 *Sir James King* and 911 *Barochan* of the "908" Class. Sir James King was the recently retired Chairman of the Caledonian Railway, while Barochan was the name of the house of his successor, Sir Charles Bine Renshaw MP. Both of these engines, together with the unnamed Nos. 912, 914 and 917, worked the crack Gourock boat trains, such as the 4.5 pm from Glasgow Central. It was a time of intense competition for the rail-steamer traffic to the Clyde resorts and, in terms of their advertising value alone, these beautiful engines must have easily justified their cost of construction.

Far outnumbering the 4-6-0s in Central were the 4-4-0s,

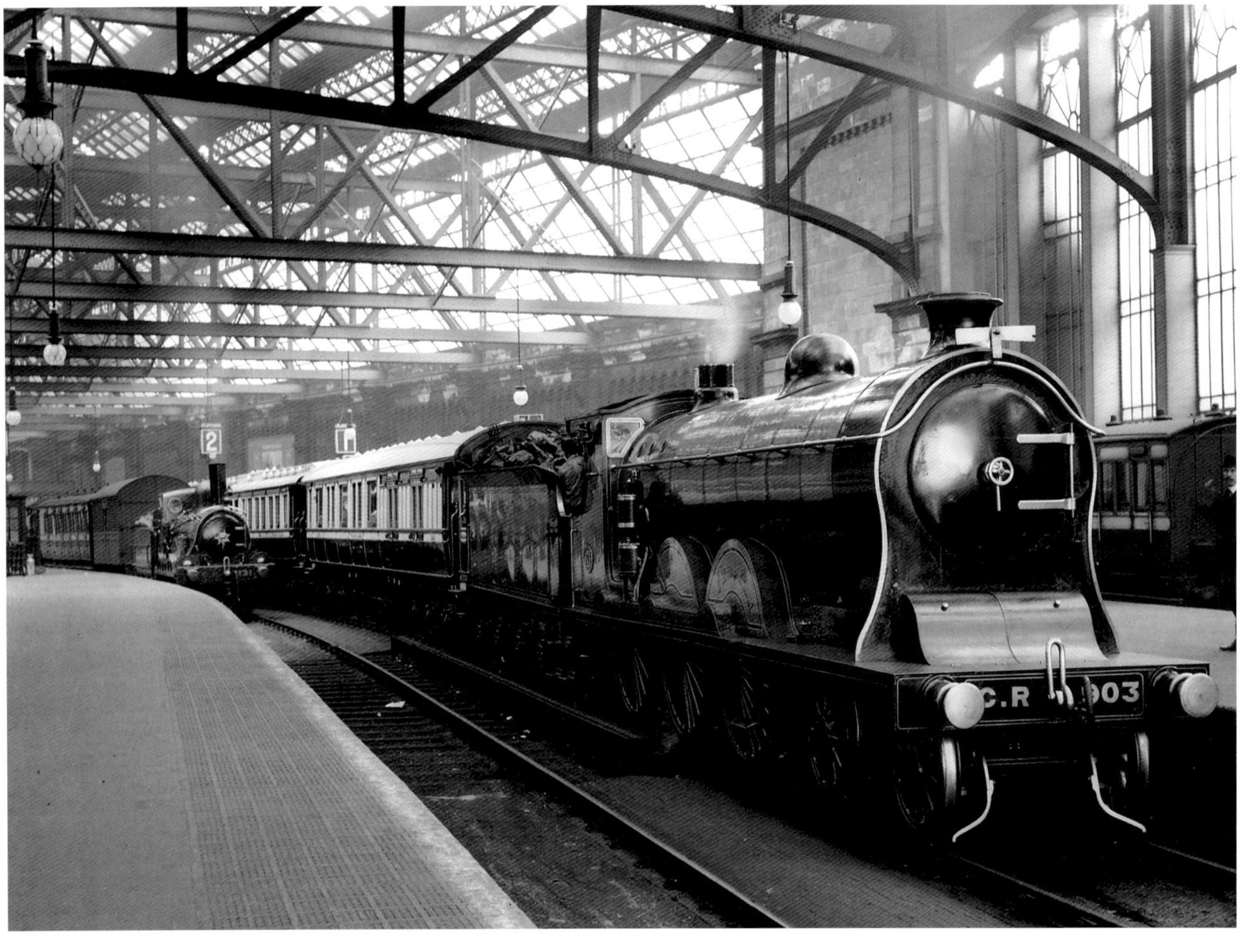

The immortal Caledonian Railway's No. 903 "Cardean" prepares to leave Central with the "Corridor". 2006 is her centenary year.

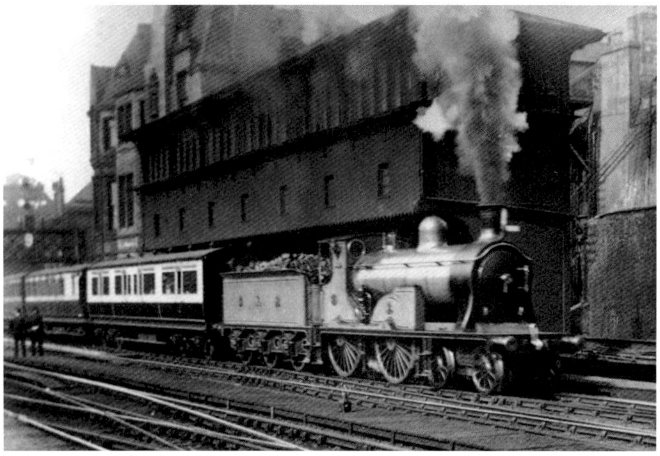

Caley "Dunalastair I" departs with its route indicator showing it to be bound for Edinburgh.

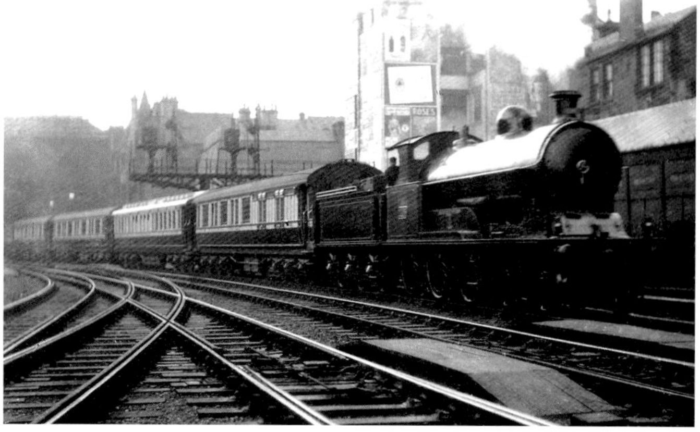

Locomotive exchanges in 1909 brought this LNWR 'Experiment' Class No. 1405 "City of Manchester" to Glasgow.

0-6-0s and 0-4-4Ts. The 4-4-0s were mostly of McIntosh's "Dunalastair" I to IV series. These worked the Carlisle "parliamentary", the Tinto, the main Edinburgh trains and the boat trains to Ardrossan, with the *Dunalastair Is* and 2s also being frequently used on the Gourock trains. When a 4-6-0 was not available for an Anglo-Scottish train, a Dunalastair III, piloted by a Drummond 4-4-0, was often substituted. The air-braked blue 0-6-0s of the "812" Class and their superheated descendants of the "30" class worked the Wemyss Bay trains, while blue "Jumbos" were prominent on many local services including those to the coast as well as those into industrial Lanarkshire. The neat little "104" Class 0-4-4Ts were employed on the Cathcart Circle, while the larger-wheeled "439" class 0-4-4Ts supported the "Jumbos" on many local services. Station piloting and empty carriage trains were mostly in the hands of Conner 6ft 2in 2-4-0s, later replaced by air-braked "670" class 0-4-2s, renewed with Lambie or McIntosh boilers.

Such was the situation prior to 1910-14 but, with the introduction of superheating in 1910, more and more reliance came to be placed on superheated 4-4-0s. In gradually increasing numbers, these acted as occasional substitutes for the big 4-6-0s as well as dominating all but the most prestigious of the long-distance services. In 1914, four of the *Dunalastair IIs* and two *Dunalastair IIIs* were rebuilt with superheaters and piston valves and four of these, Nos. 766, 769, 772 and 901were sent to Polmadie to work the top Ardrossan and Gourock boat trains from the Central.

In 1916-7, Pickersgill's "60" Class 4-6-0s emerged from St. Rollox works, and no. 61 replaced *Cardean* on the Corridor and so could be seen in the Central along with Carlisle-based Nos. 62 and 63, which worked the 10 am London train. In 1917, the closely related "944" Class 4-6-2Ts made their appearance. Nos. 944 and 945 were sent to Polmadie and, for a time, worked stopping trains between Glasgow and Edinburgh. Then, together with numbers 946–949 and, slightly later, numbers 951–953 and 955, they were put on to the Gourock and Wemyss Bay services, thus earning the sobriquet "Wemyss Bay pugs", and displaced the "908" class, which was relegated to goods train workings.

During the latter part of World War 1, the increase in traffic led to many changes. For a while, the only daytime train from London was the *Corridor,* which now departed from both Euston and Glasgow Central at 1 pm. No. 62 was observed at the Central on the up train on 8 September 1917. Another change was the 2 pm down from Carlisle, which included portions for Glasgow, Edinburgh and Perth. On 10 July 1918, this was made up of no less than 16 coaches, double-headed by two 4-4-0s, one of which came off at Carstairs. The Perth portion was taken forward by the train engine from Law Junction and the Glasgow portion was brought into the Central by "439" class 0-4-4T No. 460, running bunker first.

In 1921-2, the 4.10 pm. to Liverpool and Manchester was worked by Nos. 61 and 903, week about. Nos. 766, 769, 895 and 900–902 were the regular engines on the 4.45 pm Tinto express. No. 778, then shedded at Beattock, worked the 1.40 pm from the Central (12.45 pm on Saturdays), but was replaced by Wemyss Bay Tank No. 952 for the last three months of the year, though it returned to it for the first few months of 1923. The Caley's last, largest and

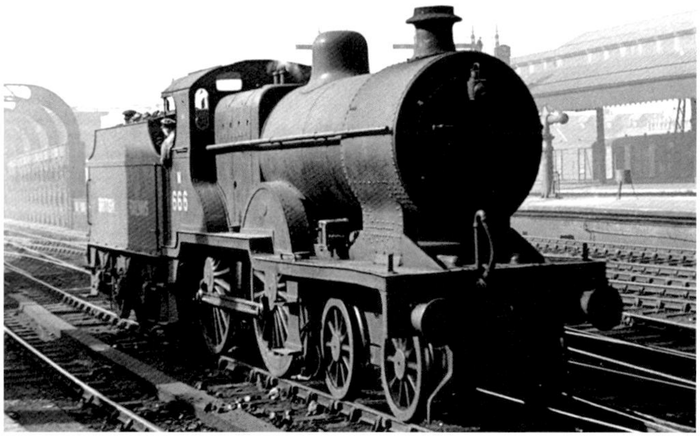

The ubiquitous LMS Class (Midland) 2P 4-4-0 No. 666 seen here in early BR livery with 'M' prefix to its number.

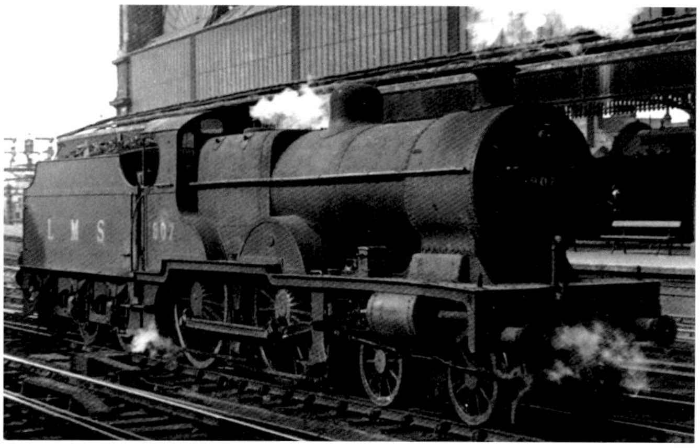

LMS Class 4P (3 cylinder Compound) 4-4-0 No. 907 backs out to turn for its next duty.

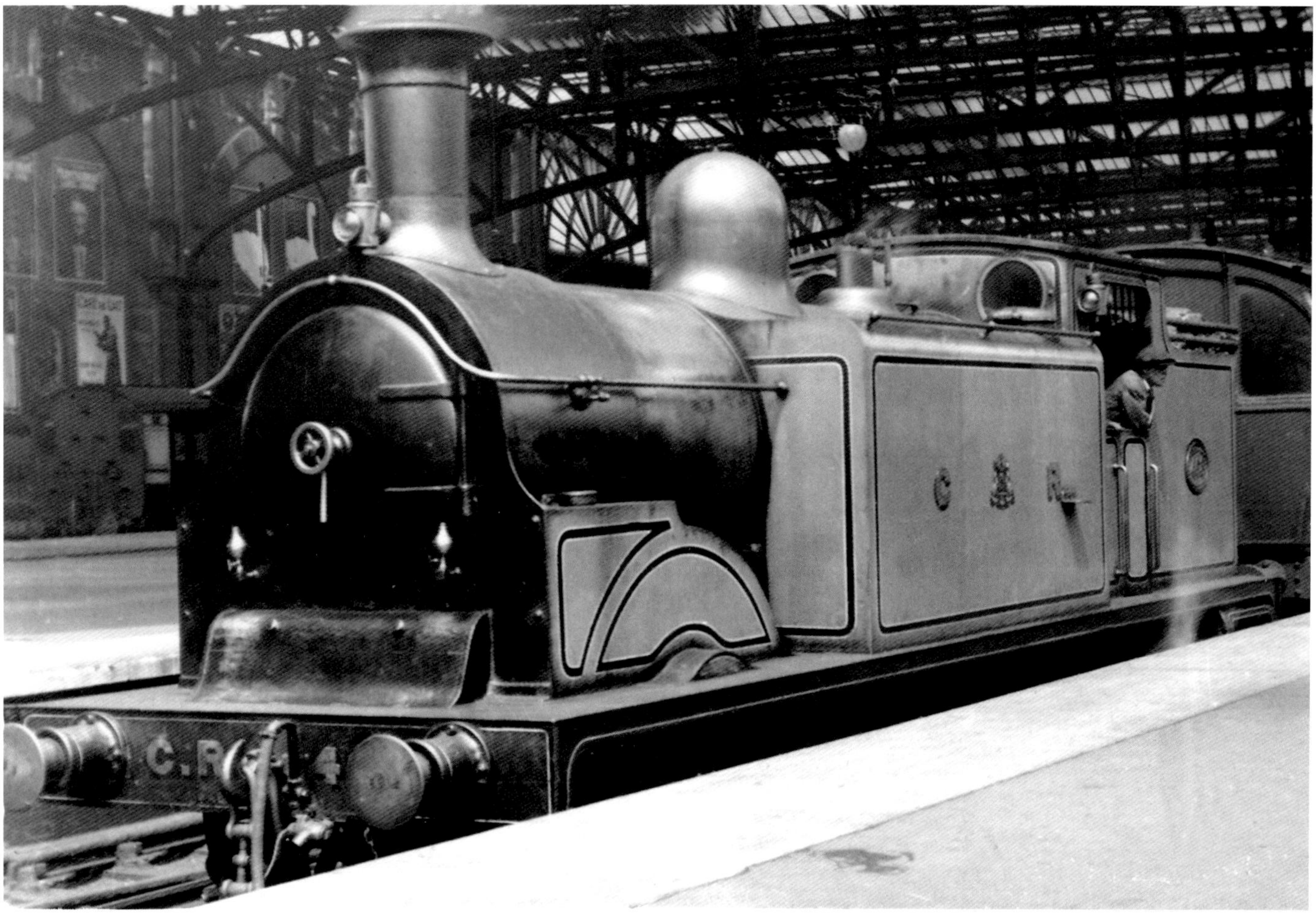

McIntosh "439" Class 0-4-4 tank locomotive No. 468.

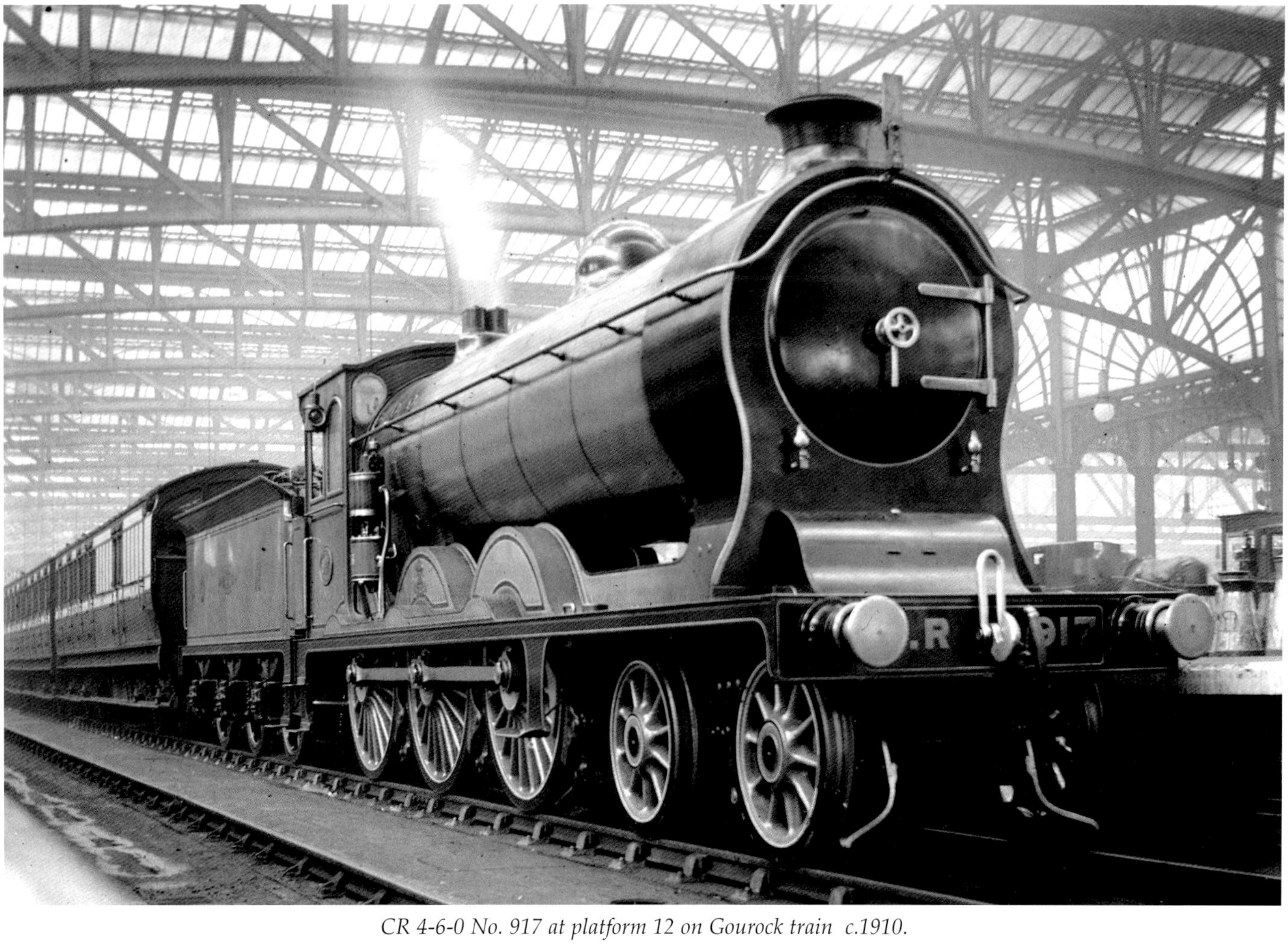

CR 4-6-0 No. 917 at platform 12 on Gourock train c.1910.

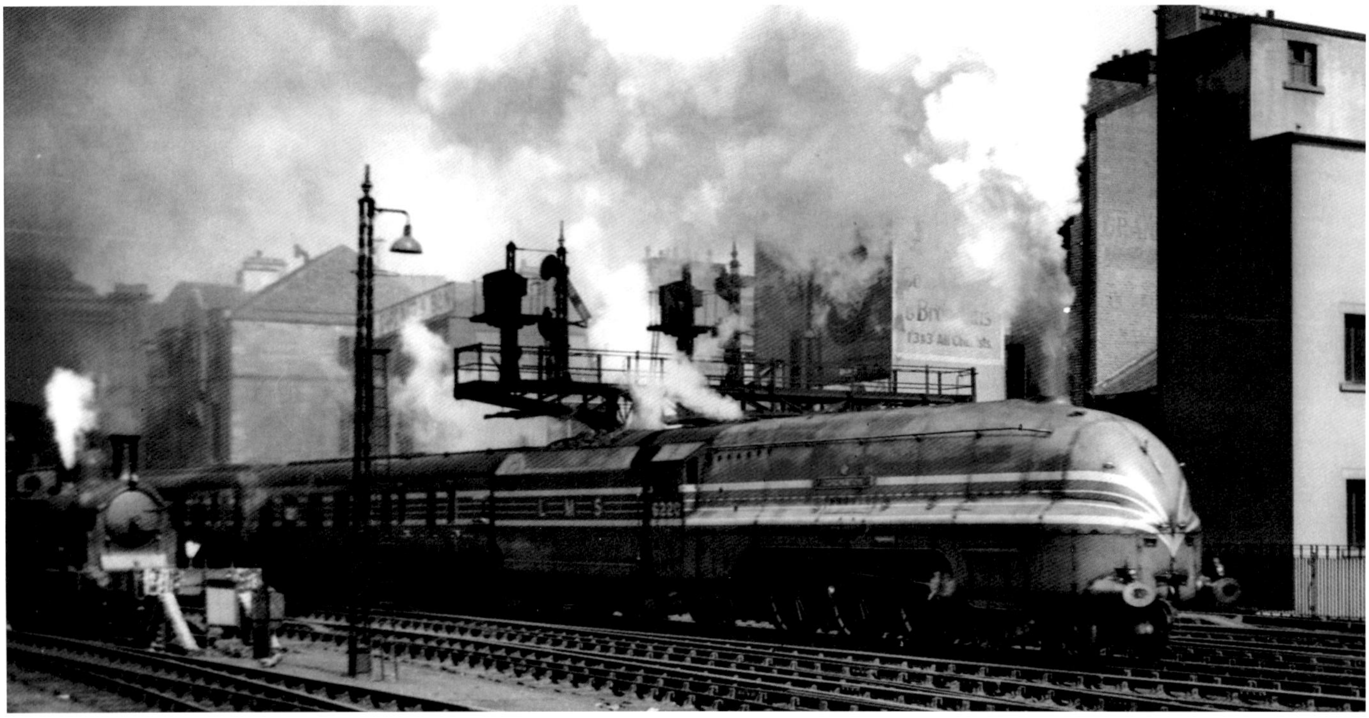

The "Coronation Scot" train in its unique blue and silver livery departs Central headed by No. 6220 "Coronation" - summer 1938.

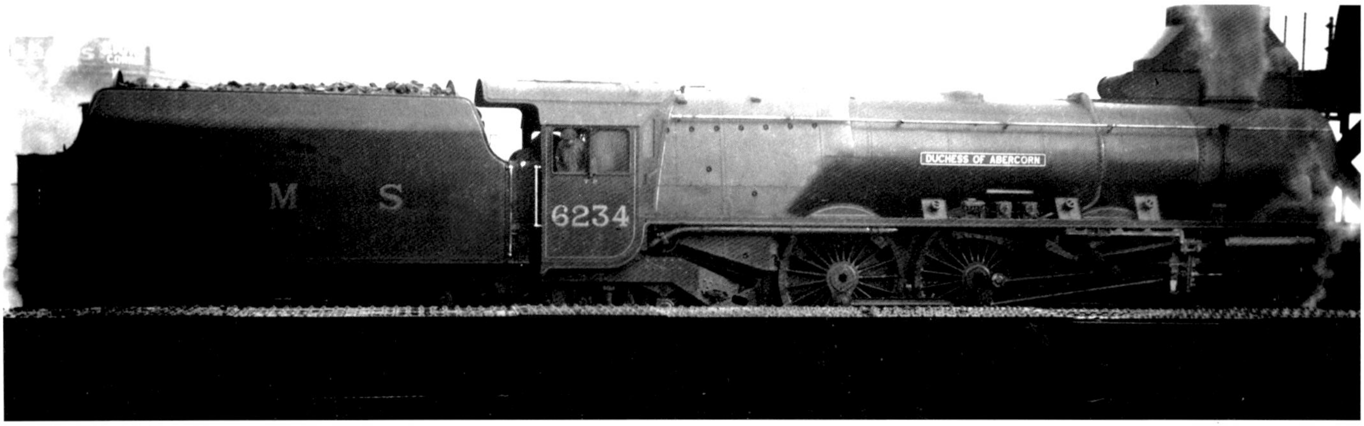

Stanier LMS 7P Pacific No. 6234 "Duchess of Abercorn", now fitted with a double chimney, heads a 600 ton test train out of Glasgow on 24 February 1939. On this run she attained the then highest power output for a steam locomotive in Great Britain. The record was only beaten in the 1980s, remarkably by a preserved locomotive, sister engine No. 46229.

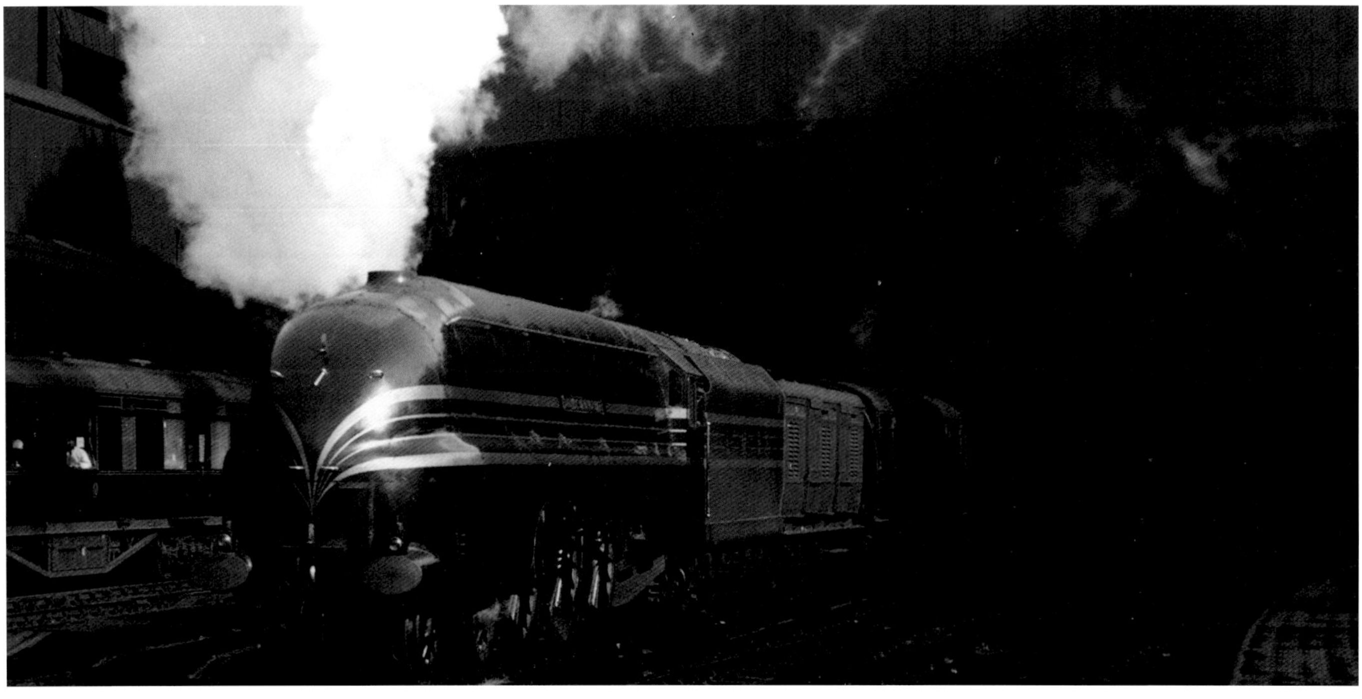

New streamlined Stanier Pacific No. 6227 "Duchess of Devonshire" in the red and gold livery makes a spirited departure from Glasgow on a Sunday "Royal Scot" service during the summer of 1938.

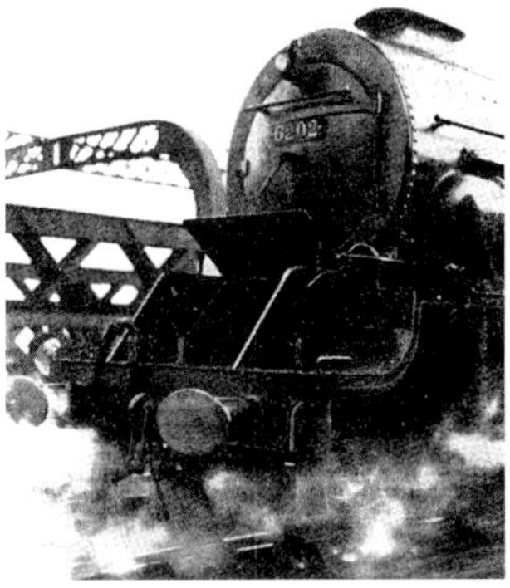

The strenuous 400 miles from Euston to Glasgow was ever a testing ground for new ideas. Here the LMS experimental "Turbomotive" No. 6202 makes its first visit to Glasgow on Monday 4 May 1936 at the head of "The Royal Scot".

most impressive design was the "956" Class 3-cylinder 4-6-0, comprising only four engines, numbers 956–959. Nos. 957 and 958 were shedded in Carlisle and began working the 10 am from Glasgow Central in April 1922, though for just how long is not clear. In the autumn of that year, however, both 3-cylinder engines were seen in the Central during the early evening, probably on the 10 am from Euston.

Blue gives way to red

The Caledonian Railway was absorbed into the London, Midland & Scottish (LMS) Railway on 1st July 1923 and, for a year or so, the only real change was the substitution

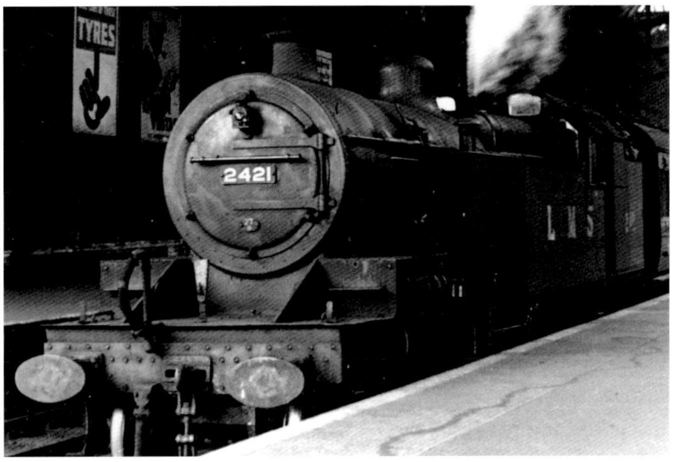

Fowler 2-6-4 tank No. 2421 on a Gourock train.

of crimson lake livery for the blue of the former Caley engines and the introduction of a new numbering system. This process took some time and, as late as 1925, no. 97, the Caley's last express engine, was observed at the head of the 10 am to Euston. Early in LMS days, underlining that the rival companies were now one, a very strange sight was seen in the Central: a Glasgow & South Western Railway (GSWR) non-superheated 4-6-0 was run round to the station and put on, of all trains, the 10 am Euston express, though with a Caley engine as pilot.

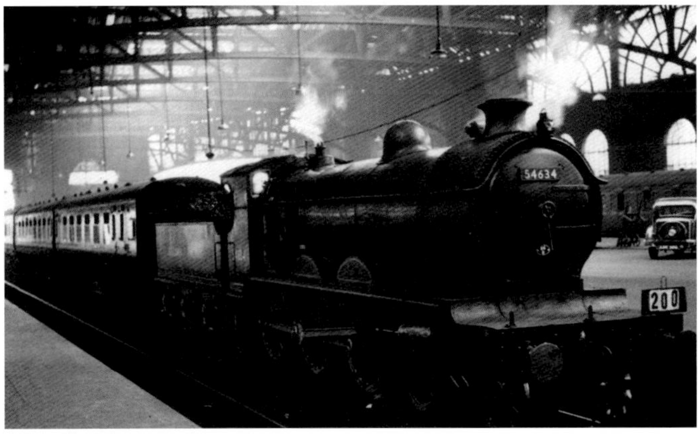

Freshly painted in black and fully lined out, CR "60" Class No. 54634 on an SLS Special - 3 May 1952.

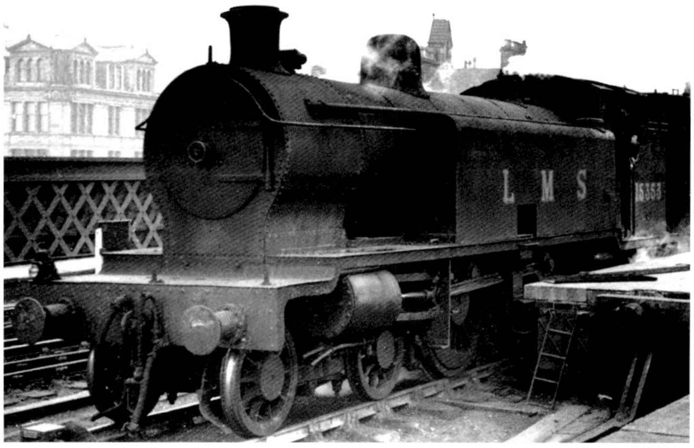

LMS No. 15353, a Pickersgill 4-6-2 "Wemyss Bay" Tank engine acts as station pilot in the mid-1940s.

One day in September 1925, LMS no. 14298, the former Caley no. 66, a Drummond 4-4-0 rebuilt with the Dunalastair 1 boiler, brought the 10 am from Euston into the Central on time, the load being 308 tons – a most creditable performance. However, by 1925, the new LMS standard Compounds were beginning to be sent to the ex-Caledonian shed of Kingmoor, Carlisle, and soon appeared in the Central at the head of the down Corridor,

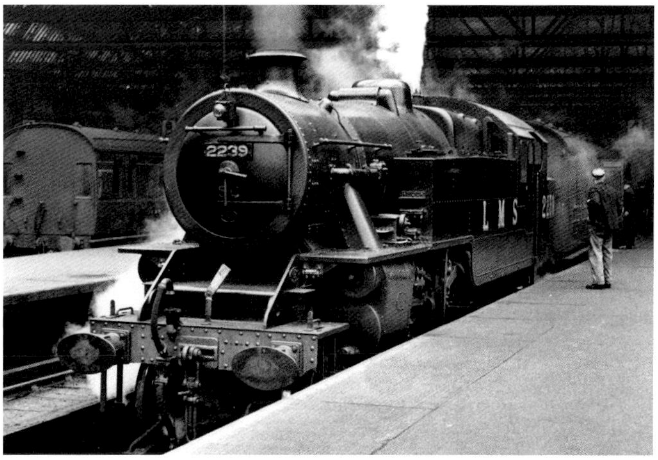

At the end of LMS days, Fairburn 2-6-4 tank No. 2239 in 1947.

at that time the 1.30 pm from Euston. It was 1927, however, before they were present in force in Scotland and responsible for most of the top-link duties, both Anglo-Scottish and internal.

However, it was "all change" again in September 1927, when the new "Royal Scot" Class 4-6-0s took over the principal London trains. Initially, numbers 6127–6132 were allocated to Polmadie and worked the Royal Scot and Night Scot to Carlisle, where English-based engines

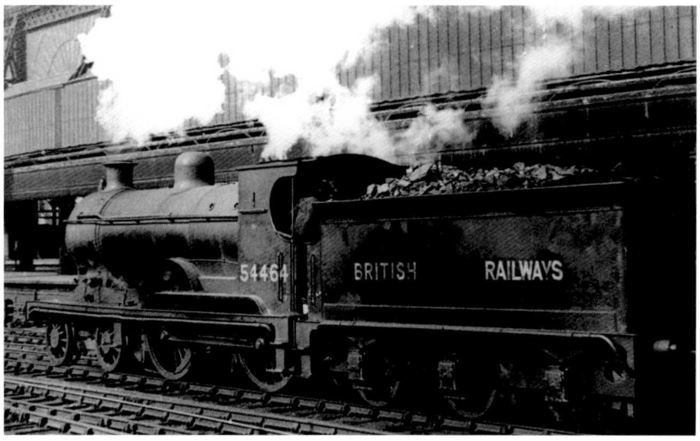

A Pickersgill Caledonian 4-4-0 3P No. 54464 - 20 June 1949.

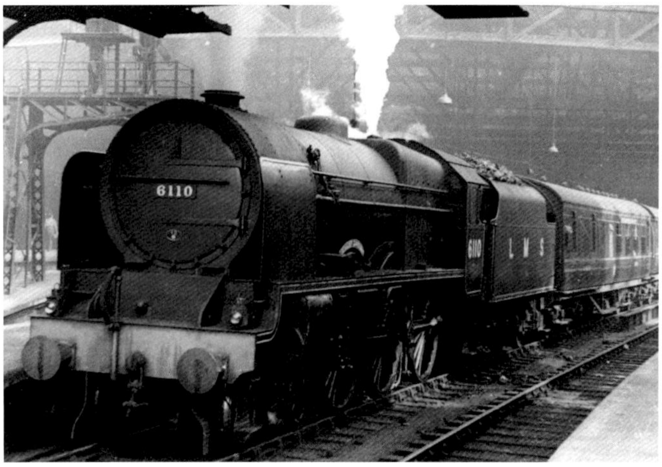

One of the original 'Royal Scot' Class No. 6110 "Grenadier Guardsman" ready to leave with a Birmingham train on 24 April 1948.

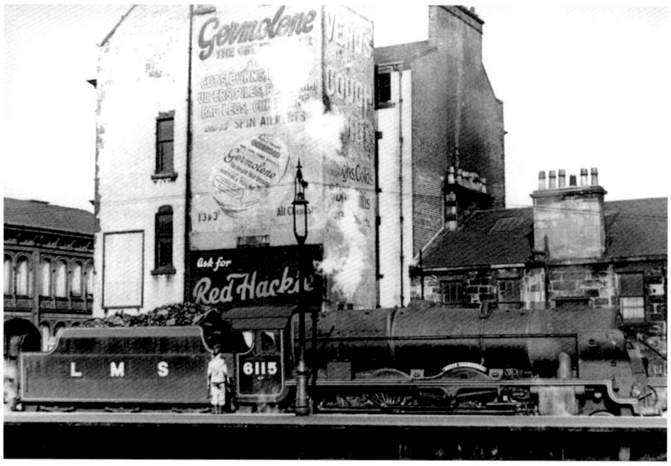

Rebuilt "Royal Scot" Class 6P 4-6-0 No. 6115 "Scots Guardsman" waits to leave with an 'up' express on 23 April 1948. The engine carries the 1946 LMS livery of black with maroon and straw lining. The advertisements on the adjoining building are worthy of note!

took over. The *Mid Day Scot,* however, was in the hands of Crewe North engines and men on alternate days, these running the full 243 miles between Glasgow Central and Crewe. Polmadie men ran the other days, but whether they manned their own engines or Crewe North engines is not clear. Although displaced from the principal London trains, the Compounds continued to work the Liverpool/Manchester trains, such as the 9.30 am with distinction, and continued to be the backbone of the Glasgow-Edinburgh services.

An important development in 1933 was the allocation of ten Fowler 2-6-4Ts to the Gourock and Wemyss Bay services, numbers 2415–2417 initially going to Polmadie and 2418–24 to Greenock Ladyburn. As the 1930s rolled on, Stanier Pacifics, "Jubilees" (mainly for the Manchester expresses), "Black Fives" and Stanier 2-6-4Ts made their presence increasingly felt. The Pacifics were rostered to run from Glasgow Central to London Euston and vice-versa without any intermediate change of engine so that, although all were initially allocated to English sheds, they appeared daily in the Central on all the London, and later, Birmingham trains. However, on the odd occasions when

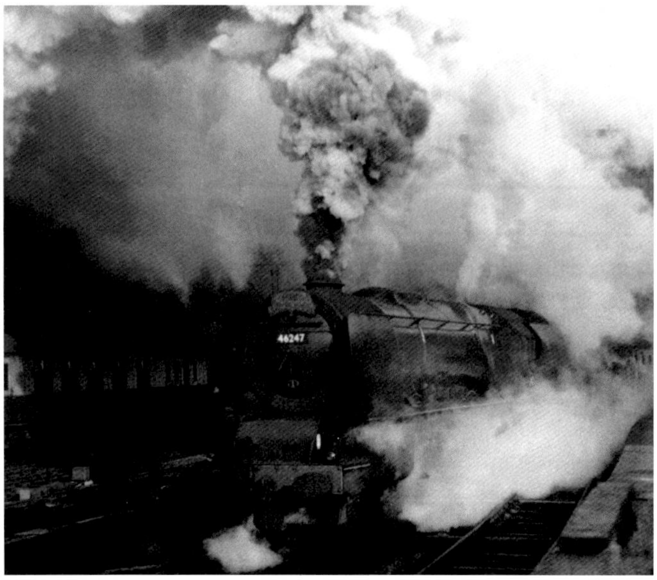

Duchess Pacific No. 46247 "City of Liverpool" makes a resounding exit from Central in the late 1950s.

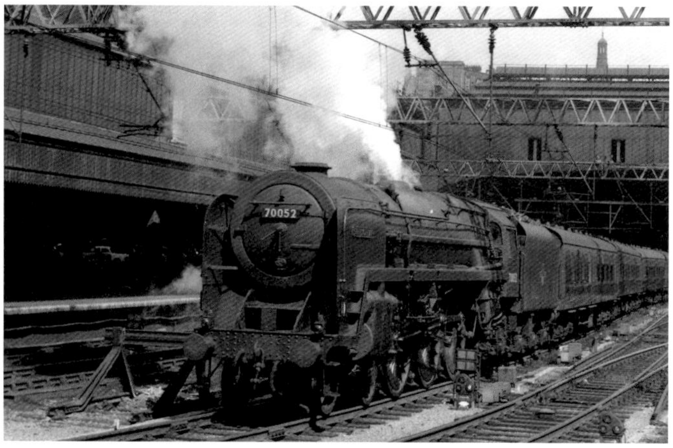

One of Polmadie's BR Standard "Britannia" Class 7P6F Pacifics, No. 70052 "Firth of Tay" leaves with the 1125 to Liverpool on 18 June 1961.

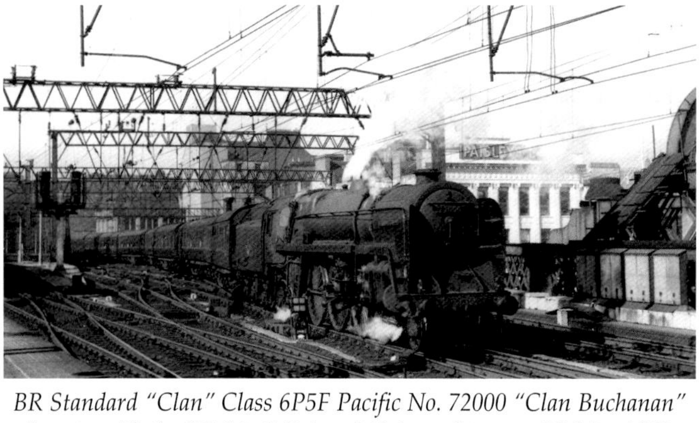

BR Standard "Clan" Class 6P5F Pacific No. 72000 "Clan Buchanan" departs with the 1716 to Edinburgh Princes Street on 23 May 1962.

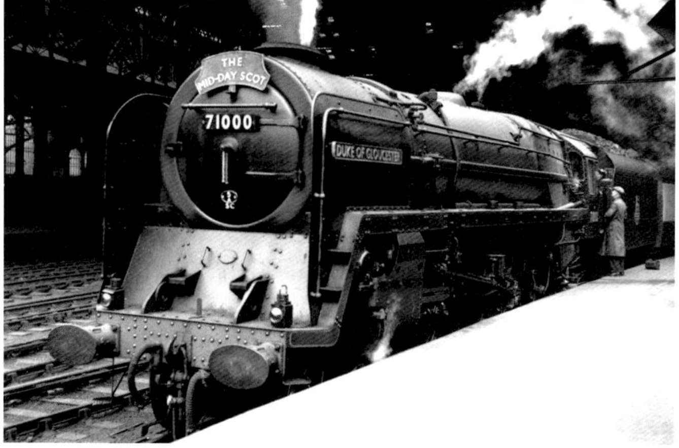

Newly in service, BR's last Pacific Class 8P No. 71000 "Duke of Gloucester" on the Mid Day Scot - 23 September 1954.

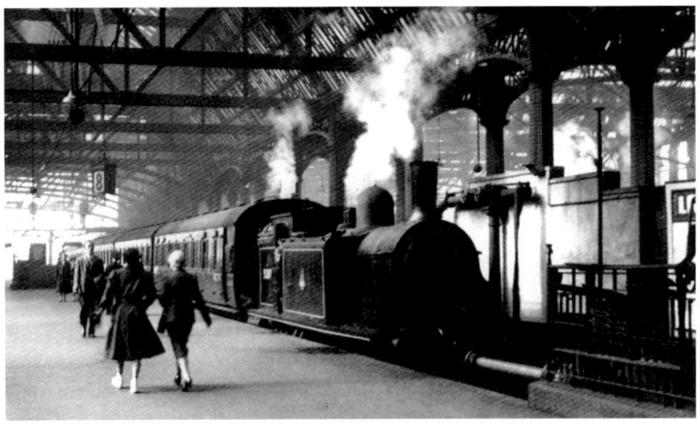

Simmering at the bufferstops after another round trip on the Cathcart Circle is one of the faithful Caley "439" Class tanks.

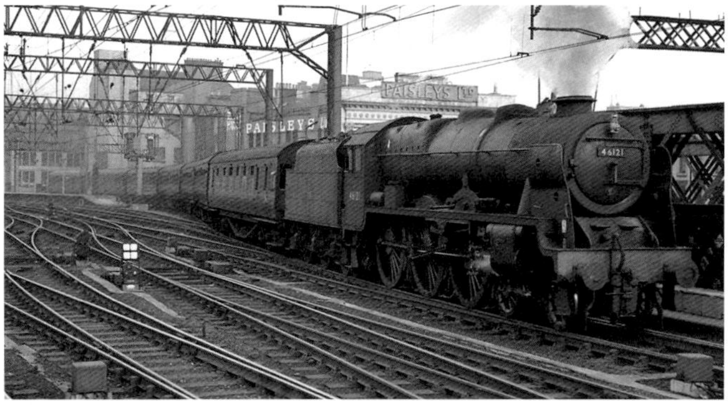

Glasgow's Own! Rebuilt "Royal Scot" No. 46121 "Highland Light Infantry, City of Glasgow Regiment" leaves Central with the 12.25pm SO to Lockerbie on 18 August 1962.

a Pacific was unavailable, the "Royal Scots" ran the full 401 miles themselves.

The year 1936 was one of considerable excitement at the Central. Firstly, there were some interesting appearances of "old" engines. From 8 January until at least 2 February, former GSWR 4-6-4T No. 15405 worked many turns on the Cathcart Circle and also ran to and from Gourock. On 1 August, McIntosh "34" Class 2-6-0 No. 17802 was noted in the station, a very rare sight indeed on passenger trains; while, on the following day, large-boilered "Claughton" No. 5948 Baltic arrived on a special train from the south. Secondly, there were the trials with the new Pacifics, no. 6202, the "Turbomotive", competing with No. 6212 on *The Royal Scot* during May, further trials being undertaken in October 1936 and June 1937.

Non-stop to Glasgow

Then in November occurred the epic performances of No. 6201, the Euston-Glasgow run being completed non-stop in 5 hours 54 minutes with seven coaches on the 16th, and the return trip to Euston the following day in 5 hrs. 44 mins. with eight coaches. However, on the same day as northbound run by No. 6201, sister engine No. 6210 brought the nine-coach *Mid Day Scot* into Glasgow Central, having beaten No. 6201 between Carlisle and Lockerbie by half a minute, despite having to start from the scheduled stop at Carlisle. The trials with No. 6201 were, of course, a preliminary to the introduction in 1937 of the most glamourous train serving the Central, the blue and silver *'Coronation Scot',* for which the new and larger streamlined "Princess Coronation" Class Pacifics, Nos. 6220–6224, were built and painted in the same livery as the train. These were followed by the red streamliners, Nos. 6225–6229, and by five non-streamlined engines of the same class for general service, especially for the other Glasgow to London trains.

A survey of engine working on the up and down *Royal Scot* on 201 occasions during the winter of 1938–9 demonstrated the predominance of the red streamliners, the numbers of the locomotives concerned and the number of journeys on which each engine performed being as follows:- 6201 (1), 6203 (2), 6204 (2), 6205 (1), 6206 (5), 6207 (2), 6208 (4), 6209 (4), 6210 (5), 6211 (1), 6212 (4), 6225 (35), 6226 (30), 6227 (32), 6228 (22), 6230 (17), 6231 (6), 6232 (6), 6233 (17) and 6234 (5). Of these, number 6234 will always be remembered for its performance on a 20-coach test train from Crewe to Glasgow Central and back in a snowstorm on 26th February 1939, when a new British record power output of 2900 equivalent drawbar horsepower (EDHP) and 3460 indicated, i.e. cylinder, horsepower (IHP) was established. This remained the record for a British locomotive until 1985 when, on three separate occasions, another engine well-known in the Central, No. 46229 *Duchess of Hamilton,* produced over 3000 EDHP and 3500-3700 IHP. By the end of the LMS in 1947, the allocation of Pacifics at Polmadie had settled down to Nos. 6220–6224, 6230–6232 and 6242, these being joined after nationalisation by No. 46227. The Fowler and Stanier 2-6-4Ts had been replaced by the new Fairburn 2-6-4Ts.

During the early years of the British Railways era, Polmadie received a large stud of the new BR Standard classes, these including "Britannia" and "Clan" Class Pacifics, Class 5 4-6-0s, and Class 4 2-6-4Ts. The unique No. 71000 appeared in the Central on *The Mid Day Scot,* a Crewe North duty, and three Peppercorn "A1" Class Pacifics, Nos. 60152, 60160 and 60161, were allocated to Polmadie around 1952 and used on the Glasgow Central to Birmingham trains; No. 60159 is also believed to have worked from Polmadie.

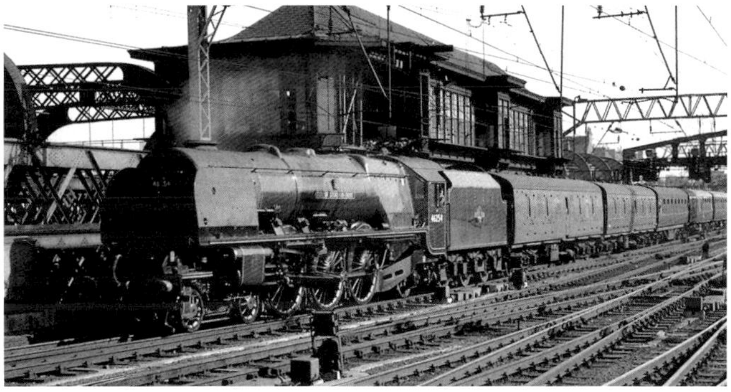

Princess Coronation Class No. 46254 "City of Stoke-on-Trent" arrives with the day Birmingham – Glasgow express on 5 July 1961.

With the run-down of steam in the 1960s, several other "East Coast" Pacifics, Nos. 60512, 60522, 60524, 60527, 60530, and 60535, worked out of Polmadie towards the end of their careers. The last official Scottish Region steam working into the Central was the 17.03 from Gourock, hauled by Fairburn 2-6-4 tank No. 42274 on 28 April 1967, but occasional steam workings from the London Midland Region continued into 1968.

"Departure"

A funeral wreath lay in the rear cab of the locomotive working "The Royal Scot" on 11 January 2001. As the train made its way south, back in the West Church, Bellshill, colleagues were bidding farewell to George Reynolds, dedicated railwayman/public relations man/golfer extraordinaire.

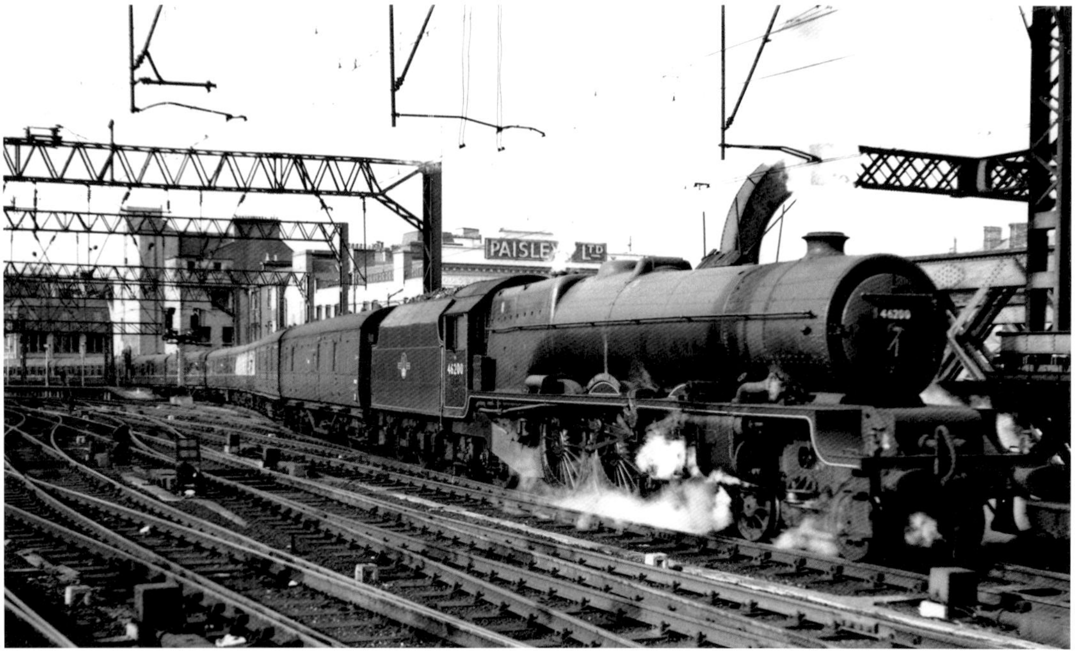

The first of Sir William Stanier's Pacifics, No. 46200 "The Princess Royal" leaves with a heavy load for the south in 1962.

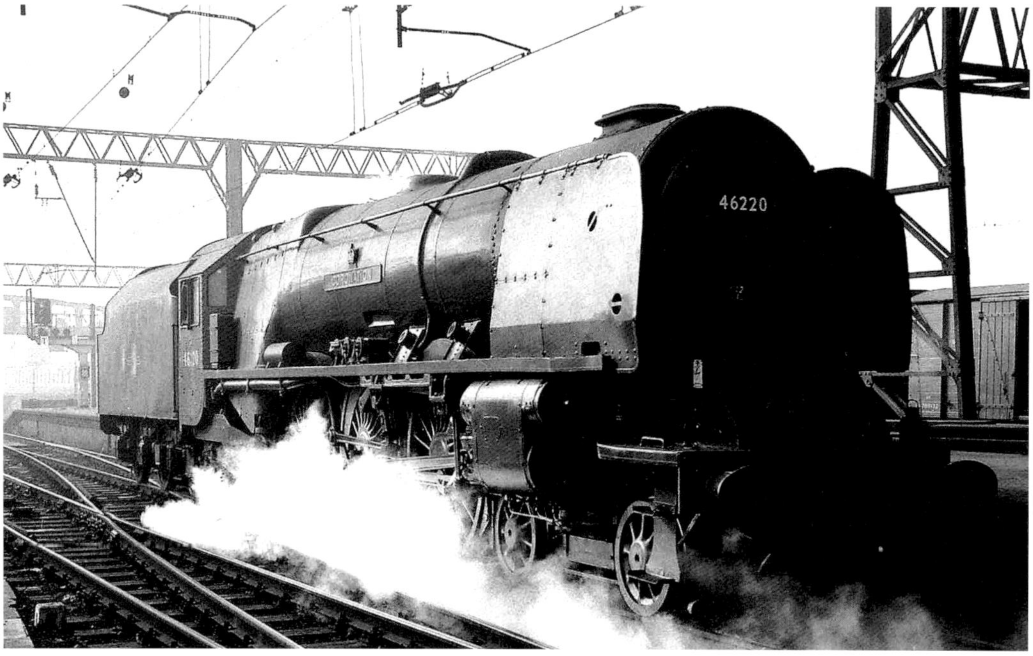

Now destreamlined, No. 46220 "Coronation" backs out of Central on its way to Polmadie for servicing having brought in the 12.10am train from London on 9 October 1962.

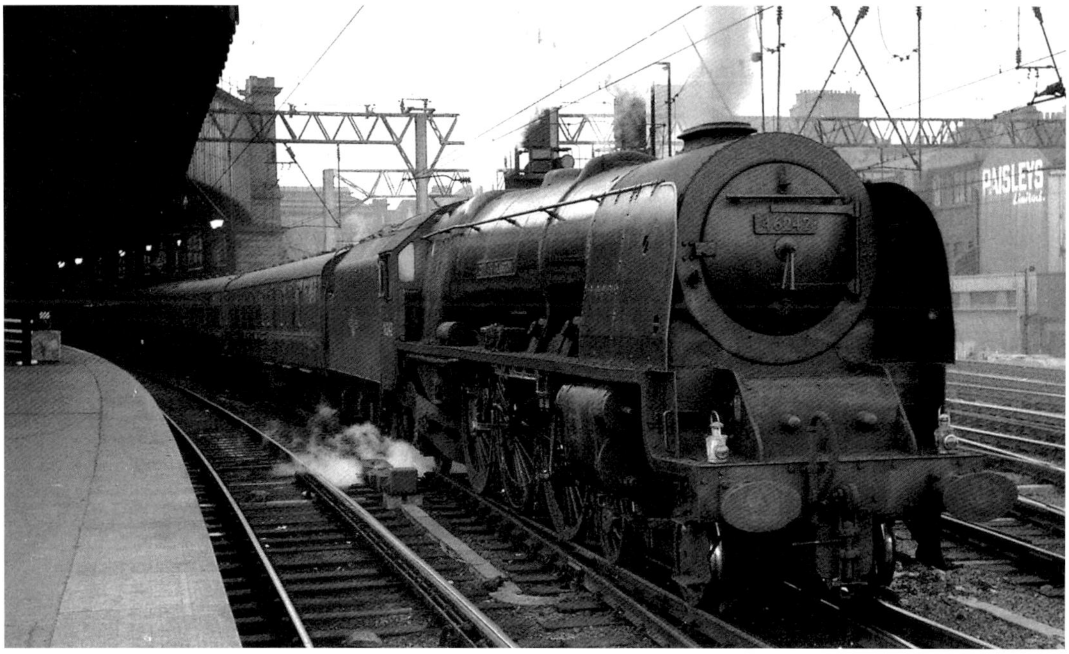

Princess Coronation Class 8P No. 46242 "City of Glasgow" waits to depart from Platform 10 with the 9.25pm train for Euston.

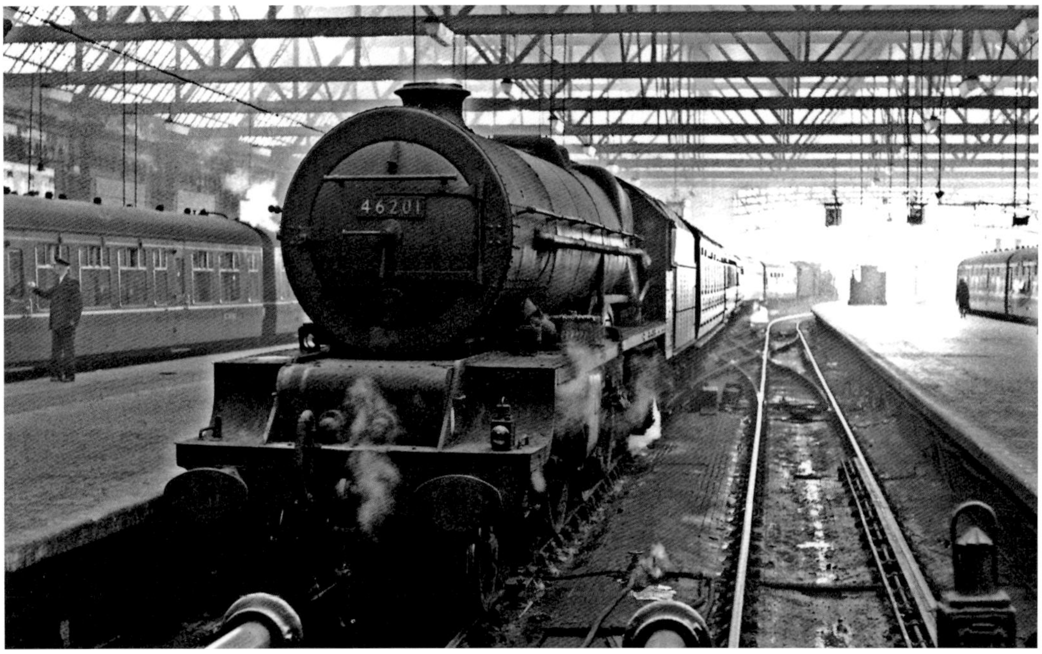

The second Stanier Pacific, No. 46201 "Princess Elizabeth", stands at the buffers having arrived with a Carlisle local on one of her last turns in 1962. Already positioned on the southern end of the coaches ready for the return working at 1225, is rebuilt Royal Scot No. 46166 "The London Rifle Brigade".

Electric, steam and diesel traction in Central's Platforms 6, 5 & 4. 'Blue Train' set No. 030 waits to leave for Motherwell while alongside sits Stanier Pacific No. 46254 "City of Stoke-on-Trent" and a driver patiently sits in his DMU.

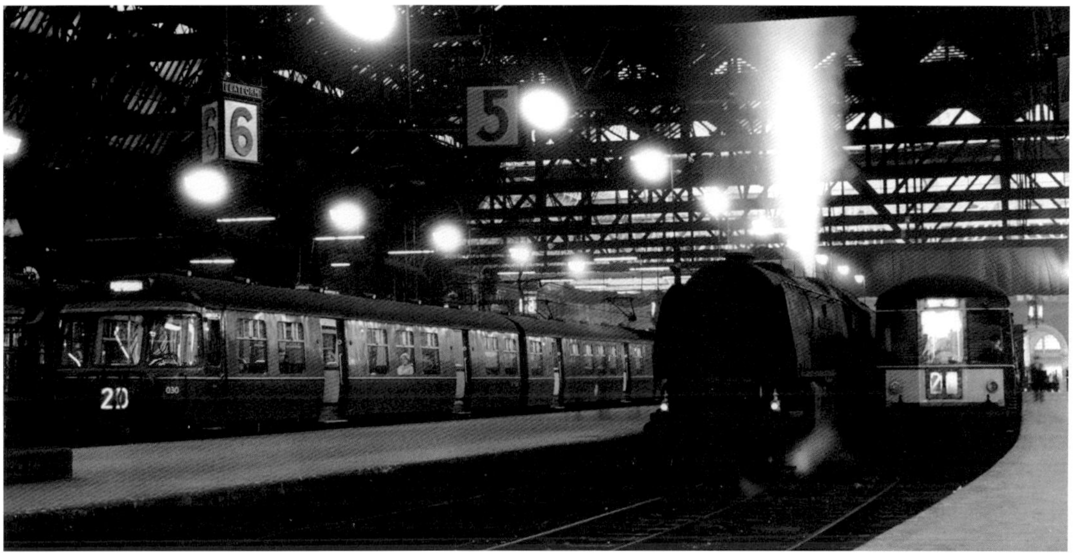

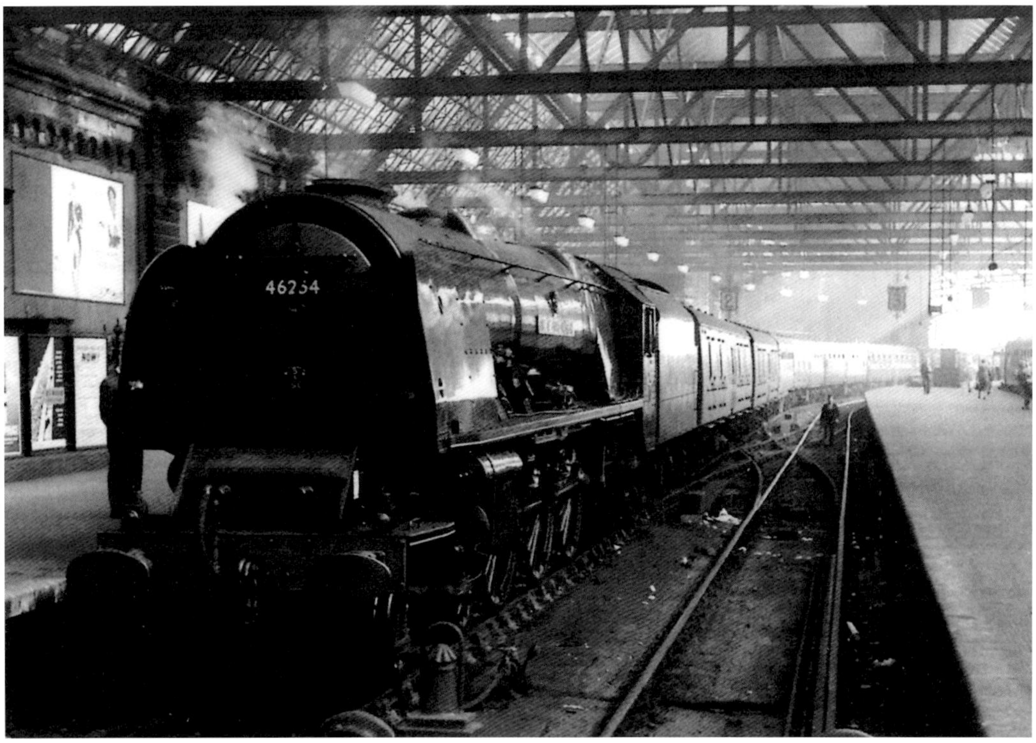

Princess Coronation Class 8P No. 46254 "City of Stoke-on-Trent" at the buffers on Platform 2 after arriving with the Birmingham train on 5 July 1961.

24 The Cathcart Circle

Jack Kernahan

" God made the country, man made the cities and the railway made the suburbs" –
Snooker Tam of the Cathcart Railway (1919)

The Glasgow and South Western Railway's terminus at St Enoch opened in 1876, followed by the Caledonian's Central Station in 1879. The availability of these fine stations in the centre of the city was the launch pad for the promotion of the suburban line to the south of the city, which, on its completion in 1894, became the famous Cathcart Circle.

On 15 November of the year Central opened, three competing schemes to bring the railway to the village of Cathcart were advertised in the newspapers. All three were designed to allow trains to operate into either St Enoch or Central station, and accordingly they required to have the backing of either the G&SWR or the CR. The G&SWR did not consider any of the projects viable and accordingly the successful line, that of the Cathcart District Railway, became allied with the Caledonian. The originally planned line from near Queen's Park to a point north of Strathbungo, permitting through running to St Enoch, was dropped.

The original line ran from Cathcart Junction, just north of Muirhouse Junction on the Central Station Extension Line, to Cathcart. Although only around two miles in length, it was not until 1 March 1886 that the line opened as far as Mount Florida, being extended to Cathcart on 25 May of that year. The first sod had been cut with due ceremony on 20 January 1883.

The works involved were difficult, involving substantial walled cuttings between Pollokshields East and Crosshill and at Mount Florida. The contract was let to the contractor offering the lowest price, but this effectively bankrupted him and the contract had to be re-let. The station building at Cathcart was not of the quality of the fine glazed canopied buildings on the island platforms of the intermediate stations, as it was not intended to be permanent. Nevertheless, the station was the first building in the village to be lit by electricity, power being brought from the recently opened G & J Weir Ltd marine engineering factory in the winter of 1887. It was also the first to use a telephone, when an innovative link, using zinc plates, was installed by a local gentleman to operate between the station and the signal box.

A few months after Cathcart District Railway opened, the directors were actively considering the completion of the circle by continuing their new line back into the city. The originally intended line through Langside and Pollokshaws would however be extended by crossing the Glasgow, Barrhead and Kilmarnock Railway (GB&K) route at Shawlands and including Maxwell Park before returning towards the city and joining the existing railway at Muirhouse Junction. This was a very different proposition from the original line, as there was only one existing area with a population to provide customers, the village of Pollokshaws which was already served by the GB&K. The extension would require no walled cuttings, but would be built on embankments between Cathcart and Pollokshaws and between Shawlands and Maxwell Park, with a major cutting through Shaw Hill just before Shawlands station, and a shallow cutting between Maxwell Park and Pollokshields West. An essential feature was the provision of several wide girder bridges across open fields, but designed for the roads anticipated as a consequence of the building developments which would follow the construction of the new line. The River Cart would be crossed twice, once at Cathcart, just to the east of the new station and again at Pollokshaws East where the station building was beautifully situated immediately above the river. The extension line opened on 2 April 1894, and the Cathcart Circle was complete.

An intense service of 42 trains per day operated on the original line to Cathcart, with 39 on Saturdays, but no Sunday service. In the first decade of the twentieth century an intense service of one train every ten minutes operated round the Circle, three trains per hour on both inner and outer circles. The line was worked by the Caledonian, which had assumed effective control of the Cathcart company after providing financial assistance to allow the completion of the original line, although the

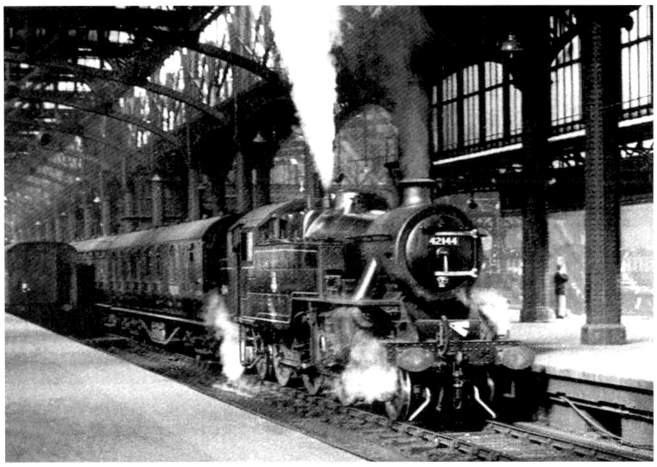

With a good head of steam Fairburn 2-6-4 tank No.42144 waits to depart from platform 10 with an Outer Circle train on 2 September 1954.

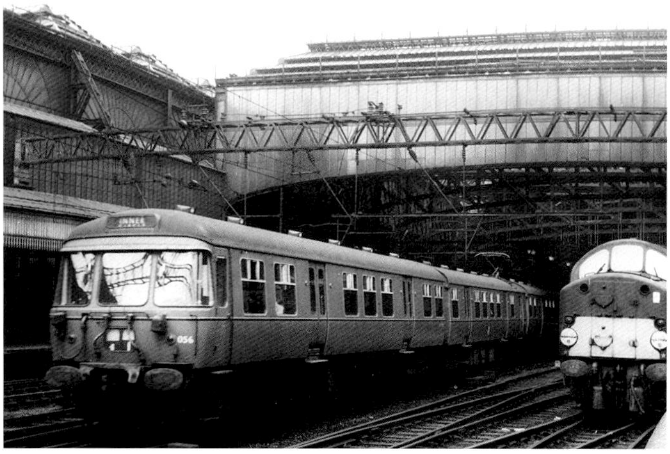

EMU set 056 in the original 'Blue Train' livery leaves with an Inner Circle service past an EE Type 4 at that time (before TOPS!).

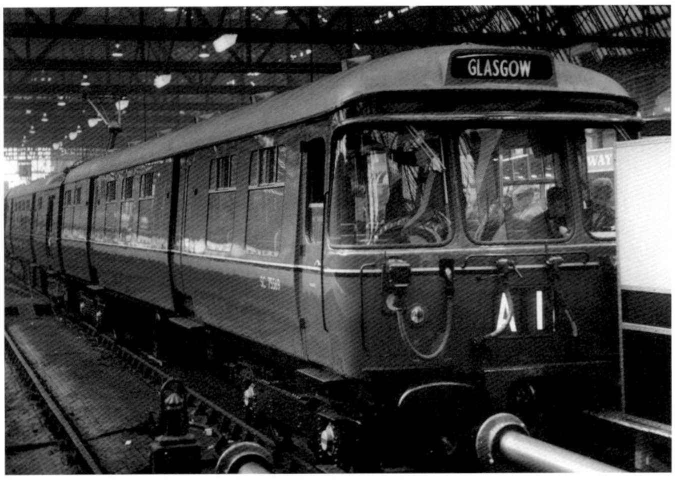

EMU unit 004 on display in Central Station during the Scottish Industries Exhibition in September 1959.

Cathcart District Railway Company remained independent until 1923. Profits were sufficient for a small dividend to be paid in the first three years after the opening to Cathcart, but reduced dramatically from 1890, due largely to tramway competition. The shareholders in the early 1890s were receiving no dividend, were watching the company's accumulated deficit mounting annually, and were financing the building of an extension through an area with little population! The income level achieved in 1889 was not reached again until 1897 after the extension was opened. Dividends then recommenced and were paid steadily at between 2 and 4% until the end of the company's independent existence.

The anticipated house building was not long in following the railway, with the goods yards at Pollokshaws East and Maxwell Park being used for unloading the stone for the new houses. By 1912 the last of the empty bridges was filled with new roads and the stations were busy, fares having been brought to a level competitive with the trams. In some areas, such as Langside and Maxwell Park, there was no other public transport, a situation which pertains to this day.

In 1903 and 1904 the extension of the Lanarkshire and Ayrshire Railway from Giffen to Newton brought additional traffic to the eastern side of the circle, not only in the form of suburban services to Kirkhill and Uplawmoor, but also fast boat trains to Ardrossan connecting with steamers to Arran and Belfast. Through running from Kirkhill to the western side of the Circle was not possible until Cathcart West Junction was remodelled in 1981.

The Cathcart Circle was signalled for the high level of service provided, with 13 signalboxes along a route of less than six miles. It was not long before this provision was found to be excessive, and Langside, Shawlands and Pollokshields West were permanently out of use from 1900. They were not officially closed and the signals removed for a further 27 years!

The greatest activity on the Circle was on days when there were big football matches at Hampden Park. While trains from furth of Glasgow used King's Park, local fans were catered for by an intense service between Glasgow Central and Mount Florida. For the return traffic, the Circle was closed to ordinary traffic and up to twenty trains stood nose to tail on the inner circle from Cathcart North Junction back as far as Pollokshaws East to be handsignalled into Mount Florida, where a third platform for this traffic had been provided on the site of the signalbox, which had closed in 1938.

The Circle trains were operated principally by tank engines. The '104' class, with 4' 6" driving wheels, were built specifically for the Circle and the Balerno branch in Edinburgh. Strangely, although the Circle had a far more intense service than the Balerno branch, out of twelve built, only four were allocated to Polmadie shed, but eight to Dalry Road, Edinburgh. To operate the ten-minute service required a minimum of five locomotives.

After the strengthening of some of the bridges in early LMS days, the line was cleared not only for the heavier '439' class tanks but also for larger engines which were frequently used tender first, so that they were turned without the necessity of using a turntable. Thus some of the Caledonian's finest locomotives, such as 'Cardean', 49 and 50 and the '60' class, have graced the Cathcart Circle. By the 1950s LMS and BR 2-6-4 tanks replaced the 0-4-4s and in 1958 the first diesel multiple units appeared. Everything changed with electrification on 27 May 1962.

The writer of a letter to The Glasgow Herald in 1953 hoped that "it would be a long time before the line was reduced to a punctual, fool-proof, characterless, push-button electric railway". The Editorial agreed, stating that the Circle was "worthy of respect and devoted preservation as an ancient monument". Many of the stations have been unstaffed since 1987, robbing the line of the many characters who composed the station staff, and the letter writer would be astonished at the closed circuit television cameras which now provide security at the stations.

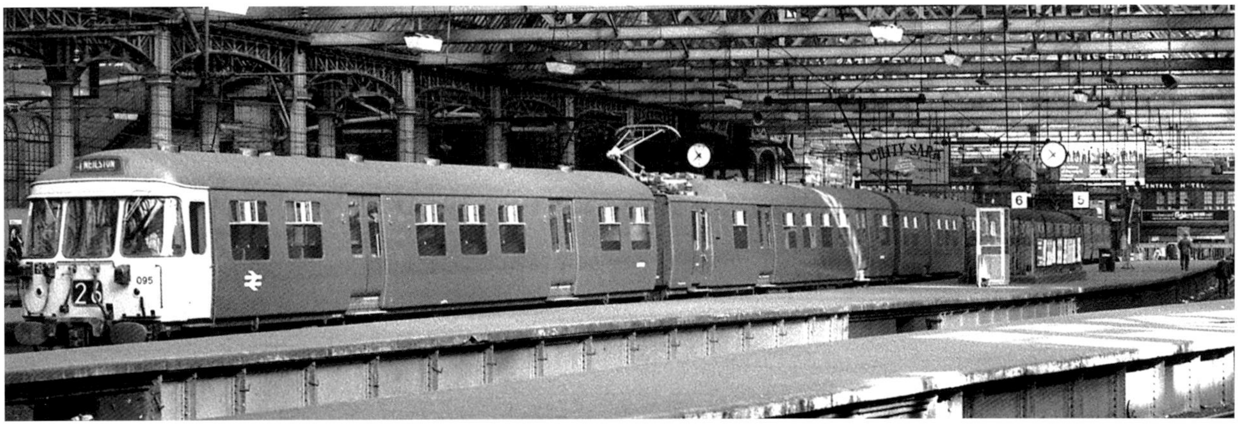

EMU set 056 in the unlined 'Rail Blue' livery sits in platform 5 with a train for Neilston.

25 With flag and whistle

Hugh Gould

As a student at Glasgow University, I spent several summer vacations in the employment of British Railways. Having learned the rudiments of station operation in 1952 at Drumchapel and 1953 at Glasgow Green, I had ambitions to be a Guard. After some machinations, in 1954, I was sent to Glasgow Central as a Porter-Guard, a hybrid grade with four hours train running and four per day on station work. The latter was tedious in the extreme, although I can at least claim to have swept the Union Street stairs.

But only a crass fool would attempt to earn an honest penny carrying luggage. This practice, known as "swadging", was the prerogative of the permanent mafia. So, after too many days thumb-twiddling, I pointed out to the Station Master Jimmy Scott that he had a far greater shortage of Passenger Guards than Porter Guards, and I was thereupon made-up to a fully-fledged Passenger Guard for the rest of the Summer. At that time, i.e. before the closure of St Enoch station, there were 53 Guards duties at Glasgow Central – four "links" of twelve duties, each rotating weekly and usually early and late turns on alternate weeks, plus a small group of miscellaneous duties. The latter included two historical turns to Ardrossan Montgomerie Pier with boat trains (formerly

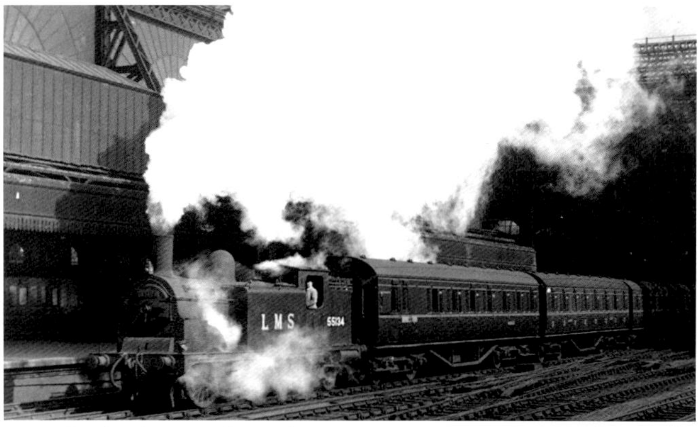

Regular haulage on the Cathcart Circle was provided by the trusted Caley 0-4-4 tanks. In June 1949, still wearing 'LMS' titles, this stovepipe chimney engine carries its new BR number of 55134.

routed via the Caledonian route, but now run over G & S.W metals). Finally, there was a small "spare link" – to which I was assigned. The duties of the "spare" were varied as to be expected; but not totally so, as a system of "link promotion" covered annual leave and absences of any length by the senior men.

So I spent a great deal of time on that great turntable, the Cathcart Circle, so often worked by Lanarkshire 4-4-0s tender-first, saving themselves a trip to Polmadie depot. Occasionally, too, a Caledonian 0-4-4T would turn up on the Circle, adding an extra touch of interest. The vast majority of the duties, however, were the preserve of the BR Standard and Fairburn 2-6-4Ts of the sheds at Polmadie, Greenock Ladyburn, and sometimes Motherwell. At peak times, many of the suburban trains were propelled empty to or from Smith Lye, the storage sidings east of Shields Road station – duties which were not as boring as might be supposed, since the Guard had control of the brake for these movements. Main line empty stock movements to and from Polmadie lacked this element of spice, but did have more interesting stock, and they frequently produced Caledonian 0-4-4Ts (the CR 4-6-2Ts had already gone).

The élite top link, whose members all seemed incredibly elderly to a young student, though none could have been over 65, had an interesting range of duties, including a lodging turn to Euston with the Royal Scot, several Carlisle turns, and most of the duties to Edinburgh Princes St. Two of these latter illustrated the benefits consequent upon the nationalisation of the separate companies of four years previous: a formerly unbalanced early duty now returned working the 1.00 pm Waverley to Queen St.; and a late duty started with the 3.00 pm Queen St. to Waverley and returned via Shotts, thereby eliminating part of a Waverley Guard's duty, which doubtless caused Trade Union ructions by treading on two traditional rivalries – Glasgow v. Edinburgh and Caley v. N.B. – both at once.

Glasgow Central Guards had very little work on the Lanarkshire lines, most of that being covered by Motherwell, Hamilton or Lanark Guards. There was,

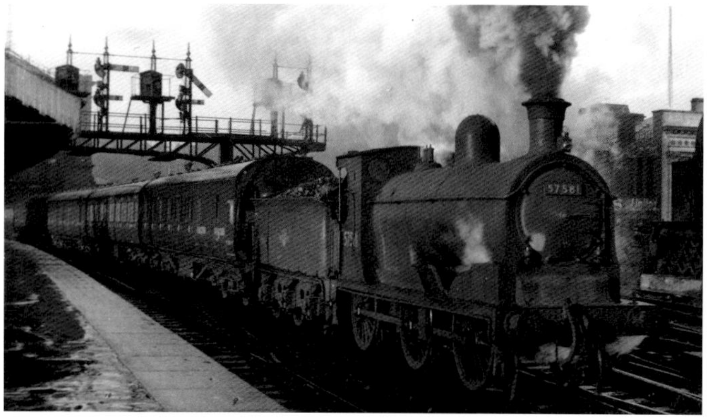

Caley 0-6-0 No. 57581 on a Kirkhill train in 1954.

however, an interesting Saturday Only duty on Turn 25, 2.20 pm to Coalburn and 4.18 pm return. Saturday late-turn duties being unpopular and therefore easy to swap, I soon found a grateful colleague to take my early duty on 18 September, and off I went on the 2.20 pm Coalburn, with loco No. 42166. I knew that the Coalburn trains went on to Bankend to turn round, but I did not know – until I got there – that the Guard had to operate the single line token instrument. So the signalman at the far end was entertained by an impressive performance on the machinery until I worked out how to do it. I returned to Glasgow mildly embarrassed and somewhat wiser.

Another minor brush with the infrastructure occurred on 23 July, on Turn 39 of No. 4 link. This involved the 7.26 am to Busby, which had to be shunted briefly into Busby goods yard to let other trains pass, before returning to Glasgow at 8.44 am. The engine that morning was Caley Jumbo No. 57448, and I was thoroughly contented as we started to propel round the blind curve into the yard at Busby. To my horror I suddenly saw that we were

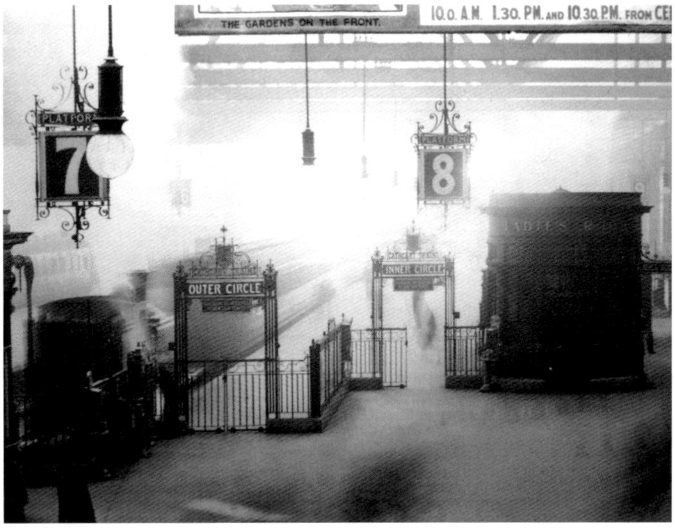

The Cathcart Circle Platforms in Caley days.

heading into a siding full of wagons. I jumped off, grabbed the point lever, and managed to move the blade, but could not get the lever fully across to lock it. All I could do was hang on grimly as the train rolled by. The expression on the Driver's face as he came into view was well worth seeing, but no harm came of the incident.

Less exciting, more amusing incidents come to mind. Three days before the Busby incident, on 20 July, I worked the 8.00 pm Cathcart Inner Circle on behalf of East Kilbride Turn 2, who was probably having tea in the guards room. The engine was No. 76002 of Motherwell, running (supposedly) tender first on one of those "turntable" jobs already mentioned. I flagged the train away and was about to leap into my van when the train took off in fine style straight into the hydraulic buffers with a very, very impressive clang. No problem, just reverse and go, but had the train been arriving instead of departing, and everyone on their feet opening doors, it might have been different.

Sometimes Guards from the "spare" link were used to cover duties at the outlying, smaller depots, and so in the first week of August, I found myself on Rutherglen Passenger Guard Turn No. 5, which was lazy but an interesting change. It consisted only of the 4.45 pm Rutherglen to Balloch, returning with the 6.50 pm Parcels Balloch to Central Low Level, and empty to Rutherglen. The 6.50 pm was featherweight, just two bogies (BGs), and on the Friday evening No. 42169 took the sharp curve at Finnieston (now Exhibition Centre) eastbound "a bit cheery" as they say, and a mountain of boxes from Westclox at Dumbarton collapsed on the van floor. Apparently the clocks were all primed, and the resultant sound was a joy to hear.

On 30 August, on Turn 45, I was on the 6.52 am Central to Bishopton when the engine, Standard tank No. 80026, suffered a double injector failure at Paisley Gilmour St, and the fire had to be dropped. I went rushing back, clutching my detonators to protect my train as taught, and on reaching Wallneuk Jn. signal box, placed three on the track (correct) but only inches apart (not correct: they should be ten yards apart). The signalman's wild gesticulations from the box baffled me at first, until the penny dropped. We were rescued very promptly by No. 57268, shunting at St James, and suddenly thrust into the limelight. Unfortunately the old faithful was not vacuum-fitted, so we made hesitant progress, stopping from time to time to release the brakes. Even so, we were only 32 minutes late at Bishopton. An interesting feature of this incident was that throughout the delay at Gilmour St., not a window was opened, not a voice was raised, not a complaint heard: folk were on their way to work. But when an early evening train, from Singer to Bridgeton Cross N.B, failed between High St. and Bridgeton, all hell broke loose, folk were jumping out of the train and running through the tunnel: they were on their way home. So, if you must have an engine failure, make sure you are going in the right direction.

Throughout my short time at Glasgow Central I enjoyed an excellent rapport with my colleagues. My tutor, Guard Bob Holland, whisked me through the rules and regulations and had me ready for the road in double-quick time. I made good friends, and as recently as the late '90s, I had coffee in a Barrhead cafe with Alastair Cameron, a No. 3 link Guard in 1954, subsequently a Station Inspector, and now in his eighties. In the Time Office, too, I had a good rapport, although the occupants there were not universally popular. They were known as the two Italians, *Signor Amgoni* and *Signor Amenti*, which I think was a little unfair, since their powers to assist were probably more limited than many realised.

I returned to Glasgow Central in the summer of 1957 as a Management Trainee, and saw the wider issues of running a large station. One delicious moment from the Information Office comes to mind:

> *"Want a train to Gourock"*
> *"Certainly. About what time?"*
> *"12.00"*
> *"Yes, there's a train at 11.50"*
> *"No wan later than that?"*
> *"Yes, there's another one at 12.10"*
> *"No wan one earlier than that?"*

Classic Glasgow indeed!

All five summers on the railway were supremely happy, probably the most carefree of my life, but although it is difficult to pinpoint specific moments, I think it was almost certainly in the congenial atmosphere of Glasgow Central in 1954 that I took the decision to seek a career on the railway. It was the best decision I ever took.

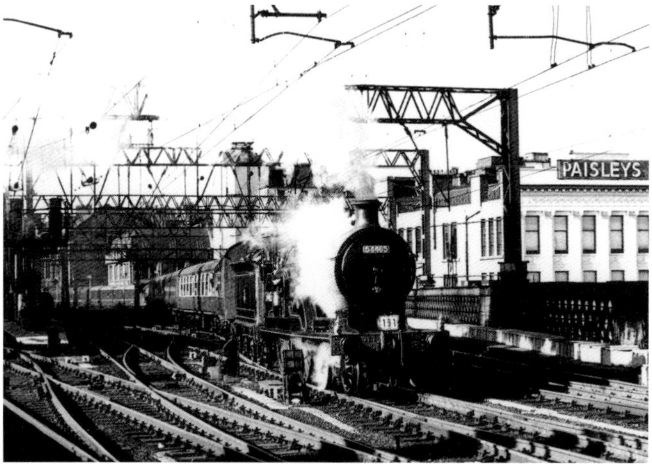

The last steam train ran on the Cathcart Circle on 26 May 1962 when a Special was hauled by Caley 'Bogie' No. 54465

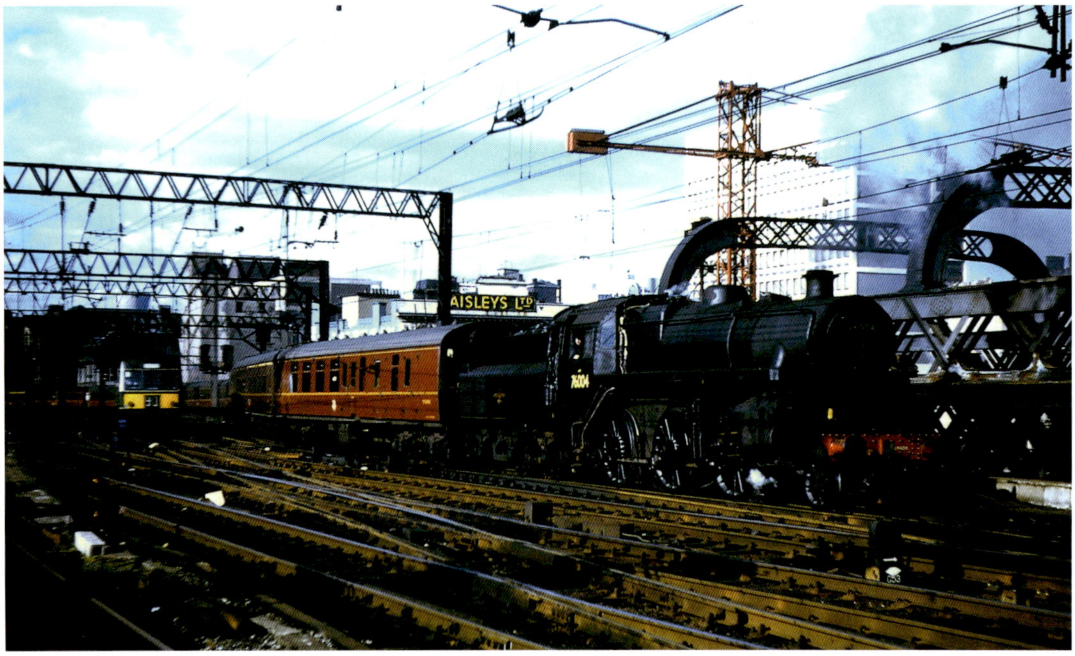

BR Standard Class 4 2-6-0 No. 76004 pulls out with empty stock on 1 August 1966

Rebuilt 'Royal Scot' Class 4-6-0 No. 46105 "Cameron Highlander" backs on to its train while an English Electric Type 4 (Class 40) stands at the head of the Up 'Royal Scot' train - April 1961.

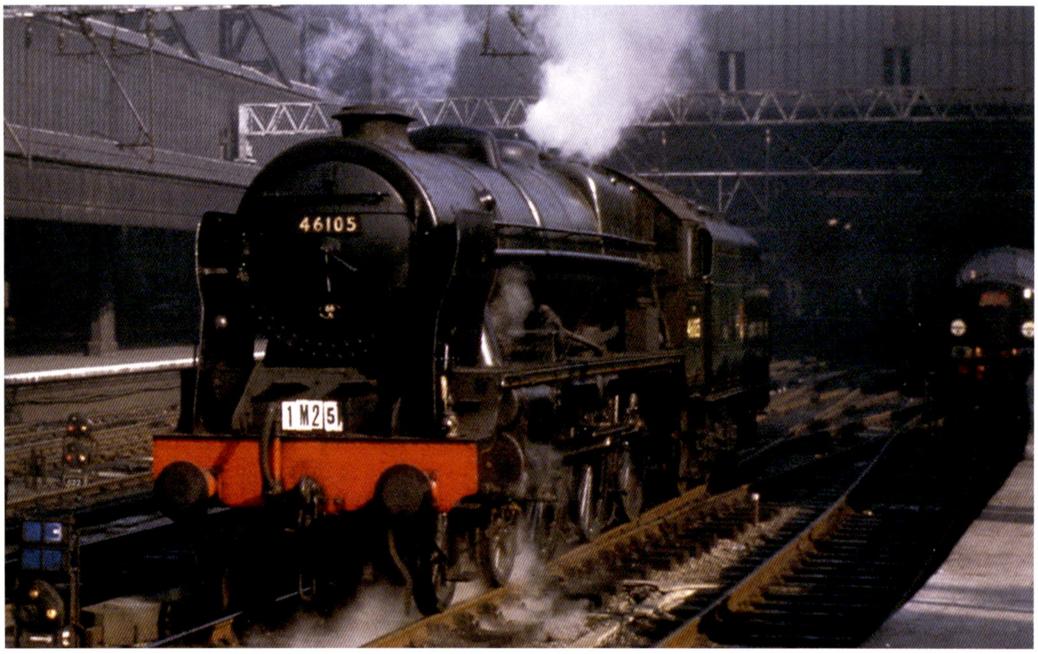

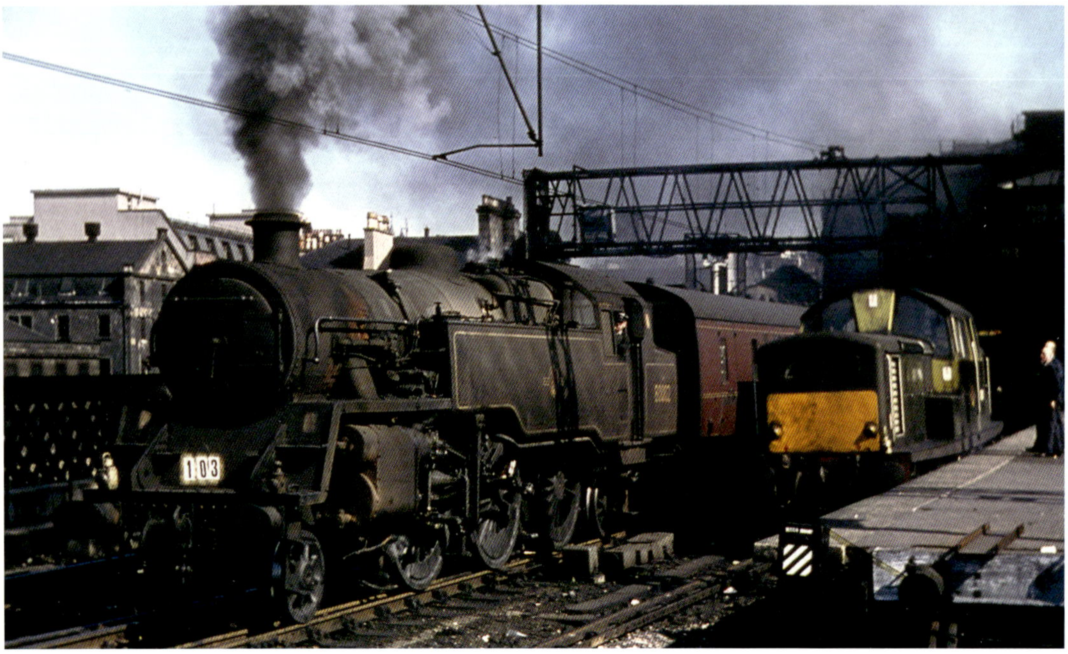

BR Standard Class 4 2-6-4 tank No. 80002 leaves with a Special express while a centre-cab Clayton diesel stands alongside - mid 1960s.

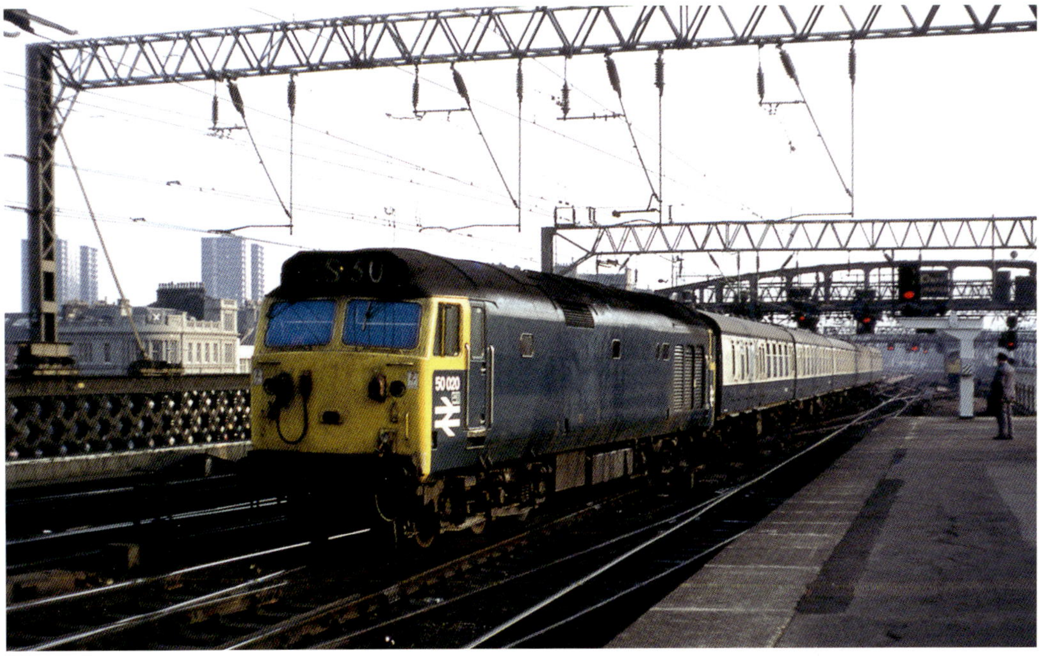

Class 50 diesel No. 50020 enters Central on a down express - 21 April 1974.

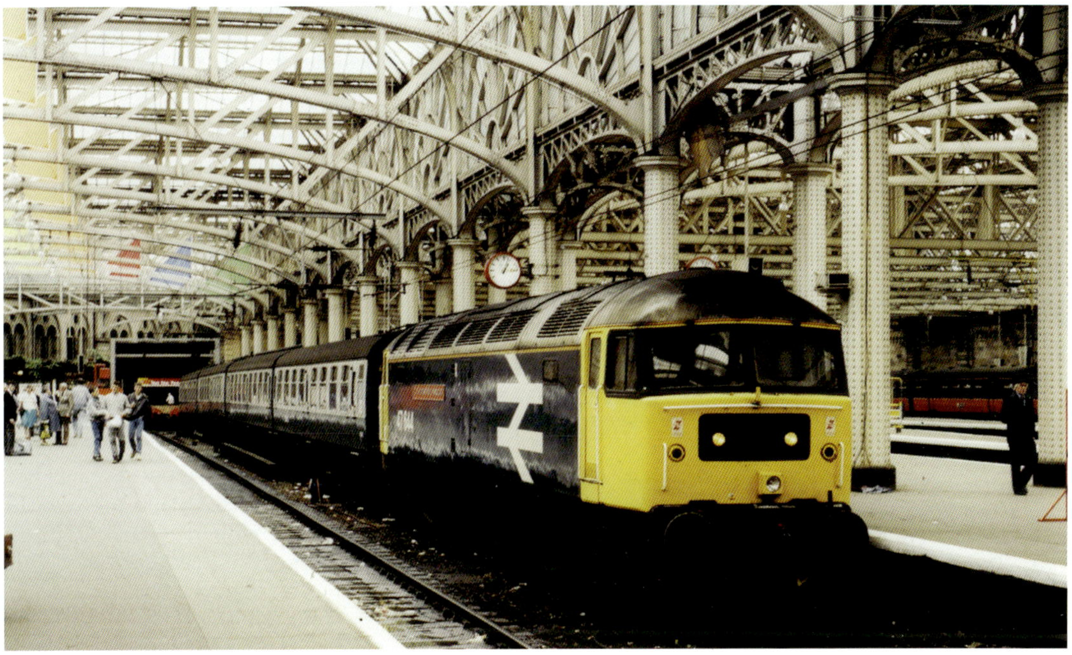

Class 47 No.47644 "The Permanent Way Institute" on a Stranraer train during the ScotRail days of the 1980s

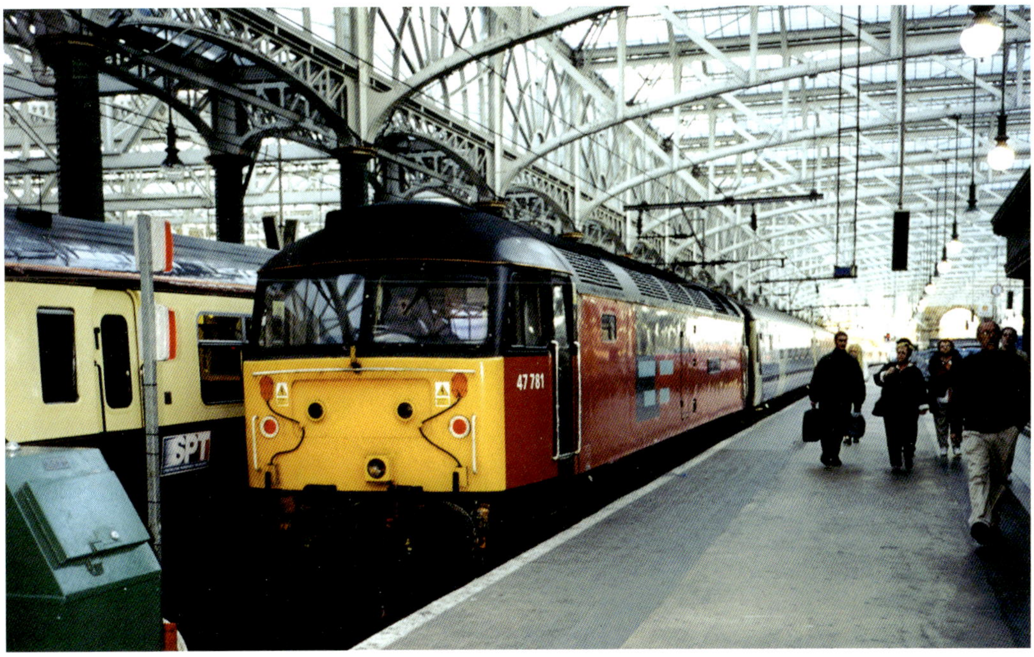

Class 47 No. 47781 "Isle of Iona" on Sleeper empty stock duty - 7 June 2001.

26 Diesels and electrics

Bob Osborne

The year 1947 was an eventful one. It marked the centenary of the opening of the Beattock to Carlisle section of the Caledonian Railway main line to the south. Further, it was the last year of the London Midland and Scottish Railway, which, having absorbed the Caledonian Railway at the Grouping a quarter of a century earlier, was now itself subsumed with the other railway companies into the nationalised British Railways (BR) from 1 January 1948.

Nationalisation in turn led to a series of profound events affecting Glasgow's railways - the Modernisation Plan (1955), the rationalisation started by the Beeching report (1963), electrification (1960s onwards), the Sectorisation of

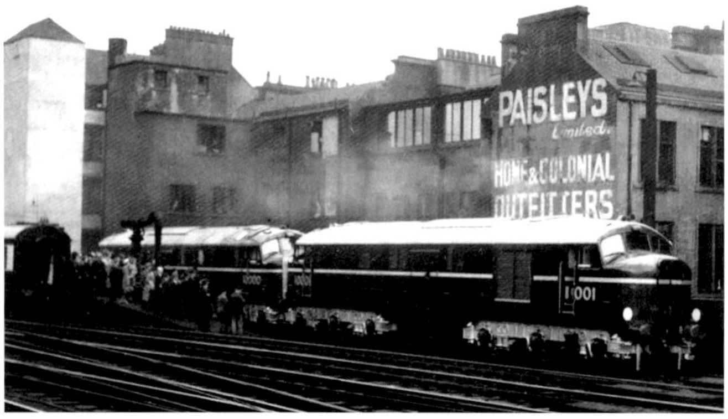

The first 'up' diesel hauled "Royal Scot" train with LMS Nos. 10000 and 10001 in charge on 2 June 1949.

the late 1980s, and finally the Privatisation of 1993-7. In the course of these changes, passenger trains hauled by steam locomotives were superseded, almost exclusively by those which needed no separate locomotive, known as multiple units, either diesel or electric (DMUs and EMUs). The year 1947 also heralded the dawn of that diesel and electric era for Glasgow's railways: on 8 December the first main line diesel locomotive, no. 10000, emerged from Derby Works. With sister no. 10001, it had a significant effect on the West Coast Main Line (WCML) from Central, reinforced by their successors.

The Anglo-Scottish Main Line services: After World War II, The Royal Scot, the most prestigious train of the route, returned on 16 February 1948, when the re-named 10 am service from Central was headed by a Duchess Pacific steam locomotive, no. 46242 City of Glasgow. However that train was to feature from the outset in the development of diesel traction. The recently-built diesels, nos. 10000/1 worked jointly on 5 October from Central to Carlisle, during a testing programme which included comparisons against steam in the form of the final "Duchess" Pacifics (nos. 46256/7), built contemporaneously. On 1 June 1949, the diesel pair completed the fourth ever non-stop run between Euston and Central, with the northbound The Royal Scot. The running was described as "dull" between "exhibitions of brilliant effort", opined observer Cecil J Allen. A regular spell of similar duties continued, with the locos performing high-mileage Anglo-Scottish diagrams of

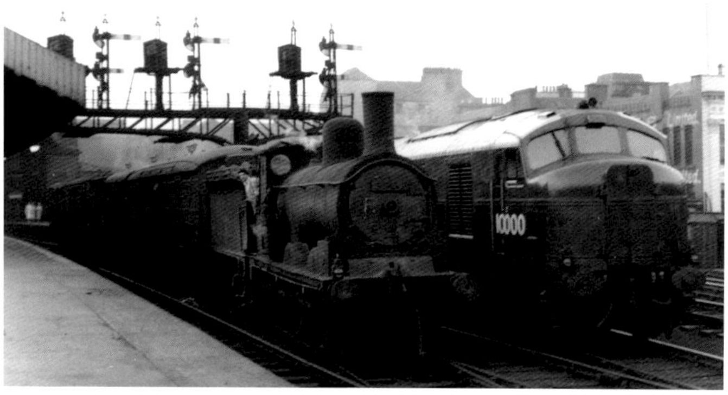

No. 10000 sits with the 9.25 pm Sleeper while a CR "Jumbo" acts as station pilot on 14 June 1957.

more than 800 miles per day on daytime/sleeper services, but typically including working (in multiple) The Royal Scot. The Southern Region had also been experimenting with diesel locomotives and between 1950 and 1954 built nos. 10201-3, which were developments of 10000/1. Subsequently, these too were directed to high mileage rosters on the WCML. Nos. 10201/2 generally worked in multiple on The Royal Scot, in contrast to 10203 which had an upgraded engine. Cecil J Allen recorded 10203 working from the Central to Beattock, and considered the locomotive was equal to a "Duchess", based on the performance that day, but felt that the diesel would be outclassed if a Pacific were to be really extended. These five experimental locomotives led to the D200 production series (Class 40) delivered from 1959 for the WCML; however, their performances were deficient when

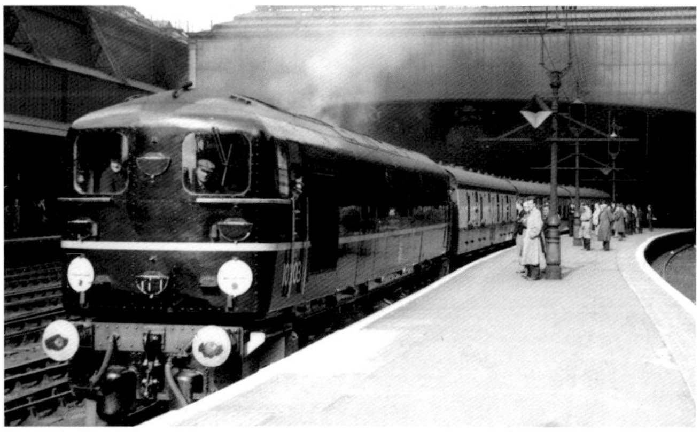

Former Southern Region diesel locomotive No. 10203 on the Up "Mid Day Scot" 19 September 1955, the first day of a four week trial running between Glasgow and Euston.

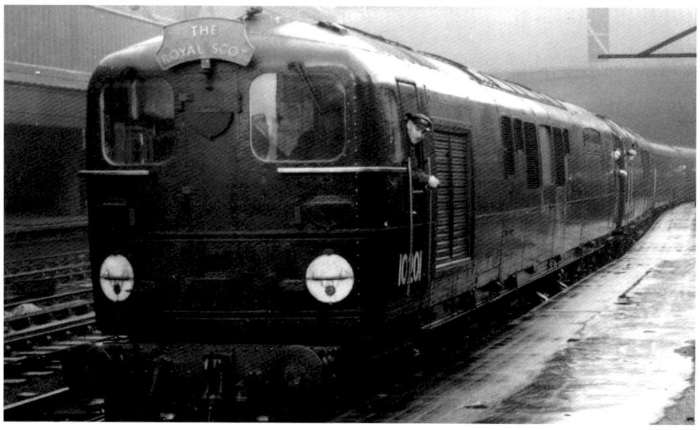

Ex-SR diesels 10201 & 10202 power "The Royal Scot" on 21 November 1957.

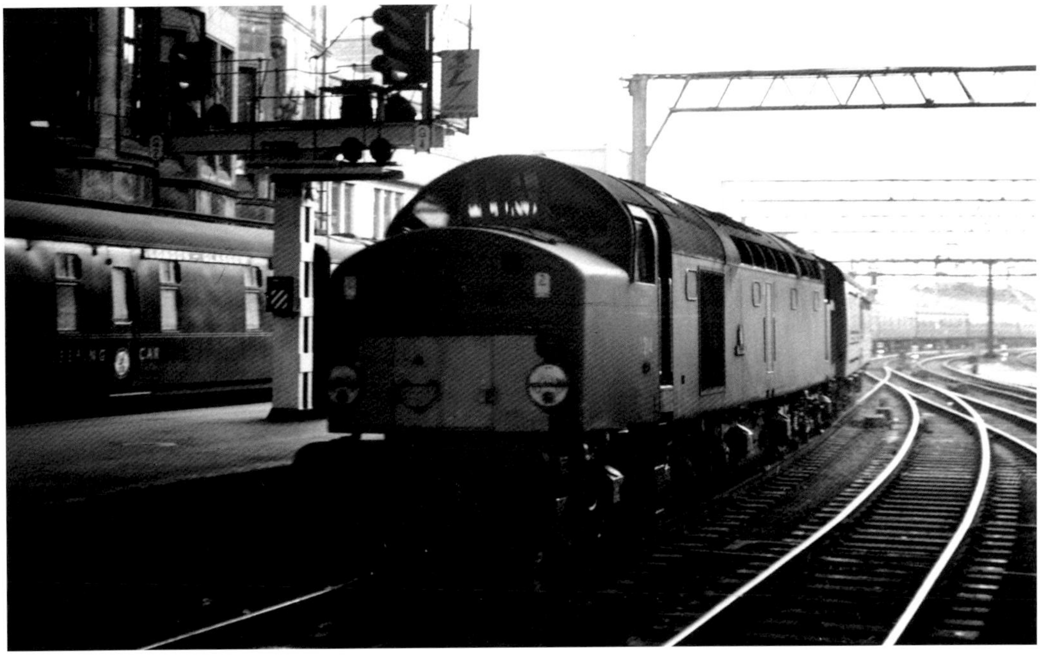

English Electric Type 4 No. D214"Antonia" enters Platform 2. The overhead masts are in place for electrification but no wires are yet attached.

Russian Premier Kosygin was in the BR Royal Train in 1967 hauled by a pair of EE Type 4s (Class 40s).

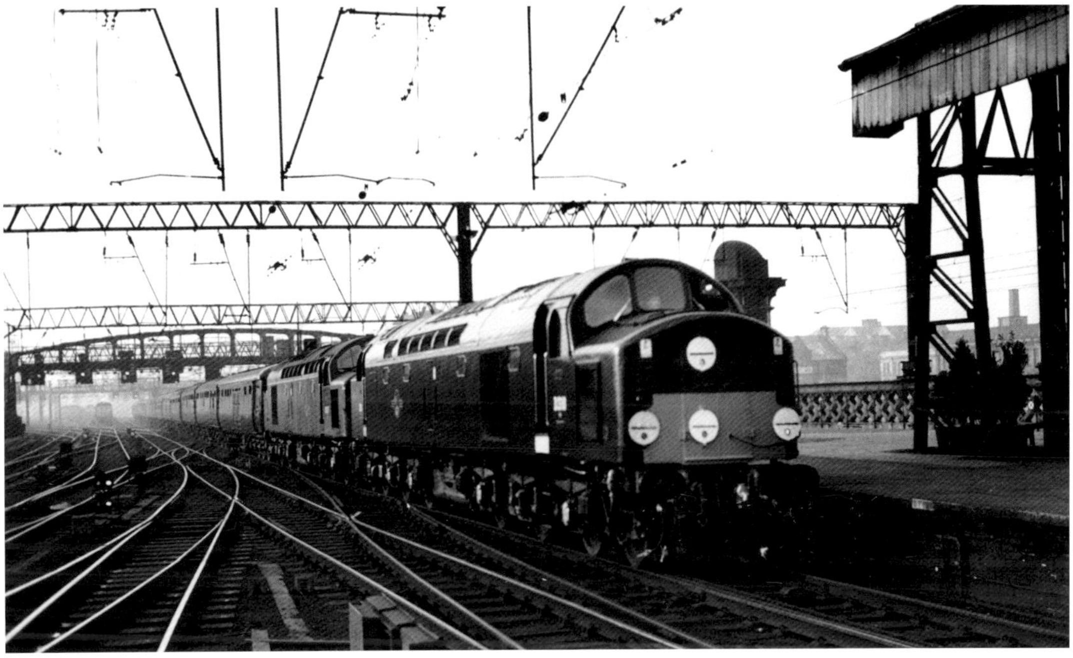

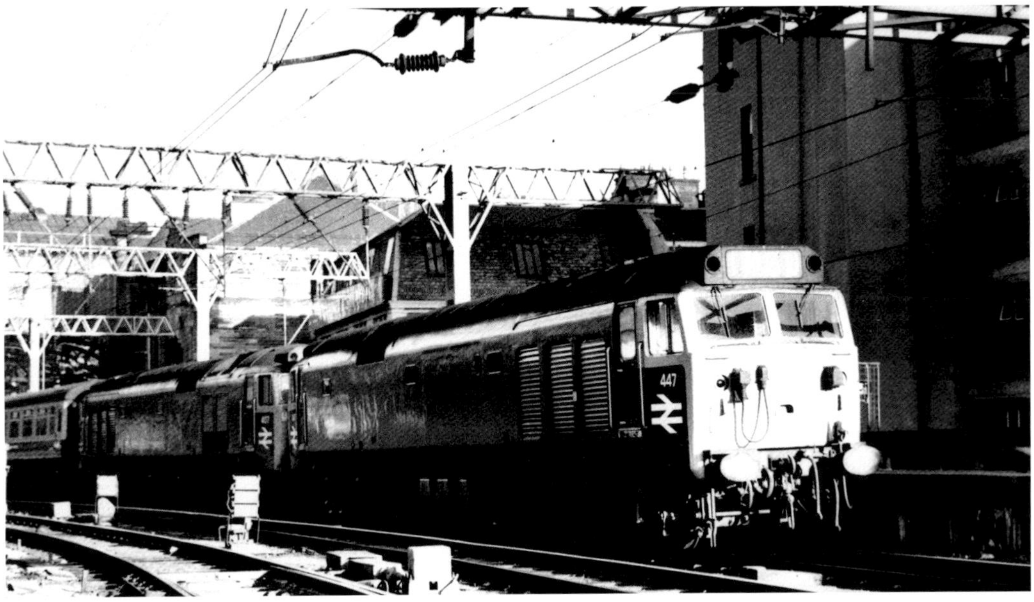

Double-headed English Electric Class 50 locomotives, Nos. 447 and 407 before the start of electric traction - early 1970s.

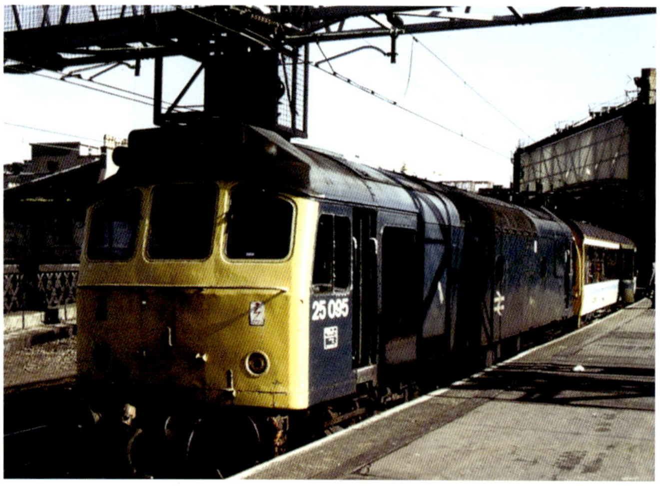

High days and holidays, an Officers' Special prepares to leave on an inspection of the line hauled by a Class 25 diesel No. 25095.

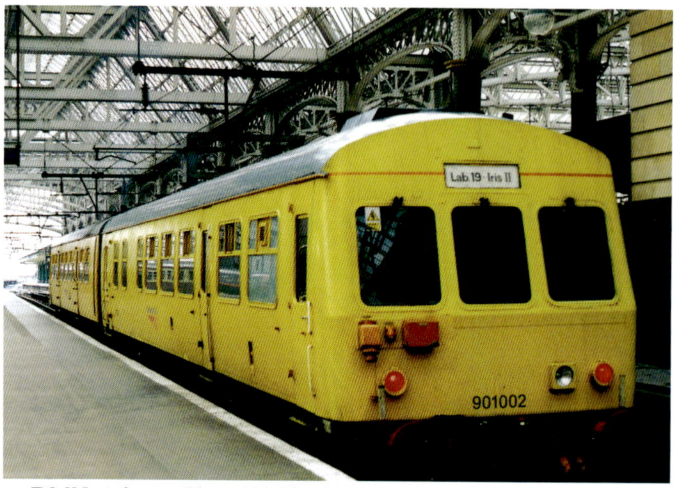

DMU stalwart Class 101 No. 901002 serving Network Rail as a mobile laboratory. Painted bright yellow and headed as "Lab 19 – Iris II" on 9 November 2005.

compared with the displaced Pacifics.

Other experimental diesel locomotives reaching Central included Deltic (DP-1), DP-2 and Kestrel. The Deltic workings into Central were limited to a trade special, although it powered Euston - Carlisle services around Christmas 1956. DP2 undertook trials between Central and London in summer 1962, but then followed Deltic to the East Coast; however its production successors – the Class 50s – became prime performers at Central. Appearances by Kestrel were few, though said to appear equal in performance to a pair of the Class 50s.

The Caledonian was introduced on 17 June 1957 as a limited load, minimum stop express, and duly eclipsed the contemporary The Royal Scot, by providing the fastest Glasgow to Euston schedule since wartime (6 hrs 40 mins). Duchess Pacific no. 46244 King George VI subsequently established a then post-war record of 5 hrs 3 mins southbound on 5 September that year. In the late 1950s, however, The Caledonian was decelerated due to electrification work, and diesels of Class 40 replacing the more powerful Pacifics from 6 February 1961. The train name disappeared in 1964, although it was briefly resurrected in the mid-1990s.

"Peak" Class 45/46 locos operated many long-distance services over the ex-Glasgow and South-Western lines from 1960/61, transferring with those trains upon closure of St Enoch. These services were progressively curtailed, and from the mid-1990s the ex-Caledonian route was dominant route from Glasgow Central to England. Brush Type 4 (Class 47) diesels had begun to be allocated to Glasgow's Polmadie depot in the mid-1960s, supplanting Class 40s on the premier expresses.

A timetable revolution resulted when electric haulage began between Euston and Crewe on 18 April 1966. The effects permeated the entire WCML, with accelerations to services to and from Central. Partly to further accelerate services on the non-electrified portion of the route north of Crewe, an order for English Electric diesel Class 50s was completed in December 1968. By 1969, they were almost exclusively devoted to Anglo-Scottish services, but the former Caledonian route via Beattock retained a speed limit of 75 mph, which dictated a non-stop schedule of about 110 minutes between Central and Carlisle for The Royal Scot with up to 13 Mark I coaches – most disappointing compared with the better steam performances.

Approval for electrification and associated work from Crewe to Motherwell finally came in 1970. Re-vamped Anglo-Scottish services commenced on 4 May that year. The Royal Scot was allocated two of the Class 50 locos and Mark II stock and was accelerated to take six hours to Euston, with some sustained 90/100 mph running expected south of Gretna. Unfortunately, the massive disruptions induced by the rebuilding of the line led to a traffic haemorrhage from which the West Coast route has

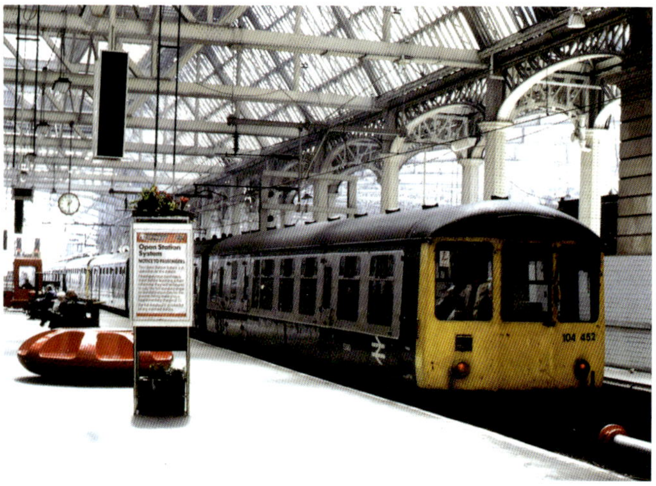

First generation DMU, Class 104 No. 104452 in the early 1980s. The notice detailing the 'Open Station System' and the red 'mushroom' seat are of interest.

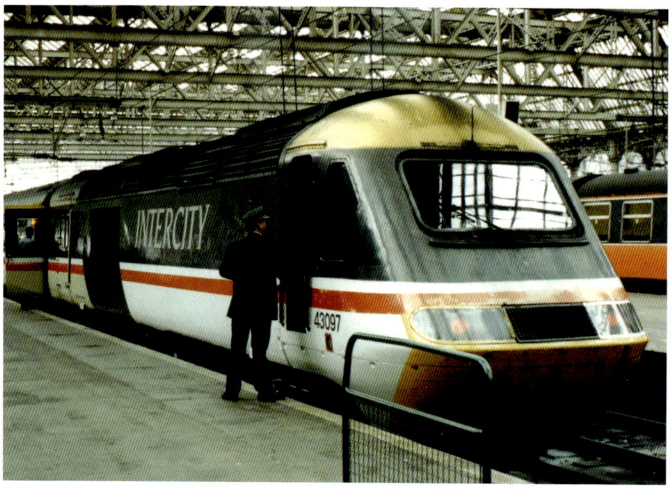

Intercity days - an HST No. 43097 stands at Platform 2.

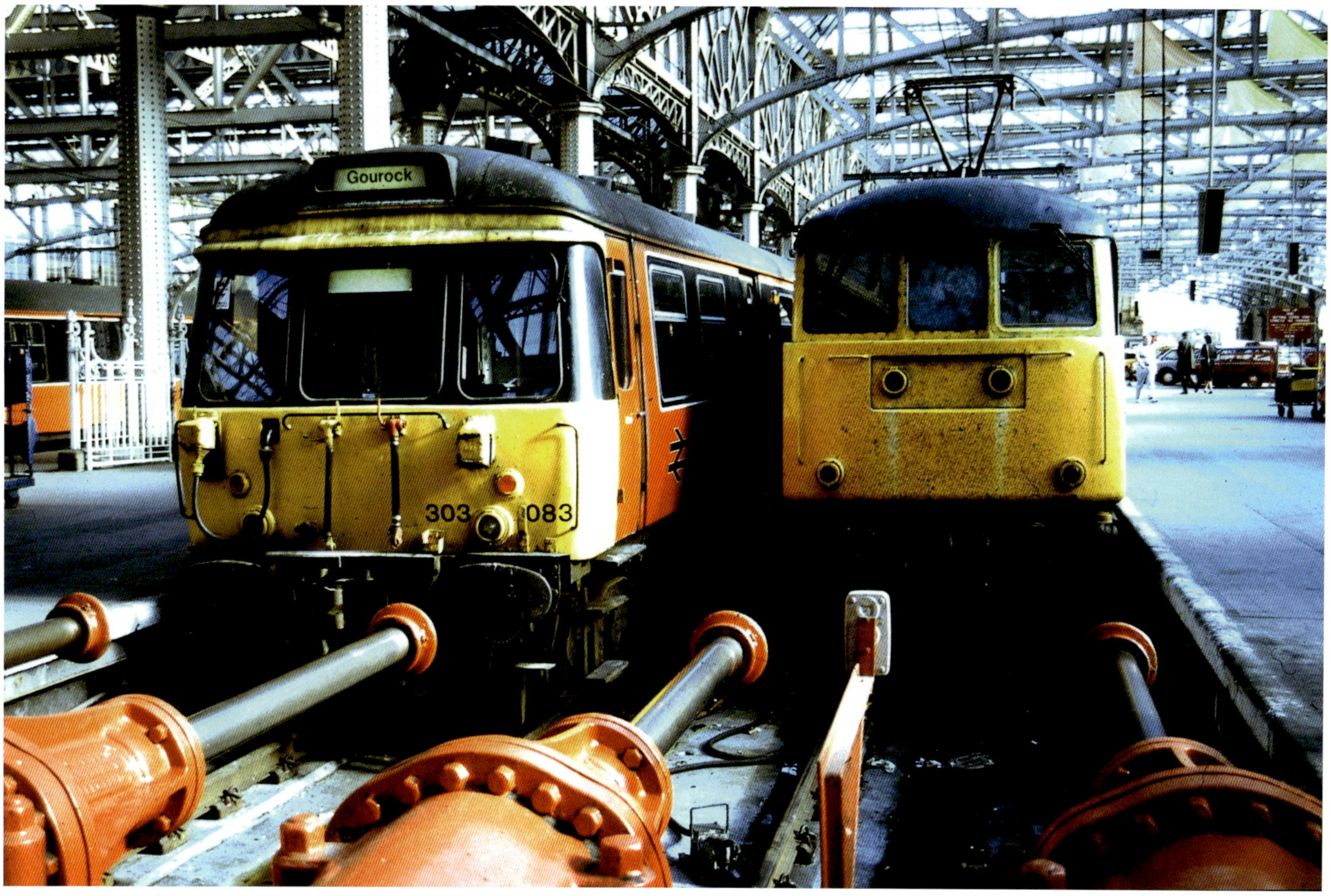

Safely berthed. Hydraulic buffers were installed to catch any train which didn't quite stop where it should, but the drivers at Central could bring several hundred tons of train assuredly to a stand at the right spot whatever the conditions. On 28 May 1990 electric suburban unit 303083 and locomotive 85034 with its long distance train have been placed in an exemplary manner.

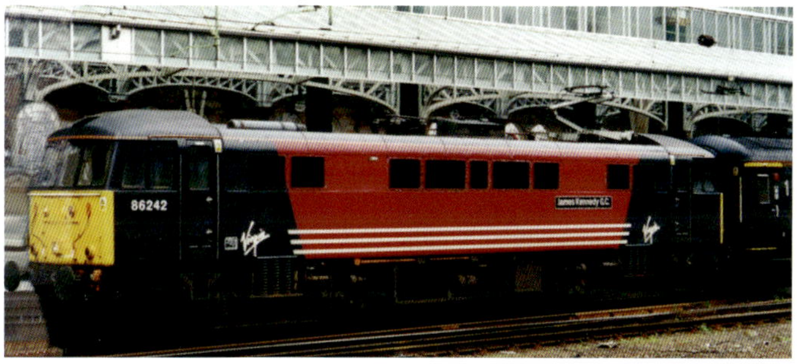

Class 86 electric locomotive No. 86242 "James Kennedy GC". The loco commemorates a very brave railwayman who, as a security officer at BREL Glasgow Works, was fatally injured during an armed robbery on 21 December 1973. The naming took place on 12 November 1981.

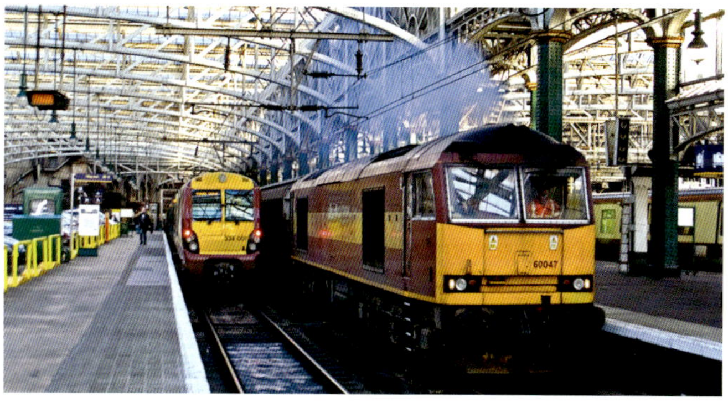

Diversionary tactics – freight at Central!

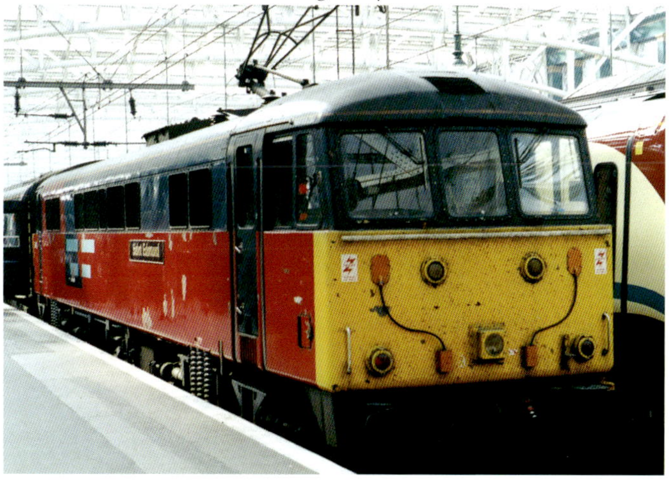

Rail Express Systems (Sector) liveried Class 86 No. 86430 "Saint Edmund" on 9 April 2002 on a Virgin CrossCountry passenger duty.

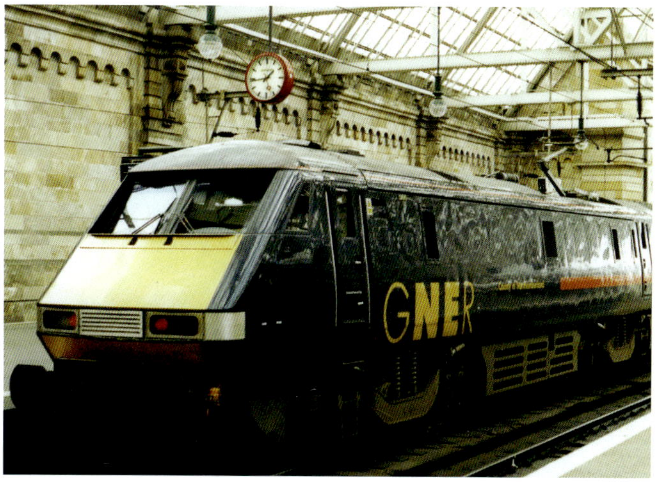

Class 91 No. 91031 "County of Northumberland", the last locomotive built in BR workshops in Crewe 1991.

perhaps never fully recovered. However, progressively, speed limits were eased, and air-conditioned Mark II stock appeared, with trains being hauled by Classes 47 or 50 north of Crewe. The principal expresses continued to be diagrammed for, but did not always receive, two of the latter. By 1973, Class 50s began to be transferred to the Western Region as their successors became available - electric locos of Classes 86 and 87; the latter particularly designed to ascend Shap/Beattock banks at high speed. During the commissioning following the electrification, no. 86202 was claimed to have well exceeded 120 mph near Beattock. Indeed, during that final diesel phase, the Class 50s were themselves returning some of their fastest work between Glasgow and Carlisle, with the veteran observer Nock describing one northbound journey as having approached the performance of an electric loco.

The full electric timetable, marketed as the "Electric Scots", transformed the route from 6 May 1974. The initial The Royal Scot behind no. 87018 took 4 hrs 56_ mins. from Euston to Central. Electric locomotives of Classes 81-87 now served Central, with the locomotives of Class 81 being allocated to Shields Road as home depot. The Advanced Passenger Train (APT) was also based at Shields Road. On test between Lockerbie and Beattock, an APT set the speed record for railways in Britain – 162.2 mph – on 20 December 1979 (until a Eurostar attained 208 mph on 30 July 2003 on the brand new Channel Tunnel Rail Link). During its short public service, the 0700 APT from Central on 7 December 1981 reached Euston in a then record time of 4 hrs 7 mins. and a non-stop farewell special completed the northbound journey in 3 hrs 52_ mins on 12 December 1984.

Further accelerations followed in 1985, using Class 87 locos with Mark III stock, after authorisation of 110 mph running for sections of the West Coast Main Line. Orders placed in 1986 included 50 electric Class 90 locos and Mark III Driving Van Trailers to enable withdrawal of elderly electric locos and Mark I stock and to introduce push-pull operation. 1989-91 saw the fastest ever loco-hauled schedule for The Royal Scot between Euston and Central of 4 hrs 43 mins. The year 1990 witnessed a revamping of the InterCity type Cross-Country trains serving Central with separate 7-coach air-conditioned Mark II sets hauled by Class 86 locos; subsequently, InterCity125 (HST) sets cascaded from the East Coast Main Line began further InterCity Cross-Country operations. Following the extension of the London Kings Cross - Edinburgh electrification to Carstairs from 1991, new direct services to/from the East Coast Main Line brought Class 91 electric locos and Mark IV stock into Central.

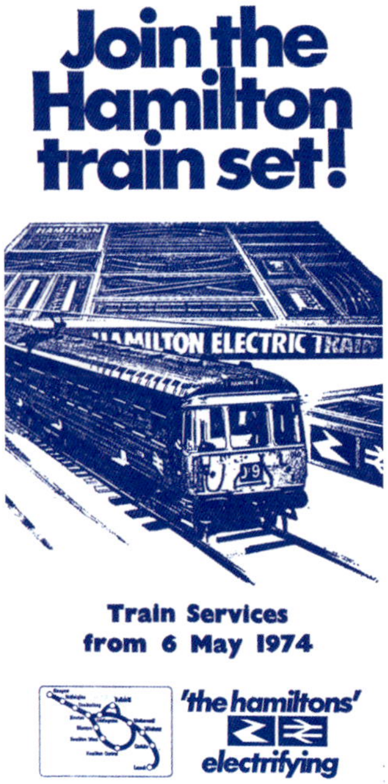

Post privatisation, Virgin "Voyager" units began displacing loco-hauled and HST sets on Cross-Country services from 17 April 2001, a process completed on 20 September 2003. Virgin "Pendolino" sets commenced WCML duties to Euston from 2002, and this transition was effectively complete at Central with the timetable change on 20 September 2004 (and a piper welcoming folk boarding the "Pendolino" forming The Royal Scot). The service was revamped with reduced times, facilitated by the tilting now possible with "Pendolinos" in the south. But in September 2004 those enhanced speeds were only permitted south of Crewe, and the The Royal Scot timing of 4 hrs 42 mins. to Euston did not compare favourably with the best loco-hauled performances of the early 1990s. It was to be 10 December 2005 before running at 125 mph could be experienced on sections of the ex-Caledonian part of the West Coast route. This date also saw the names The Royal Scot and The Caledonian again disappear.

However, the "Pendolino" sets have tremendous high-speed and potential for journey-shrinking as evidenced by set no. 309.047 "Heaven's Angels" on the high speed non-stop dash of 22 September 2006, reaching Euston in 3 hrs 55_ mins from Central; it will be fascinating to observe how they perform both in terms of that speed and as servants of the public. Less successful were the plans to operate "Eurostar" daytime and "Nightstar" sleeper services from Central to Paris and Brussels, some facilitation work having been completed and a "Eurostar" visiting Central for testing in June 1997. Perhaps they were ahead of their time as environmental considerations now question the use of air travel for relatively short distances.

Greater Glasgow Suburban services: DMUs progressively replaced steam from the late 1950s. The products from Cravens, Derby, Gloucester and Metro-Cammell (Classes 105, 107, 100 and 101 respectively) were often dedicated to particular routes, but this became progressively less absolute. Swindon-built Inter-City sets (Class 126) ventured on to the Ayrshire coast/Stranraer runs and duly appeared at Central with the transfer of services from St Enoch. Smaller diesel locomotives, such as Classes 20, 24-27 and 37 might appear on longer-distance stopping services, but the Stranraer line used Class 47-hauled rakes in the late 1980s.Such loco-hauled services and earlier DMU classes were progressively superseded by Class 156 DMUs on routes such as East Kilbride, Barrhead and Kilmarnock/Carlisle.

The North Clyde electrification through Glasgow Queen Street on 7 November 1960 had first introduced the Class 303 EMUs (the "Blue Trains") to Glasgow. Constructed locally at Linwood, these appeared in Central with the electrification of the Cathcart Circle routes. In 1979 the re-opened Argyle Line brought the first thyristor-controlled EMUs to Scotland, the Class 314s, followed by Class 318s and the more stylish Class 320s with their panels of artwork prepared by staff from the Glasgow School of Art.

A new generation of EMU, Class 334, was introduced on the Ayr line on 26 July 2001. Initial electrical faults were resolved by early 2002, enabling withdrawal of the final Class 303 "Blue-Train" on 30 December 2002, occasioning a piper's lament before its last journey from Helensburgh to Yoker depot. The Class 334 units have proved to be excellent, appearing in Central at both High Level and Low Level.

27 Changing trains

Jim Summers

Long-distance services

Glamorous "inter city" services were not the immediate reason for the vast expansion of Central High Level, whatever longer-term aspirations those prescient directors of the Caledonian might have had. Indeed in 1906 the daily number of trains for England ("Anglos" in railway parlance) was low, and remained so. It was the nationalised railway company formed in 1948 and known as British Railways, which created and nurtured the long-distance market and brought it to profitability, a state which it had probably never attained in Caledonian days.

Train working of the "Anglos" in 1906 and for long afterwards could be summarised as "few and complicated", whereas a hundred years later it had become "frequent and simple". While the few long-distance trains in the first half of the 20th century may have proclaimed a principal destination, this was nominal and in fact they conveyed through carriages for a variety of destinations. This involved much shunting en route of carriages between trains, a practice which lasted far longer on the continent than in Britain. Compared with city termini abroad, Central itself saw little such shunting of through coaches between passenger trains, though transfers were made at one time between Clyde Coast trains and Anglo services. It would have been different, had Buchanan St. and Central stations been the one location; but as it was, Central dispatched Anglos which travelled to places like Carstairs, Symington and Carlisle before being combined with portions from the north of Scotland and Edinburgh.

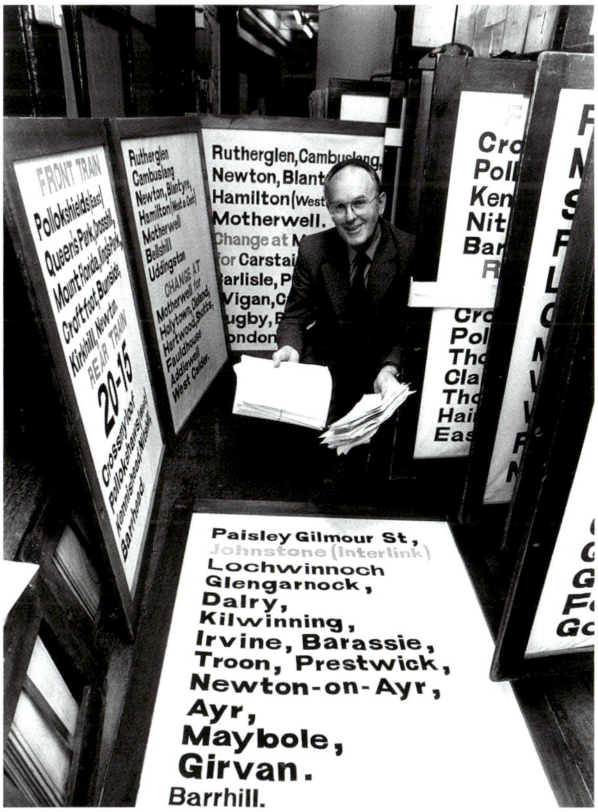

Donny McLeod, Area Manager, bids farewell to the train indicator boards, once familiar to travellers to "a' the airts".

The first up Anglo in 1906 and for years afterwards was the 10 am to Euston, which in reality was only part of a train, as it acquired a portion from Edinburgh at Carlisle; the 10.10 am was for Liverpool and Manchester; the 1200 noon had portions for Euston, Manchester and Liverpool, and gained one from Oban at Carstairs; the 2 pm Corridor for Euston conveyed also portions for Liverpool and Manchester, and acquired a portion from Edinburgh at Carlisle; and the daytime service was concluded by the 4 pm for Liverpool and Manchester. Overnight trains numbered four, one leaving as early as 4.55 pm, but really existing for postal vehicles, with others at 9.5 pm and 10.45 pm conveying sleeping carriages for London, and at 11.45 pm for Manchester and Liverpool.

At busy times, that type of train service lent itself to the expansion of capacity by elevating the portions to become full trains in their own right; but this of course implied the existence of large reserves of coaching stock, which did not do a lot for much of the year. It took the traffic costing service under Dr Beeching to establish that huge costs were incurred thereby, and that fewer resources must be made to work harder. And that could be done by simplification and acceleration of train services, firstly by dieselisation and then by electrification.

High levels of utilisation were key in the days of British Railways, so that in the 1980s the coaches for the 1000 Central to Euston, otherwise idle first thing, were scheduled to run from Ayr in the morning. It wasn't always easy for the Signalmen to cross the train from Ayr right across the throat of Central to gain Platform 1, but the benefits were valuable: an enhanced environment for Ayrshire commuters, release of other sets to relieve overcrowding, and the convenience of a through Anglo service from Ayrshire – The Royal Scot, in fact. Then there was the combination of a Manchester – Glasgow service with the traditional boat train from Manchester to Harwich to form The European, not only increasing direct journey opportunities but, more importantly, saving a set of modern carriages for other exploits. Today, such innovative flexibility is not so easily open to the franchised Train Operating Companies, but British Railways had exploited it to a fine art, and many shorter distance trains were combined to form long through services. Whereas in 1906 through carriages (to relatively

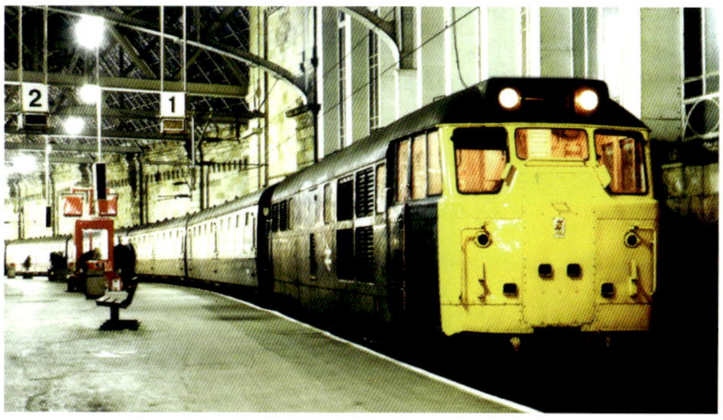

Extra relief holiday trains could not survive rigorous accountancy and foreign holidays.
A Class "31" disposes of a special train from Morcambe.

few destinations) were transferred en route between trains, British Railways began to run complete trains to a far wider range of destinations, with reduced shunting and a vastly increased frequency. The step-change on the West Coast Main Line came with electrification from Weaver Jn. to Glasgow (as the British Railways Board called it, but "Motherwell to Weaver", as the Scots chose, perversely if accurately, to describe it).

Electric Scots

Double-headed Class 50 diesel locomotives with a timing load of 450 tons had been trying to maintain a journey time to Euston of six hours or so. From 6 May 1974, electric locomotives could produce a best time of five hours, and eight trains now left for Euston (nine on Fridays, and ten on Saturdays) from 0710 at hourly intervals until 1730. Four trains now ran to Birmingham or Bristol, while the former two trains between Liverpool/Manchester and Glasgow rose to five daily. In the holiday season, a few Blackpools and the like still ran, but were subsequently reduced, as air and road alternatives improved. This train plan was essentially a "west coast" service nevertheless, and did not stretch the capacity at Central High Level unduly. The real break with tradition came when British Rail electrified the East Coast route from London King's Cross to Edinburgh and the ex-Caledonian main line onwards from Edinburgh to Carstairs.

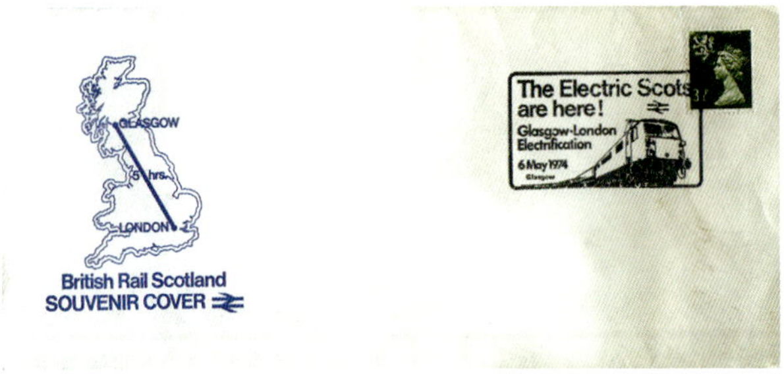

In 1906 an express service between the two major Scottish cities had been provided from the Central, via Shotts, by the Caledonian; but it could only offer the west end of Edinburgh as a destination, and eventually the unified British Railways chose and developed the longer North British route via Falkirk as the prime route. The residual service from Central via Shotts to Edinburgh by stopping train was not one of which British Rail could be proud, nor did it claim to be. However, the eventual electrified link from Edinburgh to Carstairs enabled high quality electric InterCity trains to run to Central from London King's Cross via the cities of the East Coast route to King's Cross; and they did, from 1991. Apart from the new English destinations now served directly from Central, a significant commuting business built up between Glasgow Central and Edinburgh once more.

Thus when British Railways handed over the only long-distance passenger operation in the world to run at a profit to a variety of new privatised companies, GNER inherited nine daytime trains from Glasgow Central to London King's Cross or short thereof. And – unthinkable only a few years before – those nine trains via the East Coast Main Line to King's Cross stood side by side in the Central with six, nowadays nine, Virgin trains via the rival traditional West Coast route to Euston. Besides these combined 18 trains for London, there are now 11 daily Virgin Cross Country trains for Liverpool, Manchester, Birmingham or the South Coast. These companies have developed further the simplification of train operations, leaving the nightly Caledonian Sleeper, managed by First ScotRail, as the sole example of a traditional locomotive-hauled train. Central High Level has become fuller – congested, on occasion – with long-distance trains than ever in its history. Those "through carriage" portions of the few Anglos of 1906 had, a century later, evolved into full trains on an unprecedented frequency. And in contrast to a first Up train at 1000 a century ago, in 2006, six Anglos will have left the Central before 1000, and the last arrival before midnight is 2333.

Local Services

Whilst the long-distance trains had famous LMS locomotives with names of royalty or Caledonian giants like Cardean, and had classy sets of coaches like the Coronation Scot or the sophisticated Pendolinos, the bulk of the traffic into and out of Central was handled by the humble suburban trains. It was for their comings and goings that the complicated track layout existed, along with the extensive sidings just south of the river and at Smithy Lye. Empty trains could be propelled by their incoming locomotives over the not inconsiderable distance to Smithy Lye, with a view to reducing movements of light engines.

In 1906 and, really until the end of steam, the local services on the railway system generally existed not so much for leisure as for commuting, and considerable gaps could arise during the day. Not quite so in Glasgow, for the services on routes such as the Cathcart Circle had to compete with the frequency of the trams, so that, even in 1906, the Caledonian was offering, there at least, what might nowadays be called a metro service. At that time the Hamilton Circle was scarcely a circle, because after the call at Hamilton trains set off to branch termini in deeper Lanarkshire. They combined however as a trunk to give a frequent service all day from Central as far as Hamilton. The Clyde Coast services were fairly frequent too, driven by the competitive environment with steamer connections, and the Caledonian of course offered in the Fair Holiday what were called "amplified" timetables. Some of the longer commuting runs were prestigious affairs on the old Caledonian system, and the Tinto Express from Central to Moffat was dignified with a Pullman dining car. The important Glasgow – Edinburgh Princes St. service has already been mentioned, and in its heyday it enjoyed six-wheel bogie luxurious carriages and had five buffet cars allocated to the service.

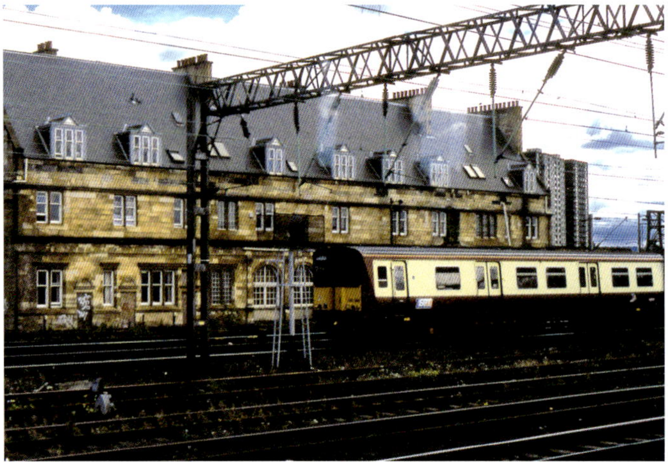

A Class "314" EMU built for the Argyle Line below Central, now used on services from the High Level Station, passes the remains of Bridge Street Station and some of the stabling sidings for suburban services.

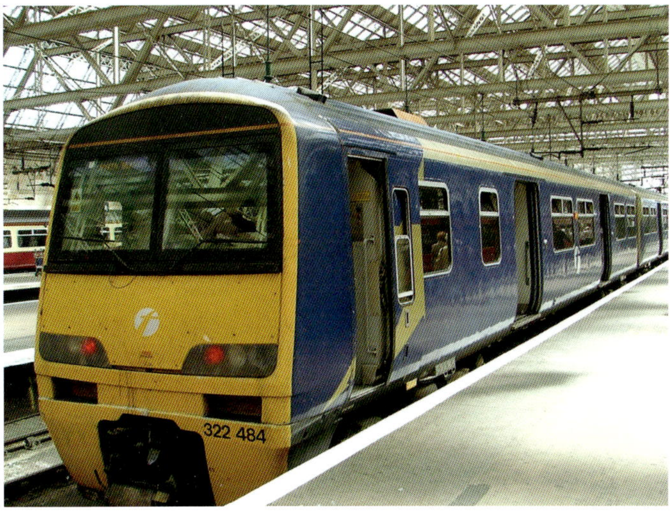

Edinburgh area suburban services are dependent for maintenance at Shields Depot, Glasgow giving rise to curiosities such as this Class "322" EMU service from Glasgow Central to North Berwick.

Dieselisation by means of multiple units was an obvious way of meeting the Beeching policy of reducing costs, and although they were introduced on the less economic extremities such as Coalburn, they could not prevent the pruning back of such services. In turn, this made more diesel multiple units available to concentrate on core local routes, such as the Hamilton Circle. A virtue of multiple units like these diesels was the ability to "dock" two or even three trains in the same platform, something not easily done with steam. This could effectively give the Central extra platforms, and is still a feature in Central, though one more popular with cunning operators than with confused passengers.

Electrification, proposed in the Inglis report of 1947, was at last on its way, however, in the shape of the famed Blue Trains. Electrification of the Cathcart Circle and allied services came on 28 May 1962. This included electrification via Kirkhill to Motherwell on the main line south – an early instance of "creeping electrification", of which the Scottish Region of British Railways later came to be an arch exponent. The track layout was also altered at Cathcart, to permit Kirkhill trains to use the Inner Circle.

A service of 630 journeys per six-day week in the steam era was increased to over 1,900 electric train journeys in a seven-day week, relatively a greater increase than had occurred on the initial "Blue Train" routes through the Glasgow Queen St. Low Level lines. Success followed: in the first week 150,000 passengers travelled, a figure practically three times the carryings of the superseded steam services. The peak-hour traffic at Glasgow Central was said to have a 50 per cent increase.

This was the period of wariness about the safe clearances between structures and the 25Kv a.c. in the overhead wires, so to save extensive bridge and tunnel reconstructions, the whole of the Cathcart Circle into Central was electrified at 6.25Kv a.c. Changeover points between 6.25Kv and 25Kv a.c. were installed on the Motherwell and Neilston lines. When electrification was extended to the main line in 1974, at 25Kv. a.c., one half of the Cathcart Circle was converted to this voltage, to provide a diversionary route for long distance trains. Subsequently, the restrictions on clearances were relaxed, and all sections of 6.25Kv could be up-rated to 25Kv.

The beneficial effects of the espousal by the public of the "Blue Trains", led to an attempt to market the still-diesel services on the Hamilton Circle as the "Green Trains", but no one was really fooled. Electrification of these routes had to wait until 1974, with the main line project. The Lanark line was not included: indeed the Scottish Office had refused to provide support. In a further piece of creeping electrification, the Scottish Region of British Railways found internally the materials and finance to reach Lanark. The electrified Hamilton Circle (marketed as the "Hamilton Train Set") saw in effect a doubling of the off-peak train service, while journey times to and from Lanark benefited dramatically.

By this time, the Passenger Transport Executive were in position and were financing the levels of service, as well as trying to develop greater use of trains and buses, with new routes if necessary. With Central now effectively full, room for expansion could only be gained by the re-opening of the closed Low Level route, and the Hamilton and Lanark services were diverted there in 1979. The Executive put much effort into this re-opening, which presaged the re-openings of other routes, together with many new station and reopened stations. Central High Level now again sees trains to Paisley Canal and to Whifflet, while the Low Level sees trains to Larkhall. Next is to be to Glasgow Airport.

The Passenger Transport Executive did its best to integrate trains and buses, beginning with the Interlink service to East Kilbride, and later Hairmyres. Under Interlink, the Central SMT company operated special bus routes to pick up passengers in the town and take them to the inconveniently situated railway station, where they would catch a limited stop train to the city, all on the one ticket: commonplace on the continent, but an innovation in the Scottish context.

The Passenger Transport Executive was of course interested in costs, and supported British Rail when it wished to convert the electrified suburban services to a system whereby only the Driver was necessary to operate the train. This led to a Guards' strike at Central, but ultimately to the sensible and pioneering solution that the trains in passenger service should have a Driver who was in charge of the operation of the train, and have a crew member in the train, who looked after the revenue and the well-being of the passengers.

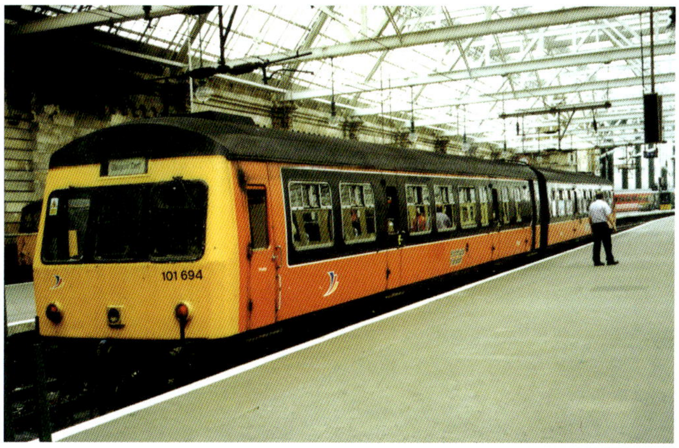

The Greater Glasgow PTE promoted through tickets and co-ordinated services between bus and rail operators on Interlink services such as to East Kilbride, worked by early generation DMUs.

28 Glasgow Central and the Advanced Passenger Train

Don Heath

Dr Beeching did many things when he became Chairman of British Railways in 1961, but one of the most far-reaching was to raise the profile of Research and Development. He recruited Dr Jones from the Radar Research Establishment at Malvern to lead a vastly expanded effort in these two fields. And one of the things which he quickly recognised was the need to apply modern mathematical theory to vehicle dynamics. He also, very perceptively, foresaw the need to give the railway a tool for competing with the airlines over the next 20-50 years. From these two initiatives, eventually came the concept of the Advanced Passenger Train (APT).

After a lot of work using gas turbines propelling skeletal vehicles, it was finally decided, in 1976, to build three 25kV electric prototypes, which emerged in 1979. These were to be principally for testing the engineering, but they would also be capable of carrying passengers, so that the final stages of the development programme could evaluate all of the various influences upon the passenger and the passenger environment.

At the time, the only electrified main line railway was the West Coast Main Line. This is a very sinuous route, where an ability to tilt the passenger vehicles would enable the train to run up to 25% faster than conventional trains, with the same degree of passenger comfort. A significant decision was then made: the prototype trains would be based in Scotland, at the Shields electric depot, not far from Central, because the West Coast Main Line was less busy at the northern end during the day. This use of the northern end of the route meant that the engineers could run the trains during normal working hours, thus avoiding the need to carry out delicate research and testing work after dark and in the middle of the night. And so Central became the "home station" for the APT: any runs involving passengers – private or paying – would therefore start and finish at Glasgow.

In 1981 the Chief Executive of the British Railways Board, Ian Campbell, became President of the Institution of Civil Engineers. His inaugural address at the beginning of November provided a wonderful launch pad to announce the entry of the train into public service. The plan was that, commencing at the beginning of that December, it would make a return trip on three days per week. Naturally, Central featured hugely in the associated celebrations arising from this very important occasion.

Unfortunately, for reasons, which have been well documented elsewhere, the release into public-carrying service proved premature. The train did a perfect return journey on its first day, but suffered a minor technical failure on the second day within half an hour of leaving Glasgow and, on the third day, it got caught in a very heavy blizzard in the Midlands of England which meant that, yet again, it did not run through to Euston. Staff at Central recall the train returning with icicles inches long.

BRITISH RAILWAYS : SCOTTISH REGION
SPECIAL NOTICE

PRIVATE AND NOT FOR PUBLICATION

MPX/N/270/84

WEDNESDAY 12 DECEMBER

EUSTON TO GLASGOW CENTRAL

Special Test APT

		1Z98			1Z98
Euston	dep	16 35	Motherwell		20/19
Carlisle		19/29			[1]
Gretna Jn		19/35½	Uddingston		20/22
Lockerbie		19/44½			[1]
		[2]	Newton		20/24½
Beattock		19/53½	Rutherglen E Jn		20/26½
Summit		19/58½	Glasgow Cen	arr	20 32½
Carstairs		20/10½		dep	20/57
Lanark Jn		20/12	Shields Jn		21/01
Law Jn		20/16	Shields ETD	arr	21/08

SPECIAL INSTRUCTIONS

Every effort to be made to ensure a clear run is given to this train as the success of the test depends on it maintaining the MAXIMUM permissible speed.

For a variety of reasons, the decision was taken to stand the train down from public service, but further development work continued over the next three years.

In the early 1980s, British Railways underwent a major re-organisation of its managerial structure, which led to the formation of business sectors. The Managing Director of the InterCity sector (Cyril Bleasdale) was very keen to ascertain exactly what the train might achieve. So, in the autumn of 1984, a special run was planned and this took place in the afternoon/evening of Wednesday 12 December that year. The aim was a 4-hour non-stop run London to Glasgow, and the timetable planners schemed a path through the busy West Coast Main Line which produced a 3 hour 57 minute schedule, with the crews working through. In the event, the train actually arrived in Platform 2 at Glasgow Central in 3 hours 52 minutes after leaving Euston, and this despite a three-minute stop at the home signal for Stafford No. 1 signal box, caused by a track circuit failure. The timing experts estimated that the net running time was actually 3 hours 45 minutes. Whilst this was clearly a special run with the line being cleared ahead of the train to ensure that it was not delayed by any other traffic, it demonstrated very clearly to over 400 people on board exactly what the train was capable of achieving. Glasgow Central participated in the celebrations by arranging a welcoming committee and conducting everybody involved in the planning and running of that service off to a special reception at the British Transport Hotel, Glasgow, Queen Street Station. It was however a swansong, as the APT project was eventually shelved.

Not until 21 years later, in December 2005, that Glasgow Central became host to a regular service of tilting trains in the form of the Virgin Class 390 "Pendolinos", with some ten Anglo-Scottish services (nine from Central and one from Waverley) in each direction, Mondays to Fridays. While the overall transits may be longer now than the magic four hours, they do include at least two intermediate stops, and have allowances built in for speed restrictions caused by track maintenance and renewals.

WEDNESDAY 12th DECEMBER 1984
1Z98 SPECIAL TEST APT: 16.35 LONDON EUSTON TO GLASGOW CENTRAL

Performance Details

London Euston ... ... depart 16h. 34m. 57s. (3 seconds early)
Glasgow Central ... ... arrive 20h. 27m. 41s. (4 mins. 49 secs. early)

The 401.3 miles from London Euston to Glasgow Central were covered in 3h. 52m. 44s., representing an actual start-to-stop average speed of 103.46 mph and setting a new record for the fastest overall journey time between these points. It is also the longest distance journey in Great Britain to have been completed at an average speed in excess of 100 mph.

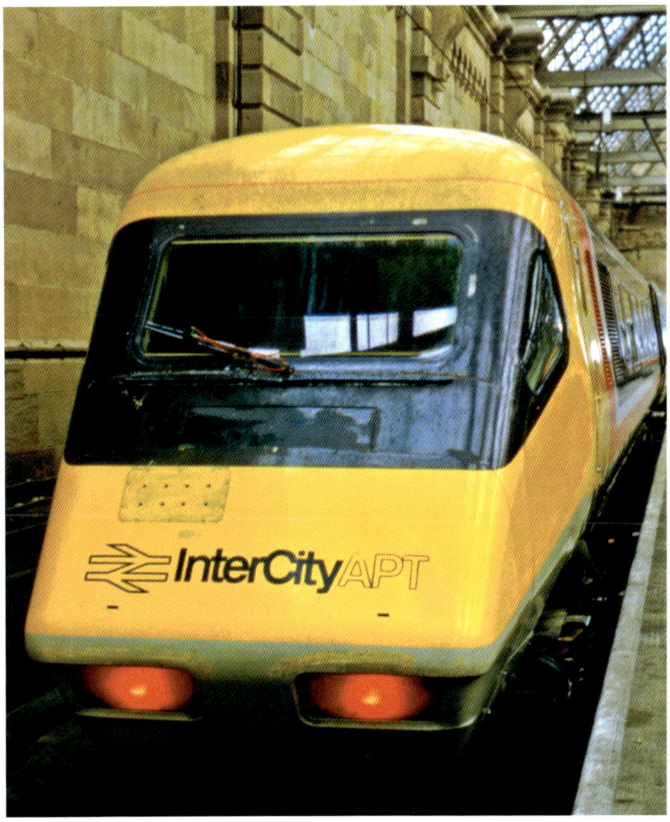

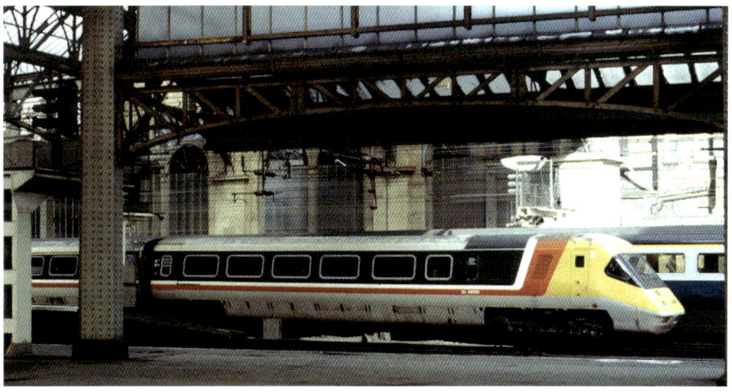

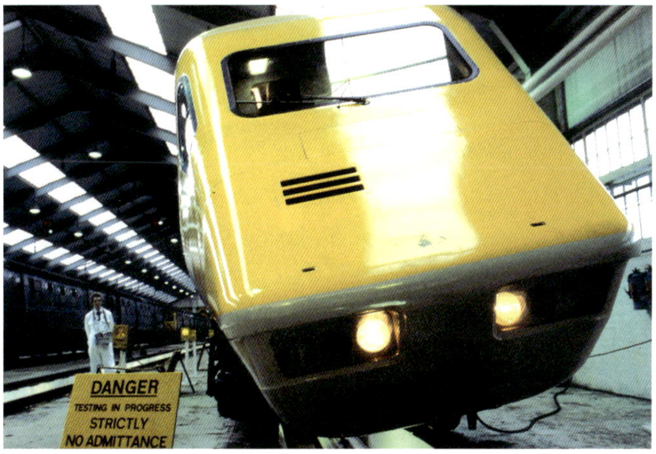

Morning of the great day: top left, the APT leaves Central for Euston. Coming home, it created the new record of 3 hours 52 minutes made possible by the British tilt technology seen demonstrated above at its base at Shields Depot, Glasgow.
(An APT achieved 162 mph on a test run between Beattock and Lockerbie – an all-time UK record speed on rail).

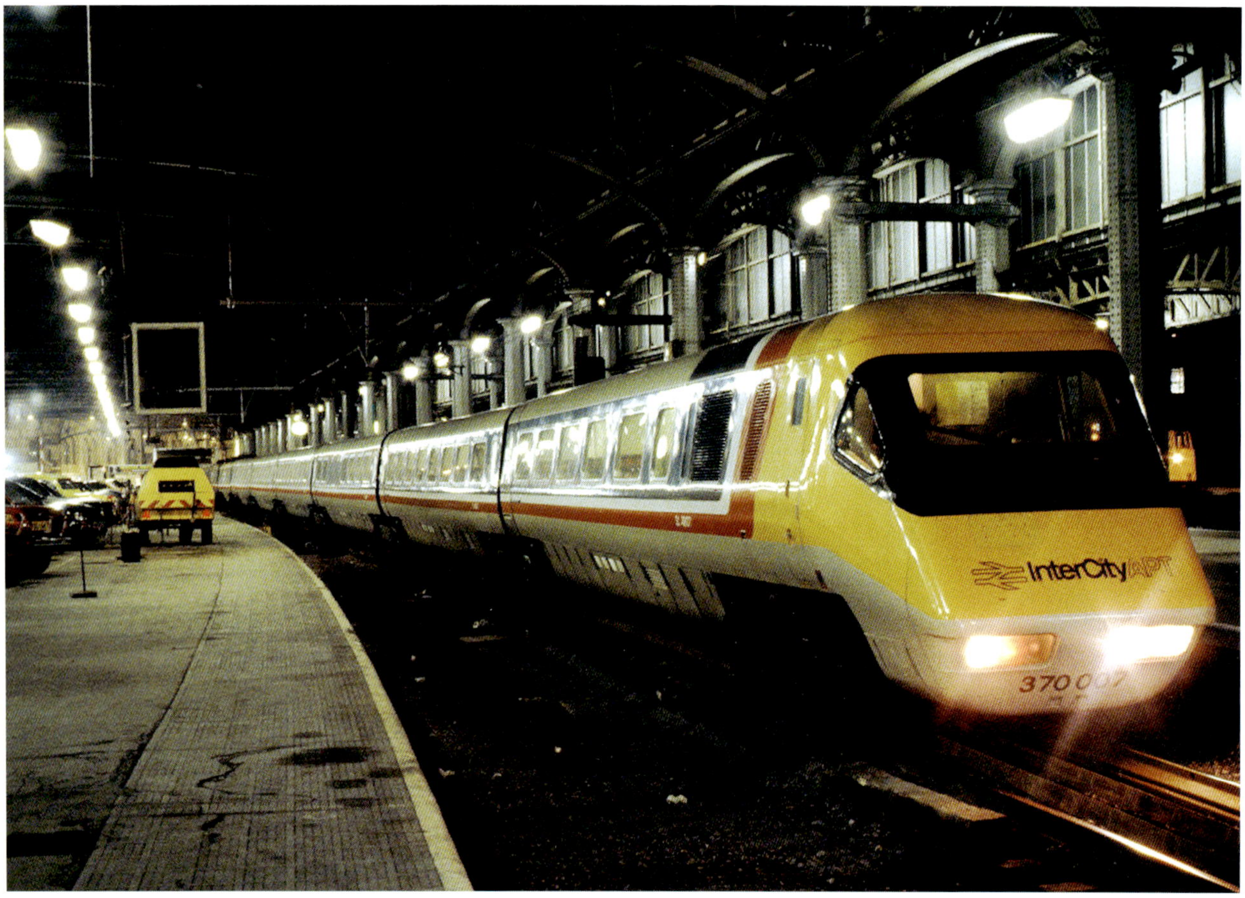

InterCity APT No. 370007 ready to depart from Central.

What might have been – Central for the Continent! Eurostar on trial 5-6 June 1997.
The Class "37" on the left is one of the ones used to haul Eurostar dead on these trial runs into the station.

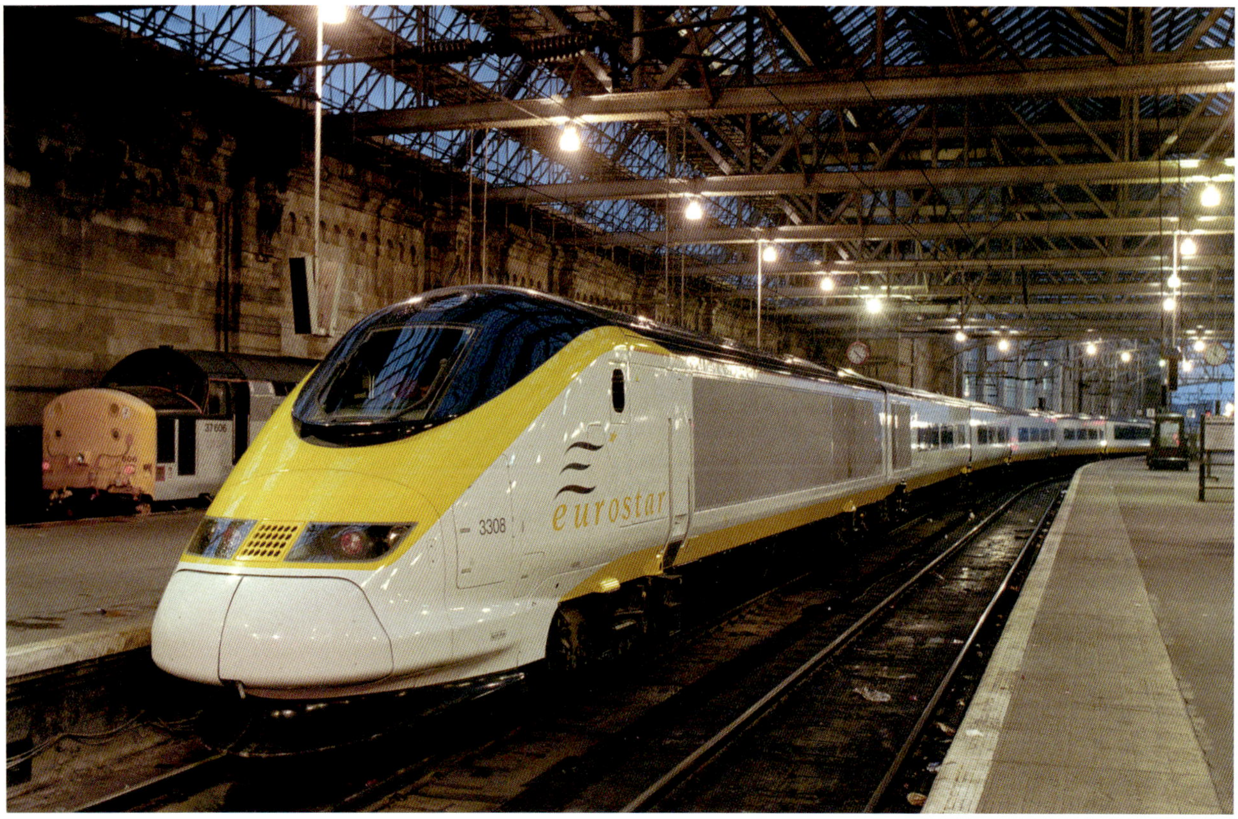

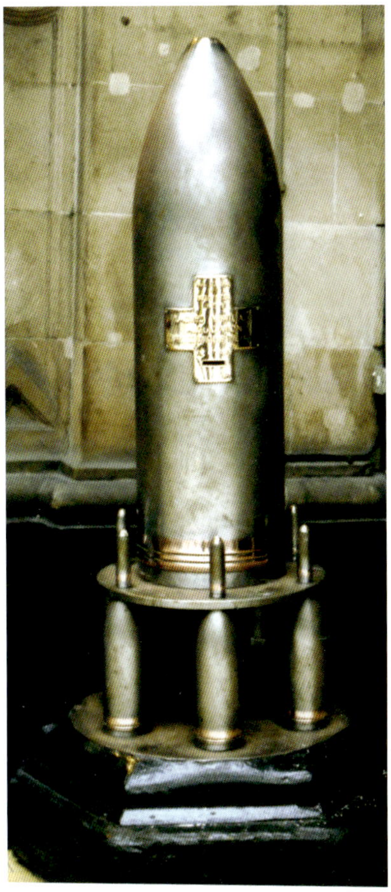

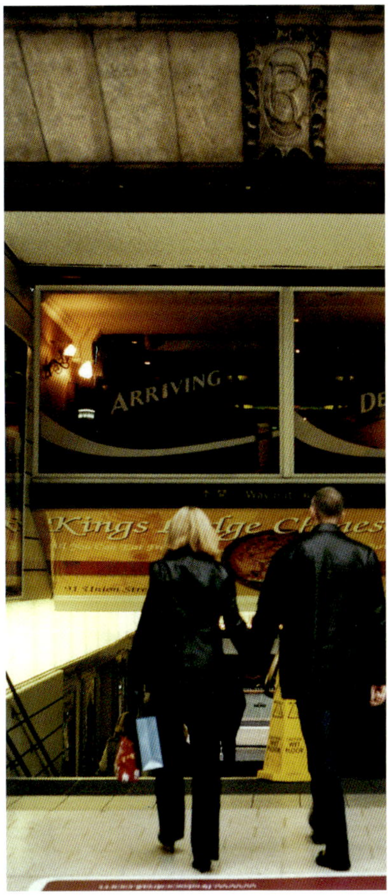

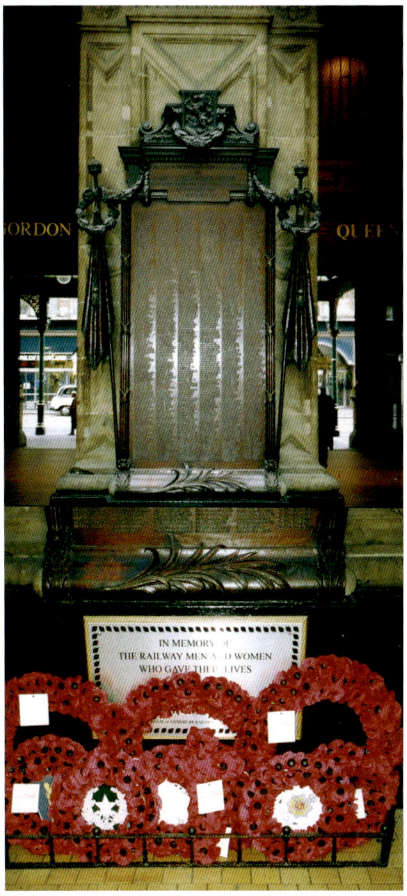

Meeting place for those looking forward and those looking back.

Central to our lives

Looking for a sign

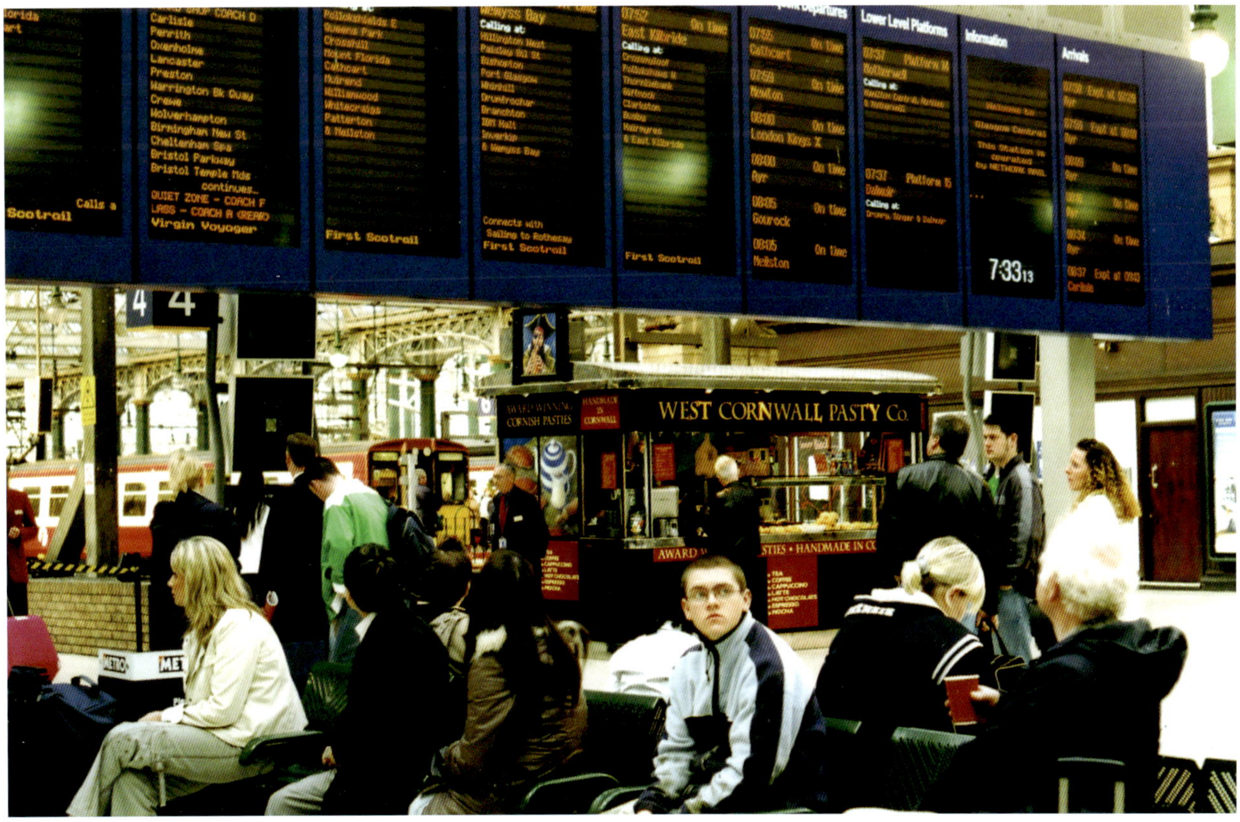

29 Central – Gateway to Scotland

Chris Green, formerly General Manager, British Rail Scotland

Glasgow Central marks the end of the gruelling 401 miles of the West Coast Main Line from London. No station could provide a more fitting terminus for a great railway – not to mention its flagship *Royal Scot* service. I have always seen Glasgow Central as one of the great cathedral stations of Britain: it was built on an epic scale, and it still has the ability to surprise arriving travellers with its sheer size and grandeur.

I became personally involved with Glasgow Central when I worked in Scotland from 1979, first as Chief Operations Manager and then as General Manager. We always saw Glasgow Central as the operational pulse for both Scotland and the West Coast Main Line and the post of Station Manager, Glasgow Central was seen as the top operational job in Scotland. I was fortunate to work with legendary Station Managers in the 1980s such as Fergus McKenzie, Donald McLeod, and Vic Gilchrist – men who won the respect of staff and customers alike both for their railway professionalism and their commitment to Glasgow Central.

Glasgow Central has had two lucky breaks. The first was to have been a late arrival on the railway scene in 1879, when the Caledonian Railway finally bridged the River Clyde. This meant that the station was largely designed as a single entity and it has remained so to this day, thanks to the far-sighted planning that went into the great 1906 Extension. The second lucky break was to have avoided being re-built as a through station to the north, as this has allowed it to keep its world-famous concourse and buildings. This was a closer shave than many people realise, as ideas for converting Central into a through station were being actively discussed in 1908 and the Caley had actually started buying land to extend the railway from Central to Buchanan St. Station!

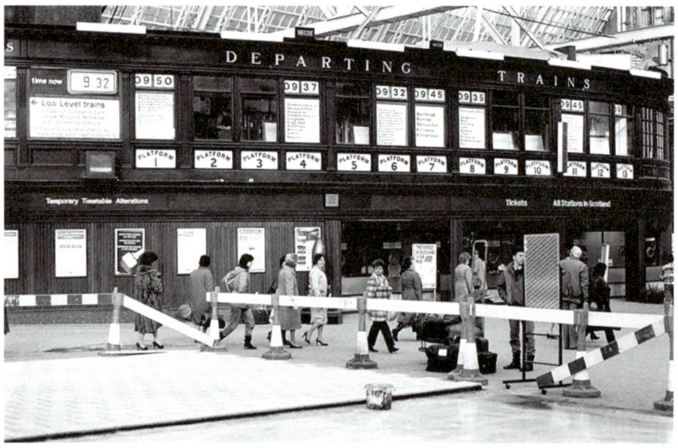

The marble tiles advance to surround the Torpedo Building with its famous platform indicators.

Few other stations outside London have the generous seven approach tracks of Central, which minimise train delays outside the station. Few other stations have the benefits of such a wide, overall roof which is entirely free of support columns or walls for the vast majority of its area. It is this wide roof area which gives the station its sense of space and ambience. And few other major stations are so well located in the business heart of a city.

Central has seen two big changes in its history. The first came in 1906, of course, when graceful wooden buildings were added to the concourse. The eastern block was originally built as the Stationmaster's Office, with its grand first floor level view of the station. The western buildings became known as the Torpedo buildings because of their distinctive shape, and together with the famous platform indicator they gave the station its special character. They have been preserved to this day through a tasteful conversion into shops and an inspired first floor buffet. Many of us have memories of the indicator being manually updated by a team of railwaymen who briefly appeared on the balcony to change the painted indicator display slats. They were greeted with the occasional groan or cheer, when a long-awaited arrival of *The Royal Scot* from England was finally displayed. The indicator had one display for each of the 13 platforms and it offered a simplicity and clarity which remains unrivalled by any modern electronic substitute!

The cathedral status of Glasgow Central made it the flagship station for Scotland. So when the network was re-born as "ScotRail" in 1984 it was natural that the cathedral station should be upgraded to reflect this significant change. Thus the second big change for Central came in a million pound upgrade in 1984, in which the entire concourse was clad in a polished white marble tile to replace the depressing black asphalt surface. The mission was to create the atmosphere of a modern airport or shopping centre, without detracting from the history of the building. Arriving visitors meet a light, spacious floor tile that reflects both daylight and electric light.

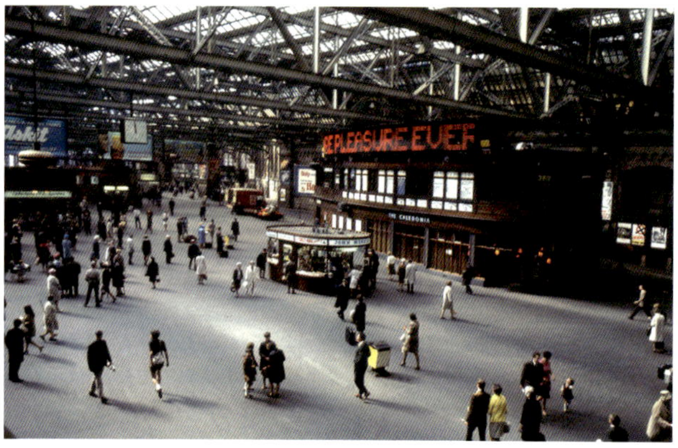
The concourse before the 1980s remodelling.

The same modernisation saw the old manual departure indicator replaced with a modern electronic indicator and the 1906 Torpedo Buildings tastefully converted into quality shops. The changeover was made in style, and a Scottish Regimental band appeared on the station in full regalia for a moving ceremony to pipe out the old indicator and switch on the new electronic board. I stood with a large crowd waiting with bated breath for the two minutes that it took to power-up the new display!

Glasgow Central has always been the place of history. My most vivid memory is of standing on Platform 1 in 1984 to welcome the Advanced Passenger Train as it snaked in from its record-breaking run from London in just 3 hours

52 minutes – a feat that has never been repeated. Other great moments at Central were the arrival of mainline electrification from London in 1974 with the *Electric Scots*, the launch of the Ayrshire Electrification in 1986, and the arrival of the East Coast electric services to Newcastle and London in 1991. But the greatest moment for me came on Monday 12 December 2005, when the 125mph tilting *Pendolino* service to London was finally launched on the West Coast – almost a generation after the APT first ran. *The Royal Scot* now offers a very respectable 4 hours 24 minutes to London with just two stops.

Glasgow Central is a station of nostalgic memories for all of us. I loved arriving on the Sleeper trains from the south. These were huge 16-coach trains – the longest in the UK – which struggled over Shap and Beattock in all weathers and rarely failed to deposit me in Glasgow Central at 8 o'clock in the morning in time for breakfast on Central and on to the first meeting. A spectacular failure was to wake up one morning around 08.00 to find myself marooned at Lockerbie by flooding, along with a hundred very un-impressed passengers. OK, so I opened the bar!

First impressions of Glasgow Central were always uplifting: a cheerful, bright, bustling station. For me it was the Gateway to Scotland and it always gave a great feeling of arriving in a new country, which I never got at London Euston. Breakfast was always in the magnificent Central Hotel – an integral part of the station, which has retained so much of its Victorian character, including the best view anywhere of the station concourse with its teeming life. Glasgow Central is not just the end of the West Coast line from London – it is a piece of Scottish history which has had the good fortune to be handed down to us in one piece. Now it is now up to us to keep it that way for future generations!

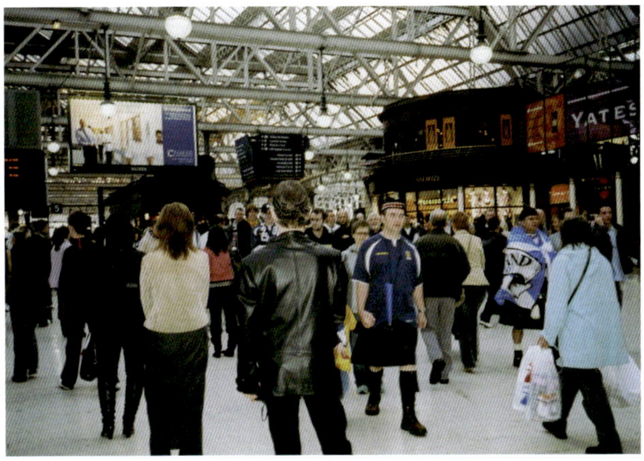

Coming and going – the concourse in 2005.

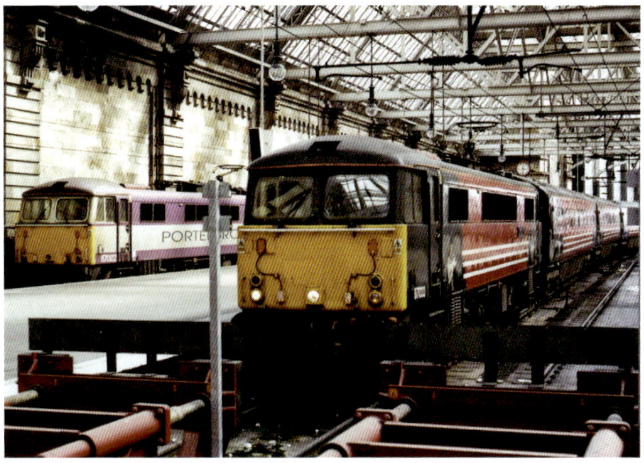
Class 87s Nos. 87002 & 87033 "Thane of Fife".

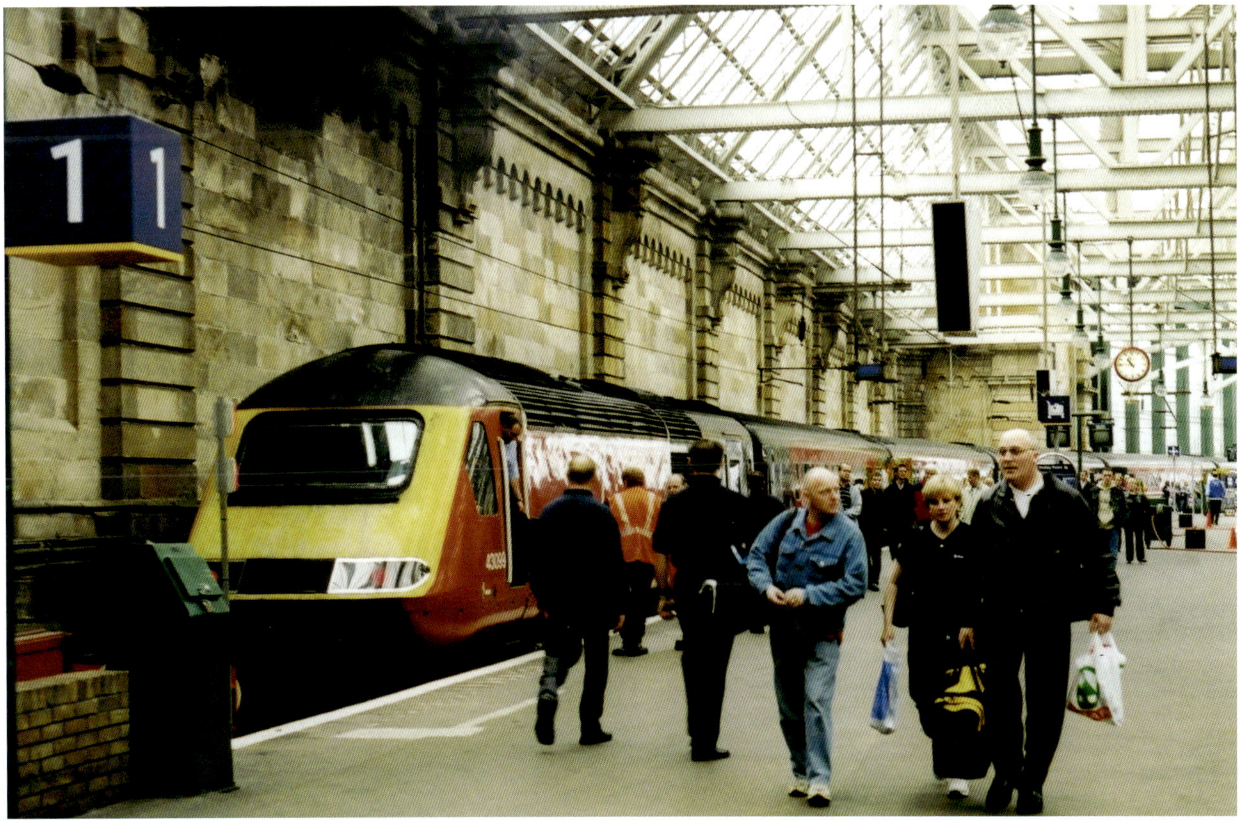

30 In Charge at Glasgow Central

Vic Gilchrist, formerly Area Manager, Glasgow Central, 1988-92

Having been brought up in the North East of Scotland and commencing my railway career in Aberdeen, the significance of Glasgow Central to the railways in Scotland was not appreciated by me at an early stage. However, when I became a Management Trainee in 1965, part of the two-year training course involved being at a large station, and in my case, this was Glasgow Central. A preliminary interview with the Station Manager was mandatory, and I vividly remember meeting the late Maurice Shand in his magnificent office overlooking the concourse, where he was provided with a panoramic view of all the station activities. While I spent a week at Central, my abiding memory is helping out with the crowd control on Glasgow Fair Saturday in 1966. At that time, the crowds were still enormous, particularly for the Clyde Coast (it was a very hot day) and some of the rolling stock provided for the trippers had clearly not turned a wheel since the previous Fair. It said much for the tolerance and good humour of the trippers that complaints were few!

Twenty-two years later, when the Area Managers' posts at Edinburgh Waverley and Glasgow Central both became vacant, I was fortunate enough to be appointed to the latter and took over in May 1988 from my predecessor, Donald Macleod. The responsibilities covered the South West of Scotland, but Glasgow Central was by far the largest concentration of railway activity. My team included the late Gordon Falconer as Station Manager. I remained in overall charge at Central for four years, before moving back to ScotRail Headquarters to co-ordinate the railway involvement in the Fatal Accident Inquiry following the Newton collision.

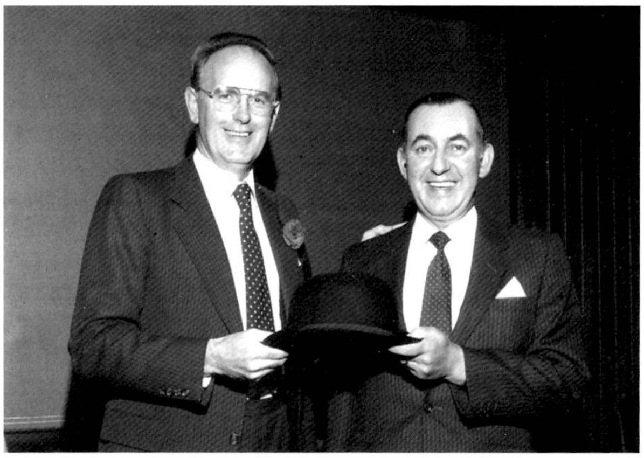

The Badge of Office.
Donny McLeod hands over to Fergus McKenzie – "apart from possessing the practical professional skills of all Station Masters, the holders of this office on the principal stations of BR were always expected to be masters of the theatrical effect as they supervised the handling of the crack expresses or welcomed notables from all walks of life. Top hats, and latterly bowlers, marked them out during such performances".

Memories of my time at Central are, of course, many; but above all I was impressed by the expertise, knowledge and dedication of the staff, many of whom had spent almost their entire careers at the station. It says a great deal for them that, during my tenure, there were few major incidents, although two EMU derailments occurred as a result of deterioration of the track at the station approaches. Severe restrictions resulted which caused major head-aches for the Station Supervisors responsible for platforming arrangements, but the effect upon train services was kept to a minimum.

The modernisation of the station and the expansion of the retail area had all been completed during my predecessor's reign, including the white tiling of the concourse. Regrettably, the money was not available at the time to renovate the magnificent station roof, and the consequences of rainwater dripping on to the tiles caused several problems for hurrying passengers. In 1989 I was honoured to receive, on behalf of the staff, the Ian Allan Ltd Best Station Award, and the plaque is proudly displayed at the Station entrance today. However, it was noticeable that, when the modernisation had been completed, nothing had been done about the station clock, a triangular monstrosity in orange, and I was pleased to be able to arrange for a replacement which fitted in with the architecture of the station as a whole.

One of the pleasures of being at Glasgow Central was the opportunity to meet arriving and departing members of the Royal family, including Prince Charles and the late Princess Diana, and other VIP's such as Michael Portillo, at that time Transport Secretary. On two occasions the arrival of Her Majesty the Queen caused considerable stress, however. In March 1990, Her Majesty was arriving at Glasgow Central, where she was being met by HRH The Duke of Edinburgh and the Lord Provost of Glasgow. About two hours before the arrival, I took a last-minute tour of Platform 1 to find to my horror that the red carpet ended about twenty yards short of the expected location of the train door from which the Royal party would emerge. Our engineering colleagues conjured up the required extra yardage, just in time, but the photograph of the arrival clearly shows the different shade of red provided at the last gasp.

When Her Majesty was arriving in May 1991 for the Gulf War Commemoration service at Glasgow Cathedral, which was being shown live on national television, the carpet was fine . . . but the diesel locomotive hauling the Royal Train succumbed near Motherwell. As a result the train was about twenty minutes late arriving, and the welcoming party was becoming very agitated indeed. Thankfully Her Majesty was unperturbed, when I took the opportunity of apologising for the delay. On a third occasion, Her Majesty's arrival was much more joyful, being the 1990 Celebrations of Glasgow, City of Culture. The station was filled with well-wishers, including a large group of lady choristers. I felt very sorry for the artist who had spent hours constructing an ice sculpture of the Eiffel Tower on the concourse, for it was hardly noticed in the excitement of the arrival.

It is not widely known, but there are several subterranean levels below Glasgow Central, and there is a virtual

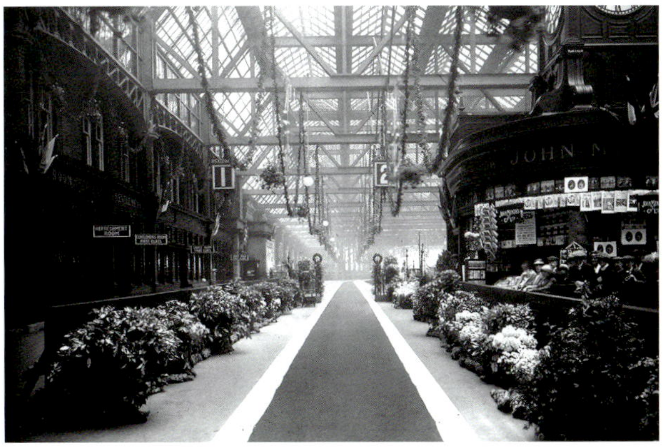

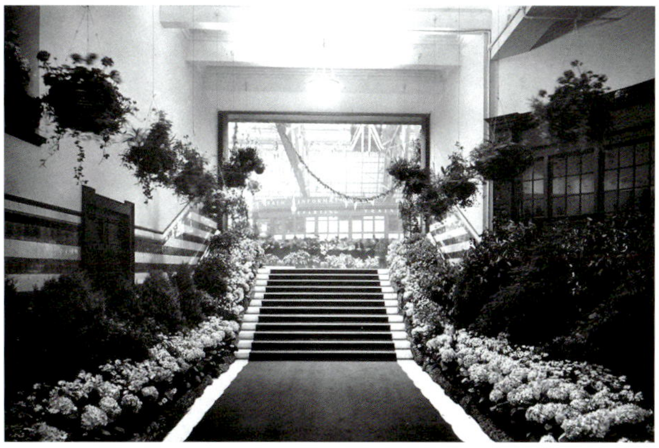

Floral decorations and red carpet await a Royal Visit by King George V for the opening of Rothesay Dock in 1907.

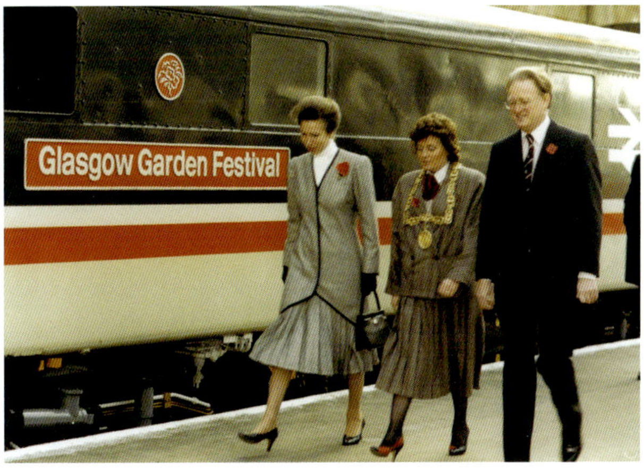

The Princess Royal, Lord Provost Susan Baird with Vic Gilchrist, Area Manager – 11 November 1988 Note that Class 87, 87006 "City of Glasgow" was temporarily renamed "Glasgow Garden Festival".

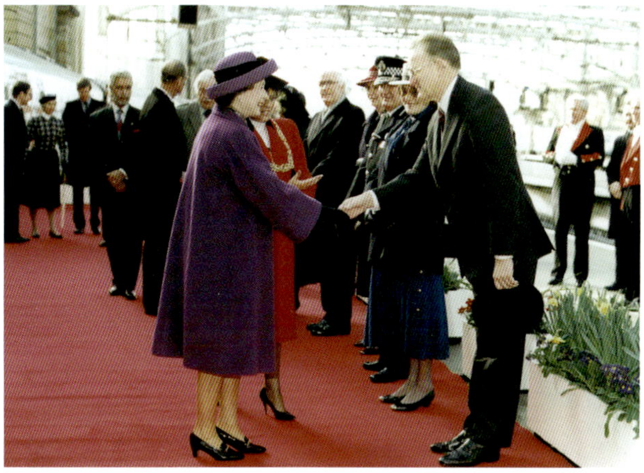

Vic Gilchrist, BR Area Manager, greets HM The Queen at Glasgow Central for "Glasgow, European City of Culture" celebrations with Lord Provost Susan Baird in attendance 2 March 1990.

rabbit-warren of passageways and archways which few people can claim to know well, if at all. Contrasting that with the view of the station roof that can be obtained from the Station Hotel gives some indication of the magnificence and extent of Glasgow Central station. And, of course, very few members of the travelling public will realise that the grey brick building located in the junction of the Ayrshire lines and the main line to the south is the Signalling Centre, controlling all movements in and out, and is an integral part of the station.

I have nothing but happy memories of my time there and of the staff with whom I worked.

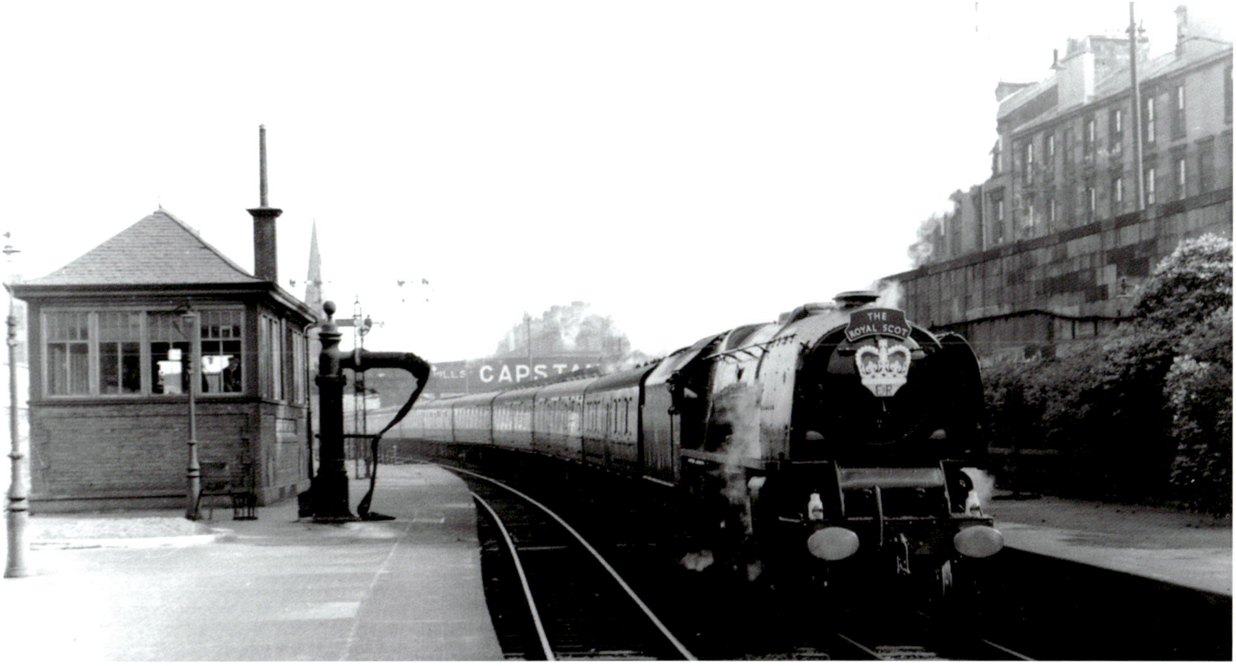

Carrying a special headboard on Coronation Day 1953, "The Royal Scot" hauled by 46220 "Coronation" passes Eglinton Street.

31 Tilting for Central

Allan McLean, Communications Manager, Scotland & North England, Virgin Trains

Scoffing scrambled egg as the Advanced Passenger Train swung at full tilt round the Lanarkshire curves was one of the more exciting culinary experiences I can recall from a lifetime of rail travel. But, thrilling though that inaugural public run of the APT from Glasgow Central on 7 December 1981 was, it failed to live up to its promise as the dawn of a new era. For that, the West Coast Main Line (WCML) had to await the delivery of Virgin's vision almost a quarter of a century later. Contrary to popular belief, the APT was to prove successful, even if its kitchen could only scramble eggs, not fry them. However, having confirmed that the tilt principle really works, Britain abandoned development.

Hence the train which has finally delivered tilt into reliable daily service between Glasgow Central and London Euston is the "Pendolino". That's the Italian title for a tilting train, indicating the source of this more subtle version of tilt than that on the APT. Assembly for Virgin

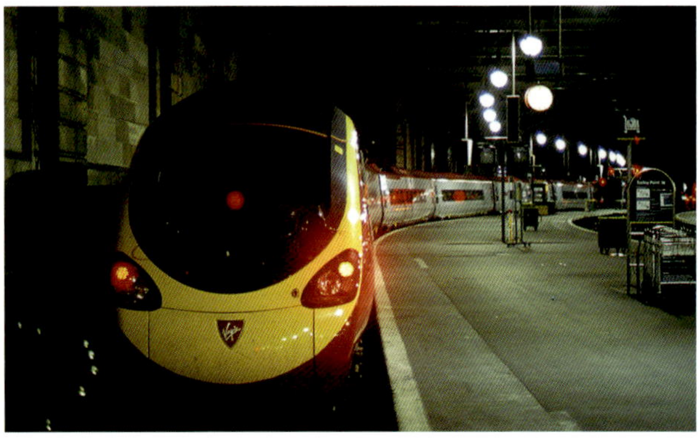

The first 'Pendolino' in Central No. 390012 29 April 2003.

Trains of the £1 billion fleet was in Birmingham, though, and the attractive sleek shape is a British design. (And Virgin's chefs can fry eggs as well as scramble them in a galley designed to prepare up to 145 First Class breakfasts.)

The WCML had been electrified south of Crewe in the 1960s and between there and Glasgow in 1974. But by 1997, when Virgin Trains arrived, it was a very tired WCML, desperate for long overdue rebuilding. Virgin refurbished the existing trains for Virgin CrossCountry and Virgin West Coast. This could only be an interim measure pending new rolling stock for the two most

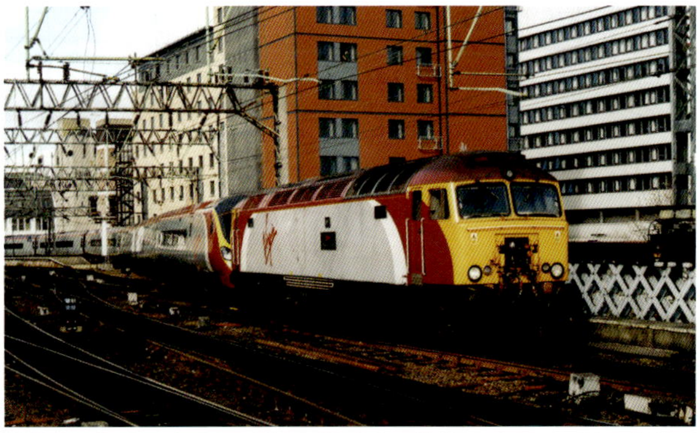

Diverted over the non-electrified Sou' West Route, a Pendolino is hauled out of Central by a "Thunderbird" Class 57.

trouble-prone inter-city franchises. The task ahead was summed up by naming the first Virgin-branded West Coast train: "Mission: Impossible".

In spite of continuing problems with worn-out kit, which would have hit any operator of these franchises, it was clear that something genuinely different was afoot. To quote just one example, Virgin's decision to have a Class 87 locomotive named "George Reynolds" at Glasgow Central in honour of my friend and colleague, who had for so long been the voice of Scotland's railways, demonstrated that here was a company with a human face.

I had abandoned my own railway career years earlier when new things didn't seem to be happening fast enough any more, but it was the Virgin vision of transformed long-distance services that brought me back into the railway fold.

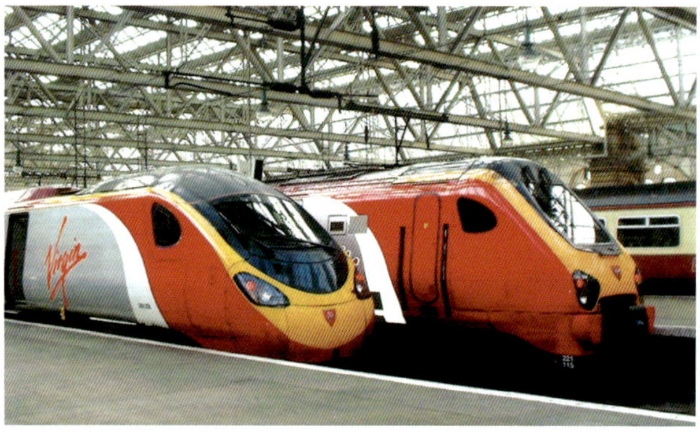

The new order, 21st Century trains, Virgin's 'Pendolino' No. 390038 and 'Voyager' No. 221115.

Playing my part as a member of the Virgin Trains team with so many lovely people, has been a source of personal joy. Great moments include sharing the enthusiasm at the naming ceremonies in Glasgow Central for *Clyde Voyager*, one of our high-speed diesel fleet for Virgin CrossCountry, and for *City of Glasgow*, one of the Virgin "Pendolinos" for the Virgin West Coast. My proudest moment at the Central, though, came on 5 January 2004, when the first Pendolino in public service all the way from London glided into Platform 1, its eight minutes early arrival welcomed by a barrage of press photographers and television crews. The positively euphoric coverage in the Scottish media was in marked

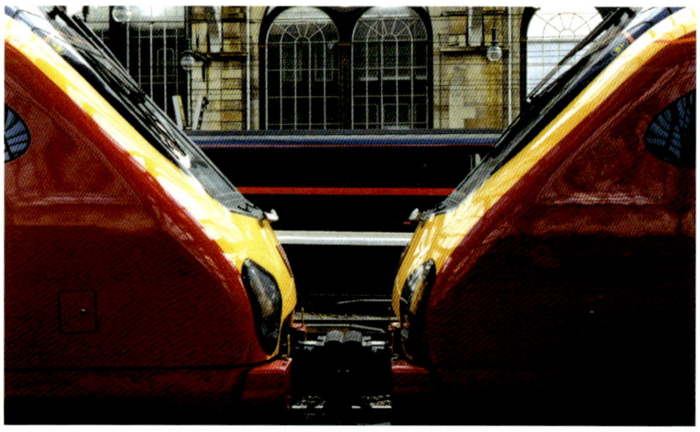

Head to head! Virgin CrossCountry Voyagers - 2005.

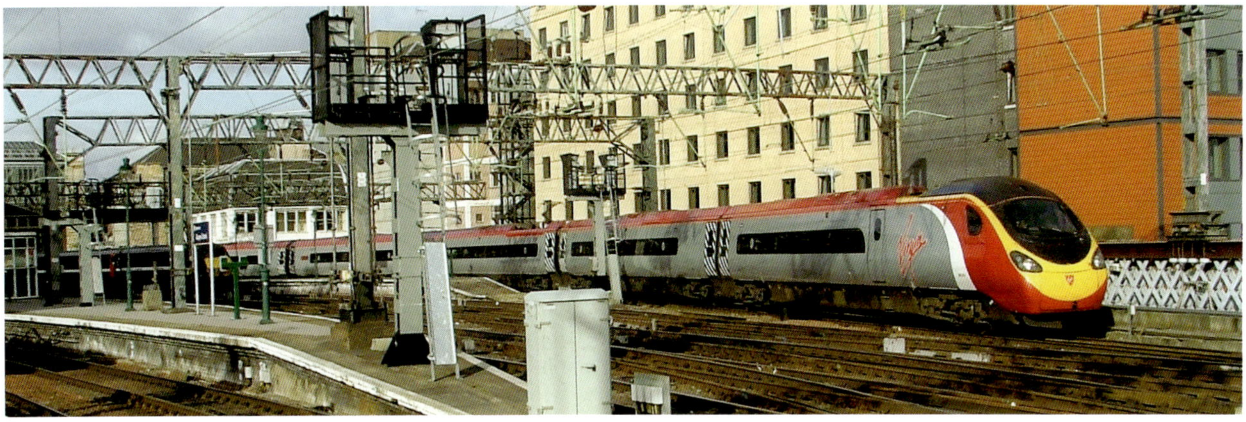

contrast to previous doom-laden reporting.

The *Daily Record* headline summed up the mood of the moment: "Tilting trains on track to be a hit." The delivery of accelerated timetables with faster, more frequent trains in September 2004 and December 2005 was followed by an unprecedented 91.1 per cent on time performance for West Coast in the four weeks to 4 February 2006.

With so many new passengers being won over to rail and real prospects for even further reductions in the best Glasgow/London timing of 4 hours 24 minutes in 2005-6, the Central can look forward to continuing success as Glasgow's increasingly popular gateway.

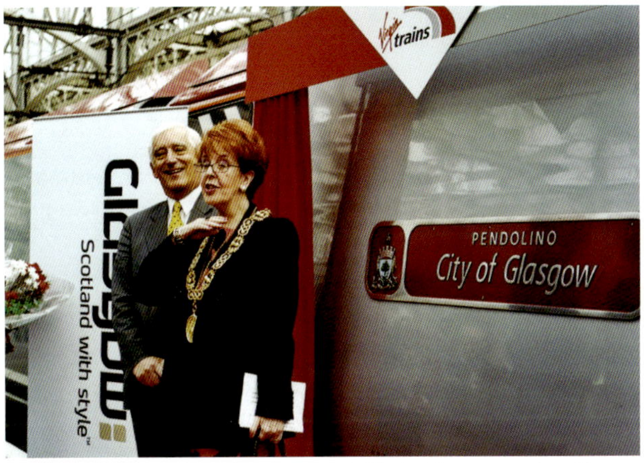

Lord Provost Liz Cameron and Chris Green naming the Virgin Pendolino "City of Glasgow" on 21 May 2004.

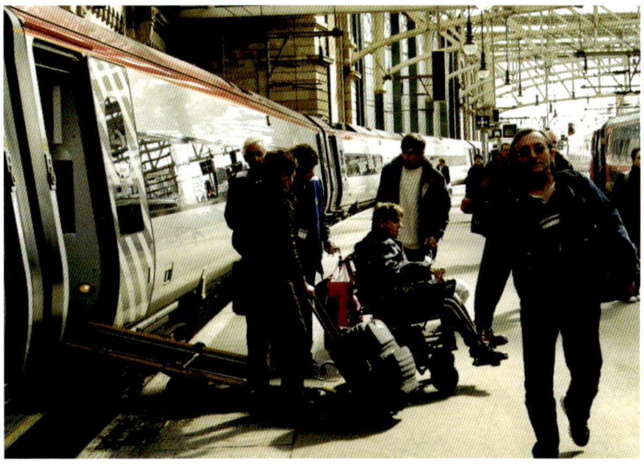

Wheelchair loading.

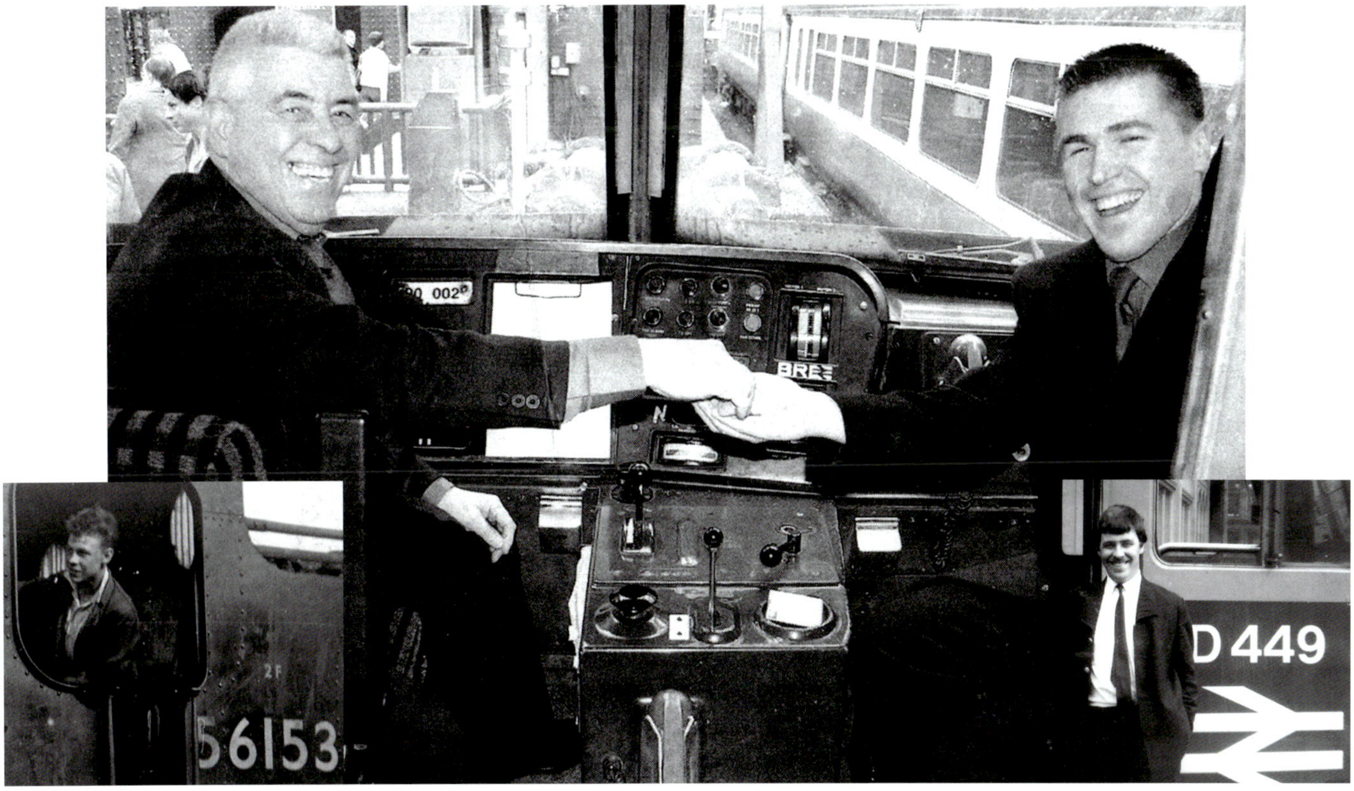

Another railway family – Driver Davie Sweeney, having brought his last train into Central, hands the keys to his Relief -his son David, in May 2004.David the elder served on steam, diesel and electric traction. David the younger serves on Pendolinos and who knows what the future may bring?

32 Changing Names at Central

Jim Summers

Nothing makes it more certain that a book on today's railways will become out of date, almost as soon as first published, than the system of franchising the train services. Every few years, the opportunity is given for new, different, or previous incumbents to bid to run the trains for the next few years. And so it has come about that, since the first printing of this book, three new faces have appeared, all with bus antecedents. Indeed, now, in 2009, there are more faces and facets than ever.

Most obviously, the new franchisees bring new liveries, but they also bring new ideas and financial plans. GNER has ceased as an operator, though the livery lingers on, while its successor, National Express gets on with repainting the trains in virginal white. Virgin itself has introduced its faster, more frequent timetable on the West Coast route, but has been forced by the Department for Transport to cut short at Birmingham its long-distance through cross-country services from Glasgow and Edinburgh. Birmingham New St. is not designed like Glasgow Central, more's the pity.

So services beyond Birmingham to the West Country or the South Coast are now in the hands of the new and hyphen-less CrossCountry Trains, really Arriva. Again by DfT decree, its Anglo-Scottish trains run from Glasgow via Edinburgh and the circuitous East Coast route, albeit with some nicely refurbished and spacious HSTs.

Another new face is that of the equally hyphenless TransPennine Express, like ScotRail a member of the FirstGroup. Its German-built Class 185 trains now cover the former Virgin route to Manchester, usefully extended to Manchester Airport. Only TPE offers porridge, and indeed catering is one of the distinguishing features when franchises change hands – National Express now offers at-seat dining in First Class, having renounced separate restaurant cars, whereas Virgin continues to include in its First Class fares an at-seat full meal service

One new livery, however, is not associated with a change in franchisee, in fact rather the opposite. The white bubbles on a blue background with a saltire motif proclaim that the trains operated by First ScotRail are now part of Scotland's Railway. The individual Strathclyde Passenger Transport and FirstGroup liveries are disappearing as the trains become due for overhaul. The new Scottish livery is intended to survive beyond any future change in operators, reducing confusion and paint consumption. Nevertheless, Central is certain to remain a fascinating place to watch the country's transport policy and colour schemes unfold.

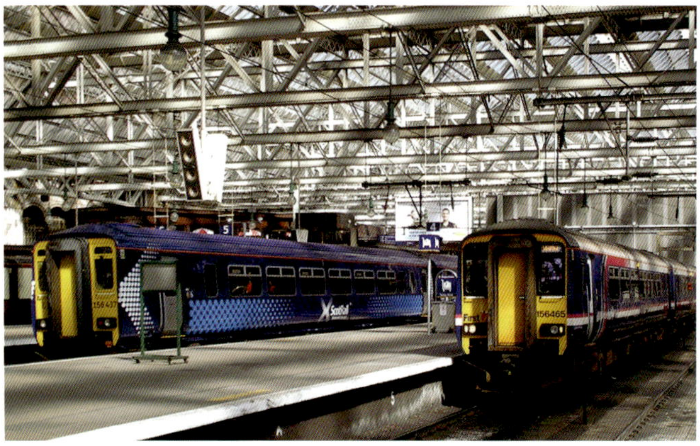

Something new - something Blue.

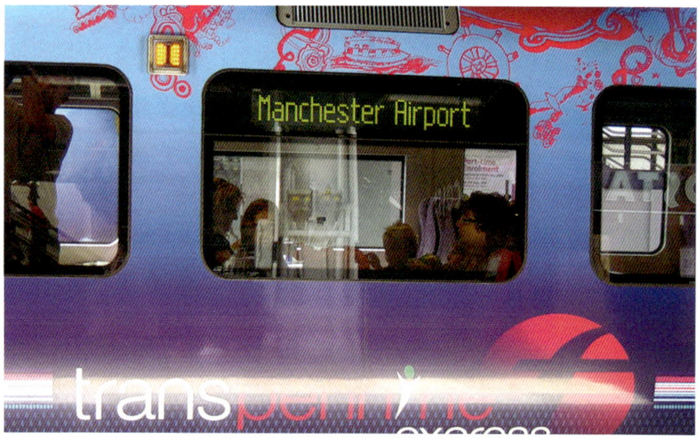

Touch down in Manchester!

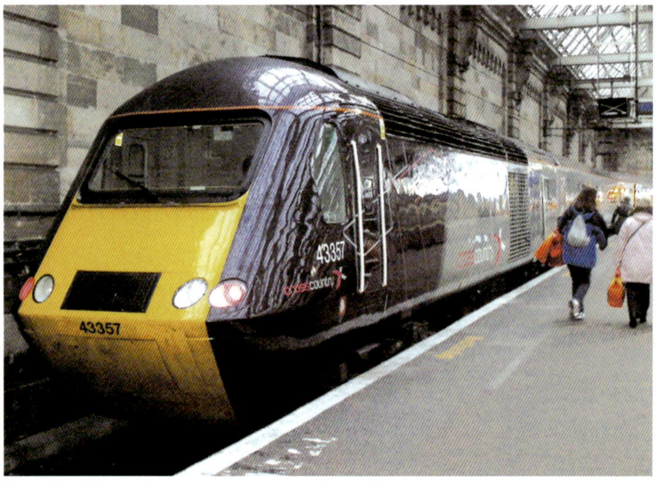

Criss-crossing England with Cross Country.

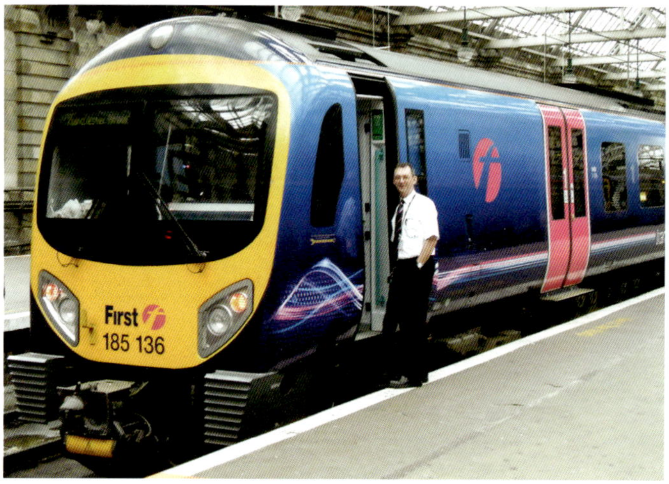

Ready for take-off.

33 Central First – Second only to London

Steve Montgomery, Managing Director, First ScotRail

Britain's largest, best-used and most punctual network anywhere outside London lies around Glasgow, and its core is Strathclyde routes operated by First ScotRail out of Central. If we include also the services which use Queen Street, the network provides 1400 trains daily to 185 stations and carries over 50 million passenger journeys annually, regularly attaining levels in excess of 90% of arrivals within five minutes of scheduled time. This results from our hard work with Network Rail and other train companies in achieving reliable trains, right-time departures, and careful regulation of the minute-to-minute running.

Electric trains provide two-thirds of suburban departures from Central High Level and all services through the Low Level platforms. Keeping this vital electric fleet delivering, day in day out, is the task of First ScotRail's maintenance depot at Shields, which provides various specialist services, including a lathe and wheel-turning facilities. A £24 million investment commenced here in May 2009 to prepare for the addition to the fleet of 16 four-car and 22 three-car Class 380 electric trains – the biggest electric train order in Scotland for a decade, creating more than 130 jobs. The Scottish Government is investing more than £200 million to bring the trains into operational use. From autumn 2010, these aluminium-bodied trains with their 23-metre carriages and distinctive front-end appearance will offer 9000 additional seats for the Ayrshire and Inverclyde routes. They will be fully air-conditioned and spacious, with full disabled access and provision for cyclists and luggage – as well as CCTV and power sockets for laptops. To accommodate trains with more carriages, Transport Scotland is also funding the lengthening platforms.

Meanwhile, Shields is busy looking after our existing electric fleets. The older trains have undergone refurbishment or programmes to improve reliability, the younger Class 318 trains have also been refurbished. And the largest and most modern electric fleet, the 90 mph Class 334, will be displaced from the Ayrshire, Inverclyde, and Argyle Lines by the new Class 380s and will migrate to the new Airdrie-Bathgate route.The diesel fleet of 48 units is maintained at Corkerhill Depot. They too have been refurbished and from December 2009 will double the service to Kilmarnock. On the Shotts route to Edinburgh they will yield to the air-conditioned 90 mph Class 158s, which will offer a new hourly semi-fast service.

No matter how attractive and reliable as our trains, our staff are our principal asset, and First ScotRail was proud to achieve Investors in People status in 2008. We are a big employer, with the West of Scotland home to most of our 4300 staff. Many people were recruited shortly after the company took over the franchise, to improve service delivery and enhance revenue protection. At our Training Academy training includes customer care, disability equality and sign language. We lay great weight on dialogue with our passengers. Most months, a "Meet the Manager" session is held on the concourse at Central or on a train. JourneyCheck and JourneyAlert systems tell individual passengers about any disruption to their trains, while the Advance club rewards our season ticket-holders. Security and reassurance of passengers is a key concern for us. CCTV has been rolled out across virtually all First ScotRail trains. Dot-matrix indications and automated announcements assist people with hearing or seeing difficulties, while all trains now carry wheelchair ramps, and we seek to achieve more step-free access at stations. A total of 184 locations on the Strathclyde network and South West Scotland already have 24-hour online CCTV, monitored from our Customer Services Centre at Paisley; this has attracted wide attention from other railways.

With passengers up by more than 20% and delays for which we are responsible down 50% since the start of the franchise, we are proud that the spring 2009 National Passenger Survey led by Passenger Focus found that customer satisfaction levels with First ScotRail remained strong. Our overall rating of 89% was up one percentage point and eight points higher than the national average among UK train operators. We out-performed national trends in 30 out of the 32 categories and improved our own results in 27 aspects.

We are delighted at the three-year franchise extension to November 2014, giving continuity for the Commonwealth Games. The agreement creates an investment fund of more than £70 million, for control by Transport Scotland, to improve further Scotland's railway. Other enhancements include additional early-morning services to allow passengers from Gourock and Ayr, and elsewhere to connect to services arriving in London before noon.

The Glasgow network may be second to London in physical size; but with our staff, our trains, our ideas, our love of the job and our partners in the industry, First ScotRail will continue to play its part with pride in all those quality matters which make Glasgow first.

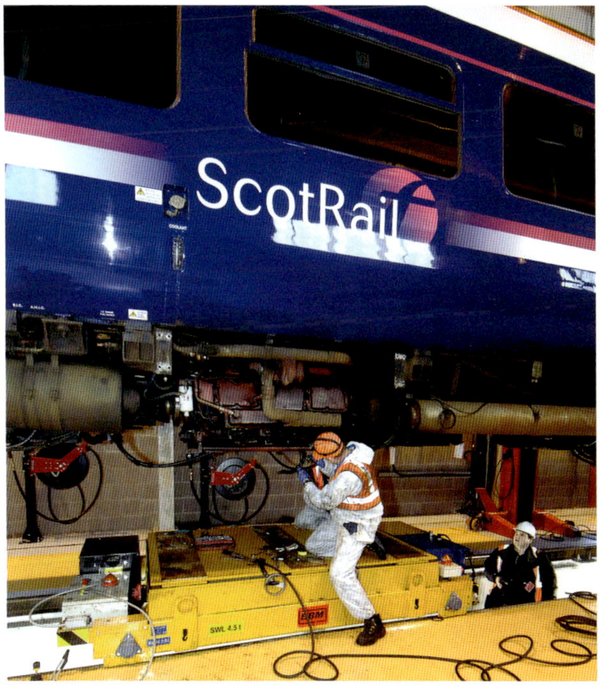

34 Footplate and Committee Room

Alistair Watson, Chairman, Strathclyde Partnership for Transport

Glasgow Central Station is rightly regarded by many as one of the finest terminus stations. With that image goes the bustle and excitement of long-distance journeys by train, but let us not forget that Central Station is part of the largest suburban rail network outside London, and is the hub of the southern half.

When I reflect on Central Station and its importance to the suburban rail network, I do so both as a train driver, and as a member of Strathclyde PTA, and latterly as its Chair. Having worked on the railways for almost 30 years now, my personal association with Glasgow Central has been quite substantial. As a Porter, Shunter, Driver's Assistant, I grasped early on the operational requirements of a railway. After I became a Driver, I intensified my association with Glasgow Central, working a whole host of different types of traction to and from the station. I no longer drive trains but am employed as a manager with Virgin Trains West Coast. I believe I have been able to put this range of transport expertise in the railway industry to good use in my role as Chair of Strathclyde Passenger Transport; and as Chair of the new West of Scotland Regional Transport Partnership, I look forward to continuing a proud history of investment in rail transport.

Central Station would not be what it is today had it not been for the creation of the Passenger Transport Authority and Executive, under Barbara Castle's far-sighted Transport Act of 1968. This recognised the significant contribution made by public transport to the economy of the conurbation, particularly in relation to rail. From 1973, the three incarnations of the passenger transport authority (Greater Glasgow PTA, Strathclyde Regional Council and Strathclyde PTA) have each made their respective marks on the suburban rail network and Central Station itself.

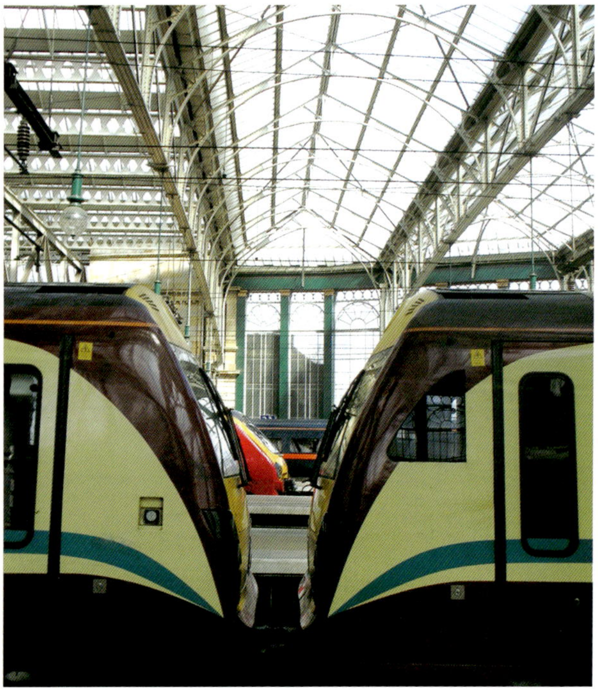

A pair of Class 334 "Juniper" sets.

It is a tribute to the PTA and its Executive that, despite having only been in existence since 1973, and being re-organised in 1975, they achieved the reopening of the Low Level Station at Glasgow Central on 1 November 1979 as part of their newly electrified Argyle Line project. It is hard to think of such a busy station operating without this asset. That project of course brought with it our investment in the Class 314 electric multiple units. And our investment in the Low Level Station continues, both to improve the passenger environment and to improve its accessibility for all, as seen in the introduction of the first disabled-access ticket office and new lifts between the two levels. I still believe that the Low Level is under-used and have, in my capacity as Chair of SPTA, proposed that it be further developed as part of the CrossRail scheme that we are currently working up. This would assist with congestion in the High Level Station.

Unfortunately the next intervention by SPT in rail services affecting Central Station, was less welcome. The growing cost of the Section 20 subsidy and industrial unrest meant that something had to be done to limit the subsidy. The

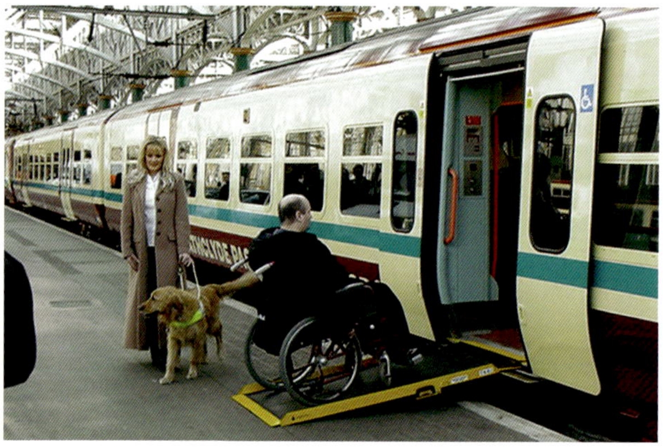

Access, a real priority.

decision was difficult and much delayed, but finally on 8 January 1983 the last train ran on the line between Glasgow Central and Kilmacolm. The substitute bus service had a declining patronage and was finally axed. This experience underpins my concern about the, once again fashionable, move by Government towards "bustitution". It is worth adding that, once times had become better financially, a train service was re-introduced in 1990, albeit by diesel, from Glasgow Central as far as Paisley Canal. I am pleased to say that this line has attracted greater patronage than projected in the business plan.

With the backing of SPT, stability was finally brought to the electrified services in 1985 when Driver Only Operation was agreed between the unions and the British Railways Board. As Chris Green, the then Managing Director of ScotRail, said at the time, without that agreement a third of the network would have had to close. This would also have made Glasgow Central a very different place from what it is today. Happier times returned in 1986 when, after protracted negotiation with the Scottish Office, the train services from Central to Ayr, Ardrossan Harbour and Largs were electrified and a new

Class 318 fleet was procured. Then in 1993 a new service from Glasgow Central to Whifflet was introduced.

Another reorganisation was to intervene in 1996, creating my own Authority. With the privatisation of rail in 1994 and a franchise for ScotRail, let to National Express in 1997, we were now dealing with a very different railway. Instead of dealing with a single fellow public body to procure our rail services, we were now faced with two providers from the private sector –Railtrack, for the operation of infrastructure, and ScotRail for the operation of services. At least in the case of ScotRail we had a contractual relationship. The position with Railtrack was further confused as, despite SPT services continuing to be the majority user of Central Station, it was the Major Stations division of Railtrack in London which was ultimately responsible for the station, not its Scottish Zone. This situation persists under the Network Rail structure and adds a layer of difficulty.

The franchise brought in 2001 a new fleet of Class 334 electric multiple units, operating out of Central Station. These are not only the first trains to achieve largely the standards set under the Disability Discrimination Act, but also, despite their teething problems on introduction, are very popular with passengers and drivers alike, due to the pleasant and comfortable environment which they provide. An additional two were procured by the SPT to enlarge the fleet to facilitate the Larkhall-Milngavie rail project. And I am delighted to say that, as part of that

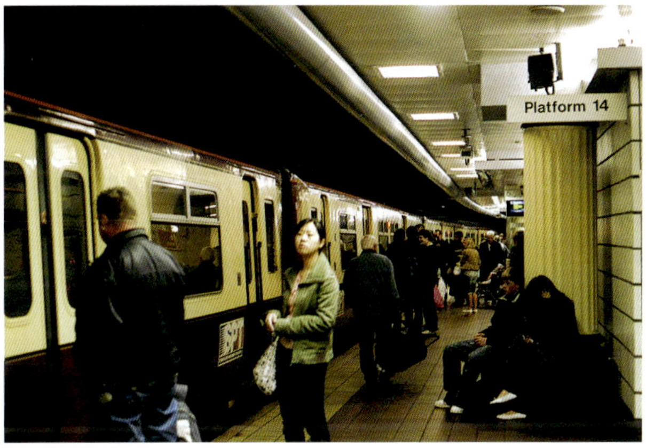

Low-level renewed with services restored to Larkhall in 2006.

project, we delivered on 9 December 2005 the new rail services between Central Station and Larkhall. Long in the planning and fraught with difficulty, because of events such as local government reorganisation, reorganisation of the railways, an attempt to apply PFI funding principles to the project, the Rail Regulator's review of Railtrack funding, the placing of Railtrack in administration, increased centralisation under Network Rail, a new franchisee, and long and difficult negotiations on funding, to name but a few, nevertheless the Larkhall –Milngavie project showed that, with perseverance, new services can still be delivered.

Now, to add to the challenge, we have the creation of Transport Scotland with its remit to develop major rail projects and to specify and manage the rail services throughout Scotland. We hope that, as with the other partners in this industry, which is growing in complexity, we will have a positive relationship in the development of the rail network in Strathclyde. It is also to be hoped that the Scottish Ministers' desire to fund the growth of the railway will continue. As with the CrossRail scheme mentioned above, our determination remains to grow the network and make better use of Central Station. As I write this, we have just submitted a Bill to the Scottish Parliament to enable the construction of a rail link from Central Station to Glasgow Airport. The project will lengthen platform 11A to allow eight-car sets to provide the service. Work to deliver the project will also provide a long-needed solution to the congestion problems between Shields and Arkleston and, as well as providing a new frequent service to the airport, it will create capacity for additional services to Ayrshire.

I started this piece reflecting on peoples' perception of Central Station, as the starting point for long-distance journeys by rail. By providing the new rail link to the airport we will bring that perception into the twenty-first century, with the distance ultimately travelled being limited only by the destinations of flights from Glasgow Airport. However, as a railwayman and politician, I live in hope that, despite the ill-fated Regional Eurostar experience, Government will accept the growing case that long-distance services by high speed rail, from a terminus like Central Station, are the only realistic alternative to the environmentally unsustainable growth in air travel.

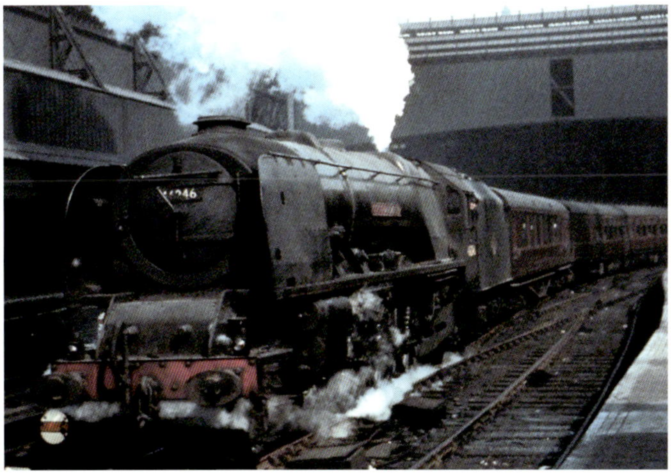

Still with a sloping smokebox top, Duchess No. 46246 "City of Manchester" leaves with an 'up' express - April 1958.

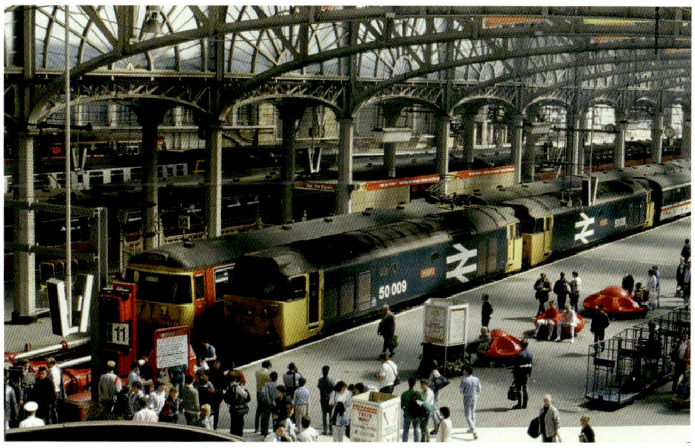

Class '50s' return to Central with the "Hoover Dambuster" Railtour on 14 May 1988 providing a reminder of the diesel era when these locomotives worked in multiple.
No. 50009 "Conqueror" and 50036 "Victorious".

35 All Change

David Simpson, Route Director, Scotland, Network Rail

The early hours of Christmas Day 2008 marked the end of an era, when Glasgow Central Signalling Centre (GCSC) was taken out of commission after 47 years of service. Over that period the box had witnessed many changes, from the final days of steam operation through to the advent of Pendolinos running to London Euston in little over four hours. Controlling one of the busiest and most complex station layouts in the UK, the box and the signallers who worked in it had adapted smoothly over the years to many different service patterns, rolling stock changes, and timetables. In fact, in its last month of operation, one of the most significant changes took place with the December 2008 timetable change, which saw a complete recast of cross-border services, including an hourly service to Euston for much of the day for the first time ever.

They faced a new challenge on 27th December, when operations commenced in the new West of Scotland Signalling Centre (WSSC), located in the triangle of tracks at Cowlairs, some two miles from Central itself. The WSSC resulted from the need to renew the signal interlocking in the Central area, which was approaching life expiry. As part of this project, new signals were fitted in and around the station, using highly reliable LEDs, which result in a much brighter aspect, as a glance from the platform ends after dark confirms. The new Signalling Centre is planned to take control progressively of much of the rail network in the west of Scotland over the next decade.

The re-interlocking project itself was a massive operation, planned over several years, and executed with as little disruption to passengers as possible. As well as completely renewing the signalling equipment in the Central station area, various other parts of the railway system were converted to be controlled from the new box. Working within the constraints of a listed building the team had many challenges to meet, including refurbishing 'Gantry 'A'' which itself is listed, and sits across the whole station throat on the Clyde bridge, a key element of the station's operation.

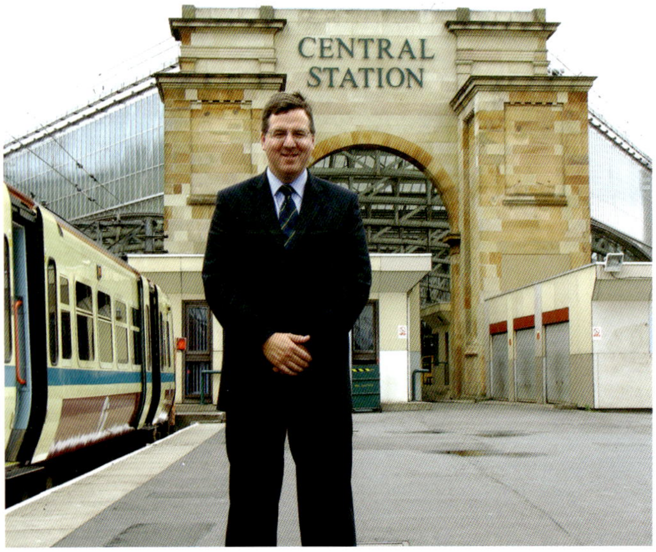

Happy to be rid of Platform 11A at long last!

Operating Central requires the highest standards of skill and expertise on the part of the signallers and timetablers. The layout provides the ability to go from 'anywhere to anywhere' – a train from platform 1 could be routed towards Shields, and from platform 15 towards Polmadie, with every combination of platform and line option in between. Maximum opportunity of this flexibility is taken in timetabling the services which use the station, but the differing platform lengths set challenges in relation to the length of trains, which can vary from a two-car Class 156 up to the long nine-car inter-city services. So, despite this flexibility, it is still necessary on occasions in peak hours to 'dock' two and even three trains at a time in one of the longer platforms. Any changes to the very complex daily plan are managed by the shift manager in WSSC in real time, and communicated to a myriad of interested parties.

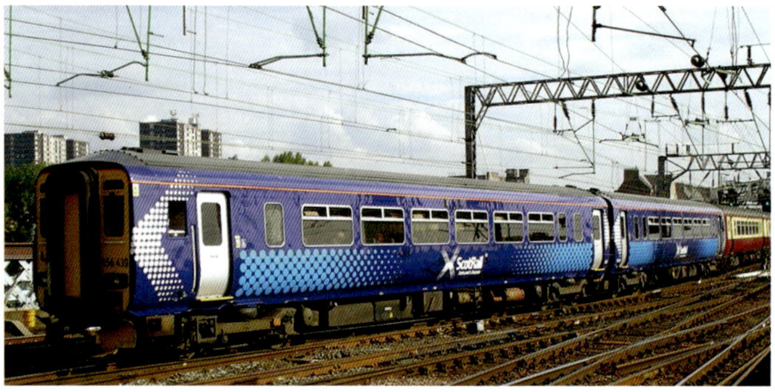

Transition - new and old!

More trains have to be fitted in over the next few years. The upgrade of the track on the Kilmarnock will allow a half hourly frequency a historically poorly served route, to provide competition with express coaches which take advantage of the upgraded M77 motorway. In addition, more trains serving Edinburgh via the Shotts line will be introduced, to improve further the range of services between Scotland's two major cities.

The platform re-numbering which took place over Christmas 2008 gave a clue about a more fundamental change, this time to the station itself – the preparations for the Airport Rail Link, offering trains every 15 minutes from Central, giving a much needed direct rail link to the airport in contrast to the often congested M8. Although the Link has since been cancelled, the extra track from Paisley and the platform works are going ahead. Two additional platforms, numbered 12 and 13, will be built on the site of the current short-stay car park between

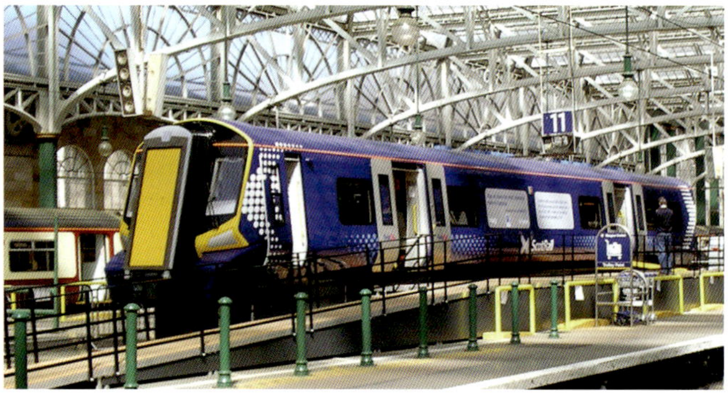

Mock-up of the new Class 380 on display.

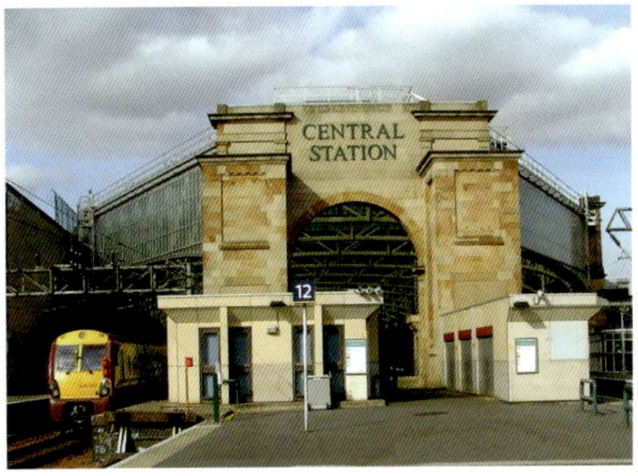

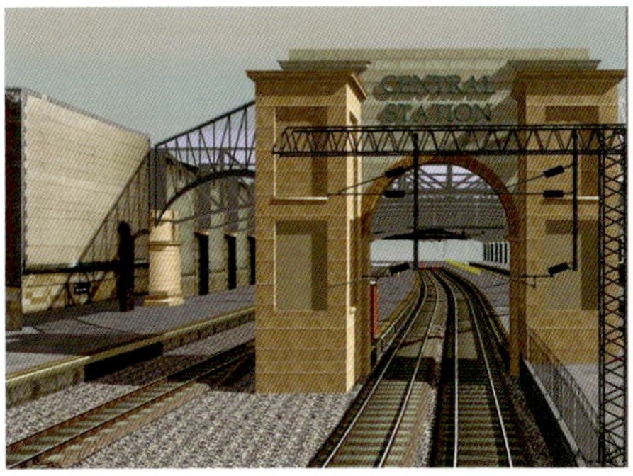

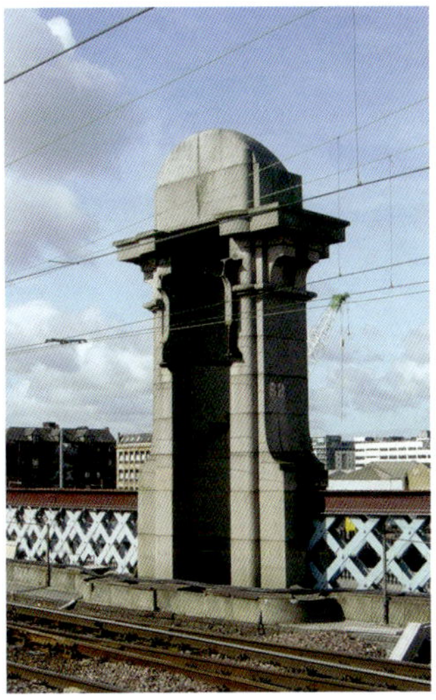

Guarding the approaches!

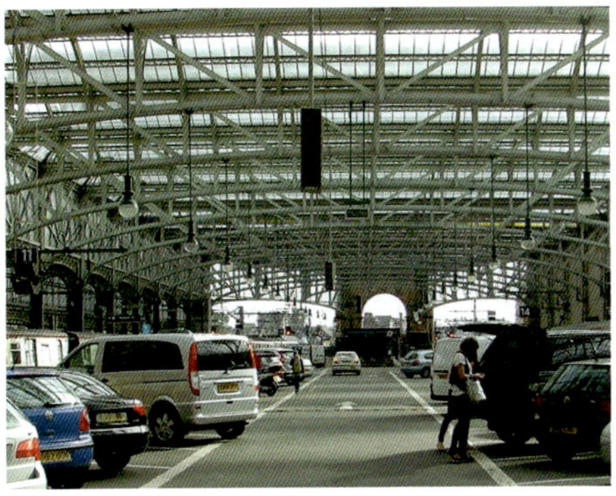

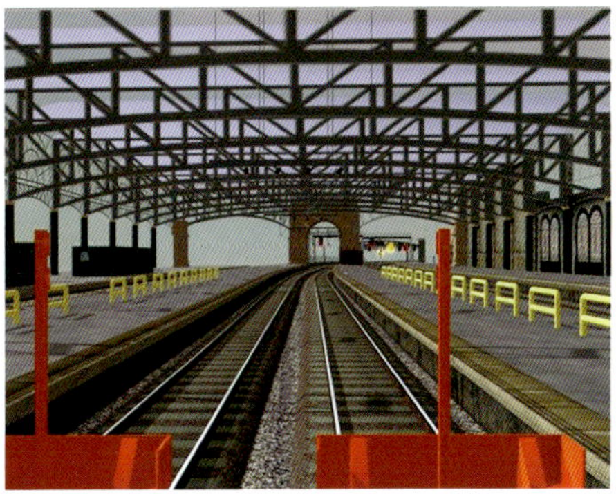

The road carriageway will give way... to rail carriages in the new platforms 12 and 13.

platforms 11 and 14. The closure of the existing platform 12 (formerly 11A), will bring to an end the long and unpopular walk towards the Clyde which this platform necessitated! New trains, in the form of class 380 EMUs will operate Ayrshire and Inverclyde services.

While all this change takes place, the station itself continues to meet the daily challenges of handling thousands of passengers. A new CCTV system is now in place to improve further the security of passengers and staff; and the renewal and upgrade of Customer Information Systems continues to ensure that the most up-to-date information is available to passengers. Central scores consistently highly in the regular customer satisfaction surveys for stations managed by Network Rail. The efforts and dedication of everyone involved in its operation will ensure that this high standard of customer service will continue in years to come.

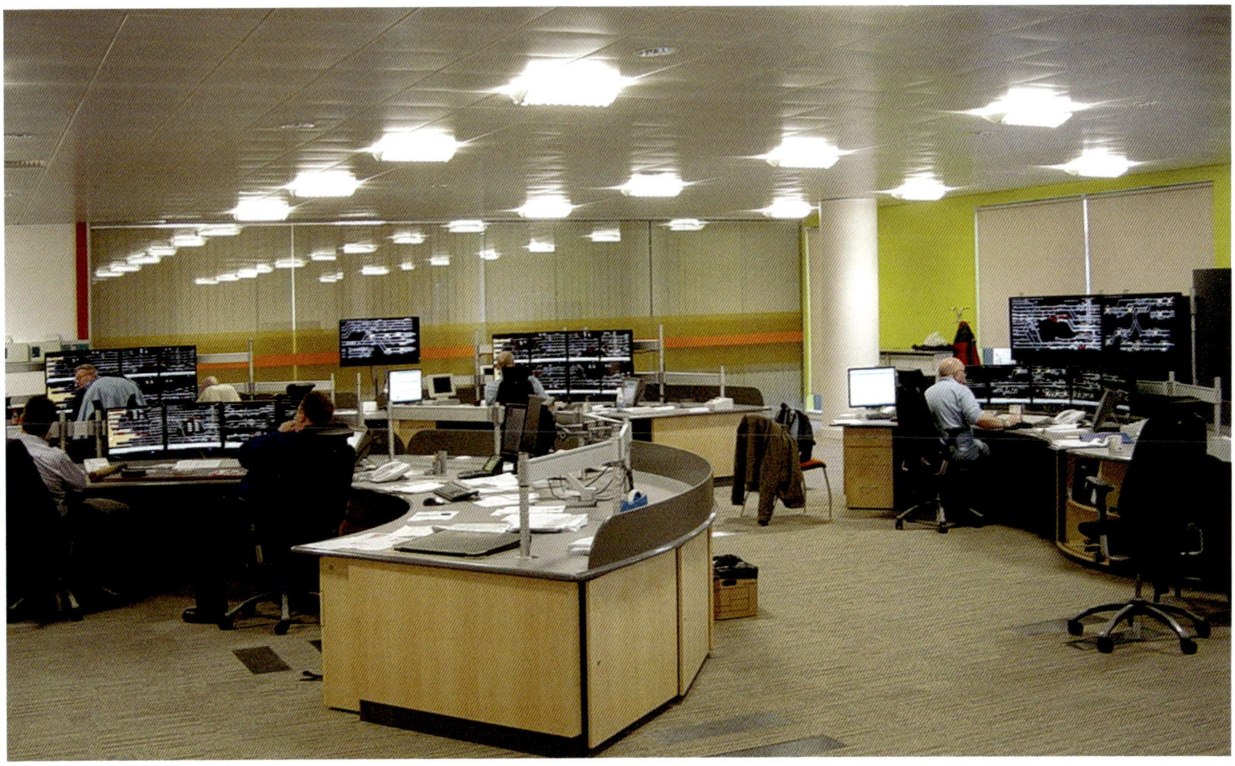

Signallers settle in to their new home in the West of Scotland Control Centre at Springburn.

36 You're welcome

Nicholas Prag, Station Manager, Glasgow Central, Network Rail

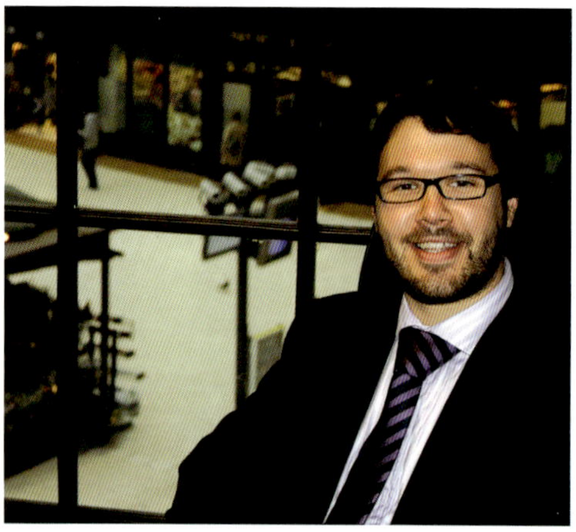

From the sprawling glass roof, to the wonderful curved wooden buildings throughout, Glasgow Central station is a fantastic environment in which to work. It has clearly been a massive part of so many peoples' lives: those who built it, those who worked here over the years, definitely not least, those thousands upon thousands of folk who use the station. It exudes a sense of history and importance for us who enjoy running it.

And that is an extremely demanding, but very rewarding job. Every day brings with it a fresh challenge, but the variety is one of its major attractions. The Station Manager is responsible for meeting these challenges through his Network Rail team, who deliver a wide range of services to the station tenants, train operating companies, contractors, British Transport Police, and not least, our travelling public, all of whom naturally have their own set of priorities. The Station Manager achieves this by continuous dialogue with all of the station partners, organising and chairing forums for discussion.

Communicating information effectively to passengers and train operating companies is one of the key elements in maintaining a smooth-running railway station. Upstairs, a busy team is dedicated to overseeing the public address system announcements and departure boards, while down on the concourse friendly Customer Service Assistants, readily identified by their blue Network Rail tabards, are always available to assist passengers with any questions; and they provide the mobility assistance service for passengers, who can pre-book this service or request it on an ad-hoc basis. In fact, the team and its two electric buggies carry out more than 12,000 "mobility assists" every year.

The safety and security of all station users will always be a top priority. In view of the increased potential of threats to stations, regular security patrols are made frequently, and an excellent network of CCTV cameras is at the disposal of staff and British Transport Police officers. Glasgow Central can rightly claim to be one of the most secure stations in the country.

The station and its staff must adapt to a future which will be fashioned by the continuing increase in demand for rail travel, and we have an ongoing drive to improve facilities. The Station Manager and his team have the ability to shape and facilitate each new project, as more money is being spent on enhancing Britain's rail network than ever before. Central station will benefit among other good things from the construction of two new platforms. These two new platforms provide more capacity within the station and will enable a greater number of services to operate. Just one of the challenges for the team at Glasgow Central is maintaining an operational station and minimising disruption to passengers and station tenants

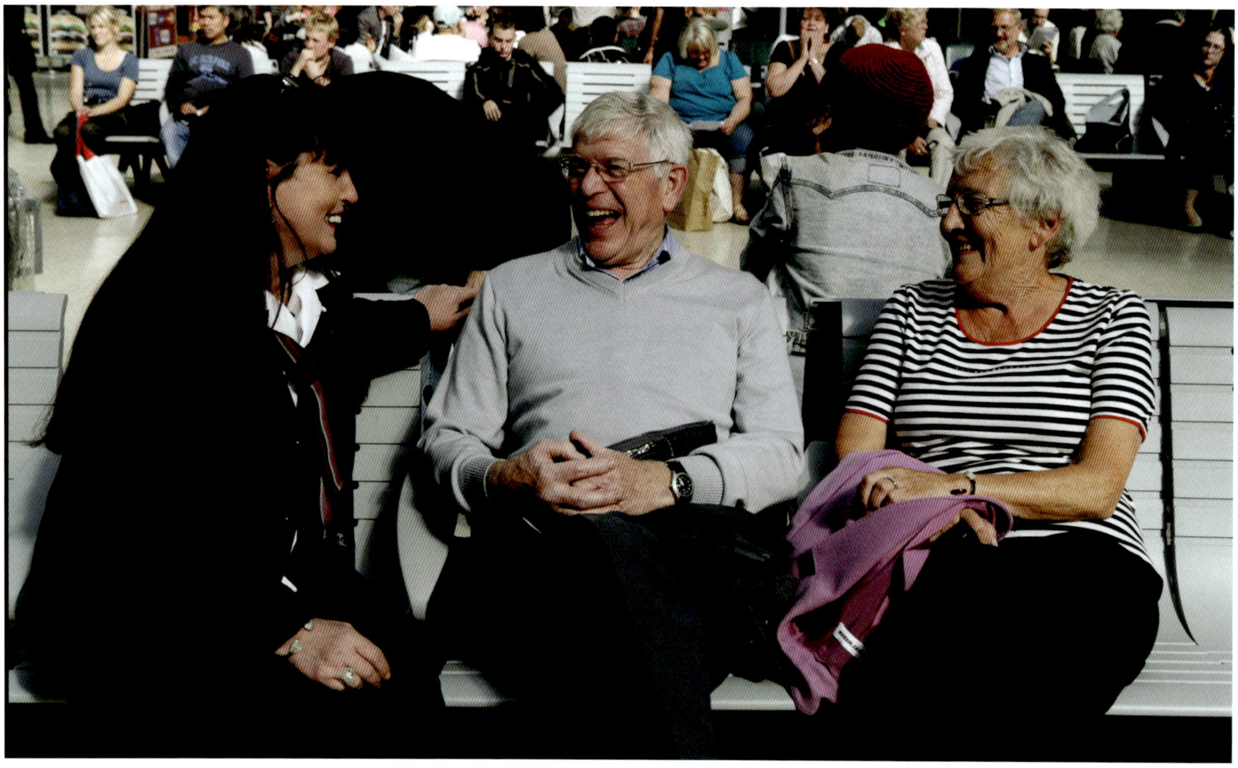

"Service with a smile" - Staff of Network Rail and the train companies work together to please the passengers.

during the considerable construction work of this project.

With each generation, Central is enhanced, expanded and enriched by those working in the station and planning for its future. The station has a proud and extensive history but, with staff committed to continuing the tradition of great service synonymous with Central, its best years are still to come.

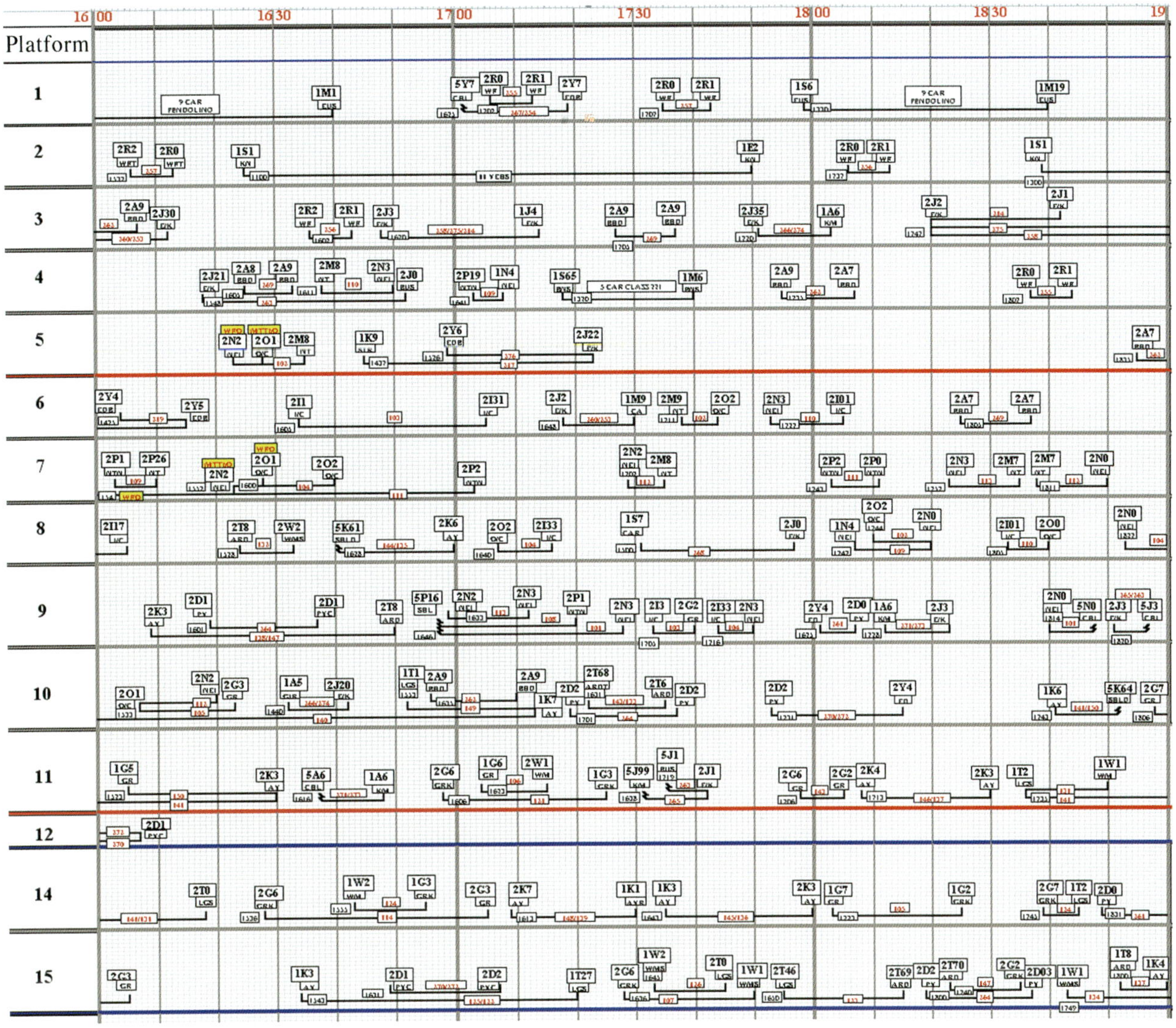

"Quart into a pint pot" - the platform occupation graph for the evening peak shows combining, double docking and not a lot of space

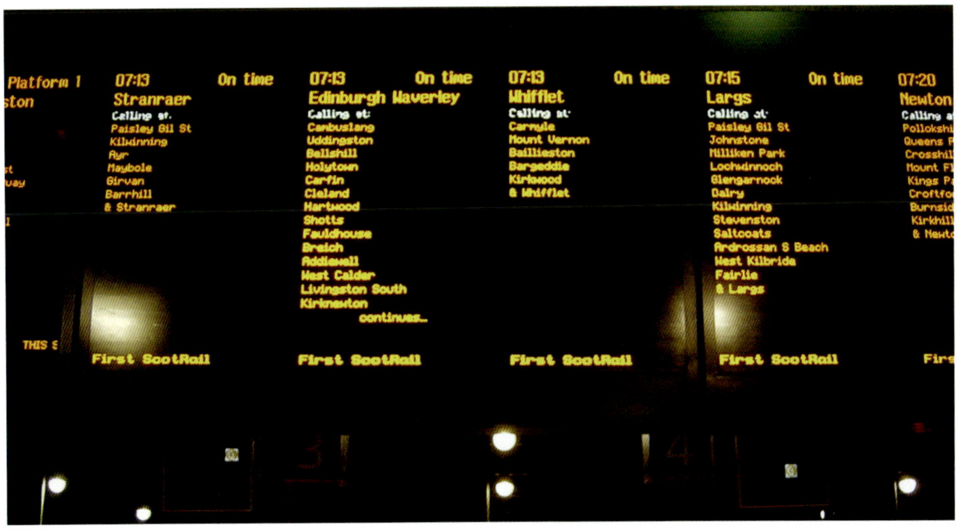

Three simultaneous departures? No problem at Central.

37 Mindful of the past, welcoming the future

Paul Lyons, Acting Deputy Manager, Glasgow Central

The year 1879 was one which was to change the landscape of Scotland for ever, as on 1 August that year Glasgow Central Station opened its doors for the first time. Today, over a century and a quarter later, the station continues to thrive and most recently Central was named Major Station of the Year 2005 at the National Rail Awards. Though much bigger – and busier – attention to detail remains at the heart of everything we do. Some may call me a romantic, but working in a place with such a rich history and exciting present as Glasgow Central Station is a very special honour indeed.

That year of opening of Central in its first form was a time of great change. Britain was embroiled in the Anglo Zulu wars and just months after Central opened, Scotland was rocked by news of the Tay Bridge disaster. It was also the year when Albert Einstein, Joseph Stalin, Padraig Pearse and Scotland's own John Maclean were born, all of whom would change the course of the 20th Century. Against this backdrop Central created opportunities for thousands of people living in the now sprawling city of Glasgow. On 'Glasgow Fair' holidays in particular, the station would be packed with people going to exotic destinations on the Ayrshire Coast, or 'doon the watter' to Wemyss Bay. The station was a portal for escaping from the smell and grime of the biggest industrial city outside London. As numbers of passengers grew, so did the need to expand. In 1899, an additional platform was added, but it was to be at a terrible cost. Gas mantles beneath the platform caused an explosion, which wiped out 65 feet of platform, and with it the lives of six men. Since that time, train movements have increased from 780 to around 1,020 every day. The popularity of rail travel has also seen annual passenger numbers double from 17 million to 34 million in recent years.

A large part of the 13-acre site that we know today as the Central dates from 1901 to 1906, when platforms 9 to 13 were built and were an instant success. An arcade of steel, octagonal columns between platforms 9 and 10 marks the boundary between the old station and the new. The mastermind, the Caledonian's Chief Engineer, Matheson, said this was to form three avenues for traffic – a central avenue for wheeling luggage and one at either side for passengers. Innovations which he used in its construction were soon picked up for use elsewhere. A steam-operated derrick crane proved so successful that the technology was later used on the other side of the Atlantic in the creation of many of New York's skyscrapers.

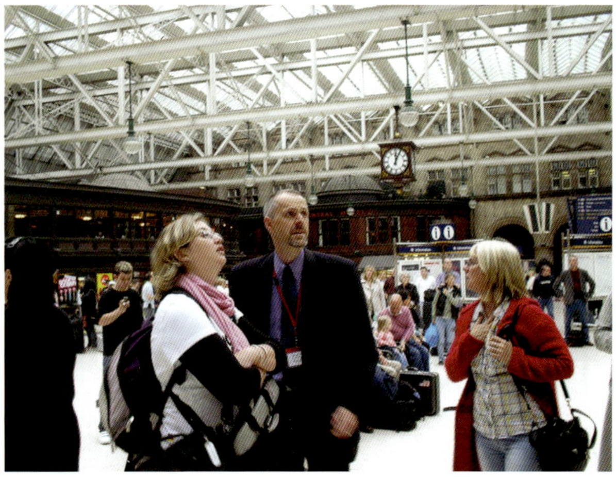

Answers the public - Paul Lyons June 2006.

It took 14,000 ordinary workers to build Central Station, all unsung heroes whose names were not recorded. The burgeoning empire required a huge workforce. Around 7,000 of the navvies who worked on Central were Irish immigrants who were escaping famine. Others were Highland Scots who moved South. Although the work was arduous and sometimes fraught with danger – the building of the railway bridge over the river Clyde in particular – they welcomed the employment. The first porters at Central were Gaels, some who had no English at all, and they were paid on a commission-only basis. Argyle Street below the station is still known as the "Hielandman's Umbrella", as this was where the Highlanders gathered to speak about their experiences and talk of home.

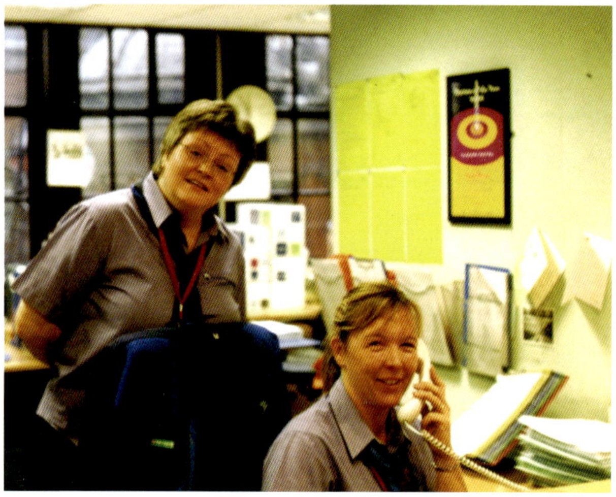

Friendly faces at Reception.

Those who have arrived, departed and passed through Central over the years include Stan Laurel and Oliver Hardy, who were often met by crowds whistling their theme tune. On one occasion, the duo arrived at Platform 1 from London to be met by a crowd of 40,000 well-wishers. The Gorbals' most beloved son, Benny Lynch, was met by similar numbers and tumultuous applause when he returned home with the accolade of being Scotland's first world champion boxer. Rudolf Hess, the deputy Nazi Fuhrer, had a less welcoming arrival to Scotland, when he was arrested during the Second World War and was later taken to Platform 1 at Central to board the train for London. It is said that, while awaiting the train, Hess asked if he could have a cigarette. When the Police Officer agreed, Hess motioned to show his hands were bound and asked to be un-cuffed. The policeman said: "Do I have it on your honour as an officer and a gentleman that you will not try to escape?" Hess smoked his cigarette, stubbed it out on the ground with his shoe and replied: "Take me away."

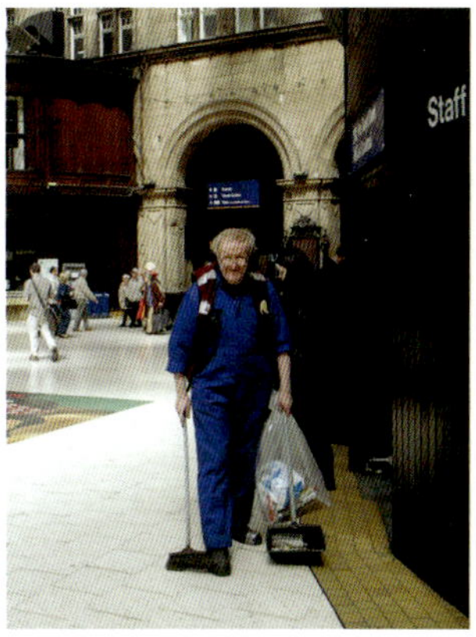

Jimmy!

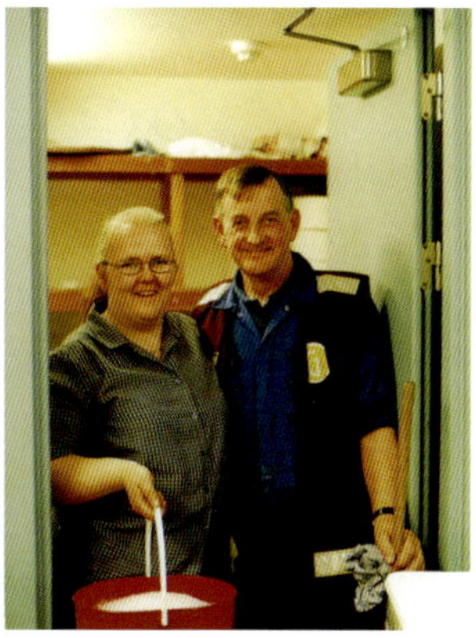

At your service!
In the 'Superloo'.

The station was also the meeting place for many thousands of troops as they left for the front in France during the First World War. Scottish soldiers suffered heavy loss of life, and the basement area was used as a temporary morgue. The Herald, Glasgow's daily newspaper, reported in July 1916: *No more a piteous sight can be seen in all of Scotland than in Glasgow Central Station where mothers and weans wait for their husbands and fathers, the lucky ones coming off in wheelchairs and many being led like blind mice off carriages.*

Central has also been a place of refuge. In 1919, thousands of people campaigned for a reduction in the working week at Glasgow's George Square. When tanks were brought in to disperse the crowd, the people became agitated and frightened. When an order was given to fix bayonets, many fled and hid in the station. Those who were caught were given terrible beatings.

Today, tides of passengers arrive and depart at Central every day, and although there is always a good atmosphere, there is a particular buzz on football match days. The station has a strong footballing link, particularly with Hampden Stadium. In the 1920s, it was confirmed as the home of all international and major domestic games, solely because the General Manager of the railway explained the lack of capacity to Ibrox or Parkhead. Shrewdly, he advised that, on the other hand, not only was there spare capacity on the Cathcart Circle lines, but there was also an abundance of land available. In order to run more trains for Hampden on match days, the signals were put out of use from Central to Mount Florida and a handsignalman was stationed each quarter mile to control the football specials.

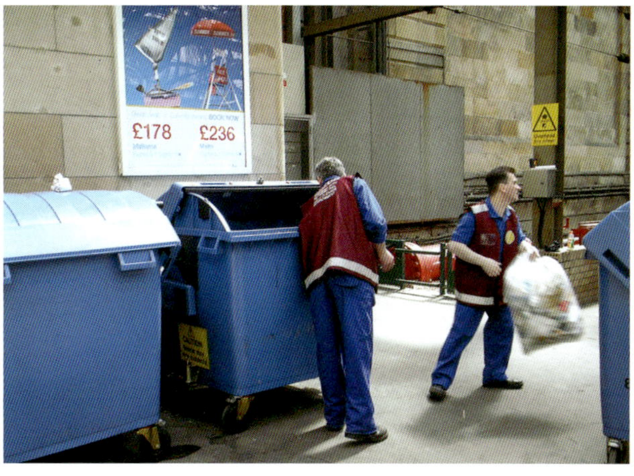

Without whom!

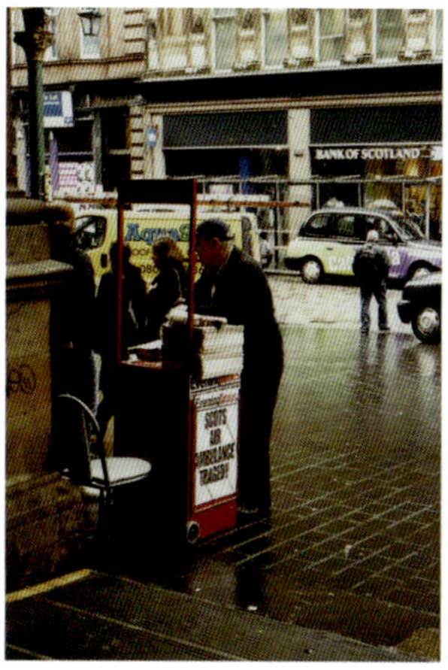

The 'Evening Times' newsvendor.

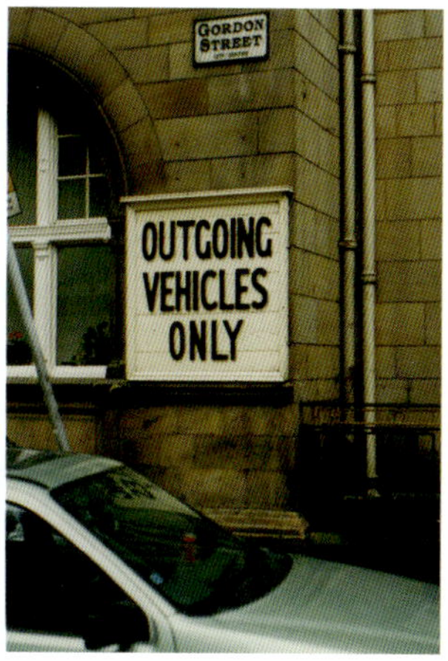

An enduring landmark.

Today's staff is highly trained and has access to state of the art technology. I like to think Matheson would have marvelled at our advances. The camaraderie between staff at Central is highly prized and, speaking personally, the kindness and friendships I have found in the railway are things I cherish. From the Customer Services buggy Driver, who regularly serenades his passengers, to the Communications worker who assisted the delivery of a baby on Platform 13 before paramedics arrived, the team is keen to help. The fact that 98,000 people use Central Station every day is testament to the success of Donald Matheson and his team. While many buildings of the same age have outlived their usefulness and lie in decline, Central is going from strength to strength. Perhaps that's why it has a special place in the hearts of the men and women who work here.

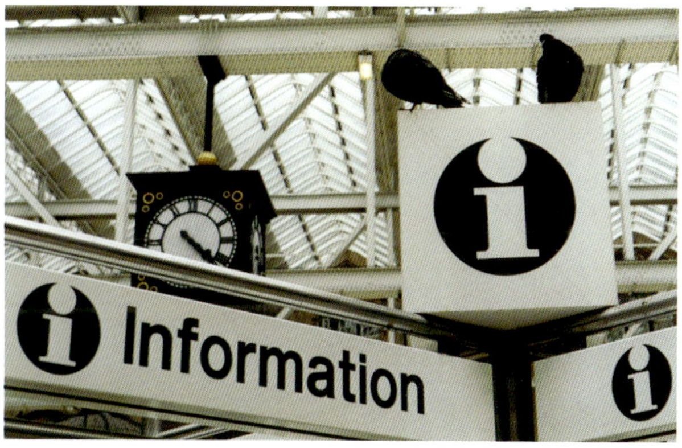

Birds eye view?

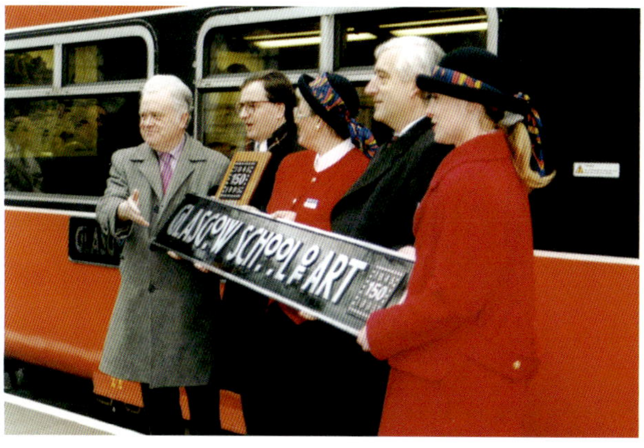

Class 320, No. 320305, named
"Glasgow School of Art 1845 – 1995" on 10 February 1995

38 Caring for Central

Ron McAulay, Director, Scotland – Network Rail

Network Rail owns and operates the railway across Great Britain. This means that in Scotland we maintain 2,736 route kilometres of track, 345 stations, and more than 14,000 other structures. These include world-renowned structures like the Forth and Tay Bridges and Glenfinnan Viaduct. Scotland's railway network is currently experiencing unprecedented levels of expansion and investment, and travelling by train is more popular now than at any time since the 1940s. With more than 80 million passenger journeys and nearly 14 million tons of freight on our railway in Scotland annually, this industry is as vital as ever to the country's economic and social development and long-term prosperity.

It is an industry which continues to grow, and this is an exciting time for rail engineers across the country. With major capacity improvements at Waverley Station completed in 2007, we are now about to begin a full renewal of the glass roof. We are also progressing well with building the new route between Glasgow and Edinburgh, via Airdrie and Bathgate, which will offer four more trains an hour between east and west. Then there are the two new platforms for Glasgow Central, now well under way, and the Forth Bridge is entering the final phase of a decade-long refurbishment programme. As the not-for-dividend company running the railways, Network Rail is delivering many of these new projects, while at the same time continuing to improve reliability and punctuality and so encouraging yet more travellers on to the rails.

Network Rail holds a host of iconic structures around Scotland in its care, but few of them play as active a role in the lives of their users as Glasgow Central station. More than 100,000 people will pass through Glasgow Central each day, and over half of all daily journeys on Scotland's rail network begin or end under the station's roof.

The station building, its imposing glazed roof, and the sheer size of the concourse cannot fail to make an impact on any traveller stepping into Central for the first time. But they are more than just a fitting reminder of the skill and ambition of the Victorian architects and engineers who created our rail network: Central lies at the heart of the city and the station has always played a key role in the economic and social life of Glasgow and its surrounding districts. Today's station, and the rail lines running into it, remain an important feature of the city's life, providing fast and efficient train services for tens of thousands of commuters each weekday and ensuring that the city's shops and leisure attractions are within reach of thousands more travellers each weekend.

Network Rail is immensely proud to be responsible for the operation and upkeep of this magnificent facility, and we look forward with enthusiasm to ensuring it meets the needs of the city and its travellers in the years to come.

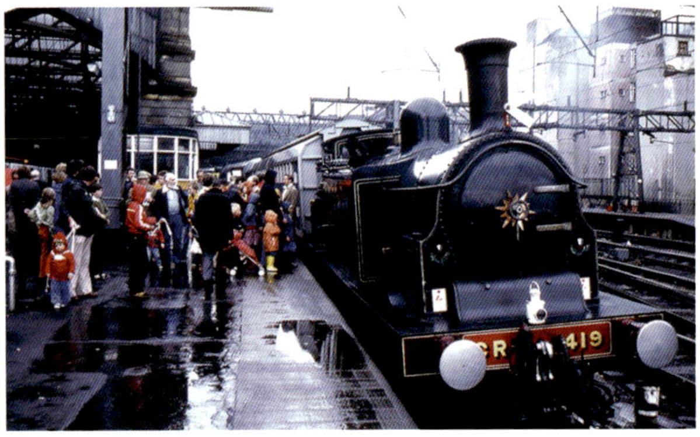

Preserved CR '439' Class 0-4-4 tank No. 419 stands on a wet day during the Station's Centenary celebrations in 1979. Its route indicator shows it to be bound for Coatbridge.

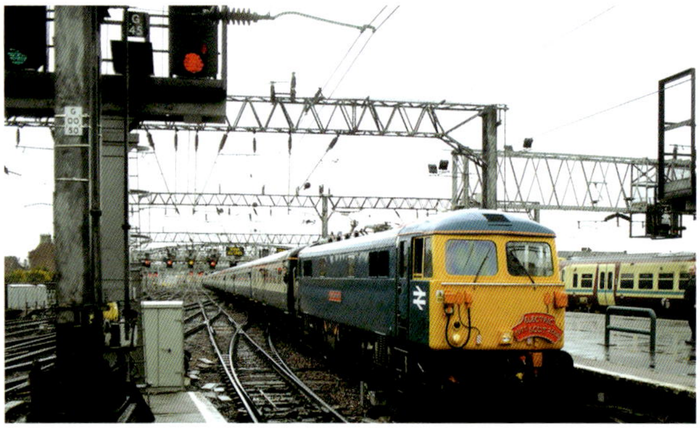

An 87 returns! 87002 on Electric Scot Special train 15 October 2008.

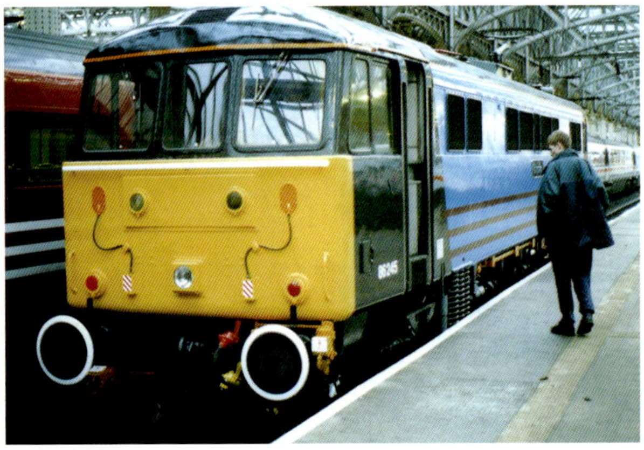

Class 86 No. 86245 "Caledonian" newly named on 15 February 1998.

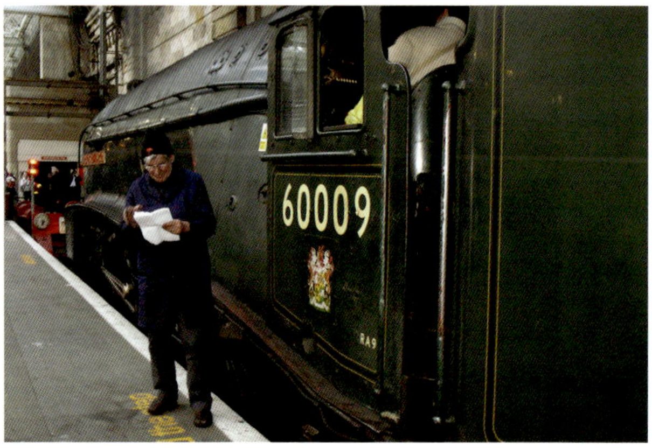

A4 No. 60009 "Union of South Africa" and its owner John Cameron, former Chairman of ScotRail, 15 April 2008.

39 A virtual railway beneath your feet

Malcolm Cook

Next time you get your ticket from the main ScotRail booking office at Central Station, spare a thought for the train drivers below your feet. As you are being served up there, down below they are dealing with emergencies, train failures and the very worst weather conditions that nature can throw at them. Underneath the main concourse of this 19th century train station, 21st century technology is in daily use by ScotRail train drivers.

ScotRail has invested £1.3 million in two state-of-the-art train driving simulators from Australia, on which drivers hone their skills and prepare for almost any eventuality. A complete virtual railway has been simulated, in which drivers of both electric and diesel trains are put through their paces, as they experience all manner of operational scenarios and practise the skills needed to deal with every eventuality.

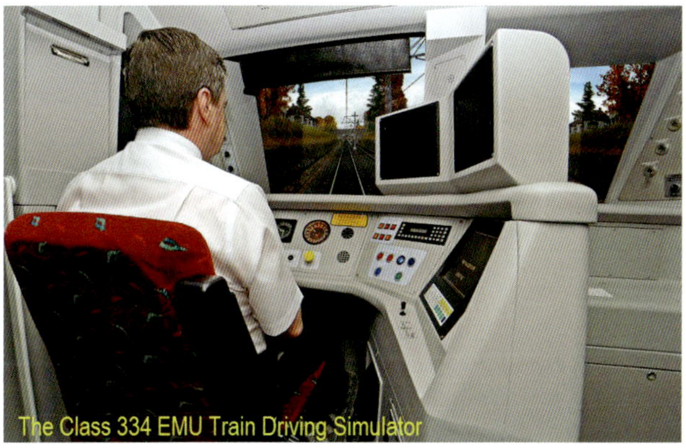
The Class 334 EMU Train Driving Simulator

The simulators are housed in a purpose-built simulation facility, located in one of the many supporting archways which make up the numerous layers of Central Station and never normally seen by the travelling public. The only clue that travellers may see, is an innocuous door, tucked away in the corner of the station near the famous "bomb".

This subterranean location has served the station well and in many guises over the years. It has previously been used as an Operational Training Centre, as a Train Crew Selection Centre, and was for many years the central cash office for the Glasgow area, routinely processing up to £2 million per week. The security precautions required to handle such large amounts of cash caused considerable problems when the location was converted into a Simulation facility. Not least of which was the removal of a 3.5 ton safe and the cutting of a doorway through steel reinforced walls into the subterranean access tunnels for the safe to pass through. This single doorway alone, took four days to complete.

All ScotRail Train Drivers have their licence to drive trains re-validated every two years and must attend the simulator for a full day before their licence can be re-issued. During their assessment they will demonstrate how they would deal with events and scenarios designed to ensure that they have had the very best preparation, for the challenging and sometimes very rare situations that can arise. These "full mission" train driving simulators faithfully replicate all the features and functions of the Class 170 Diesel Multiple Unit and the Class 334 Electric Multiple Unit traction. The driver sits in a complete and fully functioning replica of the train driver's cab.

A network of computers creates a virtual railway of more than 50 kilometres which can be driven in both directions. It includes a mainline terminal station very similar to Glasgow Queen Street, a maintenance yard similar to Yoker Depot, and many different types of terrain and signalling systems. These computer-generated images are projected on to 3m by 4m screens in front of the simulators and provide an amazingly realistic environment depicting day or night. All seasons of the year are replicated as well as flooded track, snowdrifts, fog, children trespassing on the line and, of course, autumn leaves. The drivers communicate with virtual passengers, signalmen, and traffic controllers, by using the onboard fixed radio equipment, PA systems or trackside telephones, just as in the same way as they would when in a real train or when carrying out real trackside procedures. The simulators can also realistically replicate a wide range of train and ancillary equipment failures including track and signalling faults.

So that ScotRail drivers are prepared to deal safely with any of the factors that could delay or disrupt your journey home, those Train Driving Simulators below your very feet at Glasgow Central are at the cutting edge of European Train Driving Simulator technology.

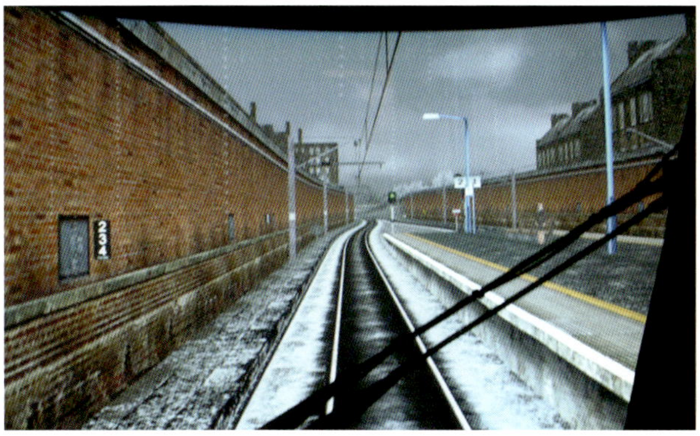
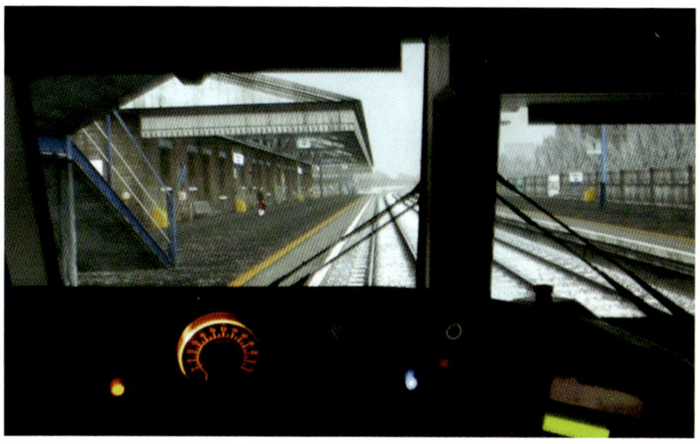

In the dry in all weathers!

From Sorrento to Glasgow

In this little spot of Italy, which has become a well-loved feature of in the northern climes of Glasgow Central, Franco d'Apice and his multinational team continue to serve the traveller. Hailing from the beautiful resort of Sorrento on the Mediterranean, Franco flitted in 1976 to the dear green place on the Clyde, as so many of his countrymen have done over the years. They have brightened our daily lives with their continental cafe cuisine and ambience. Franco has seen it all, since he has been at the Central from the days of BR, of Railtrack, and now Network Rail, opening his own business in 1989. His is in fact the longest serving "business" in the station, which he knows from top to bottom; for below the café on the High Level concourse is a wee, licensed restaurant, at the Low Level concourse, off the Hielandman's Umbrella, called – what else? - *Caffe L'Ombrellone.* adjacent to the Low level entrance. And it all remains thoroughly international, with staff from all over Europe – Albania, Estonia, Italy, Poland, and Spain – even Glasgow.

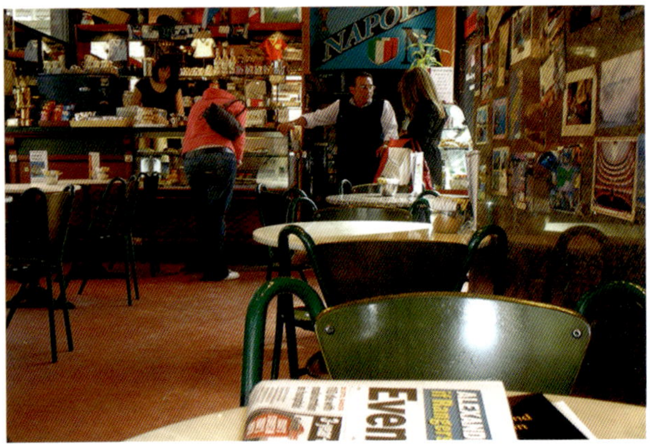

Upstairs . . . .

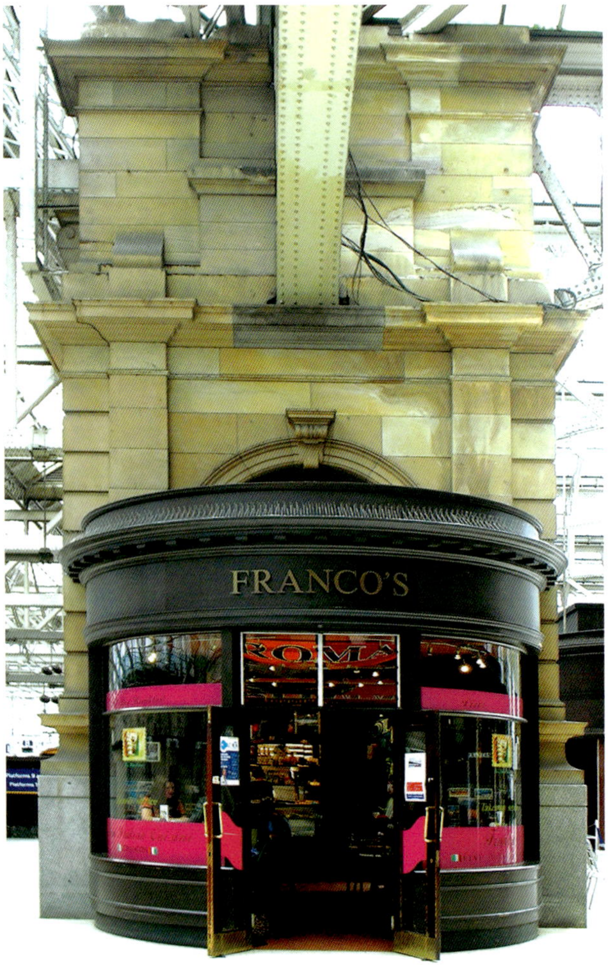

Bridging the old and the new stations – Franco sits astride the dividing line

. . . . downstairs

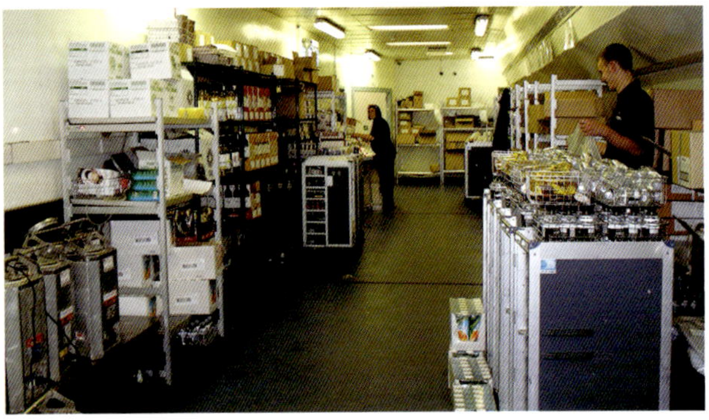

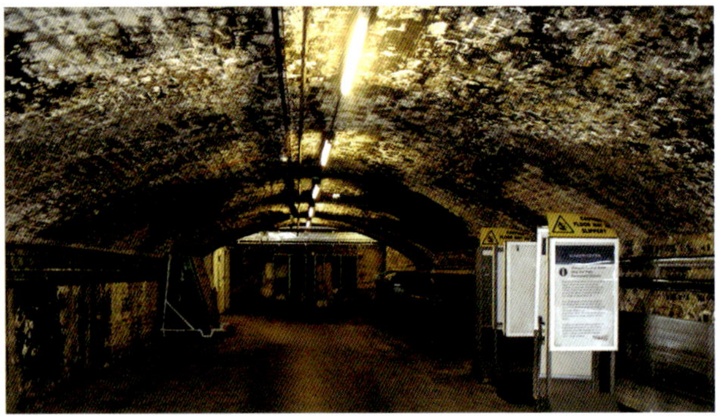

Victualling of the dining cars, trolleys, and shops aboard the trains up above is done from the stores below in the labyrinthine maze of arches underneath the platforms. Many and varied have been the uses of the arches over the years.

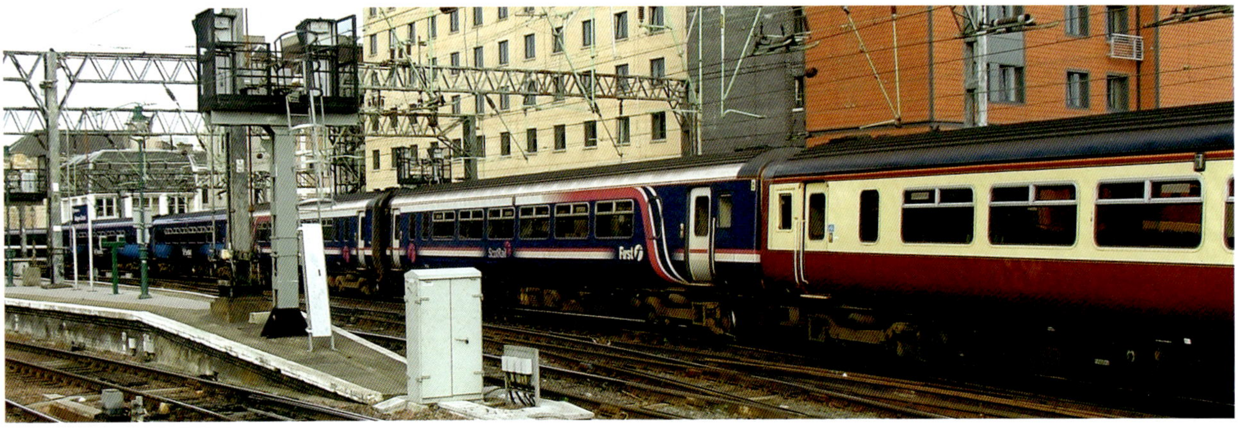

A colourful diesel cocktail – three in one!

40 Christmas with Network Rail - maintaining and renewing Central

Stephen Muirhead, Signal Engineer, Network Rail, Scotland

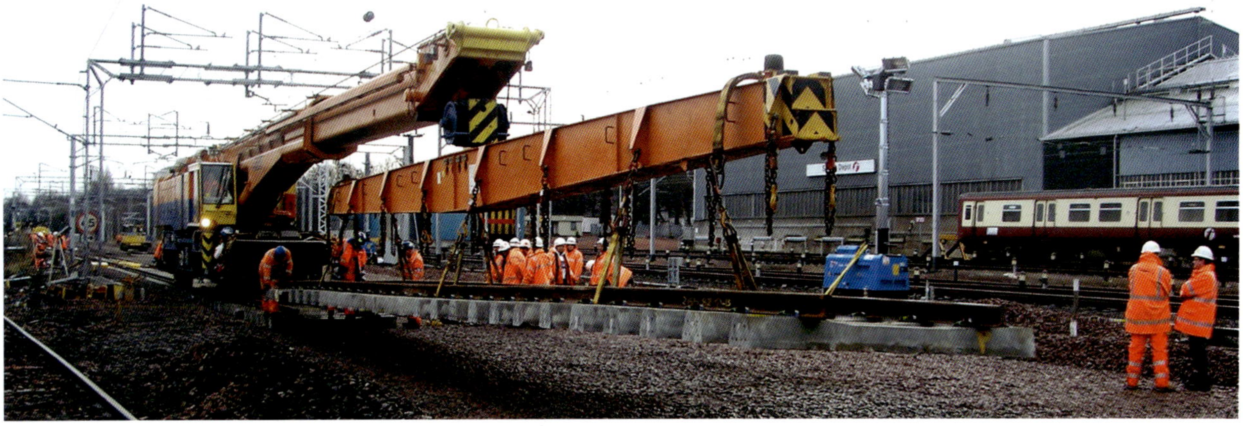

The festive season has a particular resonance for places such as Glasgow Central. This is when Network Rail can implement major changes, while minimising disruption to train operation. So it was over Christmas 2007 that the largest single renewal of a junction tackled in Scotland in recent years took place: the remodelling at Shields on the west approach to Central.

The following year it was the turn of station area itself to undergo signalling renewal. While the final acts were playing out in the old Signalling Centre in the early hours of Christmas morning, over in Springburn a new Signalling Centre was being brought to life. When the signalling in the station area was signed into use in the early hours of 30th December 2008, it was now under the new West of Scotland Signalling Centre, and the relay technology of the 1950s had been replaced by the latest solid state technology from Westinghouse. This company had supplied the previous two signalling systems for Central, in 1907 and 1960. Signallers that morning began controlling trains using a modern VDU-based control system by GE Transportation Systems. Indeed what was known as "the Glasgow Central Interlocking Renewal Project" replaced not just the Central itself but the whole area previously supervised from the old signalling centre, such as Polmadie, Rutherglen, Muirhouse, Shields, Corkerhill, Cardonald, Busby Junction and Busby Station.

This renewal project was unusual in that it did not rationalise or simplify the complex layout at Central to any extent. This was a conscious decision to preserve both the existing capacity, pending future train service improvements, and also the flexibility of the station during perturbation. Nevertheless, improvements for train drivers were incorporated, to facilitate working trains through the maze of track known locally as "The Jungle". For passengers, the noticeable change was that platforms 12 and 13 had become 14 and 15. This freed up those numbers 12 and 13 for two new platforms, one of which will replace the unpopular Platform 12 (the infamous old 11A).

Network Rail has its own sophisticated Fixed Telecom Network (FTN), which meets the extensive requirements for secure and reliable telecommunications links between the new Signalling Centre at Springburn and the infrastructure it controls. A particular challenge that Christmas was the migration to the new Centre of the 1980s-era radio equipment for driver and signaller, ahead of the latest international GSM-R technology, still under trial on the Helensburgh to Airdrie lines.

The new Signalling Centre has given rise to many changes for the people involved. The signallers and other Operations staff relocated from the old building to the new, but the front line maintainers of the equipment have remained closer to their work, at Salkeld Street Depot. A new modern Maintenance Depot has been built adjacent to the new Centre, permitting the Management / Administrative / Support staffs for the whole Glasgow area to be brought together under one roof.

The new West of Scotland Signalling Centre is aptly named: over the coming years it will gradually expand to fulfil its name as existing Centres at Cathcart, Paisley, Yoker and Motherwell are progressively brought into the new building, thereby giving Network Rail a modern and efficient centralised control of a wide geographical area – but the Glasgow Central workstation will be at its heart.

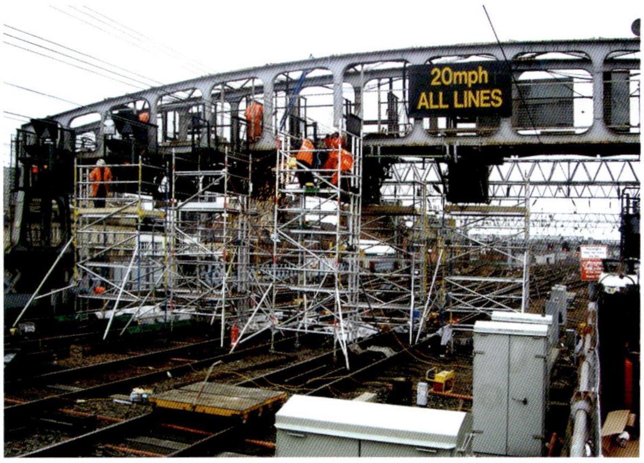

When the train service has to be suspended for a piece of major engineering (a "blockade" in the trade), the opportunity is of course taken to carry out other work.
Under the Blockade for Shields significant works were also undertaken at Gantry 'A' in Central Station converting the signal heads to the latest LED format.

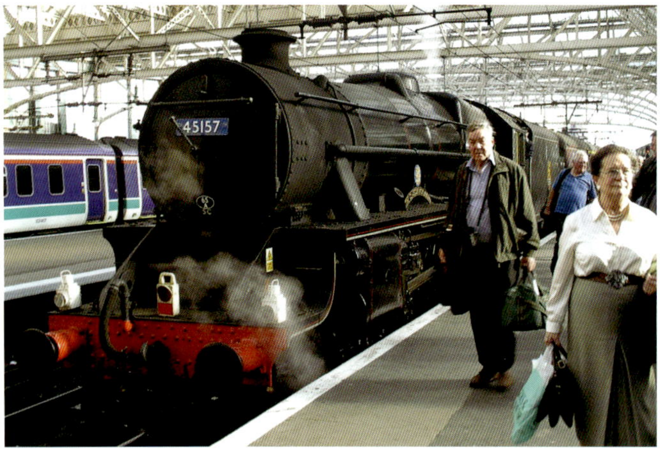

Black 5 No. 5407 poses as No. 45157 "The Glasgow Highlander" having arrived with a Special from Preston on 31 August 2006.

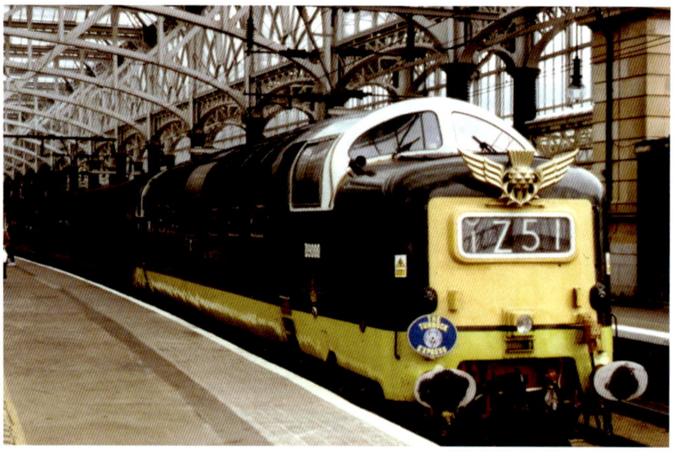

"The Tunnock Express", hauled by Deltic No. D9000 "Royal Scots Grey", also carries the 1960s 'Flying Scotsman' headboard.

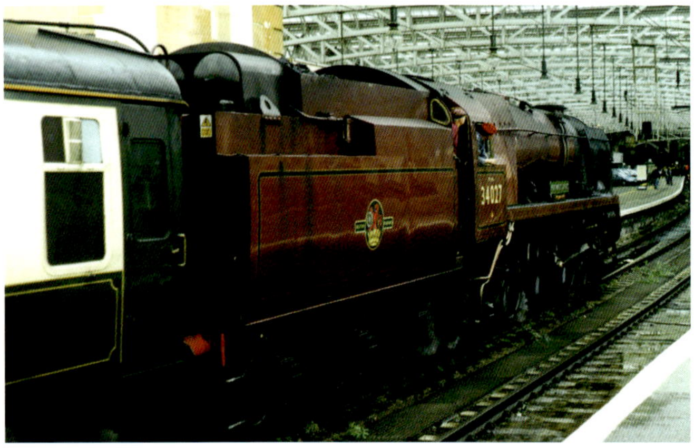

And now the Southern in Central!
'West Country' Class No. 34027 "Taw Valley" masquerades in LMS red as "Hogwarts Castle" – October 2000.

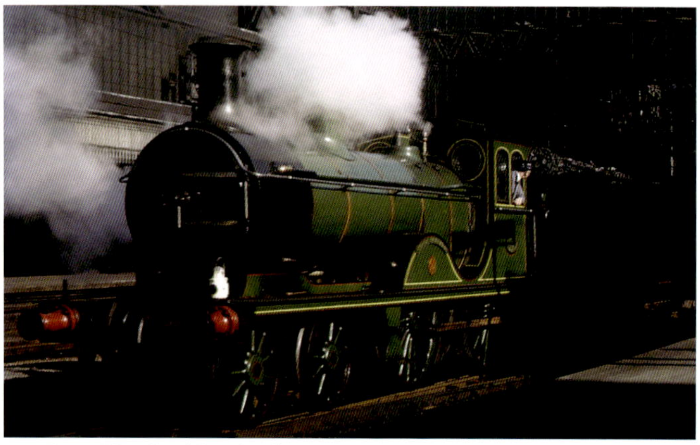

Great North of Scotland Railway No. 49 "Gordon Highlander" was also involved in the 1965 Easter Railtour - the last outings of these preserved locomotives.

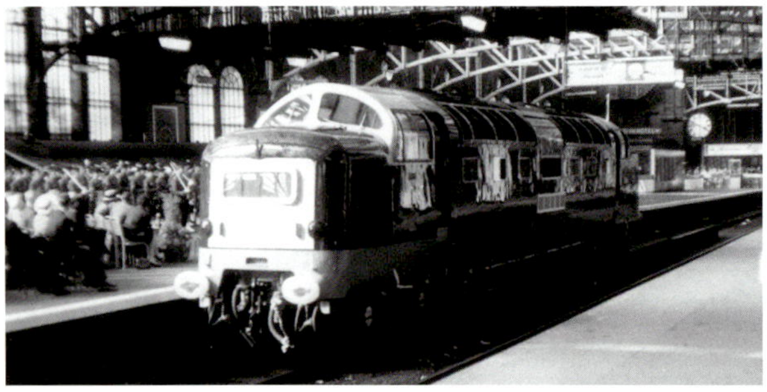

Naming of the Deltic D9019 "Royal Highland Fusilier" on 11 September 1965.

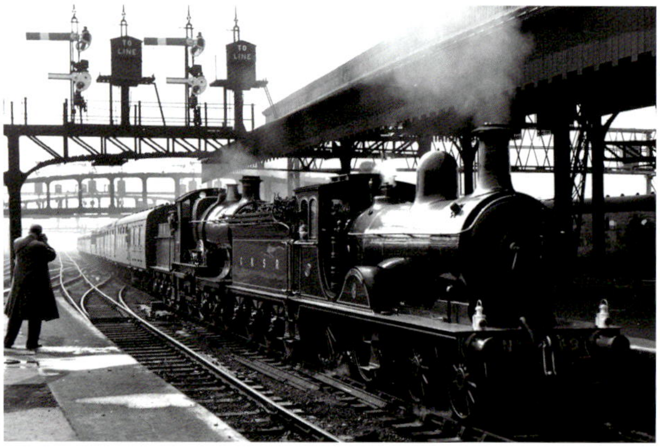

The Great Western in Glasgow! Restored GNSR No. 49 "Gordon Highlander" partners GWR No. 3440 "City of Truro" on a Scottish Industries Exhibition Special in 1959.

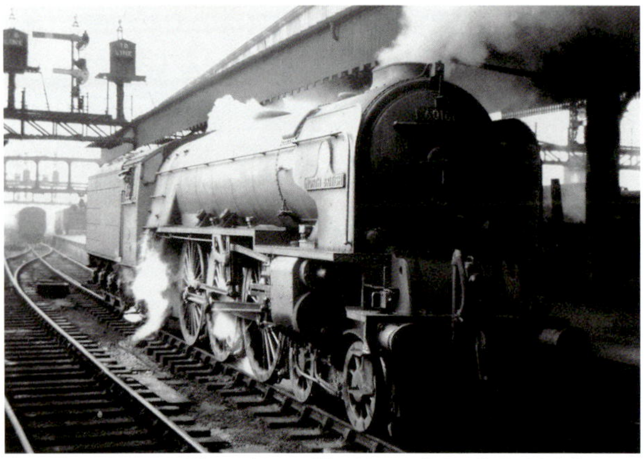

Peppercorn Class A1 pacific 60161,"North British", temporarily transferred from Haymarket shed to Polmadie around 1951 / 1953 backs out of Glasgow Central. The A1s were used on the Birminghams and the West Coast Postals.

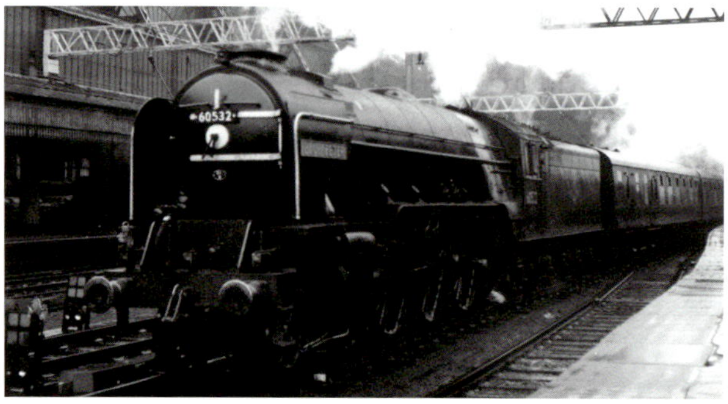

A2 Class Pacific No. 60532 "Blue Peter" departs empty as the last A2 Special from Central failed to attract sufficient patronage - October 1966.

41 Seeing and being seen – the British Transport Force at Central

David Hodgson

Familiar figures patrolling the concourse and platforms, British Transport Police officers have been seen at Central station ever since the force was formed, well over one hundred years ago. Our officers are specially trained, and their mission is to make your railways and stations safe, free from disruption and the fear of crime. Our officers do not tolerate criminality of any kind at Central, not at the High Level, not at the Low Level, not anywhere else on the rail network. Train passengers, rail staff and all who use the station have the right to go about their business without hindrance. We work closely with the train operators and Network Rail to ensure this is the case.

Times change, and new technology touches everything we do in life – it is no different for British Transport Police. Gone are the days when officers patrolled with nothing more than a lamp and a whistle to attract attention. Today, officers are in constant contact with their colleagues and control room via state-of-the-art radios, criminal records can be checked instantly, and ongoing incidents are updated using a Personal Digital Assistant.

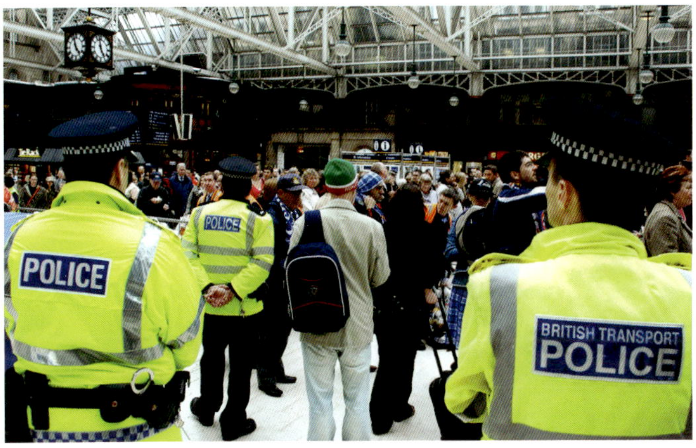

More than spectators – UEFA Cup Final 16 April 2007

Officers now have the power to issue a fixed penalty notice for a number of offences. Minor breaches of the peace and other anti-social behaviour offences are now punishable by a £40 fine on the spot. This means that a large number of offences are taken out of the court system each year, and thus our officers can spend even more time out and about patrolling the station.

Neighbourhood policing is all about building up relationships between the police and members of the public, and although BTP does not have neighbourhoods in the traditional sense, railway stations and the surrounding areas are now a real hub with social and retail outlets. So the Central now has its own dedicated Neighbourhood Police Team. These 'weel-kent' and extremely experienced officers are there to help reduce crime and reassure those who use the station every day. The team does not just undertake daily high profile and high visibility patrols in its neighbourhood, vital as these are, but is on hand to identify and address the concerns of passengers, retailers, and rail staff too.

It is working: crime on Scotland's railways has never been lower. We have seen a year-on-year decrease for the last five years. This is in no small part to the hard work, dedication and endeavours of British Transport Police officers who work hand in hand with their rail industry partners to keep it that way.

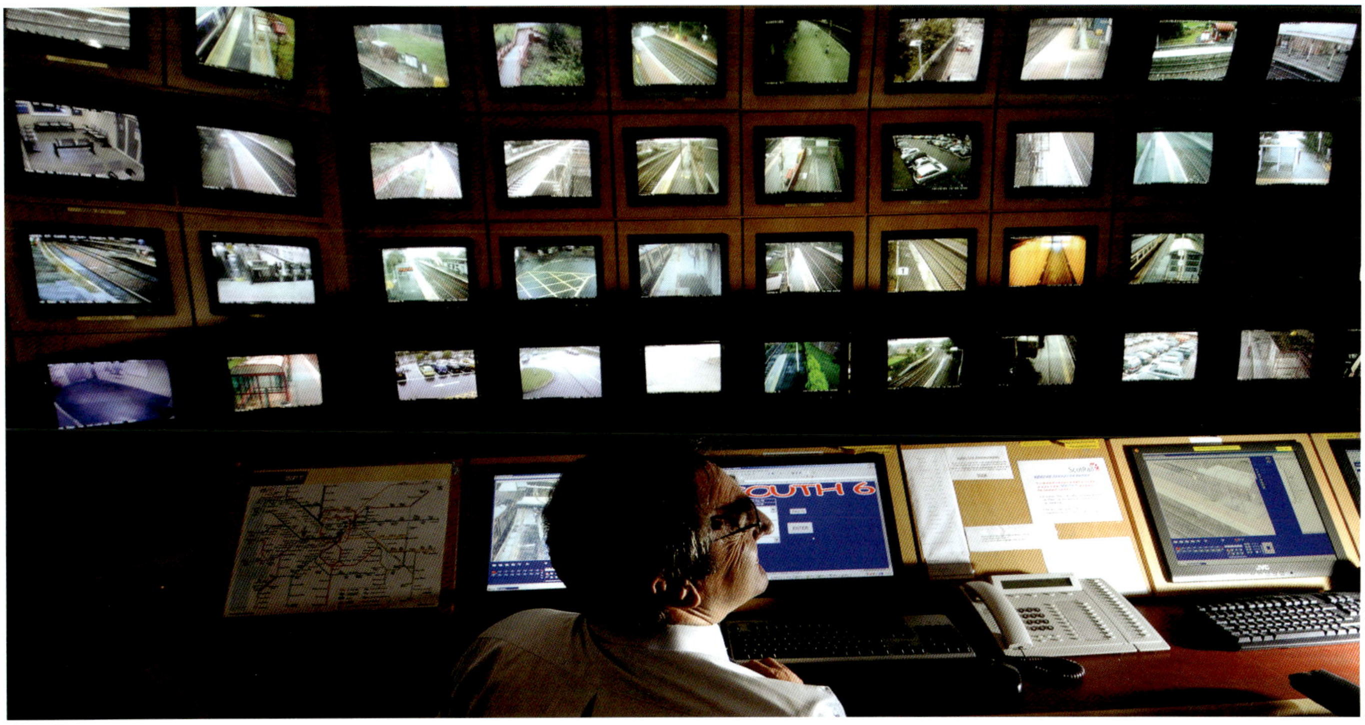

A total of 184 locations on the Strathclyde network and South West Scotland have 24-hour online CCTV, monitored from ScotRail's Customer Services Centre at Paisley, where staff view all train running and can speak to stations or individual passengers through the Help Point on each platform. This supplements the improved display on platforms of real-time information on train services.

Life and Times of Glasgow Central
A brief chronology 1879 - 1906 - 2009

1831	Opening of Garnkirk and Glasgow Railway. First railway carrying passengers to enter the city. Terminal at Glebe St.would be used by the future Caledonian Railway in 1848.
12 Aug 1840	Bridge Street Station opened serving the Glasgow and Paisley Joint Railway.
1841	Glasgow, Paisley & Greenock, and Glasgow, Paisley, Kilmarnock & Ayr railways opened throughout.
1845	Caledonian Railway incorporated.
1846	Clydesdale Junction Railway and Polloc & Govan amalgamated with Caledonian Railway; Glasgow, Garnkirk and Coatbridge sold to the Caledonian; Glasgow Barrhead & Neilston Direct Railway authorised, and leased to the Caledonian; Glasgow Southern Terminal Railway authorised to link the Caledonian near Gushetfaulds with the GB&ND, which bought it.
1847	Glasgow, Paisley & Greenock authorised to amalgamate with the Caledonian.
15 Feb 1848	Caledonian Railway line open from Carlisle, linking London to Glasgow and Edinburgh.
27 Sep 1848	Opening of South Side Station, near Gushetfaulds, temporary terminus for the Glasgow Barrhead and Neilston Direct Railway and the Caledonian (Clydesdale Junction Branch).
1 Nov 1849	Buchanan Street station opened; Anglo—Scottish traffic transferred from South Side.
1857	New South Side station opened
1864	Glasgow City Union Railway authorised to cross the river, linking the G&SW and North British networks.
1873	New South Side demolished to permit link between Barrhead and City Union lines; Caledonian authorised to cross the river and build Gordon Street (later Central) Station.
10 Oct 1876	St Enoch station opened by G&SW.
1 Aug 1879	Glasgow Central Station opened by the Caledonian Railway Company.
1 Sep 1879	Edinburgh and Carlisle trains diverted to Central, and South Side closed.
19 Jun 1885	Central Hotel opened.
15 Mar 1886	Queen Street Low Level lines of the Glasgow City and District Railway opened; amalgamated with the North British Railway in 1887.
1889	Glasgow Central Railway, being built below Argyle St., taken over by Caledonian.
10 Aug 1896	Glasgow Central Low Level line opened through Central Station.
1898	St Enoch Station enlargement and widening authorised.
1899	Glasgow Central Station enlargement and new bridge across Clyde authorised.
1 Jun 1904	Central Station extension and new bridge opened.
1 Mar 1905	Bridge Street station closed.
Sep 1906	Completion of rebuilding original part of Central and of whole station project.
3 May 1908	Completion of new power signalling at Glasgow Central.
1 Jul 1923	Caledonian Railway "grouped" into the London, Midland and Scottish Railway.
11 Jul 1927	Principal London expresses named "Royal Scot' and "Mid-day Scot".
1927	First long-distance television transmission, to Central Hotel from John Logie Baird in London.
4 May 1936	The first "Milk Bar" in a Scottish railway station was established in the Central
16/17 Nov 1936	LMS Pacific locomotive 6201 "Princess Elizabeth" completes record runs Euston-Central and Central Euston, 5hrs. 52mins. and 5hrs. 44mins.
1 Jul 1937	LMS introduces streamlined "Coronation Scot' train between Central and Euston.
1 Jan 1948	Britain's railways nationalised; LMS incorporated into British Railways.
1/2 Jun 1949	Loco nos. 10000 and10001 head first diesel-hauled up and down "Royal Scot.
1956	Modernisation of ticket office and expansion of hotel.
17 Jun 1957	"The Caledonian" express service introduced between Central and Euston.
7 Jul 1958	Diesel Multiple Units introduced, on Edinburgh (P.St) and Cathcart Circle services.
1 Jan 1961	Completion of major rationalisation and resignalling. Original bridge over River Clyde put out of use and tracks re-aligned; Eglinton Street station closed; Glasgow Central, Bridge Street Jn., Eglinton Street Jn. and Eglinton Street Station signal boxes closed. New Glasgow Central Signal Box and re-signalling brought into use.
27 May 1962	South side suburban electrification inaugurated.
19 Apr 1962	North British Locomotive Company closes.
5 Oct 1964	Central Low Level Station and line closed.
7 Jun 1966	All services from St Enoch transferred to Central.
7 Nov 1966	Buchanan Street station closed and services transferred to Queen Street.
29 Apr1967	Last scheduled Scottish Region steam-hauled service to use Central; isolated workings from Carlisle continued until 1968.
5 Jun 1967	South Bank Clyde Coast electrification inaugurated.
1967	Removal of Caledonian bridge over the Clyde.
1 Jan 1973	Automatic ticket barriers introduced Central – Gourock/Wemyss Bay.
1973	Formation of Strathclyde Passenger Transport Authority to procure train services in Greater Glasgow area and certain operational boundaries beyond.
6 May 1974	West Coast Main Line electrification north from Crewe inaugurated; route now electrified throughout Euston to Central. Also Hamilton Circle and Lanark lines.

5 Nov 1979	Central Low Level and line reopened as "Argyle Line".
20 Dec 1979	Advanced Passenger Train on a test run achieves 162 mph south of Beattock, a UK speed record.
1983	Passenger facilities at Central High Level modernised.
12 Dec 1984	APT record run 3hrs. 52 mins. Euston to Glasgow.
1985	New train indicators at platform ends, using dot matrix system, replace manual system.
Jul 1988	Last newspaper trains on West Coast Main Line.
28 Jul 1990	Paisley Canal line reopened.
1991	Start of East Coast Main Line services from Central.
14 May 1993	Last "Up/Down Special" Travelling Post Offices between Central and Euston.
1 Apr 1994	Railtrack takes over former British Rail infrastructure, including Central Station.
28 Apr 1996	First privatised train from Glasgow Central, operated by GNER.
31 Mar 1997	Last British Railways—ScotRail train from Central.
1 Apr 1997	National Express Group takes over ScotRail domestic and Sleeper services.
15 Jan 1997	Virgin Trains takes over former British Rail InterCity Cross Country routes.
15 Jan1997	Virgin Trains takes over former British Rail InterCity West Coast routes.
4/5 Jul 1997	Eurostar train, for direct services to Continent, in Central for trials – un-powered.
13 Feb 1998	Last Royal Mail train from Central. Services transferred to new Shieldmuir depot.
3 Apr 2001	Class 334 EMUs introduced on SPT services.
3 Oct 2002	Network Rail takes over infrastructure from Railtrack and ownership of Central.
Jan 2004	Last Royal Mail train from Central.
17 Oct 2004	First Group takes over ScotRail franchise from National Express.
10 Jan 2004	Cessation of mail by rail nationally.
Dec 2005	Mail by rail resumes between Shieldmuir and London, worked by GBRailfreight.
9 Dec 2005	Larkhall line re-opened, and frequencies enhanced on Argyle Line.
	Major conference in Glasgow advocates a new Anglo-Scottish High Speed Line.
12 Dec 2005	Accelerated Virgin "Pendolino" service to Euston, fastest train 4hrs 24mins.
Sep 2006	Centenary of the expansion of Glasgow Central Station.
1 Jan 2006	Transport Scotland now responsible for Scotland's railways.
1 Apr 2006	The Strathclyde Partnership for Transport takes over the roles and functions of the Strathclyde Passenger Transport Authority and Executive.
22 Sep 2006	New record time Glasgow – Euston of 3 hours 55 minutes 27 seconds by Pendolino
11 Nov 2007	CrossCountry assumes former Virgin routes via East Coast to West Country
9 Dec 2007	First TransPennine takes over Manchester services
9 Dec 2007	National Express replaces Great North Eastern Railway on East Coast route
14 Dec 2008	Virgin "very high frequency" timetable launched on West Coast route.
2 Feb 2009	Central Hotel closed
13 April 2009	CCTV system throughout station commissioned
17 Sep 2009	Glasgow Airport Rail Link cancelled
17 Sep 2009	Central wins is first in the Best Major and Best Overall stations categories of the National Rail Awards
27 Sep 2009	Car park closed to permit construction of new platforms 12 and 13
25 Dec 2009	Existing platform 12 (formerly 11A) closes for rebuilding

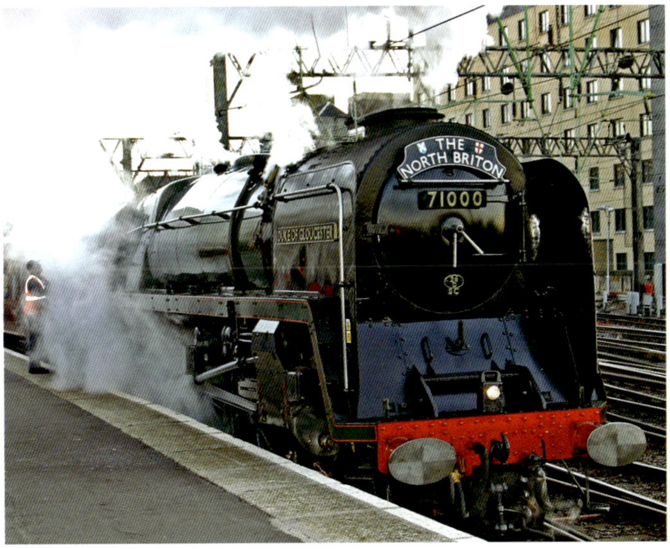

After a gap of forty years or so, amazingly restored BR Pacific No. 71000 leaves Central on the next leg of "The North Britain" tour, 16 April 2008.

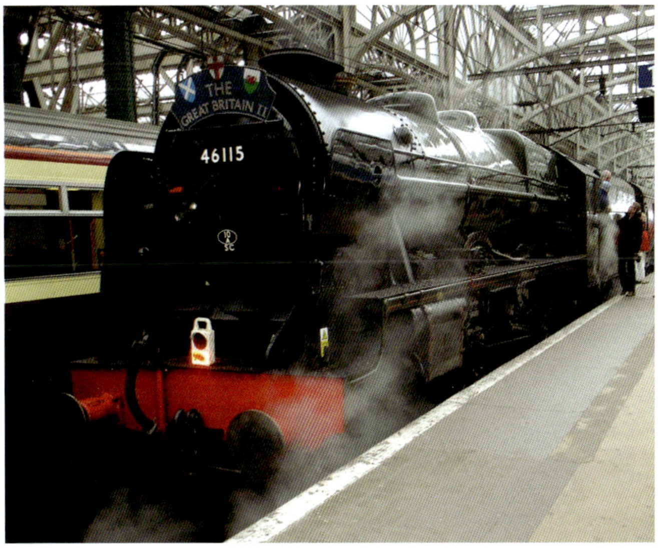

Royal Scot, No. 46115 "Scots Guardman" makes a welcome sight in Platform 11 with a special on 9 April 2009.

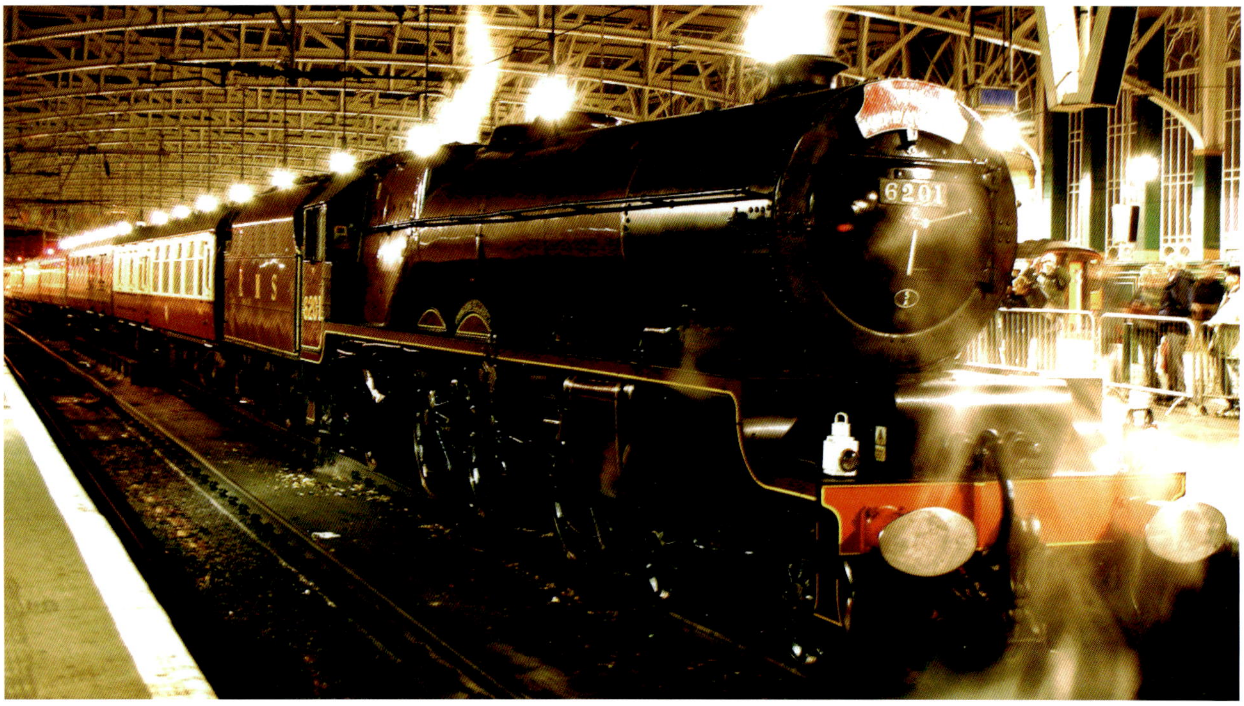

On 17 November 2006 No. 6201 "Princess Elizabeth" celebrates the 70th anniversary of her record run to Euston. The locomotive has been beautifully preserved in running order by the 6201 Society for future generations to enjoy.

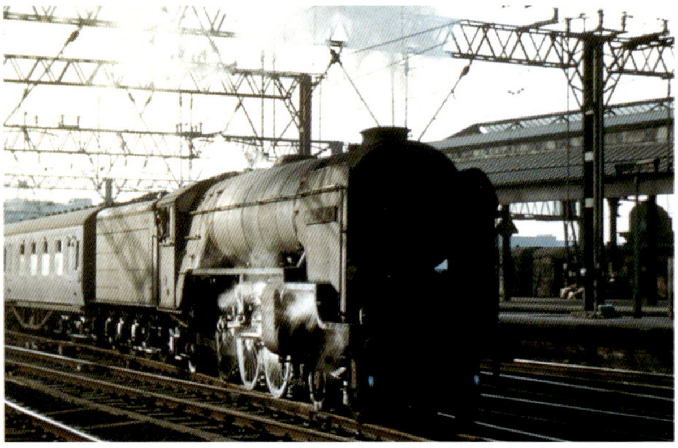

Former LNER A2/3 No. 60512 "Steady Aim" was one of the A2s transferred to Polmadie in late 1963 seen entering on a local.

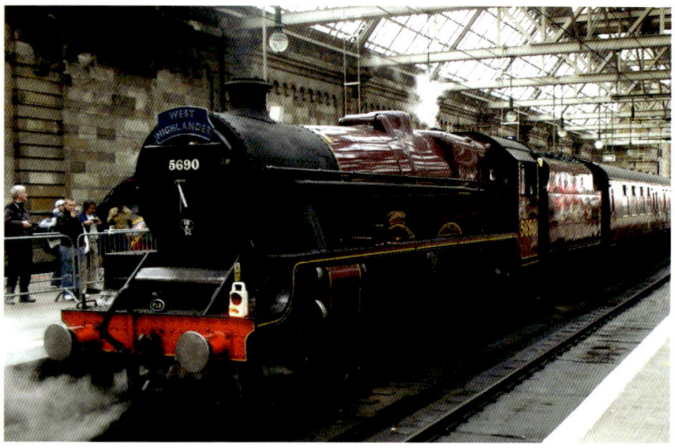

Return of a "Jubilee", No 5690 "Leander" fresh from climbing Shap and Beattock and spot on time on 25 September 2009.

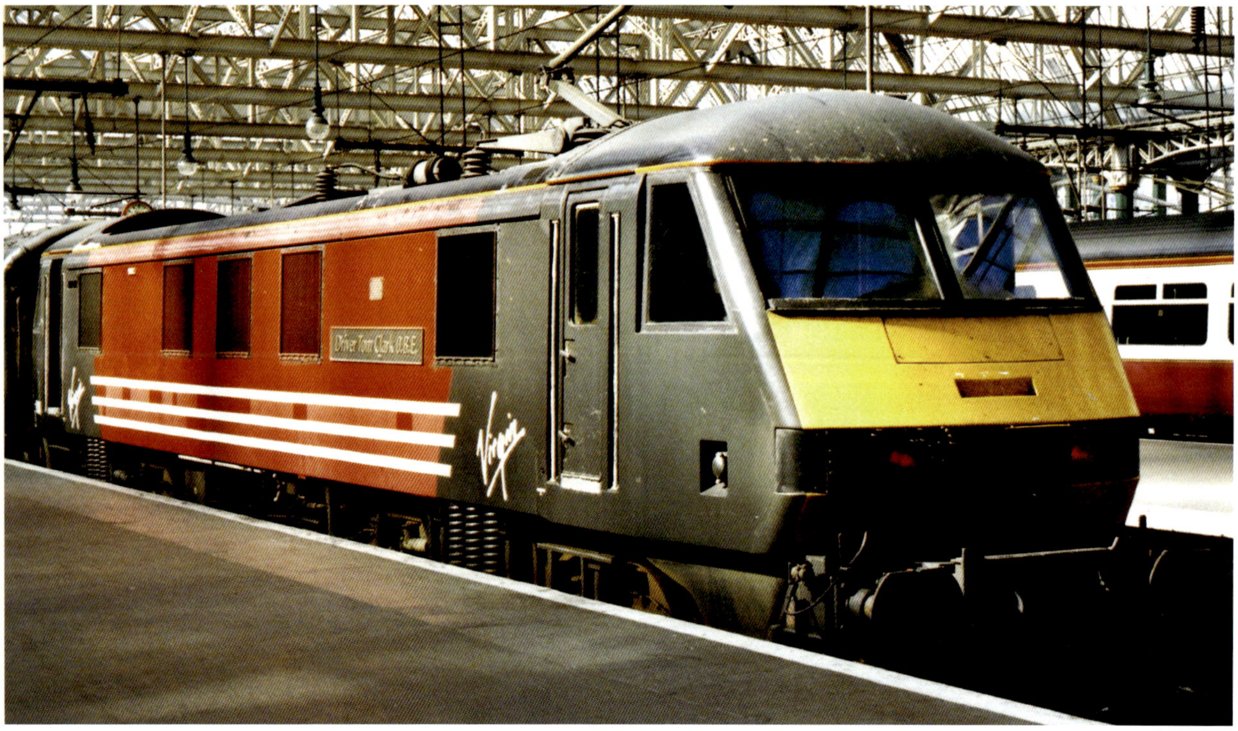

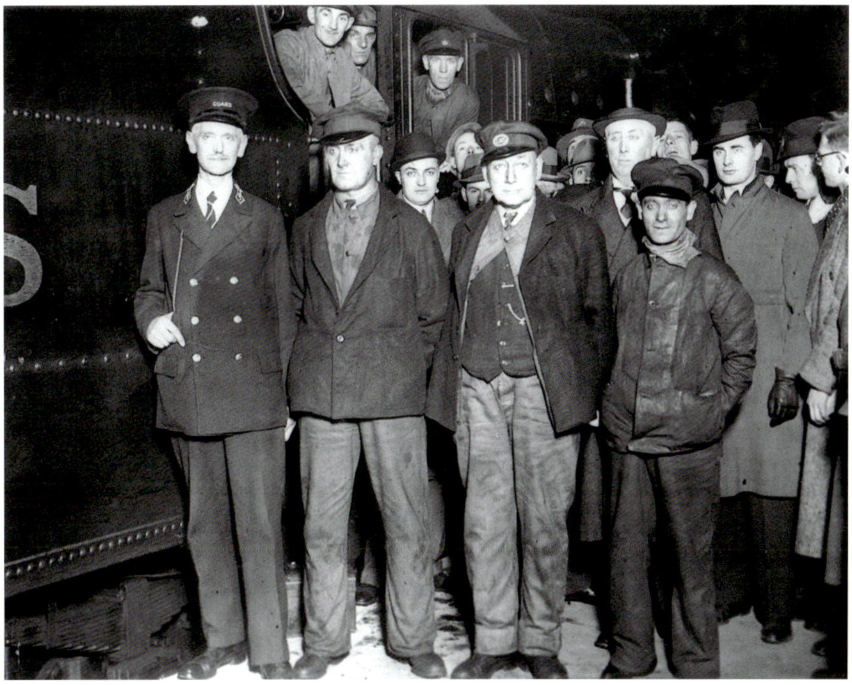

70 years apart!
Driver Clark with Firemen Shaw and Fleet pose with No. 6201 "Princess Elizabeth" at Central after the record northbound run of 5 hours 52 minutes on 16 November 1936 and on the following day the return journey was made in 5 hours 44 minutes.
Driver Russell Southworth prepares to depart from Central on 22 September 2006 going on to achieve a new southbound record of 3 hours 55 minutes and 27 seconds.
It was the first non-stop run between Glasgow and London since 1949 and the first ever sub four hour Glasgow to London.

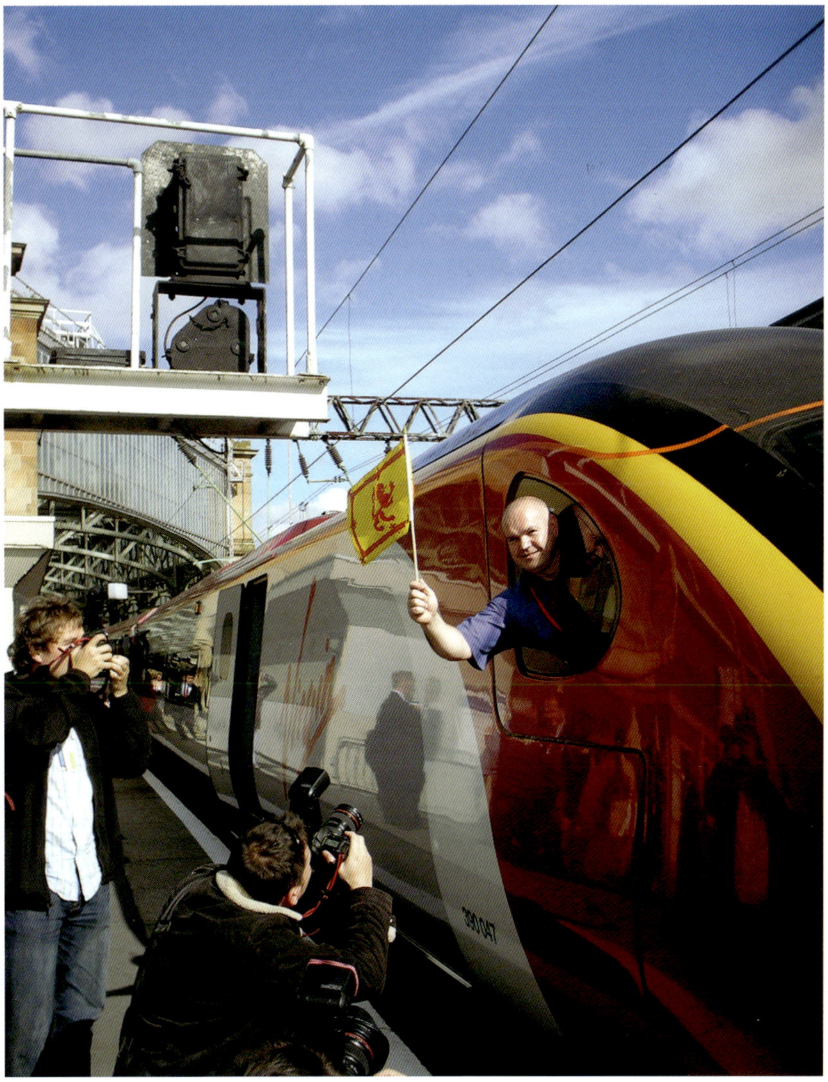

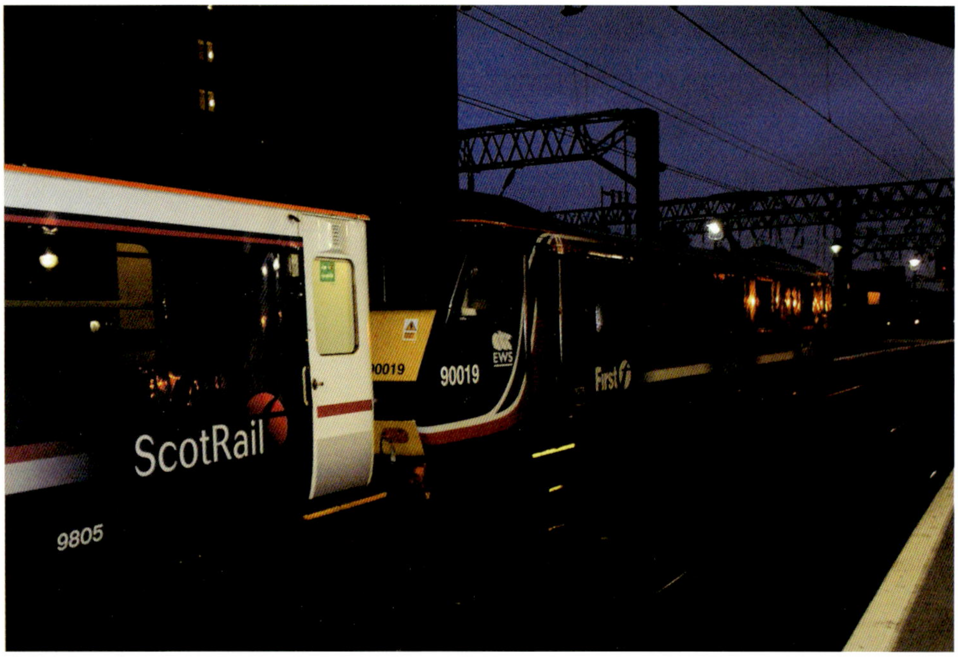

And so to bed on wheels – leaving Central for another day.